MEMOIRS OF A REVOLUTIONARY

Victor Serge

Memoirs of a Revolutionary
1901-1941

TRANSLATED AND EDITED BY
PETER SEDGWICK

OXFORD UNIVERSITY PRESS

Oxford University Press, Walton Street, Oxford OX2 6DP

OXFORD LONDON GLASGOW
NEW YORK TORONTO MELBOURNE WELLINGTON
IBADAN NAIROBI DAR ES SALAAM CAPE TOWN
KUALA LUMPUR SINGAPORE JAKARTA HONG KONG TOKYO
DELHI BOMBAY CALCUTTA MADRAS KARACHI

ISBN 0 19 281037 5

Mémoires d'un révolutionnaire *par Victor Serge* © *Éditions du Seuil 1951*
English Translation © *Oxford University Press 1963*
First published by Oxford University Press, London 1963
First published, with corrections, as an Oxford University Press paperback 1967
and reprinted 1975, 1978

*Printed in Great Britain by
Morrison & Gibb Ltd,
London and Edinburgh*

CONTENTS

INTRODUCTION

Victor Serge, who was born in 1890 and died in 1947, was an anarchist, a Bolshevik, a Trotskyist, a revisionist-Marxist, and, on his own confession, a 'personalist'. Belgian by place of birth and upbringing, French by adoption and in literary expression, Russian by parentage and later by citizenship, he eventually became stateless and was put down as a Spanish national for purposes of his funeral documents. He was a journalist, a poet, a pamphleteer, a historian, an agitator, and a novelist. Usually he was several of these things at once; there were few times in his life when he did not combine at least two or three nationalities, ideologies, and professional callings. Nevertheless, although there is no way of describing him in brief without an inventory of discordances, he was very much an integral man. To read his memoirs is to receive the impression of a strong and consistent personality, of an approach to life and to politics which is complex but unified, of a heart which, however it may be divided, is so because reality tears it asunder, not because its loyalties are confused. When we list the varying political trends that entered into Victor Serge's make-up, we are simply recording his continual sensitivity to certain perennial dilemmas of action. Serge hated violence, but he saw it, at times, as constituting the lesser evil. He believed that necessity in politics might sometimes be frightful, but was necessity no less; only he was not inclined to glorify it into a virtue. He mistrusted the State, but he recognized it as an inevitable form in the progress of society. So general a statement of political predicaments is doubtless banal, but it is in fact rather rare to find a public figure (let alone a revolutionary public figure) who plainly registers both extremes of a dilemma with equal sensitivity, even though his ultimate choice may incline very definitely towards one pole or the other.

An appreciation of the complexity of political choice probably does not conduce to effective Left-wing theory or leadership. The improvising politician, concerned above all to seek the key to social transformation, has almost of necessity to over-emphasize some features of social reality at the expense of others. But the revolution-

ary of mixed origins and impulsions may well make a very good
witness to the great upheavals of his time. Standing at the confluence
of several radical traditions, he will be able to judge the programmes,
actions, and ideas of the competing parties with a certain detachment; and yet his detachment will not be of the uncomprehending,
noncommittal kind which would make it impossible to describe the
revolution at all, except perhaps as a sequence of despotic acts.
Thus it is N. N. Sukhanov, an ex-Social Revolutionary, ex-Menshevik Bolshevik sympathizer, who is responsible for a brilliant and
uniquely valuable history of the revolutionary year of 1917.[1] To the
subsequent epoch of the Revolution, its opening and continuing
phases of mass violence, terror, and degeneracy, Serge brings a mind
already matured in the experience of heroism and its corruption.
When he entered the service of the Revolution, at the age of twenty-
eight, he had behind him several years of disgust with the commer-
cialized Social-Democracy of Belgium, three years of mounting
disillusionment with anarchist terrorism, and five years' unspeakable
existence as a convict among convicts. Steeped in the 'individualist'
psychology of his libertarian past, he retained an intense and wary
consciousness of the many-sidedness of human motivation, of man's
potential both for Titanic endeavour and for regression to the brute.

In the writings of Serge particular political tendencies stand displayed as the expression of moral and psychological resources
within the individual. Not Marxism or reformism, Stalinism or
liberalism are primary, but will, fear, sensitivity, dishonesty, courage, mental rigidity, psychic dynamism, and their opposites or
absences. Serge tells you that a certain man is an obsessive, or that he
leans too much upon favour, and this information is intended to
mean quite as much as the facts about his party alignment; indeed,
the political characterization is perhaps causally dependent on the
more personal one. Serge often manages his evocation of the person
by means of physiognomic detail: how this face was puffed (*bouffi*),
that one solid-looking (*carré*), how certain eyes were gentle, or harsh,
or firm. On his return to Western Europe, in 1936, Serge drew a
long train of political conclusions (which stood the test of time considerably better than the more catastrophic expectations of his
comrades) from one simple anatomic observation: that the Belgians

---

[1] N. N. Sukhanov, *The Russian Revolution, 1917: A Personal Record* (edited and
abridged by Joel Carmichael), Oxford University Press, 1955.

were now *fat*.

Serge's fascination with the expressive externals of people is of particular use to ın.m in the many thumbnail portraits of revolutionists, writers, and plain folk that fill the pages of the *Memoirs*. As Serge progresses on his various expeditions with the political and the literary vanguard, he leaves behind him a trail of single paragraphs or sparse sentences each bearing the vivid imprint of a summarized personality: Gramsci, Toller, Lukács, Yesenin, Balabanova, Gide, Trotsky, Vandervelde, Pilniak, Barbusse—the improbable list could be extended indefinitely, though there would be little point in trying to do so since much of Serge's appeal lies in the most obscure of his characters. While these portrayals are succinct and bold they are not, generally speaking, caricatures, for Serge maintains a scrupulous fairness towards his memories. He can summon up a trio of German Social-Democrats, a clique of Comintern functionaries or a collection of deadbeat *illégalistes*, and project their living presence into the odd paragraph or so with utter sympathy and at the same time with transparent fidelity to his own point of view. There is a passage in his novel *L'Affaire Toulaév* in which he shows us Stalin, at the height of the purges, not as a sadist or a villain but as a hopelessly solitary man, viewed in the white light of compassion. And yet Serge's concern for human beings is by no means the same type of concern that a non-political writer would display, confronted by the same personages. Although Serge's portraits of political characters are rounded, nuanced, and humane, he is all the time seeing and selecting their traits from a specifically revolutionary standpoint; basically he is asking himself, 'Is this man the kind of person who will help to make the revolution? Or will he perhaps help to make the wrong kind of revolution?' Towards the end of the *Memoirs*, and again in his diaries, Serge remarks that one of the greatest problems in politics is that of reconciling intransigence, which he thought indispensable to any worthwhile convictions, with the equally necessary principles of criticism towards ideas and respect towards men. 'Intransigence is steadfastness, is *living* . . . Nietzsche was quite right to consider "possession of the truth" as allied to the will to dominate.' It is Victor Serge's exceptional merit as a revolutionary witness, not only that he conceived of the problem at all, but also that he himself so often resolved it in a mode of perception that fused both intransigence and love.

The marked independence of Serge's vision can be detected very early in his Bolshevik career. Writing in May 1921 from Petrograd to a French anarchist comrade, he reflects that 'the prime error of the present Russian regime is to have created an entire bureaucratic mechanism to manage production instead of leaving it to the workers organized by industry (i.e. syndicalism). It has failed principally in attacking, through methods of centralized discipline and military repression, any individual initiative, opposition, or criticism (even a fraternal and revolutionary one), any aspiration towards liberty; in short, in being guided by a spirit contrary to that of anarchism'. Well before a fraction of the party leadership itself (around Trotsky, Zinoviev, and Kamenev) will rally an opposition to the regime's bureaucratization, Serge voices a libertarian and syndicalist protest, reviving his old allegiance to anarchy's black flag:

To be precise, what we need is a new anarchism, equipped with a practical programme, enriched by all the experience of the proletarian revolution, capable of guiding the movement of the masses. Its basis, like that of the reorganisation of production itself, can lie only in syndicalism.

The propagation of any views such as this had in March 1921 been declared incompatible with Party membership at the C.P.S.U.'s Tenth Congress, and would, soon after Serge wrote, become anathematized as an international heresy at the Comintern's Third Congress—whose sessions he attended as a staff member. Small wonder that he asked his correspondent to 'destroy this letter or at any rate don't leave it lying around'.[1]

In his public writing Serge was more guarded but still went to the very limits of caution. In August 1921 a French Socialist publishing-house brought out his booklet, *Les Anarchistes et l'expérience de la révolution russe*; it had been written in the summer of 1920, before the banning of the party factions whose positions had corresponded most closely with his own. In it (as he himself hints on p. 114 of the *Memoirs*) we find, sometimes in rudimentary but often in quite developed form, all the basic concepts deployed by Serge in his later analyses of the Red dictatorship and its totalitarian leanings. Fundamental to his critique is a distinction between the avoidable and the unavoidable aspects of degeneration in revolutions. Unlike most

[1] Letter of 29 May 1921 to 'camarade Michel' (otherwise unidentified), now in the Musée Social, Paris. I am indebted to Colette Chambelland for access to the Victor Serge papers held there.

other supporters of Bolshevism, he does not idealize the existing regimentation, or deny it for what it is. 'The proletarian dictatorship has, in Russia, had to introduce an increasingly authoritarian centralism. One may perhaps deplore it. Unfortunately I do not believe that it could have been avoided' (p. 29). However, the role of necessity must not be invoked as an unrestricted excuse licensing any conceivable measure of despotism: 'The rise of a Jacobin Party and its exclusive dictatorship do not then appear to be inevitable; and at this point everything depends on the ideas which inspire the party, on the men who carry out these ideas, and on the reality of control by the masses' (p. 31). What is more, 'Every revolutionary government is by its very nature conservative and therefore retrograde. Power exercises upon those who hold it a baleful influence which is often expressed in deplorable occupational perversions (*déformations professionnelles*)', (p. 34; *cf. Memoirs*, p. 99).

All the greater, therefore, was the responsibility of free-thinking revolutionaries: 'It will be the task of libertarian Communists to proclaim by their criticism and activity that the crystallization of the workers' State must be avoided at all costs' (p. 34). The solution to the problem of all-embracing State ownership must be 'production to the producers, that is to the trade unions' (p. 39), even though this policy holds the danger that the unions will themselves turn into a new State bureaucracy. Anarchism is vindicated in its proclamation of 'the terrible harm residing in authority, the harmfulness of Statism and authoritarian centralism' (*ibid.*). Indeed, in the very successes of the Revolution 'little credit is due to Authority. Many things have been achieved in spite of it' (p. 41); here Serge seems to prefigure his later emphasis on the economic disadvantages of Stalinism (*cf. Memoirs*, p. 378). All the same, anarchists must be 'with the Revolution, unhesitating and ubiquitous, or they will be nothing' (p. 43). They will be Communists, but 'in contradiction to numerous others they will strive to preserve the spirit of freedom, and so will be gifted with a more critical approach and a sharper awareness of ultimate ends. Within any Communist movement their lucidity will make them the most formidable enemies of the climbers, the budding politicians and commissars, the formalists, pundits and intriguers.'

It is this continuous record of fundamental unorthodoxy that makes Victor Serge's record so different from most other ex-Communist autobiographies. Through his personal tenacity and his intellectual pluralism Serge could mentally balance the various risks of political action, hedging, as it were, expectations which for others were staked upon a fanatic's throw of all or none, and so insuring himself against the chances both of blind commitment and of stark disillusion. Harking back to the turbulent and frightful years of his youth, he could remark simply *je ne regrette rien pour moi*, and there is the same absence of personal remorse when he recounts his Bolshevik career. The vividness and immediacy of Serge's recollections do not strike us as being artificially tinted by hindsight; and in fact the judgements he passes on Russian events are very often repeated identically in writings separated by decades, quoted back and forth with a touch of clairvoyant's vanity.

Over the last twenty-five years or so considerable controversy has waxed over the question: is Stalinism the logical, organic, and inevitable continuation of Bolshevism? Most Western observers have replied with a simple affirmative; and an equation of similar form, but with the signs of all quantities reversed from negative to positive, was propounded until quite recently by political algebraists within the Soviet sphere of influence. On the other hand, the Trotskyist school of Marxism has long insisted that Stalinism is the 'direct negation' of Bolshevism, while official Soviet theory after 1956 has increasingly tended to posit much the same kind of polar opposition between 'Leninist norms' and at least some of the 'excesses, abuses, and crimes' of Stalin's day. Victor Serge's answer to the problem was persistently double-sided. As against Trotsky and his followers he stresses the fatal rigidities and ambiguities of Leninist and Marxist doctrine, and the sources of degeneracy in such early Soviet institutions as the Cheka. As against the pairing of Bolshevism with Stalinism, he simply describes what, in his experience, Bolsheviks and Stalinists were like, and details the severe limitations set upon a free development of Soviet Socialism by the Civil War and its aftermath of havoc. Serge was suspicious of any notion tending to establish historical fatalism, and this set him both against the easy appeal to necessity which Leninists and Stalinists employed in their apologias of butchery, and against the common Western habit of regarding the degenerescence of revolutions into tyranny as virtually the only Iron Law which it is still permissible to detect within history. One locus in Serge's polemical writings is particularly worth citing in this respect.[1] In 1938 and 1939 Trotskyist and libertarian circles were hotly involved in debating the nature of the Kronstadt rising of 1921, whose ruthless liquidation by the Bolsheviks lent itself to obvious comparison with the ongoing Great Purge. Serge entered into combat both with Trotsky, who had no qualms at all about the Bolshevik treatment of the mutineers, and with a Yugoslav ex-Trotskyist, Anton Ciliga, who saw the Kronstadt rising as a pro-letarian revolution against the bureaucracy, and its suppression as a proof of the linear descent of Stalin's Party from Lenin's. Trotsky had brusquely dismissed Serge's earlier reminiscences of the Kronstadt massacres: 'Whether there were any needless victims I do not know. On this score I trust Dzerzhinsky more than his belated critics. . . . Victor Serge's conclusions on this score—from third hand—have no value in my eyes.' Serge retorted that his information on Kronstadt came from anarchist eyewitnesses he had interviewed in prison immediately after the rising; whereas Dzerzhinsky's conclusions were 'from seventh or ninth hand', the head of the Cheka having been absent from Petrograd at the time. 'The single fact that a Trotsky did not know what all the rank and file Communists knew—that out of inhumanity a needless crime had been committed against the proletariat and peasantry—this fact, I repeat, is deeply significant. . . .'

On the other hand, Serge maintained against Ciliga that the socio-political composition of the non-Party masses at the time of Kronstadt was very far from progressive. 'In 1921, everybody who aspires to Socialism is inside the Party. . . . It is the non-party workers of this epoch, joining the party to the number of 2,000,000 in 1924, upon the death of Lenin, who assure the victory of its bureaucracy.' The conscious revolutionaries in the leadership of the mutiny 'con-stituted an undeniable élite and, duped by their own passion, they opened in spite of themselves the door to a frightful counter-revolution.' Serge's comment on the general issue in question could well be taken as a summing up of his lifelong attitude to the Revolu-tion: 'It is often said that "the germ of all Stalinism was in Bolshevism at its beginning". Well, I have no objection. Only, Bolshevism also contained many other germs—a mass of other germs—and those who lived through the enthusiasm of the first years of the first victorious revolution ought not to forget it. To judge the

[1] *New International*, February 1939, pp. 53–4.

living man by the death germs which the autopsy reveals in a corpse —and which he may have carried in him since his birth—is this very sensible?'

In one sense the political career of Victor Serge terminated with the demise of the European Left after the fall of France in 1940.[1] He was never again able to participate in any social movement with a recognizable influence upon public events. The last six or seven years of his life passed in virtual political solitude; his refugee status forbade any intervention by him in Mexican affairs, and he could find no wider international audience to hear him out. None the less, Serge never at any stage retired from his vocation as a revolutionary writer. He went on writing his fine novel on the Purges during the rout of France, in the fugitives' warren of Marseilles, and on the troubled voyage that took him to his final asylum. Once in Mexico, he wrote without respite: novels, essays, poems, articles, biography and autobiography. Anxious to keep abreast of the major social and cultural developments of the time, he devoured every significant book, periodical or journal that he chanced on, in Russian, French, Spanish, German, or English. He kept a voluminous diary, amassed material on Mexican history and culture, and sent off long political letters to his circle of friends abroad, as well as to any prominent foreign publicists that he felt like criticizing. The lengthy studies he undertook as *rapporteur* to a small Socialist exile group, destined for the eyes of a mere handful, are composed with the same measure and density as the works he intended for publication. All these millions of words were typed by Serge in cramped single-spacing on reams of the cheapest flimsy, with rarely an erasure or amendment. When one manuscript was finished he went straight on to the next without looking back. Reading over the text of the *Memoirs*, his friend Julián Gorkín remarked that the book was 'condensed and excessively laconic, through the adoption of this telegraphic style'; surely material so rich should be developed and expanded? Serge gave a sceptical smile, and answered, 'What would be the use? Who would publish me? And besides, I am pressed for time. Other books are waiting.' He worked on, sometimes with a haunting sense that his

---

[1] Except where otherwise stated, the material for the following outline of Serge's last years is drawn from Julián Gorkín's invaluable appendix to the 1957 edition of the *Memoirs*, from Serge's published notebooks, or from the issue of the review *Témoins* containing his letters to Antoine Borie. Details of these are to be found in the bibliography.

faculties might be weakening through the sheer vacuity that surrounded him. 'Terribly difficult,' he notes, 'to create in the void, lacking the least support, the least real environment.' He speaks of 'writing for the desk-drawer alone, past the age of fifty, unable to exclude the hypothesis that the tyrannies will outlast the remainder of my life . . .'; and 'I am beginning to wonder if my very name will not be an obstacle to the novel's publication.'

This oppressive sense of failure was not without its foundation in recent experience. As soon as Serge arrived in Mexico he paid the familiar penalty for his clairvoyance. His book on the Nazi aggression against Russia (*Hitler Contra Stalin*) proved to be too frank for the public taste, since it predicted disastrous Soviet reverses in the early stages of the war, with the peasants actually welcoming Hitler's invaders. As a result, the small firm that had published the book expired in ruin. Serge's dark forecasts turned out of course to be perfectly accurate. Public meetings addressed by Serge, Gorkín, and others from their circle were brutally assailed by Communist groups, on one occasion by an armed gang of 200 men. Several times he and his friends had to go into hiding. At his lodgings, which he seldom left if he could help it, he had a spy-hole cut into the front door so that he could identify callers before opening to them. The danger was not always so bluntly physical. A protracted barrage of slander was directed against Serge and his circle by the many organs of the Mexican Press influenced by the Communists and their powerful associates (such as the trade-union leader Lombardo Toledano). The strong German Stalinist emigration (*Freies Deutschland*), including such veteran propagandists as André Simone (Katz) and Paul Merker, added their quota of venom to the campaign.[1] Serge's friends were Socialist militants of long standing like Marceau Pivert, the leader of the pre-war French Socialist Left; Gustav Regler, lately a political commissar with the International Brigades in Spain; Julián Gorkín, the former international secretary of the independent Marxist party P.O.U.M.; and other Spanish comrades of that complexion. Nevertheless, they (and Serge and

---

[1] Some of the slanderers were subsequently themselves targets for the same type of treatment. In January 1953 Paul Merker was accused by the East German régime of having, during his Mexican exile, made *Freies Deutschland* into a 'propaganda journal for Zionist ideas'; he and his old collaborator Jungmann were arrested and imprisoned. This purge was conducted as part of 'the lessons of the Prague Trials' of November 1952, as a result of which Simone-Katz was hanged as a British Intelligence agent, allegedly recruited by Noël Coward in 1939.

Gorkín particularly) were incessantly denounced as Nazi agents, enemies of the United Nations, allies of the *sinarquistas* or local Fascists, founders of a new Trotskyist International, and fomenters of railway strikes. One by one, Mexican publications closed their columns to this obscure band of troublesome foreigners. The editor of one weekly which still admitted Gorkín as its foreign editor, and Serge as a contributor, was called in to see Miguel Alemán, the Minister of the Interior and future President of the Republic; there he was informed that the Soviet and British Ambassadors were pressing the Mexican Government to withdraw from Serge and Gorkín all public means of expression. Although the editor refused to accede, his journal afterwards acquired a new management enjoying the favour of the Soviet Embassy, and he, Gorkín, and Serge were all unceremoniously ousted. The boycott was now total, and Serge found it increasingly hard to keep body and soul together. Only one more book of his saw print during his life, a novel published in Canada and (in translation) in the United States. He tried in vain to get the *Memoirs* published in the U.S.A. 'In every publishing-house', he bitterly concluded, 'there is at least one conservative and two Stalinists; and nobody has the slightest understanding of the life of a European militant.' He died penniless, and his friends had to make a collection among themselves to pay the expenses of his burial.

The estrangements and dissensions typical of *émigré* political groups bore particularly heavily upon Serge. Within the independent Socialist colony he was the only member with a specifically Bolshevik background. His collaboration with Socialists from other traditions was warm and unstinted, but we can gain some inkling of a certain isolation that he felt, to judge from a note he entered in his diary in mid-January 1944. Here he records his pleasure at the resumption of friendly relations with Trotsky's widow Natalya, noting how they, 'the sole survivors of the Russian Revolution here and perhaps anywhere in the world, used to be separated so completely by sectarianism; and this was not like the human spirit of the real Bolsheviks . . .' He reflects that Natalya is going to be pained by certain anti-Trotskyist observations in a book which he had just brought out in co-authorship with his friends; 'she will perhaps not realize my solitude in these collaborations'. He concludes sadly, 'There is nobody left who knows what the Russian Revolution was

really like, what the Bolsheviks were really like—and men judge
without knowing, with bitterness and basic rigidity.'

Yet in other respects Serge was far too much of a revisionist for his
more traditional Marxist comrades, many of whom were nursing
hopes for their post-war return to the Old World on the crest of a
European Revolution. Serge had no such hopes. For him the Second
World War was a 'war of social transformation' (and not simply a
classical imperialist war as nearly all his comrades thought), usher-
ing in an era of controlled and planned economies that would,
under the conditions of post-war reconstruction, burst the fetters of
capitalist private property even in the absence of proletarian upheavals. 'European big capital, weakened and discredited by the
war it has brought on, will find itself in *opposition* to the growth of
production and the common good, *now in clear evidence*.'[1] Serge
believed that this inevitable collectivist transformation would have a
marked totalitarian bias, which could, however, be largely counteracted by class-struggle on the political level. Parliaments, munici-
palities, trade unions, and workers' councils offered a possible focus
for this countervailing influence by the masses. Serge maintained
this perspective well after the war: 'I wonder if some kind of
collectivism, quasi-totalitarian but *enlightened*, guaranteeing the
human rights that have been acquired over several centuries,
will not eventually establish itself for the reconstruction of the
old continent; such a system I would find acceptable if it were
directed by technicians and effectively controlled by the masses.'[2]

So pessimistic an outlook, based (despite its undoubted insights)
upon speculative impressionism rather than on any thorough
economic analysis, could not fail to irritate most of his comrades.
Their charges of 'technocratism' ('Just one more little "deviation"
in my life-history', as he remarked) irked him, and he in his turn
could not take seriously their pipe-dreams for an insurrectionary
post-war settlement in Europe. There was no basis for the growth of
mass revolutionary parties in the conditions of Occupied Europe,
and in any case nowadays 'a popular revolution which possesses no
aeroplanes will inevitably be beaten'. There could be no question
any longer of a specifically proletarian hegemony; the 'vanguard'
must be sought preponderantly within the growing social strata of

[1] Unpublished MS., *Economie Dirigée et Démocratie* (no date).
[2] Letter to Borie, 26 September 1947.

technicians and white-collar employees. 'The education of the working class has to be managed afresh. . . .'

Serge's reflections on the Western social order are suggestive but
often highly ambiguous. He was on surer ground as a commentator
upon Soviet perspectives, which he indeed saw as determining the
direction of all politics, and especially Socialist politics, in the rest of
Europe. He shared none of the current illusions that the Grand
Alliance of Churchill, Roosevelt, and Stalin would survive the end
of hostilities with Germany. As early as January 1944 we find him
noting that 'Stalinist hegemony over Europe would not be a liberation but a new nightmare' and that 'it would also mark the beginning of the Third World War'. Serge's last years were increasingly
clouded by this prospect of 'the permanent war' (as he terms it in a
diary entry for October 1944), anticipated by him at a time when
Western politicians often displayed the most grotesque naïvety over
Stalin's intentions. Rarely can his sense of 'the appalling powerlessness of accurate prediction' have afflicted him so acutely as when
he watched the unfolding of the promised nightmare: Stalinist sub-
jugation of Eastern Europe, extremist demands for preventive
nuclear war on the Western side. The letters and notebooks of this
period reflect the division of his fears between the threat of Stalinism
and the threat of war. It would be possible to excerpt fragments of
these sources in such a way as to present either a pro-Western
Victor Serge or a kind of 'New Left' archetype, repelling both
capitalism and Communism with a libertarian disgust. The
truth must be that within a man of Serge's loyalties the Cold War
engendered contradictions which he could only express, never
surmount.[1]

Serge was convinced that the sources of Soviet expansionism lay
in the extreme inner weakness of the social organism underneath the
totalitarian armour. In an unpublished essay written in English[2] he
observes: 'The training of a popular revolution who [which] has
survived against the worst odds has formed in the governmental
circles a mentality of offensive bluff and courageous risk, daily
expediency, belief only in force and fact. In the greatest danger the
régime will not think of retreat, evolution, compromise, but of an

---

[1] For a discussion of one particular crux in Serge's correspondence, see Appendix, *Victor Serge and Gaullism*, p. 383.
[2] Unpublished MS., *On the Russian Problem* (October 1945).

offensive struggle in which compromises are expediency, more apparent than real.' In Serge's view the post-war era might evolve along any of three possible directions. If the Soviet system yielded neither to internal nor external pressure, there would be war. Alternatively the régime might back down in the international field while refusing any concessions at home; 'war is then postponed, but not removed altogether'. Or again, 'under the combined pressure of the masses at home and of the international conflicts which will arise in various ways, the régime may try and evolve towards a democratization. Upon the slightest relaxation of terrorist totalitarianism, immense possibilities are opened out, which may cause the emergence in Russia of a Socialist-inclined or Socialist democracy, and permit a peaceful collaboration with the world outside. The nightmare of war is then removed.'[1]

It was in fact this last possibility that aroused Serge's closest interest. His papers and letters refer repeatedly to the idea of something quite odd and unforeseen happening in Russia, which would transform the situation most favourably for its people and for the world outside. Serge is deliberately vague as to what this change might consist of. It is certainly not an anti-Stalinist revolution of the kind advocated by Trotsky. He calls the prospect one of 'internal crisis',[2] 'change of régime in Russia',[3] or of a 'great Soviet reform'.[4] One illuminating episode of March 1944, recorded subsequently in his diary, indicates the strength of Serge's conviction on this score. He had met Trotsky's grandson, Siova Volkov, on a bus. Siova was about seventeen years old at this time, and was understandably bitter about things Russian. In the course of his childhood his mother had been driven to suicide in Berlin and his father had disappeared forever in Russia. Having taken refuge with his grandfather in Mexico, the boy had had to crouch beneath a bed, wounded in the foot, amidst a hail of machine-gun bullets directed throughout the house by the artist Siqueiros; he had lived in the same house in the time when Trotsky was murdered by an agent who had ingratiated himself with the whole family. Siova now told Serge that he had completely forgotten the Russian language. 'You'll have to learn it, then,' said Serge. 'What for?' Siova replied violently, 'Out of sentimental attachment? No, thank you!' And Serge answered,

---

[1] Unpublished MS., (no title, no date).   [2] Letter to Borie, 26 September 1947.
[3] *Ibid.*, 16 April, 1947.   [4] *On the Russian Problem.*

'Russia will be changing a great deal, before very long. We must remain faithful to her, and keep up great hopes.'

This long-term optimism of Serge, which now seems uncannily prescient, arose from the same source as his dark immediate fore-bodings: from his certain belief, based on long personal experience in Russia, that the terrorist edifice of Stalinism was founded on un-endurable social strains, which had been accentuated even further by the ruin of the Second World War. He probably, too, still believed that what he called 'the moral capital of the Socialist revolution' had still not been exhausted even by the long years of blood and lies. Serge had been one of the first people (before any-body else, he thought) to use the word 'totalitarian' of the Soviet State, but unlike some Western thinkers he did not mean it to imply a finished, impervious, and stable structure, governed omni-potently at the top by considerations of pure power. The detail of his prediction, where there was detail at all, might be fanciful; a few days before he died, he told his son Vlady, 'I won't live to see this but you probably will—monuments to Trotsky and to Stalin in the public squares of Russian cities.'[1] There is no reason to sup-pose that he would have regarded the present Russian régime as the 'Socialist-inclined or Socialist democracy' of his hopes. Never-theless, in broad outline and to an astonishing degree, Serge's sense of Soviet reality, of its double-sidedness for the future as well as for the past, has been justified by the turn that events have in fact taken.

To say this much is not to elevate Serge into an expert oracle, a sort of Nostradamus of twentieth-century revolutionism. Because his background and experience were so intensively Russian, he is some-times a much less valuable guide to certain areas of politics outside the frontiers of the Soviet Union itself. His references to colonial nationalist movements, in the *Memoirs* as elsewhere, are nearly always distant or disparaging. Later in life he tended to regard all non-Russian Communist Parties (of whom he had never held a very high opinion) as little more than extensions of the Kremlin and N.K.V.D. apparatus. When, in late 1944, he encountered the sug-gestion that Communist-led resistance movements might develop an autonomous character, free of Muscovite control, his response was wholeheartedly scornful: there were only 'totalitarian-Communist

[1] Information supplied by Vlady.

condottieri of the Mao-Tse Tung or Tito type, cynical and *convinced*, who will be "revolutionary" or "counter-revolutionary"—or both simultaneously—depending on the orders they receive, and capable of an about-face from one day to the next'.[1] It would of course be senseless to reproach Serge for not foreseeing the Yugoslav and Chinese schisms of Communism; but enough has been said to suggest that his clairvoyance was principally that of an exceptionally sensitive eyewitness and participant of the Bolshevik movement.

About Victor Serge's death, as in his life, there was a retiring quality. He had been in poor health over a number of years, with a record of heart-attacks going back to his convict years in France. The high altitude of Mexico City did not suit his condition, and even his long, lyrical excursions into country parts could offer small convalescence after the years of deprivation and persecution. In the middle of 1947 he suffered two attacks of angina. He looked frightfully old and tired, but was optimistic and full of plans. There were offers of publication (for *L'Affaire Toulaév*) from Canada, France, and the U.S.A., of collaboration with Mexican reviews, even of a possible visa for the United States. Early in the small hours of Monday, 17 November, he read his wife a poem he had just written. It was a meditation on a Renaissance terracotta of a pair of hands, old and with knotted veins. Serge had tears in his eyes as he read the poem out; the hands symbolized generations of human suffering and resistance, and the knots on them were so like those of his own veins. He went to bed after typing the poem, and had his breakfast around ten the next morning, discussing anthropology with his wife, something about the mystical significance of gold. She had to go.to work then; there is no record of the rest of Serge's day until eight in the evening, when he went out to see his son Vlady. He wanted to have a talk about Vlady's paintings, but his son was not at home. He met his friend Julián Gorkín in the street; they talked for a while, and shook hands when they parted. This would be around 10 p.m. Not long after that, doubtless feeling himself ill, Serge hailed a taxi, sank back into the seat, and died without telling the driver where to take him. His family found him stretched out on an old operating-table in a dirty room inside a police-station. Gorkín recounts what

---

[1] *Carnets*, p. 172–3; cf. also Serge's letter on '*Stalinism and The Resistance*' in *Politics*, February 1945.

he looked like: his upturned soles had holes in them, his suit was threadbare, his shirt coarse. Really he might have been some vaga-bond or other picked up from the streets. Victor Serge's face was stiffened in an expression of ironic protest and, by means of a bandage of cloth, the State had at last closed his mouth.

Liverpool, 1963 Leeds, 1977   PETER SEDGWICK

EDITOR'S NOTE TO THE 1978 IMPRESSION

Since the first publication of the *Memoirs* in English, many titles have been added to the repertory of Serge's available works. The Bibliography has been updated, and the Appendix and Introduction revised in the light of newly available material.

It is fitting to note at this point the considerable indebtedness of English-speaking Serge readers to the efforts of Dr. Richard Greeman, whose work on the translation and promotion of the novels—a task of genuine scholarship as well as of devotion—deserved a better appreciation. The indefatigable labour and devotion of Jean Rière has re-established and republished many Serge texts—though the name of Victor Serge is still nowhere to be found in any directory or history of modern French literature. With the main body of Victor Serge's work now in print or on its way to publication, I will bow out as translator by adding a short unpublished poem of his (sent to me by his son Vlady), along with an English version, composed for the wedding of my comrades Jim and Ellen Edmondson:

> *O nuit pleine de toi, ô nuit pleine d'étoiles*
> *j'ai besoin, pour t'aimer, de comprendre le monde*
> *pour comprendre le monde, j'ai besoin de t'aimer.*

> A night filled with stars, a darkness filled with you:
> So that I could love you I had to understand the world
> And before I could understand the world, I had to love you.

ACKNOWLEDGEMENTS

The text of this translation is shorter, by about an eighth, than the French original. With the exception of the final chapter, which is intact, pruning has taken place throughout the length of the book. The paragraphing of the original is generally longer than here and Serge's frequent habit of dissolving the end of a sentence in three dots (. . .) has on the whole been abandoned in the translation. Purely mechanical errors on the part of Serge (e.g. in the translation of foreign names) have been corrected wherever they have been noted.

In the preparation of this edition I am greatly indebted to Victor Serge's son Vlady for the loan of material from his father's archives, and for a lively, moving, and deeply informative correspondence; both forms of assistance have been of considerable help to me in the Introduction. I am also grateful to Jean Rière, Julián Gorkín, J.-P. Samson, Enid Starkie, André Malraux, Paul Avrich, Richard Greeman, Michael Futrell, Gero Neugebauer, Jean Maitron, Pierre Naville, Paul Schmierer, Pierre Frank and Boris Björklund for their help with footnotes and editorial material. Many of the most awkward points in the text itself were resolved with the help of Pierre Marteau, Philip Burnett, and Gill Seidel. On a matter of history: it was George Orwell to whom Serge first transmitted the manuscript of Serge's *Memoirs* for publication in English; and Isaac Deutscher who supported my request to the Oxford University Press to be allowed to translate and edit the present edition.

1

WORLD WITHOUT ESCAPE
1906–1912

Even before I emerged from childhood, I seem to have experienced, deeply at heart, that paradoxical feeling which was to dominate me all through the first part of my life: that of living in a world without any possible escape, in which there was nothing for it but to fight for an impossible escape. I felt repugnance, mingled with wrath and indignation, towards people whom I saw settled comfortably in this world. How could they not be conscious of their captivity, of their unrighteousness? All this was a result, as I can see today, of my upbringing as the son of revolutionary exiles, tossed into the great cities of the West by the first political hurricanes blowing over Russia.

On 1 March 1881, nine years before my birth, on a day of shining snow, a fair-haired young woman, her face calm and determined, who was waiting near a St. Petersburg canal for the passing of a sledge escorted by Cossacks, suddenly waved a handkerchief. There was an echo of muffled, soft explosions, the sledge came to a sudden halt, and there on the snow, huddled against the canal wall, lay a man with greying side-whiskers, whose legs and belly had been blown to shreds: the Tsar Alexander II. The party called *People's Will* published his death-sentence on the following day. My father, a non-commissioned officer in the cavalry of the Imperial Guard, was at that time stationed in the capital; he sympathized with this underground party, which demanded 'bread and liberty' for the people of Russia, and had no more than about sixty members and two or three hundred sympathizers. Among those responsible for the assassination, Nikolai Kibalchich,[1] a chemist and distant relative of my father, was arrested and hanged, together with Zhelyabov, Ryssakov, Mikhailov, and Sofia Perovskaya, daughter of a former Governor of St. Petersburg. In court, four of the five condemned to death defended their libertarian demands with dignity and courage; on the scaffold, they embraced one another and died calmly.

My father had joined in the struggle, entering a revolutionary military group in the south of Russia which was soon completely broken; for several days he hid in the gardens of the oldest monastery in Russia, St. Lavra of Kiev; he crossed the Austrian frontier by swimming under the bullets of the police; and he went on to Geneva, in a land of sanctuary, to start a new life.

He intended to become a physician, but geology, chemistry, sociology, and philosophy also interested him passionately. I never knew him as anything but a man possessed with an insatiable thirst for knowledge and understanding which was to handicap him during all his remaining years in 'the struggle for life'. Along with the rest of his revolutionary generation, whose masters were Alexander Herzen, Belinsky, and Chernyshevsky (then a deportee in Yakutia), and also by reaction against his religious training, he became an agnostic, after Herbert Spencer, whom he heard speak in London.

My grandfather on my father's side, a Montenegrin by origin, was a priest in a small town in the Chernigov province; all I knew of him was a yellowing daguerreotype of a thin, bearded cleric with a high forehead and a kindly expression, in a garden full of bonny, bare-footed children. My mother, born of Polish gentry, had fled from the bourgeois life of St. Petersburg, and she too went to study at Geneva. I was born at Brussels, as it happened, in mid-journey across the world, because my parents, in quest of their daily bread and of good libraries, were commuting between London (the British Museum), Paris, Switzerland, and Belgium. On the walls of our humble and makeshift lodgings there were always the portraits of men who had been hanged. The conversations of grown-ups

---

[1] Nikolai Ivanovich Kibalchich (1854–81) was, as well as the manufacturer of the bombs that blew up the Tsar, a leading theoretician of the *Narodnaya Volya*. In his death-cell he prepared a design for a flying-machine propelled by rockets, which is claimed by present-day Soviet science as an antecedent to the Sputniks.

dealt with trials, executions, escapes, and Siberian highways, with great ideas incessantly argued over, and with the latest books about these ideas. In my childhood's memory I accumulated images of the world: Canterbury Cathedral, the esplanade of old Dover Castle above the sea, the dismal red-brick street in Whitechapel, the hills of Liége. I learned to read through cheap editions of Shakespeare and Chekhov, and, dozing off to sleep, I dreamt for hours of blind King Lear leaning, in his journey over the cruel waste-land, on the tender attentions of Cordelia. I also acquired bitter experience of that unwritten commandment: 'Thou shalt be hungry.' I think that if anyone had asked me at the age of twelve, 'What is life?' (and I often asked it of myself), I would have replied, 'I do not know, but I can see that it means "*Thou shalt think, thou shalt struggle, thou shalt be hungry*".'

It must have been some time between the age of six and eight that I became an evildoer. Through this episode I was to learn another commandment: *Thou shalt fight back*. I was a well-loved child, being the first-born; but for some years I became, inexplicably, a criminal child. With a devilish cunning, the criminal child worked his mischief as if he wanted to avenge himself against the universe and even, what was most cruel, against those he loved. The precious pages of my father's scientific notes were found torn up. The milk, stored for supper in the cool of the window-ledge, was found dosed with salt. My mother's clothes were mysteriously burnt with matches or else slashed with scissors. Ink was surreptitiously spilt on newly-ironed linen. Objects disappeared without trace. Nobody could intercept the hands of the criminal child—my hands. I was harangued at length, I was admonished, I often saw my mother's eyes fill with tears; I was beaten too, and punished in a hundred ways, because my petty crimes were mad, exasperating, incomprehensible. I drank the salted milk, I denied everything (naturally), I melted into wretched promises, and then went to bed, in inconsolable grief, thinking of King Lear leaning on Cordelia. I became taciturn and introverted. Now and then the crimes would stop, and life would become bright, until the coming of another dark day which I had learnt to expect with a vigilant inner certainty. Eventually a time came when I acquired a sure foreknowledge of evil: I knew and felt, inwardly, that my mother's pinafore would be dirtied or slit with scissors. I waited upon chastisement, and

lived amid rebuke—and yet I used to play and climb trees as if evil
had never existed. I had entered an unfathomable mystery, I had
become wise; I carried the problem inside my head and let its solution ripen. The end of this episode, which I am sure made a deep
impression on my character, left me with the most exalting memory
of tenderness that I have ever experienced. I was about to learn that
two individuals could, with a deep gaze and an embrace, understand
one another utterly and conquer the worst evil. We were living
on the outskirts of Verviers, in Belgium, in a country house which
had a big garden. Two days before, some gross misdeed, whose
precise nature I no longer remember, had cast a shadow over the
household. However, I spent that particular day in the garden with
my little brother Raoul. As twilight appeared, my mother called
us back into the big kitchen, where a delicious smell of warm bread
hovered in the air. First she busied herself with my brother, washing
him, feeding him and putting him to bed. Then she made the
wicked child sit on a chair, knelt before him, and washed his feet.
We were alone, lapped in an unforgettable sweetness. My mother
looked straight up at me and suddenly, in a tone of reproach, asked,
'But why do you do all this, my poor little man?' and then the truth
flashed out between us, because a strange power was bursting within
me: 'But it isn't me,' I said, 'it's Sylvie! I know everything, everything!'

Sylvie was an older adolescent cousin adopted by my parents
and living with us, a blonde and graceful girl, but cold-eyed. I had
accumulated so many observations and proofs, and with such
analytic power, that my headstrong, tearful exposition was irrefutable. The matter was closed, with a full and permanent recovery of
trust. I had fought back steadfastly against evil, and had been
delivered from it.

My first great experience of hunger dates from a little later, at the
age of eleven. I used to recall how one day in England we fed on
grains of wheat prised out of the ears which my father had picked
up from the side of a field; but that was nothing. We spent a hard
winter at Liége, in a mining district. Above our lodging a café
proprietor used to work: *Mussels and Chips!* Exotic odours. . . . He
gave us a little credit, but not enough, for my brother and I were
never satisfied. His son would steal sugar to trade with us for bits of
string, Russian postage stamps, and various oddments. I became

accustomed to finding exquisite delicacy in the bread we soaked in black coffee (which was well-sugared, thanks to this commerce), and it was evidently good enough for me to survive on. My brother, two years my junior—eight and a half at that time—did not take to this diet, and grew thin, pale and depressed; I saw him wasting away. 'If you don't eat,' I told him, 'you're going to die'; but I had no idea what it was to die, and he even less, so it did not frighten us.

The fortunes of my father, who had been appointed to the Institute of Anatomy of the University of Brussels, took a sudden turn for the better. He summoned us to his side, and we ate sumptuously. Too late though for Raoul, who was confined to bed, sinking fast but fighting back for a few weeks. I put ice on his forehead, I told him stories, I tried to convince him that he would get better, I tried to convince myself; and I saw something incredible happening within him: his face became that of a little child again, his eyes glittered and grew dim at the same time, and all the while the doctors and my father came into the dark room on tiptoe. Alone together, my father and I took him to the cemetery at Uccle, on a summer's day. I discovered how alone we were in this seemingly happy town—and how alone I was myself. My father, believing only in science, had given me no religious instruction. Through books, I came across the word 'soul'; it was a revelation to me. That lifeless body that had been bundled away in a coffin could not be everything.

Some verses of Sully Prudhomme that I learned by heart gave me a kind of certainty which I dared not confide to anyone:

> *Blue eyes, dark eyes, loved and lovely,*
> *Exposed to endless dawn,*
> *From beyond the tomb still see*
> *Tight though their lids be drawn.*

In front of our lodging there was a house topped with a finely wrought gable, which I found a magnificent sight. Golden clouds used to rest over it every evening. I called it 'Raoul's House', and often dawdled to gaze at this house in the sky. I detested the lingering hunger of the poor children. In the eyes of those I met, I thought I saw Raoul's look. They were nearer to me than anybody else, they were my brothers, and I felt that they were condemned. These feelings were rooted deeply, and have remained with me. After forty years, when I returned to Brussels, I went to see that gable in the sky on the road to Charleroi; and throughout the rest of my life it has been my fate always to find, in the undernourished urchins of the squares of Paris, Berlin, and Moscow, the same condemned faces of my tribe.

My first friendship dates from the following year. Wearing a Russian smock in white and mauve check, which my mother had just finished, I was going home along a country street in Ixelles carrying a red cabbage; proud of my smock and feeling a little ridiculous on account of the cabbage. An urchin of my own age, thick-set and bespectacled, squinted at me sarcastically from across the road. I deposited my cabbage in a doorway and walked up to him, meaning to pick a quarrel with him by calling him bat-eyed. 'Glass-face! Goggles! Want me to push your face in?' We measured each other up like the small gamecocks that we were, jostling one another's shoulders a little. 'Just you dare!' 'Get started!'; all without fighting, however, but forming from then on a friendship which was, through all its enthusiasms and tragedies, never far from conflict. And when he died on the scaffold at the age of 20, we were still friends—and foes. It was he who, after the squabble, came and asked me if I wanted to play with him, and thus established a dependence on me against which, despite our affection, he ever afterwards rebelled in his inmost heart. Raymond grew up as far as he could in the street, anything to get away from the stifling back room that was his home, behind a cobbler's stall where his father patched the shoes of the district from morning till night. His father was a spiritless drunk, an old Socialist disgusted with Socialism. From the age of thirteen I lived alone, owing to the journeys and estrangements of my parents; Raymond often came to seek refuge with me. Together we learnt to forsake the tales of Fenimore Cooper for Louis Blanc's great *History of the French Revolution*, whose illustrations showed us streets, just like those that we haunted, overrun by *sansculottes* armed with pikes. Our favourite pastime was to share two sous' worth of chocolate between us, reading these gripping stories. They moved me particularly because their legends of the past lent substance to the ideals of men I had known of since the first awakenings of my intelligence. Together, though much later, we were to discover Zola's overwhelming novel *Paris* and, in an effort to relive the despair and rage of Salvat, trapped in the Bois de Boulogne after his essay in murder, we wandered for hours through the Bois de la Cambre in the autumn rain.

My father, a university teacher of small means, kept up his anxious *émigré* existence. I saw him in close combat with the money-lenders. His second wife, worn out with child-bearing and poverty, underwent terrible crises of hysteria. From the 1st to the 10th of each month, the household (which I seldom visited) ate reasonably well, from the 10th to the 20th less well, and worst of all from the 20th to the 30th. Certain memories, already old, remained embedded in my soul like nails in flesh: for example (when we were living somewhere in the new district behind the Cinquantenaire park), my father going out one morning with a cheap little coffin of yellow wood under his arm. His emotionless face: '*Thou shalt seek to obtain thy bread on credit.*' On his return, he retired to the solitude of his anatomy and geology atlases. I had never been to school, for my father despised this 'stupid bourgeois instruction for the poor', and could not pay for a college education. He worked with me himself, not often and not well—but the passion for knowledge and the radiance of a constantly armed intelligence, never allowing itself to stagnate, never recoiling from an inquiry or a conclusion, shone from him so powerfully that I was quite hypnotised by it, and went the rounds of museums, libraries, and churches, filling up my notebooks and ransacking encyclopaedias. I learned to write without ever knowing grammar; I was eventually to learn French grammar by teaching it to Russian students. For me, learning was not something separate from life, it was life itself. The mysterious relationships between life and death became clear through the very unmysterious importance of the fruits of the earth. The words 'bread', 'hunger', 'money', 'no money', 'credit', 'rent', 'landlord' held, in my eyes, a crudely concrete meaning which was, I think, to predispose me in favour of historical materialism. . . . Still, my father wanted to make me take up higher education, despite his professed contempt for certificates. He spoke of this often, hoping to influence me in that direction. A pamphlet by Peter Kropotkin[1] spoke to me at that time in a language of unprecedented clarity. I

---

[1] Peter Kropotkin (1842–1921): outstanding Anarchist writer; imprisoned for agitation in Russia, he escaped from jail to England (1876) where he settled after various wanderings in Europe. Returned to Russia after the February Revolution of 1917.

have not turned back to it since, and at least thirty years have elapsed since then, but its message remains close to my heart. 'What do you want to be?' the anarchist asked young people in the middle of their studies. 'Lawyers, to invoke the law of the rich, which is unjust by definition? Doctors, to tend the rich, and prescribe good food, good air, and rest to the consumptives of the slums? Architects, to house the landlords in comfort? Look around you, and then examine your conscience. Do you not understand that your duty is quite different: to ally yourselves with the exploited, and to work for the destruction of an intolerable system?'

If I had been the son of a bourgeois university teacher, these arguments would have seemed a trifle abrupt, and over-harsh towards a system which, all the same. . . . The theory of a Progress that advanced ever so gently as the ages passed would probably have seduced me. . . . Personally, I found these arguments so luminous that those who did not agree with them seemed criminal. I informed my father of my decision not to become a student. It was a fitting time to tell him: the disastrous end of the month.

'What are you going to do then?'

'Work. I'll study without being a student.'

To tell the truth, I was too afraid of sounding pompous or of starting a great disputation of ideas, to dare to reply, 'I want to fight as you yourself have fought, as everyone must fight throughout life. I can see quite clearly that you have been beaten. I shall try to have more strength or better luck. There is nothing else for it.' That is pretty near what I was thinking.

I was just over fifteen. I became a photographer's apprentice, and after that an office-boy, a draughtsman and, almost, a central-heating technician. My day's work was now ten hours long. With the hour and a half allowed for lunch and an hour's journey, there and back, that made a day of twelve and a half hours. And juvenile labour was paid ridiculously low wages, if it was paid at all. Plenty of employers offered two years' apprenticeship without pay, in return for teaching a trade. My best early job brought in forty francs (eight dollars) a month, working for an old businessman who owned mines in Norway and Algeria. . . . If, in those days of my adolescence, I had not enjoyed friendship, what would have I enjoyed?

There was a group of us young people, closer than brothers.
Raymond, the short-sighted little tough with a sarcastic bent, went
back every evening to his drunken old father, whose neck and face
were a mass of fantastically knotted muscles. His sister, young,
pretty, and a great reader, passed her timid life in front of a window
adorned with geraniums, amid the stench of dirty old shoes, still
hoping that, some day, someone would pick her up. Jean, an
orphan and a part-time printer, lived at Anderlecht, beyond the
stinking waters of the Senne, with a grandmother who had been
laundering for half a century without a break. The third of our
group of four, Luce, a tall, pale, timorous boy, was blessed with
'a good job' in the *L'Innovation* stores. He was crushed by it all:
discipline, swindling, and futility, futility, futility. Everyone
around him in this vast, admirably organized bazaar seemed to be
mad, and perhaps, from a certain point of view, he was right to
think so. At the end of ten years' hard work, he could become
salesman-in-charge, and die as the head of a department, having
catalogued a hundred thousand little indignities like the story of the
pretty shop-assistant who was sacked for rude behaviour because
she refused to go to bed with a supervisor.

In short, life displayed itself to us in various aspects of a rather
degrading captivity. Sundays were a happy release, but that was
only once a week, and there was no money. Now and then we would
wander along the lively streets of the town centre, gay and sardonic,
our heads full of ideas, spurning all temptations with contempt.
We were too prone to contempt. We were lean young wolves,
full of pride and thought: dangerous types. We had a certain
fear of becoming careerists, as we considered many of our elders
to be who had made some show of being revolutionary, and afterwards. . . .

'What will become of us in twenty years' time?' we asked ourselves
one evening. Thirty years have passed now. Raymond was guillotined: 'Anarchist Gangster' (so the newspapers). It was he who,
walking towards the worthy Dr. Guillotin's disgusting machine,
flung a last sarcasm at the reporters: 'Nice to see a man die, isn't
it?' I came across Jean again in Brussels, a worker and trade-union
organizer, still a fighter for liberty after ten years in gaol. Luce has
died of tuberculosis, naturally. For my part, I have undergone a
little over ten years of various forms of captivity, agitated in seven

countries, and written twenty books. I own nothing. On several occasions a Press with a vast circulation has hurled filth at me because I spoke the truth. Behind us lies a victorious revolution gone astray, several abortive attempts at revolution, and massacres in so great number as to inspire a certain dizziness. And to think that it is not over yet. Let me be done with this digression; those were the only roads possible for us. I have more confidence in mankind and in the future than ever before.

We were Socialists: members of the *Jeunes-Gardes*.[1] Ideas were our salvation. There was no need to prove to us, textbook in hand, the existence of social conflict. Socialism gave a meaning to life, and that was: struggle. There were intoxicating demonstrations under heavy flags that were awkward to carry when you had not slept or eaten properly. And then we would see, ascending the balcony of the *Maison du Peuple*, the slightly satanic forelock, the domed forehead, the twisted mouth of Camille Huysmans.[2] There were the warlike headlines of *La Guerre Sociale*. Gustave Hervé, leader of the insurrectionist element of the French Socialist Party, organized a poll among his readers: 'Should he be killed?' (This was under a Clemenceau government). In the wake of the big antimilitarist trials, French deserters brought us the whiff of the aggressive trade unionism of Pataud, Pouget, Broutchoux, Yvetôt, Griffuelhes, Lagardelle.[3] (Of these men, most are now dead;

---

[1] *Jeunes-Gardes Socialistes:* Belgian federation of Socialist youth groups, founded in 1890 and still in active existence at the present day. Affiliated to the Belgian Socialist Party.

[2] Camille Huysmans (1871–1968): prominent Belgian Socialist, secretary of the Second International before the First World War; later an eminent Parliamentarian, being President of the Chamber 1936–9 and 1954–8, Minister of Education 1925–7 and 1947–9, and Prime Minister in 1946–7.

[3] Pouget, Yvetôt and Griffuelhes dominated the French trade union scene in this decade. Emile Pouget (1860–1932) was a brilliant journalist, editor of the explosive anarchist journal *Le Père Peinard*, then of the C.G.T. organ *Voix du Peuple*; organizer, pamphleteer and advocate of the eight-hour day. Georges Yvetôt (1868–1942) was secretary of the trade-union Labour Exchanges from 1901, an antimilitarist, and author of *L'A.B.C. Syndicaliste*. Victor Griffuelhes (1874–1923) was the untheoretical but highly effective secretary of the C.G.T. from 1902 to 1909. Emile Pataud was an electricians' leader, co-author (with Pouget) of a syndicalist Utopia. Benoît Broutchoux was a syndicalist miners' leader and journalist. Hubert Lagardelle (1874–1958) founded the review *Le Mouvement Socialiste* (1898); in 1904 he joined the Socialist Party and advocated a variety of Sorelian syndicalism; went to Italy after the rise of Fascism and became economic adviser and confidant to Mussolini; was Pétain's Minister of Labour (1942–3).

Lagardelle lived to become an adviser to Mussolini and Pétain.) Men escaped from Russia told us of the Sveaborg mutiny, of the dynamiting of an Odessa prison, of executions, of the 1905 general strike, of the days of liberty. The first public discussion I ever opened was on these topics, for the Ixelles branch of the *Jeunes-Gardes*.

Our young contemporaries talked about bicycles or girls in a most loathsome way. We were chaste, expecting better things both from ourselves and from fortune. Without benefit of theory, adolescence opened up for us a new aspect of the problem. In a sordid alley, at the end of a dark passage hung with gaudy washing, there lived a family we knew: the mother gross and suspicious, nursing the vestiges of her beauty; a lecherous daughter with bad teeth; and a stunning younger girl, of pure Spanish beauty, her eyes all charm, innocence, and softness, her lips like blossom. It was all she could do, when she passed us chaperoned by her dam, to manage a smiling 'Hello' to us. 'It's obvious', said Raymond, 'they're sending her to dancing lessons and keeping her for some rich old bastard.' We discussed problems like this. Bebel's *Woman and Socialism* was on our reading-list.

Gradually we entered into battle, not with Socialism, but with all the anti-Socialist interests that crawled around the working-class movement: crawled around it and seeped into it and ruled over it and smeared dirt on it. The halting-points on the routes of local processions were arranged to suit certain tavernkeepers associated with the workers' Leagues—impossible to suit them all! Electoral politics revolted us most of all since it concerned the very essence of Socialism. We were at once, it now seems to me, both very just and very unjust, because of our ignorance of life, which is full of complications and compromises. The two per cent. dividend returned by the co-operatives to their shareholders filled us with bitter laughter because it was impossible for us to grasp the victories behind it. 'The presumption of youth!' they said: but in fact we were athirst for the absolute. The Racket exists always and everywhere, for it is impossible to escape from one's time and we are in the time of money. I kept finding the Racket, flourishing and sometimes salutary, in the age of trade and in the midst of revolution. We had yearned for a passionate, pure Socialism. We had satisfied ourselves with a Socialism of battle, and it was the great age of reformism.

At a special congress of the Belgian Workers' Party, Vandervelde,[1] young still, lean, dark, and full of fire, advocated the annexation of the Congo. We stood up in protest and left the hall, gesturing vehemently. Where could we go, what could become of us with this need for the absolute, this yearning for battle, this blind desire, against all obstacles, to escape from the city and the life from which there was no escape?

Socialism meant reformism, parliamentarism, and unrelieved Talmudism. Its intransigence was incarnated in Jules Guesde,[2] who made one think of a city of the future in which all the houses would be alike, with an all-powerful State, harsh towards heretics. Our way of correcting this doctrinal rigidity was to refuse to believe in it. We had to have an absolute, only one of liberty (without unnecessary metaphysics); a principle of life, only unselfish and ardent; a principle of action, only not to win a place in this stifling world (which is still a fashionable game), but to try, however desperately, to escape from it since it was impossible to destroy it.

That principle was offered us by an anarchist. He of whom I am thinking has been dead many years. His shadow lingers on, greater than the man himself. A miner from the Borinage, recently released from prison, Emile Chapelier had just founded a communist—or rather communitarian—colony in the forest of Soignes, at Stockel. At Aiglemont, in the Ardennes, Fortuné Henry, brother of the guillotined terrorist Emile Henry, was running a similar Arcady. 'To live in freedom and work in community, from this day on. . . .' We went along sunlit paths up to a hedge, and then to a gate. Buzzing of bees, golden summer, eighteen years old, and the doorway to Anarchy! There was an open-air table, loaded with tracts and pamphlets. The C.G.T. *Soldier's Handbook*, *The Immorality of Marriage*, *The New Society*, *Planned Procreation*, *The Crime of Obedience*, *Citizen Aristide Briand's Speech on the General Strike*. Those voices were alive. A saucer full of small change, and a notice, 'Take what you

---

[1] Emile Vandervelde (1866–1938): Belgian Socialist leader, prominent in the Second International; entered the Cabinet during the First World War. Foreign Minister 1925–7.

[2] Jules Guesde (1845–1922): Republican revolutionary under the Empire, jailed for opposition to the Franco-Prussian War. Exiled in Switzerland after the suppression of the Commune, he espoused Bakuninist ideas, before turning to State 'collectivism'. Joined the 'Cabinet of National Defence' at the outbreak of war.

want, leave what you can'. Breathtaking discovery! The whole city, the whole earth was counting its pennies, one was presented with money-boxes on special occasions: No Credit, Trust Nobody, Shut the Door Firmly, What's Mine is Mine, yes? Monsieur Th——, my employer, a colliery-owner, issued all postage-stamps himself; impossible to cheat this millionaire out of ten centimes! We were amazed at the pennies abandoned by Anarchy to the sky.

A little farther on, and we came to a small white house under the trees: *Do What You Will* over the door, which was open to all-comers. In the farmyard, a big black devil with a pirate's profile was haranguing a rapt audience. A real style to the man, his tone bantering, his repartee devastating. His theme: free love. But how could love not be free?

Printers, gardeners, a cobbler, a painter were working here in comradeship, together with their womenfolk. It would have been idyllic, if only. . . . They had started with nothing, like brothers; they still had to tighten their belts. Usually these colonies collapsed quite quickly, for lack of resources. Although jealousy was formally prohibited in them, quarrels over women, even though resolved by bursts of generosity, did them the greatest mischief. The libertarian colony of Stockel, transferred to Boitsfort, spun out for several years. There we learned to edit, set up, proof-read and print, all by ourselves, our paper *Communiste*, which consisted of four small pages. Some tramps, a short, prodigiously intelligent Swiss plasterer, a Tolstoyan-anarchist Russian officer, Leon Gerassimov, with a pale, noble face, who had escaped from a defeated insurrection and, the following year, was to die of hunger in the Fontainebleau woods; also a redoubtable chemist, from Odessa via Buenos Aires—all these helped us to investigate the solutions of many a great problem.

The individualist printer: 'Friend, there is only yourself in the world. You must try not to be a bastard or a ninny.'

The Tolstoyan: 'Let us be new men. Salvation is within us.'

The Swiss plasterer, a disciple of Luigi Bertoni:[1] 'All right, so long as you don't forget your hob-nailed boots: you'll find those in the factories.'

---

[1] Luigi Bertoni (1872–1947): Swiss printer and publisher of anarchist literature, firstly of the bilingual journal *Le Réveil* (*Il Risveglio*) from 1900 to 1940, then of various pamphlets; in opposition to both World Wars. Publisher of Kropotkin, Malatesta, and other anarchist writers.

The chemist, having listened long, said in his Russo-Spanish accent: 'All this is claptrap, comrades; in the social war we need good laboratories.' Sokolov was a cold-blooded man, moulded in Russia by inhuman struggles, apart from which he could no longer live. He came out of the storm, and the storm was within him. He fought, he killed, he died in prison.

The idea of 'good laboratories' was of Russian origin. From Russia, swarming through the whole world, came men and women who had been formed in ruthless battle, who had but one aim in life, who drew their breath from danger. The comfort, peace, and amiability of the West seemed stale to them, and angered them all the more since they had learned to see the naked operations of a social machinery which no one thought of in these privileged lands. In Switzerland, Tatiana Leontieva killed a gentleman she mistook for a minister of the Tsar. Rips fired on the *Gardes Républicains* from the top deck of a bus in the Place de la République. A revolutionary, in the confidence of the police, executed the head of the Okhrana's secret service in a hotel room at Belleville. In a mean quarter of London called Houndsditch (a name appropriate to such squalid dramas), Russian anarchists withstood a siege in the cellar of a jeweller's shop; the picture of Winston Churchill, then a young Cabinet Minister, directing the siege became a photographer's cliché. In Paris, Svoboda was blown up while trying out his bombs in the Bois de Boulogne. 'Alexander Sokolov' (whose real name was Vladimir Hartenstein) belonged to the same group as Svoboda. In his little room behind a shop in the Rue de la Musée, he had installed a complete laboratory, just a few yards from the Royal Library, where he spent part of his day writing to his friends in Russia and Argentina, in Greek characters but in Spanish.

It was a time of pot-bellied peace; the atmosphere was strangely electric, the calm before the storm of 1914. The first Clemenceau government had just drawn working-class blood at Draveil (in 1908), where police had entered a strike meeting only to shoot and kill several innocent people, and at the funeral demonstration for these victims, where troops opened fire. (This demonstration had been organized by the secretary of the Food Workers Union, Métivier, an extreme-Left militant and police spy who the previous day had received his personal instructions from the Minister of the Interior, Georges Clemenceau himself.) I remember our anger when we learnt of these shootings. That same evening a hundred of us youngsters showed the red flag in the neighbourhood of the Government buildings, willingly battling with the police. We felt ourselves close to all the victims and rebels in the world; we would have fought joyfully for the men executed in the prisons of Montjuich or Alcala del Valle, whose sufferings we recalled each day. We felt the growth within us of a wonderful and formidable collective awareness.

Sokolov laughed at our demonstration, mere child's play. He himself was silently preparing the real reply to the workers' murderers. At the end of a sad train of events, his laboratory was discovered; he found himself hounded down, without means of escape. Flight was impossible because of his face, notable for its intense eyes and conspicuous in a crowd because the top part of his nose had been crushed (apparently with a blow from an iron bar). He shut himself up in a furnished room at Ghent, loaded his revolvers and waited; and when the police came, he fired on them as he had fired on the Tsar's police. The peaceful sergeants of Ghent paid for the Cossacks' pogroms and Sokolov laid down his life, 'whether here or there matters little, so long as one lays it down on the great day, for the awakening of the oppressed'.

In the Rue de Ruysbroek, at the shop of a little grocer-cum-bookseller who was suspected of being an informer, I had met Edouard, a metal-turner; he was thick-set, with the physique of some outlandish Hercules, and a heavy, muscular face lit up by his timorous, shifty little eyes. He had come from the factories of Liége and was fond of reading Haeckel's *Riddle of the Universe*. Of himself, he said, 'I was well on the way to becoming a splendid ruffian! I was lucky to begin to understand. . . .' And he told me how on the barges of the Meuse he had lived a ruffian's life ('Just like the others, only tougher, of course'), terrorizing the women a little, working hard, with the odd bit of pilfering from the docks, 'Without knowing what a man is or what life is.' He asked to be admitted into our group. 'What ought I to read, do you think?'

'Elisée Reclus,' I answered.[1]

'It isn't too difficult?'

'No,' I replied, but already I was beginning to see just how

---

[1] Elisée Reclus (1830–1905): French geographer, one of five brothers outstanding in the subject; an associate of the First International. Banished to Belgium after the suppression of the Commune.

tremendously difficult it was. We let him join, and he was a good comrade. Our times together were not clouded by the foreknowledge that he would die, by his own hand, close to me.

Paris called us, the Paris of Salvat, of the Commune, of the C.G.T., of little journals printed with burning zeal, the Paris of our favourite authors, Anatole France and Jehan Rictus; the Paris where Lenin from time to time edited *Iskra* and spoke at *émigré* meetings in little co-operative houses; the Paris where the Central Committee of the Russian Social-Revolutionary Party had its headquarters, where Burtsev lived, who had just unmasked, in the terrorist organization of this party, Evno Azev, engineer, executioner of Minister von Plehve and of Grand Duke Sergei, and police spy. I took my leave of Raymond with bitter irony. I noticed him on a street corner, unemployed, handing out advertisements for a tailor's shop. 'Hello there, Free Man!' I said, 'Why not Sandwich-Man?'

'Perhaps it will come to that,' he said, laughing, 'but no more towns for me. They are nothing but treadmills. I want to work or bust on the open road; I shall at least have fresh air and countryside. I've had a bellyful of all these deadpans. I'm only waiting to get enough to buy a pair of shoes.' He went off with his mate by the Ardennes roads, to Switzerland and the open spaces, helping with the harvest, raising limestone with masons, cutting timber with woodcutters, a floppy old felt hat over his eyes, a volume of Verhaeren in his pocket:

> *Drunk with the world and with ourselves, we bring*
> *Hearts of new men to the old universe.*

I have often thought since then that poetry was a substitute for prayer for us, so greatly did it uplift us and answer our constant need for exaltation. Verhaeren, the European poet nearest to Walt Whitman (whom we did not yet know), flashed us a gleam of keen, anguished, fertile thought on the modern town, its railway stations, its trade in women, its swirling crowds; and his cries of violence were like ours: '*Open or break your fists against the door!*' Fists were broken, and why not? Better that than stagnation. Jehan Rictus lamented the suffering of the penniless intellectual dragging out his nights on the benches of foreign boulevards, and no rhymes were richer than his: *songe-mensonge* (dream-lie), *espoir-désespoir* (hope-despair). In springtime '*the smell of crap and lilacs. . . .*'

One day I went off, all at random, taking ten francs, a spare shirt, some work-books, and some photos which I always kept with me. In front of the station I chanced to meet my father, and we talked of the recent discoveries on the structure of matter which had been popularized by Gustave Le Bon.

'Are you off?'

'Yes, to Lille for a fortnight.'

I believed it; I was never to come back, never to see him again, but the last letters I had from him in Brazil when I was in Russia, thirty years later, still spoke of the structure of the American continent and the history of civilizations.

Europe at that time knew no passports, and frontiers hardly existed. I stayed in a mining village at Fives in Lille; two and a half francs a week (fifty U.S. cents), payable in advance, for a clean garret. I wanted to go down the mine. Some cheery old miners laughed in my face: 'You'd be finished in two hours, friend.' On the third day, I had four francs left. I went to look for work, rationing myself; every day a pound of bread, two pounds of green pears, a glass of milk (bought on credit from my kind hostess), twenty-five centimes to spend. Annoyingly enough, the soles of my shoes began to let me down, and on the eighth day of this routine, attacks of giddiness forced me to seek the haven of benches in the public gardens. I was obsessed by a dream of bacon soup. My strength was ebbing, I was going to be good for nothing, not even for the worst possible existence. An iron footbridge over the railway-line in the station began to exert an absurd fascination over me, when I was saved by a providential meeting with a comrade who was supervising drain-digging in the street. Almost at once I found work with a photographer at Armentières, at four francs a day—a fortune. I was unwilling to leave the mining village, and went out at dawn in the sad morning mist with the workers in their leather helmets. I travelled to work amongst slag-heaps, then shut myself up all day in a poky laboratory where we worked alternately by green light and red. In the evening, before fatigue could prostrate me, I would spend a little while reading Jaurès' *L'Humanité*, with mingled admiration and annoyance. A couple lived behind the partition. They adored one another, and the man used to beat his wife savagely before taking her. I could hear her murmur through her sobs, 'Hit me again, again.' I found inadequate the studies of working-class women which I had hitherto read. Would it after all take centuries to transform this world and these human beings? Yet each one of us has only one life in front of him.. What was to be done?

Anarchism swept us away completely because it both demanded everything of us and offered everything to us. There was no remotest corner of life that it failed to illumine, at least so it seemed to us. A man could be a Catholic, a Protestant, a Liberal, a Radical, a Socialist, even a syndicalist, without in any way changing his own life, and therefore life in general. It was enough for him, after all, to read the appropriate newspaper; or, if he was strict, to frequent the café associated with whatever tendency claimed his allegiance. Shot through with contradictions, fragmented into varieties and sub-varieties, anarchism demanded, before anything else, harmony between deeds and words (which, in truth, is demanded by all forms of idealism, but which they all forget as they become complacent). That is why we adopted what was (at that moment) the extremest variety, which by vigorous dialectic had succeeded, through the logic of its revolutionism, in discarding the necessity for revolution. To a certain extent we were impelled in that direction by our disgust with a certain type of rather mellow, academic anarchism, whose Pope was Jean Grave in *Temps Nouveaux*.[1] Individualism had just been affirmed by our hero Albert Libertad. No one knew his real name, or anything of him before he started preaching. Crippled in both legs, walking on crutches which he plied vigorously in fights (he was a great one for fighting, despite his handicap), he bore, on a powerful body, a bearded head whose face was finely proportioned. Destitute, having come as a tramp from the south, he began his preaching in Montmartre, among libertarian circles and the queues of poor devils waiting for their dole of soup not far from the site of Sacré Coeur. Violent, magnetically attractive, he became the heart and soul of a movement of such exceptional dynamism that it is not entirely dead even at this day. Libertad loved streets, crowds, fights, ideas, and women. On two occasions he set up house with a pair of sisters, the Mahés and then the Morands. He had children to whom he refused to give State registration. 'The State? Don't know it? The name? I

---

[1] Jean Grave (1854–1939): anarchist militant and author, founder of the journal *La Révolte*; novelist and essayist. Manufactured a bomb, but never threw it.

don't give a damn, they'll pick one that suits them. The law? To the devil with it.' He died in hospital in 1908 as the result of a fight, bequeathing his body ('That carrion of mine', he called it), for dissection in the cause of science.

His teaching, which we adopted almost wholesale, was: 'Don't wait for the revolution. Those who promise revolution are frauds just like the others. Make your own revolution, by being free men and living in comradeship.' Obviously I am simplifying, but the idea itself had a beautiful simplicity. Its absolute commandment and rule of life was: 'Let the old world go to blazes.' From this position there were naturally many deviations. Some inferred that one should 'live according to Reason and Science', and their impoverished worship of science, which invoked the mechanistic biology of Félix le Dantec,[1] led them on to all sorts of tomfoolery, such as a saltless, vegetarian diet and fruitarianism and also, in certain cases, to tragic ends. We saw young vegetarians involved in pointless struggles against the whole of society. Others decided, 'Let's be outsiders. The only place for us is the fringe of society.' They did not stop to think that society has no fringe, that no one is ever outside it, even in the depth of dungeons, and that their 'conscious egoism', sharing the life of the defeated, linked up from below with the most brutal bourgeois individualism.

Finally, others, including myself, sought to harness together personal transformation and revolutionary action, in accordance with the motto of Elisée Reclus: 'As long as social injustice lasts we shall remain in a state of permanent revolution.' (I am quoting this from memory.) Libertarian individualism gave us a hold over the most intense reality: ourselves. *Be yourself.* Only, it developed in another 'city without escape'—Paris, an immense jungle where all relationships were dominated by a primitive individualism, dangerous in a different way from ours, that of a positively Darwinian struggle for existence. Having bade farewell to the humiliations of poverty, we found ourselves once again up against them. To be yourself would have been a precious commandment and perhaps a lofty achievement, if only it had been possible; it would only have begun to be possible once the most pressing needs of man, those which identify him more closely with the brutes than with his

---

[1] Félix le Dantec (1869–1917): Lamarckian biologist, theorist of evolution and rationalist.

fellow humans, were satisfied. We had to win our food, lodging and clothing by main force; and after that, to find time to read and think. The problem of the penniless youngster, uprooted or (as we used to say) 'foaming at the bit' through irresistible idealism, confronted us in a form that was practically insoluble. Many comrades were soon to slide into what was called 'illegalism', a way of life not so much on the fringe of society as on the fringe of morality. 'We refuse to be either exploiters or exploited,' they declared, without perceiving that they were continuing to be both these and, what is more, becoming hunted men. When they knew that the game was up they chose to kill themselves rather than go to jail.

One of them, who never went out without his Browning revolver, told me, 'Prison isn't worth living for! Six bullets for the sleuth-hounds and the seventh for me! You know, I'm lighthearted.' A light heart is a heavy burden. The principle of self-preservation that is in us all found its consequence, within the social jungle, in a battle of One against All.

A positive explosion of despair was building up in us unbeknown. Man is finished, lost. We are beaten in advance, whatever we do. A young anarchist midwife gave up her calling 'because it is a crime to inflict life on a human being'. Years later, awakened into hope by the Russian Revolution, I wanted to reach Petrograd, then in flames, and agreed to pass through a sector of the Champagne front, at the risk either of being left there in a common grave or of killing men better than myself in the opposite trench. I wrote: 'Life is not such a great benefit that it is wrong to lose it or criminal to take it.'

René Valet, my friend, was a lively, restless spirit. We had met in the *Quartier Latin*, we had discussed everything together, usually at night, around the St. Geneviève hill, in the little bars jostling on the Boulevard St. Michel: Barrès, Anatole France, Apollinaire, Louis Nazzi. Together we muttered scraps of Vildrac's *White Bird*, Jules Romains' *Ode to the Crowd*, Jehan Rictus' *The Ghost*. René was law-abiding and prosperous, he even had his own locksmith's workshop, not far from Denfert-Rochereau. I can see him there now, standing up like a young Siegfried, criticizing Anatole France's treatment of the destruction of this planet. Having had his say, René would sink slowly down on the asphalt of the boulevard, with a sly grin. 'What is certain is that we are all mugs. Yes, mugs!'

I remember his fine, square-set ginger head, his powerful chin, his green eyes, his strong hands, his athlete's bearing (an emancipated athlete, naturally). He liked to wear the navvy's wide corduroy trousers, with a waistband of blue flannel. Once, on an evening of riots, we wandered together around a guillotine, ridden by our gloom, sickened by our feebleness, mad with anger. 'We have a wall in front of us,' we told each other, 'and what a wall.' 'Oh, the bastards!' muttered my ginger-headed friend, and next day he confessed to me that all that night his hand had been closed upon the chill blackness of a Browning revolver. Fight, fight, what else was there to do? And if it meant death, no matter. René rushed into mortal danger out of his sense of solidarity with his defeated mates, out of his need for battle and, at the heart of it, out of despair. These 'conscious egoists' were going to get themselves slaughtered for friendship's sake.

I had arrived in Paris a little after the death of Libertad. The luxurious Paris of Passy and the Champs-Elysées, and even of the great boulevards of commerce, were for us like a foreign or enemy city. Our own Paris had three centres: the great working-class town that began somewhere in a grim zone of canals, cemeteries, waste plots, and factories, around Charonne, Pantin, and the Flandre bridge; it climbed the heights of Belleville and Ménilmontant, and there became a plebeian capital, lively, busy and egalitarian like an ant-heap; and then, on its frontiers with the town of railway stations and delights, became cluttered with shady districts. Small hotels for a 'short time', 'sleep-sellers' where for twenty sous one could gasp in a garret without ventilation, pubs frequented by procurers, swarms of women with coiled hair and coloured aprons soliciting on the pavements.

The rumbling trains of the *Métro* would suddenly plunge into a tunnel under the town, and I would linger in a circle of passers-by to hear and see Hercules and the Boneless Wonder with their fantastic patter, clowns with a waggish dignity who always needed just another fifteen sous before they would perform their best tricks, upon an old rug spread on the pavement. And inside another circle, as evening came on and the workshops emptied, the blind man, his stout female assistant and the soulful orphan-girl would sing the popular songs of the day: '*The riders of the moo-oon. . . .*'

and in the ballad there was also some mention of 'dusky night' and
'desperate love'.

Our Montmartre adjoined, but never met, the Montmartre of
artists' taverns, bars haunted by women in feathered hats and
hobble-skirts, the *Moulin Rouge*, etc. We acknowledged only old
Frédé's *Lapin Agile*, where people sang old French songs, some perhaps going back to the days of François Villon, who was a wandering,
despairing, merry young sprig, a poet, a rebel like us—and a gallows-
bird. The old Rue des Rosiers, where the generals Lecomte and
Clément Thomas were shot under the Commune, now renamed the
Rue de la Chevalier de la Barre, had, since the time of the barricades,
only changed its appearance at one point along its extent. There, at
the top of the slope, the basilica of Sacré Coeur de Jésus was sloth-
fully nearing completion, in a sort of fake-Hindu, monumentally
bourgeois style. Hard by the stone-yards here, young radical thinkers
had put up a statue of the young Chevalier de la Barre who had
been burnt by the Inquisition.

The basilica and the white marble Chevalier looked down on the
roofs of Paris: ocean of grey roofs, over which there arose at night
only a few dim lights, and a great red glow from the tumultuous
squares. We would pause there to take stock of our ideas. At the
other end of the street, a lopsided square stretched at the crossing
of two roads, one a steep incline, the other rising in flights of dull grey
steps. In front of a tall and ancient shuttered house, the journal
Causeries Populaires and the offices of *L'Anarchie*, both founded by
Libertad, occupied a shabby building, filled with the noise of
printing-presses, singing, and passionate discussion. There I met
Rirette,[1] a short, slim, aggressive girl-militant with a Gothic profile,
and Emile Armand[2] the theoretician, sickly and goateed, his
pince-nez all askew, once a Salvation Army officer, lately a convict
in solitary confinement, a stubborn, often subtle dialectician who
used to argue purely on the basis of self. 'I only propose, never
impose,' he would almost splutter; yet out of his spluttering emerged

[1] Rirette and Serge were in fact lovers, and later married during his imprisonment at Melun. She joined him in Spain, but had to return to France and thence
lost contact with him, except by correspondence.

[2] Emile Armand—pseudonym of Ernest Jouin (1872–1962): after being influenced by anarchism during his period in the Salvation Army, founded a
Christian-Tolstoyan-anarchist journal (*L'Ere Nouvelle*), then turned to individualist
anarchism and edited *L'Anarchie* and subsequently *L'En-Dehors*.

the most disastrous theory possible: that of 'illegalism'. This transformed lovers of liberty, 'outsiders', enthusiasts for comradely living, into technicians of obscure and illicit crafts.

The most important subject of our discussions, some of which ended in shooting and blood-letting among comrades, was 'the importance of science'. Should scientific law regulate the whole life of the New Man, to the exclusion of irrational sentiment and of all idealism 'inherited from ancestral faiths'? Taine's and Renan's blind cult of science, here reduced to almost algebraic formulae by fanatical popularizers, became the catechism of individualist revolt: 'Myself alone against all', and 'Nothing means anything to me', as the Hegelian Max Stirner[1] once proclaimed. The doctrine of 'comradely living' slightly counteracted the unpardonable isolation of these rebels; but out of it was emerging a constricted coterie, equipped with a psychological jargon demanding a long initiation. I found this coterie at once fascinating and repellent. I was at some distance from those primitive conceptions; other influences were at work on me, and there were other values which I neither could nor would abandon: basically, the revolutionary idealism of the Russians.

I had happened to find work easily at Belleville, as a draughtsman in a machine-tool works, ten hours a day, twelve and a half including the journeys, starting at 6.30 a.m. In the evenings I went, by the funicular railway and the *Métro*, to the Left Bank, the Latin Quarter, our third Paris—the one I liked best, to tell the truth. I had an hour and a half at my disposal to read at the St. Geneviève Library, with eyes that stubbornly refused to stay open over political economy, and a tired intellect functioning now only at half-cock. I took to alcohol to help me to read, but I only forgot everything the following day.

I left the brutalizing atmosphere of my 'good job', the pallid fascination of the Chaumont hills in the morning and the fascination of evening, when the street was full of lights and the eyes of working-girls. I proceeded to settle myself in the garret of an inn, in the Place du Panthéon, trying to live by teaching French to Russian students and by doing jobs of routine brain-work. It was better to

---

[1] Max Stirner (1806–56): German anarchist philosopher, author of *The Ego and His Own*: 'Nothing means anything to me', is the opening of this work (*Ich hab' mein' Sach' auf Nichts gestellt*, a quotation from Goethe).

feel a faint pinch of hunger reading in the Luxembourg Gardens than to eat my fill by sketching crankshafts till I could no longer think.

From my window I could see the square, the Panthéon gate, and Rodin's 'Thinker'. I would have liked to know the exact spot on which Dr. Tony Moilin had been shot in 1871 for tending the Commune's wounded. The bronze Thinker seemed to me to be meditating on that crime, and waiting to be shot himself. After all, how insolent he was, doing nothing but thinking; and how danger- ous if he ever came to a conclusion.

A Social-Revolutionary had introduced me to the members of his party among the Russian emigration. He was a large, hairless gentleman of Americanized manners, often sent off by the party on missions to the United States. The Russian Social-Revolutionary Party was passing through a serious crisis of morale, since several police agents had been unmasked in its Battle Organization; for example, Azev and Zhuchenko. The militant who had greeted me on my arrival, with whom I had often discussed Maeterlinck and the meaning of life all night long, was called Patrick. He led an exemplary life, kept faith amid the general demoralization, and cultivated a healthy optimism. When the Paris archives of the Okhrana's secret service were opened in 1917 we found that Patrick was also a police agent, but that was really no longer of any importance.

I led a many-sided life; I was attracted by the partisan warriors of Paris, that sub-proletariat of *déclassé*, 'emancipated' men, dream- ing of freedom and dignity and constantly on the verge of im- prisonment; and among the Russians I breathed a much purer air, distilled in sacrifice, energy and culture. I taught French to a stunning young woman who always wore red dresses, a Maximalist,[1] one of the rare survivors of the attempt at Aptekarsky Island, in St. Petersburg. There three Maximalists had presented themselves in uniform at a reception in the villa of the Prime Minister, Stolypin, and suffered themselves to be roasted in the hall, so as to make sure that the villa would be blown up to practically nothing. People around me spoke of them as if they had only just gone out of the

[1] The Maximalist party split from the Social-Revolutionaries in 1906, advocat- ing the socialization of industry as well as of land, together with a wider applica- tion of terrorism (to include pillage and incendiarism of estates, as well as individual assassination). The movement's general position was in some ways close to that of the Anarchists. By 1908 the movement was virtually extinguished, though it did make a brief reappearance after 1917.

room; of Salomon Ryss, alias Medved, the Bear, who had joined the Okhrana to disrupt and disorganize it, had been caught and recently hanged; of Petrov, who had done the same at St. Petersburg, and had lately assassinated the head of the secret police; of Gershuni, who refused a pardon out of contempt for the Tsar— they dared not hang him all the same—then escaped, and died here, not far from us, of tuberculosis; of Yegor Sazanov who twice offered up his life, first when he threw a bomb under von Plehve's carriage, and again when he killed himself in jail, a few months before he was due for release, in protest against the maltreatment of his comrades.

Coming from these discussions, I would meet old Edouard Ferral, selling his copies of *L'Intransigeant* on the corner of the Boulevard St. Michel and the Rue Soufflot. *L'Intran, L'Intran!*: he proclaimed his wares in a soft, trembling voice. He sported an improbable pair of worn-out boots, and a complete, authentic tramp's outfit. A disgraceful yellow straw hat sat like a halo on his head. Bearded like Socrates, a lively glow in his eyes (which were the colour of Seine water), he lived, wanting even elementary necessities, among the lowest of the low. I never knew under what strains he had been brought so low, for certainly his was one of the finest intelligences of the libertarian movement, naturally heretical, loved and admired by the young. Deeply learned, reciting and translating Virgil with lyrical passion in down-at-heel pubs in the Place Maubert (where we willingly followed him), a disciple of Georges Sorel and himself a theoretician of syndicalism, he blended this theory with the ideas of Mécislas Golberg,[1] who practically died of hunger in the Latin Quarter affirming that the highest revolutionary vocation was the thief's.

It was Ferral who introduced me to the terrifying world of utmost poverty, spiritless degradation; the borderline of humanity under the rubble of the great city. There, a tradition of total, overwhelming defeat had been kept up—as it still is—for at least ten centuries. These wretches were the lineal descendants of the first beggars of Paris, perhaps of Roman Lutetia's meanest plebs. They were older than Notre Dame, and neither St. Geneviève nor the blessed

[1] Mécislas (Mieczyslaw) Golberg (1870–1907): Polish anarchist and Bohemian, resident in Paris after 1894; an associate of Apollinaire, Picasso and other literary-artistic figures of the time, Golberg edited a periodical for the unemployed, evolved a theoretical basis for Cubism (*La Morale des Lignes*, 1908), and acted as a lively influence in the thinking of his milieu.

Virgin had ever been able to do anything for them: proof, of course, that they were beyond redemption. I saw them in the pubs of *La Maub'*, drinking their draught wine, eating the pork-shop's refuse, repairing the dressings (sometimes spectacularly faked) on their sores; I heard them discuss the affairs of their guilds, the allotment of a particular begging-pitch that had become vacant through the passing of a certain member, lately found dead under a bridge. Others would be replenishing their trays with matches and shoe-laces, others again delousing themselves discreetly. I observed, terrified, what the city could do to man, the mangy, pestiferous, kennelled cur's existence to which it reduced him; and this helped me to understand Peter Lavrov's *Historical Letters*,[1] concerning social justice.

The *clochard* is a spent individual, squeezed dry of personal initiative, who has learnt to enjoy, feebly but stubbornly, the meagre vegetable existence which is all that he has. The rag-pickers were a world apart, adjacent but separate, centring on the Barrière d'Italie at St. Ouen; some of the less abandoned managed to accumulate a positive treasure by exploiting an abundant raw material: the town's refuse. The genuine human refuse could not even do that, having too little energy and too much sloth to pursue the systematic efforts of the dustbin brigade.

I translated Russian novels and poems—Artzybashev, Balmont, Merezhkovsky—for a charming Russian journalist under whose signature they appeared. Thanks to this employment I was enabled to buy onion soup for Ferral at the stroke of midnight by a brazier in Les Halles beneath the squat, massive silhouette of St. Eustache. One of the peculiar features of working-class Paris at this time was that it bordered extensively on the underworld, that is, on the vast world of irregulars, outcasts, paupers, and criminals. There were few essential differences between the young worker or artisan from the old central districts, and the ponce from the alleys by Les Halles. A chauffeur or mechanic with any wits about him would pilfer all he could from the boss as a matter of course, out of class consciousness ('It's all on the guv'nor!') and because he was 'free' of old-fashioned prejudice. Working-class attitudes, aggressive and anarchic, were pulled in opposite directions by two antagonistic

[1] Peter Lavrov (1823–1900): Russian Populist Socialist of the non-insurrectionary school.

movements, the revolutionary syndicalism of the C.G.T. which, with a fresh and powerful idealism, was winning the real proletariat to the struggle for positive demands, and the shapeless activity of the anarchist groups. Between and beneath these two currents, restless and disaffected masses were being borne along. Two extraordinary demonstrations of this time marked an epoch for me and for the whole of Paris; I think that no historian will be able to ignore their significance.

The first one took place on 13 October 1909. On that day we heard the news of an incredible event: the execution of Francisco Ferrer,[1] decreed by Maura and permitted by Alfonso XIII. The founder of the Modern School in Barcelona, condemned absurdly for a popular uprising of some days' duration, fell back into the ditch at Montjuich shouting to the firing-squad: 'I forgive you, children! Aim straight!' (Later on he was 'rehabilitated' by Spanish justice.)

I had written, even before his arrest, the first article in the great Press campaign conducted on his behalf. His transparent innocence, his educational activity, his courage as an independent thinker, and even his man-in-the-street appearance endeared him infinitely to the whole of a Europe that was, at the time, liberal by sentiment and in intense ferment. A true international consciousness was growing from year to year, step by step with the progress of capitalist civilization. Frontiers were crossed without formalities; some trade unions subsidized travel for their members; commercial and intellectual exchanges seemed to be unifying the world. Already in 1905 the anti-Semitic pogroms in Russia had roused a universal wave of condemnation. From one end of the Continent to the other (except in Russia and Turkey) the judicial murder of Ferrer had, within twenty-four hours, moved whole populations to incensed protest.

In Paris the movement was spontaneous. By hundreds of thousands, from every *faubourg*, workers and ordinary folk, impelled by a terrible indignation, flowed towards the city centre. The revolutionary groups followed rather than guided these masses. The editors of revolutionary journals, taken aback by their sudden influence, spread the call: 'To the Spanish Embassy!' The Embassy would

[1] Francisco Ferrer (1859–1909): pacifist, anarcho-syndicalist, and educational reformer. His *Escuela Moderna* in Barcelona taught rationalist and libertarian principles to its pupils. Much influenced by the French C.G.T., he translated and distributed French syndicalist material and founded the journal *Solidaridad Obrera*.

have been ransacked had not Lépine, the Police Commissioner, barricaded all entries to the Boulevard Malesherbes. Angry riots started in these prosperous thoroughfares, lined with banks and aristocratic residences.

The backwash of the crowds carried me among newspaper kiosks blazing on the pavements and overturned omnibuses whose horses, painstakingly unharnessed, gazed stupidly at their empty contraptions. Police cyclists charged, weaving their machines to and fro at random. Lépine was shot at from ten yards by a revolver from somewhere in a group of journalists belonging to *La Guerre Sociale*, *Le Libertaire*, and *L'Anarchie*. Weariness and the onset of night calmed the outburst, which left the people of Paris with an exultant sensation of strength. The Government authorized a legal demonstration two days after, led by Jaurès; we marched along, 500,000 of us, surrounded by mounted *Gardes Républicains* who sat all subdued, taking the measure of this newly-risen power.

There was a natural transition from this demonstration to the second. Miguel Almereyda[1] had participated in the organization of the first, and was the moving force behind its successor. I had helped him hide in Brussels, where he had brusquely ridiculed my momentary Tolstoyan fancies. In short, we were friends. I told him, 'You're just an opportunist. Your people have started off quite wrong.' He answered 'As far as Paris is concerned you are an ignoramus, my friend. You can purify yourself with Russian novels, but here the revolution needs cash.'

He incarnated human achievement in a measure so far practically unknown to me. He had the physical beauty of the pure-bred Catalan—tall forehead, blazing eyes—allied with an extreme elegance. A brilliant journalist, a captivating orator, a capable libertarian politician, adroit in business, he was able to handle a crowd or fix a trial, to brave the bludgeons of the police, the revolvers of certain comrades or the spite of the Government, and to concoct fantastic intrigues. In the ministries, he had his connexions; in the slums, his devoted friends.

He was behind the disappearance from Clemenceau's drawer

[1] Miguel Almereyda (Bonaventure Vigo) (1883–1917): revolutionary militant and writer; organized the *Jeunesses Révolutionnaires* (1908), then founded the political-satirical review *Le Bonnet Rouge*, which led a 'defeatist' campaign in 1916–17 until it was suppressed. Almereyda was then accused of receiving German funds and arrested.

of a receipt for 500 francs signed by an *agent-provocateur* in the syndicalist movement. He then presented himself at the Assize Court and was acquitted with the jury's congratulations. He organized the circulation of *La Guerre Sociale*, whose guiding spirit he was, together with Gustave Hervé ('The General') and Eugène Merle, who was to become Paris's most powerful and Balzacian journalist. Almereyda had experienced a scarifying childhood, partly in a reformatory for a minor theft. It was he who, after the Ferrer demonstration, seized upon the Liabeuf affair. This was the prelude to a number of other dramas.

It was a battle of low life. Liabeuf, a young worker of twenty who had grown up on the Boulevard de Sébastopol, fell in love with a little street-walker. The vice-squad, those persecutors of girls, saw them together and had him condemned as a ponce. This he was not; on the contrary, his dream was to rescue this girl from 'the game'. The officially-provided defence counsel did not turn up at the trial, the accused man's protests were naturally of no avail, the petty sessions magistrate hurried through the proceedings in five seconds (as usual with these matters) and the police were, of course, on oath. Liabeuf felt branded with infamy. Once out of prison, he armed himself with a revolver, donned spiked armlets under his cloak, and went in quest of vengeance. To arrest him they had to nail him to the wall with a sabre blow. He had wounded four policemen, and was condemned to death. The left-wing Press indicted the vice-squad and demanded a pardon for Liabeuf. Commissioner Lépine, a short gentleman capable of a cold hysteria, whose goatee presided every year over the bludgeoning of the May Day demonstrators, demanded his execution. Almereyda wrote that if they dared to set up the guillotine, there would be more blood around it than beneath it. He appealed to the people of Paris to stop the execution by force. The Socialist Party lent its support to the movement.

On the night of the execution assorted crowds, from all the *faubourgs*, all the bounds haunted by crime and misery, converged upon that unique spot in Paris, always ghastly by day and sinister by night: the Boulevard Arago. On one side, bourgeois houses, insensitive to everything, with their windows neatly drawn on 'every man for himself' (and 'God for all', if you please), on the other, two lines of stout chestnut trees, beneath the wall—a wall of great cemented stones, dull greyish-brown, that most silent, most pitiless of walls, the prison wall: twenty feet high. I had come with Rirette, with René the Angry, with old Ferral who, positively fanatical in affliction, seemed to float along, unbelievably weak, inside his ragged suit. The militants from all the groups were there, forced back by walls of black-uniformed police executing bizarre manœuvres. Shouts and angry scuffles broke out when the guillotine wagon arrived, escorted by a squad of cavalry. For some hours there was a battle on the spot, the police charges forcing us ineffectively, because of the darkness, into side-streets from which sections of the crowd would disgorge once again the next minute. Jaurès was recognized at the head of one column and nearly brained. Almereyda manœuvred in vain to break through the human barrier. There was plenty of violence and a little bloodshed—one policeman killed. At dawn, exhaustion quietened the crowd, and at the instant when the blade fell upon a raging head still yelling its innocence, a baffled frenzy gripped the twenty or thirty thousand demonstrators, and found its outlet in a long-drawn cry: '*Murderers!*' The barriers of policemen now moved only lethargically. 'Do you see it?—The wall!' René shouted to me.

When in the morning I returned to that part of the boulevard, a huge policeman, standing on the square of fresh sand which had been thrown over the blood, was attentively treading a rose into it. A little farther off, leaning against the wall, Ferral was gently wringing his hands: 'Society is a filthy trick.'

From this day dates the revulsion and contempt that is aroused in me by the death-penalty, which replies to the crime of the primitive, the retarded, the deprived, the half-mad or the hopeless by nothing short of a collective crime, carried out coldly by men invested with authority, who believe that they are on that account innocent of the pitiful blood they shed. As for the endless torture of life imprisonment or of very lengthy sentences, I know of nothing more stupidly inhuman.

After the fight for Ferrer the philosopher, the battle for Liabeuf the desperado proved (although we did not see it) the seriousness of the deadlock in which the revolutionary movement of Paris was situated, no tendency being exempt. Energetic and powerful in 1906–7, the *Confédération Générale du Travail* began to decline, mellowed after a mere few years by the development of highly-paid sections among the working class. The 'insurrectionism' of Gustave Hervé and Miguel Almereyda revolved in a vacuum, expressing nothing in the end but a craving for verbal and physical violence. Bloated Europe, whose wealth and prosperity had grown to an unprecedented degree in the thirty years since 1880, still based its social system upon ancient injustices, and thereby created in its great cities a limited but numerous social stratum to whom industrial progress brought no real hope, and only that minimum of consciousness that sufficed to shed light upon its own misfortune. More: through its excess of energy, as well as the incompatibility of its historical structure with the new needs of society, the whole of this Europe was drawn towards resolving its problems in violence. We breathed the oppressive air of the prelude to war. Events heralded the catastrophe clearly enough. The Agadir incident, the partition of Morocco, the massacre at Casablanca; Italy's aggression against Tripolitania began the dismemberment of the Ottoman Empire, and the 'futurist' poet Marinetti detailed the splendour of bowels steaming in the sun of a battlefield. The Austrian Empire annexed Bosnia-Herzegovina. The Tsar continued to borrow money from the French Republic and to hang and deport the best of the Russian intelligentsia. From the two ends of the globe the Mexican and Chinese revolutions flamed out to illumine our enthusiasm.

On the Left Bank, bordering the Latin Quarter, I had founded a study-circle called 'Free Inquiry' (*La Libre Recherche*), which met upstairs in a Socialist co-operative in the Rue Grégoire-de-Tours, down dark corridors cluttered with barrels. The houses near by were brothels, with red lamps, large numerals, brightly-lit doors and signs in seventeenth-century script: *The Basket of Flowers*. The crowded thoroughfare of the Rue de Buci, packed with stalls jutting on to the pavement, unsavoury little bars, and costermongers, gave me the sensation (or so I thought) of going back to the Paris of Louis XVI. I was familiar with all the old doors along the street and on the peeling façades above the advertisements for the hire of evening-dress, I discerned the brand, invisible to others, of the Reign of Terror.

In public meetings, I would dispute with *Le Sillon*'s Christian Democrats,[1] who were fond of tough, strong-arm tactics, and with

---

[1] *Le Sillon:* journal of social Catholicism founded by Marc Sangnier in 1894; condemned by Pius X in August 1910.

the Royalists, who were roused to white-hot frenzy by Léon Daudet.[1] When the tall Léon appeared on the platform with his plump profile, rather like that of a declining Bourbon or an Israelite financier (the similarity between these would be exact), we would form a battle-square in a corner of the hall we had picked beforehand, and as soon as his thunderous voice proclaimed 'The monarchy, traditional, federalist, anti-Parliamentarian!' etc., our jeering interruptions would chime in: 'A century behind the times! Coblenz![2] The guillotine!', and I would demand leave to speak, protected by a rampart of stalwart comrades. The *Camelots du Roi*[3] waited for this moment to charge our square, but we were not always defeated.

By contrast Georges Valois,[4] a former anarchist himself but recently converted to royalism, was very willing to discuss his syndicalist-royalist doctrine; he invoked Nietzsche, Georges Sorel, 'the social myth', the communal guilds of the Middle Ages, national sentiment. Meanwhile, certain comrades suggested that I should again take up the editing of *L'Anarchie*, now transferred from Montmartre to the Romainville Gardens, and threatened by splits among the different tendencies. I made it a condition that the previous editorial and printing staff, a collection of 'scientific individualists' whose leading light was Raymond, should get out and that I should be allowed to recruit my own colleagues. Nevertheless, for a month two staffs co-existed, the old one and mine.

For a while I caught up again with Raymond and Edouard. They were intoxicated with their algebraic formulae and in thrall to their dietary discipline (absolute vegetarianism, no wine or coffee, tea or infusions, and we who ate otherwise were 'insufficiently evolved'). They were already, or were becoming, outlaws, primarily through the influence of Octave Garnier, a handsome, swarthy, silent lad whose dark eyes were astoundingly hard and feverish. Small,

---

[1] Léon Daudet (1868–1942): son of Alphonse Daudet; co-founder of the monarchist and extreme Right *L'Action Française*. Novelist and anti-Semitic writer.

[2] Coblenz: the base of the Royalist *émigrés* during the French Revolution.

[3] *Camelots du Roi*: nickname given to the young toughs who sold *L'Action Française*.

[4] Georges Valois (Alfred Gressent) (1878–194?): first an anarchist and organizer of the first bookshop assistants' union (1903); subsequently a leader of *L'Action Française*, and founder of the first French fascist movement (*Les Faisceaux*) (1925–8); later reverted to a left-wing, anti-State position. A prolific writer through his various phases, Valois died in a Nazi concentration-camp.

working-class by origin, Octave had undergone a vicious beating on a building site in the course of a strike. He scorned all discussion with 'intellectuals'. 'Talk, talk!' he would remark softly, and off he would go on the arm of a blonde Rubensesque Flemish girl, to prepare some dangerous nocturnal task or other.

No other man that I have met in my whole life has ever so convinced me of the impotence and even the futility of the intellect when confronted with tough primitive creatures like this, rudely aroused to a form of intelligence that fits them purely technically for the life-struggle. He would have made an excellent seafarer for a Polar expedition, a fine soldier for the colonies; or, at another period, a Nazi storm-troop leader or an N.C.O. for Rommel. There was no doubt of it, all he could be was an outlaw. His was a restless, uncontrolled spirit, in quest of some impossible new dignity, how or what he did not know himself. Petty quarrels multiplied. Raymond, Edouard, and Octave departed soon enough, and I transferred our print-shop, in which we lived together as comrades, to the top of Belleville behind the Chaumont hills, in an old workingmen's house in the Rue Fessart. I set out to give a new emphasis to the paper, in the form of a turn from individualism to social action. I opened a polemic against Elie Faure the art historian who, citing Nietzsche, had just proclaimed the civilizing function of war. I noted, almost enthusiastically, the suicide of Paul and Laura Lafargue, the son-in-law and daughter of Karl Marx; Lafargue, having reached the age of sixty, an age at which, he decided, active creative life was over, administered poison to himself and his wife. I sought to affirm a 'doctrine of solidarity and revolt in the here and now', quoting Elisée Reclus: 'Man is Nature become conscious of itself.' Of Marx I knew practically nothing. We denounced syndicalism as a future Statism, as terrible as any other. The cult of 'the workers', a reaction against the politicians (who were primarily lawyers interested in their Parliamentary careers), struck us as being over-rigid and as carrying within itself the seeds of an anti-intellectual careerism.

The end of 1911 saw dramatic happenings. Joseph the Italian, a little militant with frizzled hair who dreamed of a free life in the bush of Argentina, as far away as possible from the towns, was found murdered on the Melun Road. From the grapevine we gathered that an Individualist from Lyons, Bonnot by name (I did not know the man), who had been travelling with him by car, had killed him, the Italian having first wounded himself through fumbling with a revolver. However it may have happened, one comrade had murdered or 'done' another. An informal investigation shed no light on the matter and only annoyed the 'scientific' Illegalists. Since I had expressed hostile opinions towards them, I had an unexpected visit from Raymond. 'If you don't want to disappear, be careful about condemning us.' He added, laughingly, 'Do whatever you like! If you get in my way I'll eliminate you!'

'You and your friends are absolutely cracked', I replied, 'and absolutely finished.' We faced each other exactly like small boys over a red cabbage. He was still squat and strapping, baby-faced and merry. 'Perhaps that's true,' he said, 'but it's the law of nature.'

A positive wave of violence and despair began to grow. The outlaw-anarchists shot at the police and blew out their own brains. Others, overpowered before they could fire the last bullet into their own heads, went off sneering to the guillotine. 'One against all!' 'Nothing means anything to me!' 'Damn the masters, damn the slaves, and damn me!' I recognized, in the various newspaper reports, faces I had met or known; I saw the whole of the movement founded by Libertad dragged into the scum of society by a kind of madness; and nobody could do anything about it, least of all myself. The theoreticians, terrified, headed for cover. It was like a collective suicide. The newspapers put out a special edition to announce a particularly daring outrage, committed by bandits in a car on the Rue Ordener in Montmartre, against a bank cashier carrying half a million francs. Reading the descriptions, I recognized Raymond and Octave Garnier, the lad with piercing black eyes who distrusted intellectuals. I guessed the logic of their struggle: in order to save Bonnot, now hunted and trapped, they had to find either money, money to get away from it all, or else a speedy death in this battle against the whole of society. Out of solidarity they rushed into this squalid, doomed struggle with their little revolvers and their petty, trigger-happy arguments. And now there were five of them, lost, and once again without money even to attempt flight, and against them Money was ranged—100,000 francs' reward for the first informer. They were wandering in the city-without-escape, ready to be killed somewhere, anywhere, in a tram or a café, content to feel utterly cornered, expendable, alone in defiance of a horrible world. Out of solidarity, only to share this bitter joy of trying to be killed, without any illusions about the struggle (as a good many told me when I met them in prison afterwards), others joined the first few, such as red-haired René (he too was a restless spirit) and poor little André Soudy. I had often met Soudy at public meetings in the Latin Quarter. He was a perfect example of the crushed childhood of the back-alleys. He grew up on the pavements: T.B. at thirteen, V.D. at eighteen, convicted at twenty (for stealing a bicycle). I had brought him books and oranges in the Ténon Hospital. Pale, sharp-featured, his accent common, his eyes a gentle grey, he would say, 'I'm an unlucky blighter, nothing I can do about it.' He earned his living in grocers' shops in the Rue Mouffetard, where the assistants rose at six, arranged the display at seven, and went upstairs to sleep in a garret after 9 p.m., dog-tired, having seen their bosses defrauding housewives all day by weighing the beans short, watering the milk, wine, and paraffin, and falsifying the labels. . . . He was sentimental; the laments of street-singers moved him to the verge of tears, he could not approach a woman without making a fool of himself, and half a day in the open air of the meadows gave him a lasting dose of intoxication. He experienced a new lease of life if he heard someone call him 'comrade' or explain that one could, one must, 'become a new man'. Back in his shop, he began to give double measures of beans to the housewives, who thought him a little mad. The bitterest joking helped him to live, convinced as he was that he was not long for this world, 'seeing the price of medicine'.

One morning, a group of enormous police officers burst into our lodgings at the press, revolvers in hand. A bare-footed little girl of seven had opened when the bell rang, and was terrified by this irruption of armed giants. Jouin, the deputy Director of the *Sûreté*, a thin gentleman with a long, gloomy face, polite and almost likeable, came in later, searched the building, and spoke to me amiably, of ideas, of Sébastien Faure[1] whom he admired, of the deplorable way in which the outlaws were discrediting a great ideal.

'Believe me', he sighed, 'the world won't change so quickly.' He seemed to me neither malicious nor hypocritical, only a deeply distressed man doing a job conscientiously. In the afternoon he

[1] Sébastien Faure (1858–1942): after a period of Guesdism, became an anarcho-communist writer and publicist; editor of *L'Encyclopédie Anarchiste*.

sent for me, called me into his office, leant on his elbows under the green lampshade, and talked to me somewhat after this fashion:

'I know you pretty well; I should be most sorry to cause you any trouble—which could be very serious. You know these circles, these men, those who are far away from you and those who have a gun in your back, more or less. They are all absolutely finished, I can assure you. Stay here for an hour and we'll discuss them. Nobody will ever know anything of it and I guarantee that there'll be no trouble at all for you.'

I was ashamed, unbelievably ashamed, for him, for myself, for everybody, so ashamed that I felt no shock of indignation, nor any fear. I told him, 'I am sure that you must be embarrassed yourself, talking to me like this.'

'But not at all!' All the same, he was doing the dirty job as if he were overwhelmed by it.

In a cell of La Santé, behind a wall in the specially guarded section reserved for men condemned to death, I began to study seriously. The worst of it all was the constant hunger. From a legal point of view I could easily have cleared myself, since the paper's management and editorship was in the name of Rirette; but I was determined to assume all responsibility.

The murders and collective suicide continued. Of these I picked up only distant echoes. Meanwhile the reward of 100,000 francs was burrowing into the brains of certain 'conscious egoists', and the arrests began; Bonnot was besieged for a whole day at Choisy-le-Roi, defending himself with a pistol and writing, in the intervals of the firing, a letter which absolved his comrades of complicity; he lay between two mattresses to protect himself against the final onslaught, and was killed, or else killed himself, no one really knows which. Octave Garnier and René Valet, caught up at Nogent-sur-Marne in a villa where they were roughing it with their women, underwent an even longer siege, taking on the civil police, the *gendarmerie* and the Zouaves. They fired hundreds of bullets, viewing their attackers as murderers (and themselves as victims) and, when the house was dynamited, blew out their own brains. Rebellion's just another dead-end, nothing we can do about it; we may as well hurry up and re-load! At heart, they resembled the *dynamiteros* of Spain who stood up in front of tanks shouting *Viva la Fai!*; bidding defiance to the world. Raymond, betrayed by a woman for a considerable sum, was surprised and arrested. André Soudy, betrayed by an anarchist writer, was arrested at Berck-Plage where he was nursing his tuberculosis. Edouard Carouy, who had no part in these events, was betrayed by the family hiding him, and arrested, although armed like the others, without any attempt at self-defence; this athletic young man was exceptional in being quite incapable of murder, though bent on suicide. The others too were all betrayed. Some of the anarchists shot at those informers, one of whom was killed. Nonetheless, the shrewdest one of them continued to edit a little Individualist review on the blue cover of which the New Man could be seen struggling up from the shadows.

My examination was short and pointless, since I was actually accused of no offence. The first magistrate who interrogated me for identification purposes, an ageing, refined personage, nearly threw a fit of temper as he meditated on my future. 'A revolutionary at twenty! Yes—and you will be a plutocrat at forty!' 'I do not think so,' I replied in all seriousness, and I am still thankful to him for that outburst of revealing anger. I endured the long, enriching experience of cell-life, allowed no visits or newspapers, with only the squalid statutory rations (which were picked at by all the thieves on the staff) and some good books. I understood, and ever since have always missed, the old Christian custom of retreats which men spent in monasteries, meditating face to face with themselves and with God, in other words with the vast living solitude of the universe. It will be good if that custom is revived, in the time when man can at last devote thought to himself. Some very simple rules will suffice for that end: physical and intellectual discipline, exercise (absolutely necessary for the man in a cell), walks for meditation (I did my six miles around the cell every day), intellectual work, and recourse to that exaltation, or slight spiritual tipsiness, which is furnished by great works of poetry. Altogether, I spent around fifteen months in solitary confinement, in various conditions, some of them hellish.

The trial of 1913 assembled on the benches of the Assize Court about twenty prisoners, of whom maybe half a dozen were innocent. In the course of a month, 300 contradictory witnesses paraded to the bar of the court. Against the half-dozen main culprits there was no worthwhile evidence since they denied everything. Six witnesses out of forty contradicted each other in their identifications of the most incriminated defendants; but sometimes, in this hotchpotch of confused testimony, a single word would hit the mark and convince the jury. Someone had recalled a word pronounced with a certain accent, a shout of Soudy's ('The man with the rifle') in the middle of a minor street-fight: 'Come on, fellows, let's blow!' And no further doubt was possible because of the tone, the accent, the slang. It was hardly a piece of scientific evidence, but it was human evidence all the same.

On some days, it became a trial of the police, who were pumping a star witness, an old half-blind, half-deaf peasant woman, to make her identify photographs. The head of the *Sûreté*, Xavier Guichard, a man of aesthetic pretensions, admitted having hit a woman, shouting at her: 'You're young. You can still become a tart! As for your kids, they can go to hell on the Public Assistance!'

Dr. Paul, an expert in forensic medicine, pomaded, elegant and somewhat fleshy, lectured on the corpses with visible relish. He had been conducting post-mortems on all the murder victims of Paris for the last forty years—after which he would go off to a good lunch, select a tie to wear for tea and, leaning against the mantelpiece of some drawing-room, recount his 10,000 anecdotes of crime. Beaming M. Bertillon, the inventor of anthropometry, modestly admitted that he could be mistaken over finger-prints: there was a probability of error of about one in a billion. The lawyer who, in an attempt to embarrass Bertillon, had elicited this bombshell from him, could not recover from his own confusion.

The principal defendants, Raymond Callemin, André Soudy, Monier, a gardener, and Eugène Dieudonné, a joiner, denied everything and, in theory, had a plausible case. In reality, irrefutable signs of guilt were killing them, apart from Dieudonné who was in fact innocent, not of all complicity but of the particular aspect in which he stood accused. His arrest had arisen from a resemblance between his dark eyes and another pair of eyes, still darker, which were in the graveyard. He alone shouted his innocence in frenzy, with no sign of apathy; which made a striking contrast with the real culprits, insolent and jeering, whose whole behaviour was a calm challenge: 'We dare you to prove it.' Since everyone knew the truth, proof was superfluous, as they themselves were aware, but they continued acting after their vocation as desperadoes; smiling, blustering, taking notes. Raymond 'denied the right of the court to judge', but weakened in the face of authority, directing little sallies, like a peevish schoolboy, at the President of the court. Soudy, cross-examined as to whether a rifle was his property, replied, 'Not mine, but as you know, Proudhon said that property is theft.'

The prosecution had intended to unearth (for the benefit of the public) an authentically novelettish conspiracy, assigning me to the role of its 'theoretician', but had to abandon this project after the second session. I had believed that I would manage to be acquitted, but now understood that in such an atmosphere the acquittal of a young Russian, and a militant at that, was impossible, despite the entire clarity of the facts of the case; for no direct or indirect responsibility for these tragedies could be laid against me. I was there only because of my categorical refusal to talk; that is, to become an informer. I demolished the prosecution's case on various points of detail (which was easy). I defended our principles—of uninhibited analysis, solidarity and rebellion (which was much more difficult); and I annoyed the 'innocent' culprits by demonstrating that society manufactured crime, criminals, desperate ideas, suicides, and the poison of money.

Bonds of genuine sympathy were formed between the defendants and their counsel—except for Paul Reynaud, who defended some accessory or other with reasonable skill, but still remained aloof. Moro-Giafferi, leonine in appearance, a Napoleon in a neck-tie, thundered on behalf of Dieudonné. His grand, arm-waving eloquence, invoking the crucified Christ, the French Revolution, the grief of mothers, the nightmare fears of children, sickened me at first. By the end of twenty minutes of it, I was hypnotized, just like the jury and the gallery, by the power of his astounding dialectic. A relationship almost of friendliness drew me towards Adad (who committed suicide in Paris some years ago—and what better course was there for an old, penniless lawyer?) and to César Campinchi, a cool, brilliant debater who appealed only to reason, though with a certain irony. I was to see him again much later, seriously wounded in the First World War, and Minister of the Navy in the Second. (One of those who favoured resistance to the death, he died under house-arrest in Marseilles in 1941, just as I was embarking for America.) I reflected that if these desperadoes had been able, before their struggle, to meet men like this, understanding, cultured and liberal-minded, both from inclination and by profession (perhaps more apparently than really so, but even that would have been

C

enough), they would not have entered upon their paths of darkness. The most immediate cause of their revolt and ruin seemed to me to lie in their isolation from human contacts. They were living in no company but their own.

During the trial we were confined in the tiny cells of the Conciergerie, dark holes honeycombed in the ancient stonework of the same buildings where tourists still go to visit the prison of the Girondins and Marie-Antoinette's cell. Going to court, we would reassemble, escorted by *Gardes Républicains*, beneath old archways which gave us the feeling of being underground. We would walk up a corkscrew staircase inside one of the pointed towers which overlooked the Seine and, passing through a little side-door, enter the great court-room of the Assizes, which would be buzzing with the presence of a crowd. The last session took twenty hours and the verdict was announced at dawn. We waited for it, sitting together in two anterooms, in a strange atmosphere rather like our old meetings in Montmartre. The usual arguments started all over again. Our lawyers, pale-faced, came to fetch us. Then, the sweltering silent court-room, and twenty prisoners, tense, erect and hard-faced. Four death-sentences, several condemned to hard labour for life. The only acquittals were for the women, who were in any case innocent, but apart from this Parisian juries were reluctant to find women guilty. (They had acquitted Mme Steinheil, who was accused of murdering her husband; they acquitted Mme Joseph Caillaux, wife of the former Prime Minister, who had killed the editor of *Le Figaro*; later they acquitted the anarchist Germaine Berton, who had killed a Royalist leader.)

Dieudonné was condemned to death even though no one doubted his innocence (which was compromised by his faulty alibis); once more he shouted his guiltlessness and, alone among the accused, seemed on the verge of collapse. Raymond, who had demanded an acquittal, jumped up, his face crimson, and interjected violently: 'Dieudonné is innocent—it's me, me that did the shooting!' The President requested him to sit down, for the pleadings were over and confession no longer had any juridical value.

I myself received five years' solitary confinement, but I had managed to get Rirette acquitted; two revolvers discovered on the premises of the paper served to justify my conviction, which was provoked, no doubt, by my calm hostility during the hearings.

I found this justice nauseating; it was fundamentally more criminal than the worst criminals. This was incontestably obvious; it was just that I was an enemy, of a different sort from the guilty ones. As I pondered the judgement, its enormity did not surprise me. I only wondered if I would be able to live that long, for I was very weak— at any rate physically. I made up my mind to live it out, and was very ashamed to be thinking of myself like this, next to others who. . . .

We said our farewells to one another beneath the high vaults of the Terror. Through a frightful slip, while I was talking to Raymond I used an expression for which I have never forgiven myself. 'You live and learn,' I remarked, I cannot now say why, perhaps because I had just decided in favour of living. He stared, and then broke into laughter: 'Living is just the problem!'

'Forgive me,' I broke out.

He shrugged his shoulders. 'Of course, man! My mind's set.'

An hour later, in the pale light of morning, I was once again pacing around my suffocating cell. Somebody was sobbing incessantly in the next cell, and it got on my nerves. A little old warder, kindly and sad, came in, averting his face: 'Carouy (Edouard) is dying. Can you hear him?' I could indeed hear a queer panting noise, coming from beyond the sobs next door. 'That's him gasping away. . . . He took some poison which he'd got hidden in the soles of his shoes. . . . Well, well, what a life!' He had not been condemned to death.

The obviously innocent Dieudonné was reprieved, in other words given forced labour for life. For eighteen years he fought fantastically against his servitude, escaping several times and spending years in solitary confinement. After his final escape he reached Brazil. Through the good offices of Albert Londres,[1] he was able to return to France.

Raymond was so stolid in the death-cell that they did not keep the date of the execution from him. He spent the waiting period in reading. In front of the guillotine he noticed the group of reporters and shouted to them: 'A nice sight, isn't it?'

Soudy's last-minute request was for a cup of coffee with cream and some fancy rolls, his last pleasure on earth, appropriate enough for that grey morning when people were happily eating their

[1] i.e. through a Press campaign on his behalf.

breakfasts in the little *bistros*. It must have been too early, for they could only find him a little black coffee. 'Out of luck', he remarked, 'right to the end.' He was fainting with fright and nerves, and had to be supported while he was going down the stairs; but he controlled himself and, when he saw the clearness of the sky over the chestnut trees, hummed a sentimental street-song: 'Hail, O last morning of mine'. Monier, usually taciturn, was crazy with anxiety, but mastered himself and became calm. I learned these details only a long time afterwards.

So ended the second explosion of anarchism in France. The first, equally hopeless, was that of 1891–4, signalled by the outrages of Ravachol, Emile Henry, Vaillant, and Caserio.[1] The same psychological features and the same social factors were present in both phases; the same exacting idealism, in the breasts of uncomplicated men whose energy could find no outlet in achieving a higher dignity or sensibility, because any such outlet was physically denied to them. Conscious of their frustration, they battled like madmen and were beaten down. In those times the world was an integrated structure, so stable in appearance that no possibility of substantial change was visible within it. As it progressed up and up, and on and on, masses of people who lay in its path were all the while being crushed. The harsh condition of the workers improved only very slowly, and for the vast majority of the proletariat there was no way out. The declassed elements on the proletarian fringe found all roads barred to them except those which led to squalor and degradation. Above the heads of these masses, wealth accumulated, insolent and proud. The consequences of this situation arose inexorably: crime, class-struggles and their trail of bloody strikes, and frenzied battles of One against All. These struggles also testified to the failure of an ideology. Between the copious theorizing of Peter Kropotkin and Elisée Reclus, and the rage of Albert Libertad, the collapse of anarchism in the bourgeois jungle was now obvious. Kropotkin had grown up in a completely different Europe, one less stable, where the

[1] Ravachol exploded bombs in the homes of two officials connected with a recent anarchist trial; he was guillotined in 1892. Vaillant was executed for a bomb-explosion in the Chamber of Deputies in December 1893, which killed nobody. Emile Henry threw a bomb in the Café Terminus, which (much against his intentions) caused only minor injuries; executed in May 1894. Caserio, a young Italian anarchist, stabbed President Carnot to death in June of the same year.

ideal of liberty seemed to have some future and people believed in revolution and education. Reclus had fought for the Commune; the confidence inspired by the greatness of its thwarted vision had lasted him for the rest of his days; he believed in the saving power of science. On the eve of war in Europe, science was functioning solely to assist the progress of a traditionalist and barbaric social order. One felt the approach of an era of violence: inescapable.

In other lands, namely Poland and Russia, the revolutionary movement confronted régimes of a mongrel character, half-absolutist and half-capitalist: there the movement was able to concentrate these diffuse energies and channel them along ways of sacrifice, at the end of which lay victories that were not only possible but popularly desired.

The men, the situations and the conflicts were almost the same, only with a historical complexion different from that in France, the 'Rentier State' as Yves Guyot[1] put it. In Poland, Joseph Pilsudski's Socialist Party (P.P.S.) was raiding Treasury vans and tax-offices, attacking governors and policemen. In Russia, the Social-Revolutionary Party was conducting a similar campaign, and the combat groups of the Bolshevik fraction of Social-Democrats— including the extraordinary terrorist Kamo,[2] the intellectual and laboratory-maker Krassin, the skilful organizer Koba-Stalin, the man of action Tsintsadze and the courier Litvinov—were conducting the struggle for the Party's income on the highways, the public places of Tiflis and the ships of Baku, bomb and revolver in hand. In Italy, in *Pagine Libere* of 1 January 1911, a young Socialist agitator, Benito Mussolini, was chanting the praises of the anarchist desperadoes.

Of this hard childhood, this troubled adolescence, all those terrible years, I regret nothing as far as I am myself concerned. I am sorry for those who grow up in this world without ever experiencing the cruel side of it, without knowing utter frustration and the

---

[1] Yves Guyot (1843–1928): free-trade economist, Deputy, and Minister of Public Works from 1889 to 1892.

[2] 'Kamo': the Party name of S. A. Ter-Petrosian (1882–1922), Bolshevik revolutionary who committed numerous robberies, was four times sentenced to death, and feigned insanity for four years in Germany in order to prevent his extradition to Imperial Russia. 'Koté' Tsintsadze, Kamo's less sensational colleague, undertook similar activities in the pre-revolutionary period; later became a prominent Georgian Bolshevik, at odds with Stalin; was arrested in 1929, and died in captivity in 1931.

necessity of fighting, however blindly, for mankind. Any regret I have is only for the energies wasted in struggles which were bound to be fruitless. These struggles have taught me that, in any man, the best and the worst live side by side, and sometimes mingle—and that what is worst comes through the corruption of what is best.

2

LIVE TO PREVAIL
1912–1919

Of prison I shall say here only a little. It burdened me with an experience so heavy, so intolerable to endure, that long afterwards, when I resumed writing, my first book (a novel) amounted to an effort to free myself from this inward nightmare, as well as performing a duty towards all those who will never so free themselves (*Les Hommes dans la Prison*). It is reasonably well known in France and the Spanish-speaking countries. In the jail where I did the most time, there were three or four hundred of us in torment, mostly doing long sentences between eight years and life. Among these men I encountered the same proportions of weak spirits, human scum, average types, and exceptional men, gifted with some spark of divinity, as anywhere else. Generally speaking, with only a few exceptions, the warders, of whatever grade, were on a much lower level. They were criminals, respectably but obviously so, gifted with a guaranteed immunity from punishment and superannuation at the end of their unspeakable lives. They included sadists, inflexible hypocrites, morons, racketeers, scroungers and thieves; and, incredible as it may seem, some who were good and almost intelligent.

The French prison itself, organized as it is according to ancient regulations, is nothing but an absurd machine for breaking those men who are thrown into it. Life there is a kind of mechanized madness; everything in it seems to have been conceived in a spirit of mean calculation how best to enfeeble, stupefy and numb the prisoner, and poison him with an inexpressible bitterness; his return to normal life must evidently be made quite impossible. This end is attained by an organization impregnated with the penal traditions of the pre-revolutionary order, with the religious idea of chastisement (an idea which now, lacking any basis in faith, is only a psychological justification for social sadism), and with the footling detail of our vast modern administrations. The hotchpotch mixing of malefactors, semi-lunatics, and victims of all descriptions; under-nourishment; the rule of complete and perpetual silence imposed at every moment upon all common activity; arbitrary punishments designed to humiliate, torture, and weaken; prohibition of any knowledge whatsoever concerning life outside, even if it be war, invasion, or national peril; the maximum possible deprivation of intellectual exercise, prohibition of study, even of reading more than one book a week, to be chosen from the idiotic novelettes of the prison library (fortunately it also contained Balzac). In the long run this treadmill turns out sexual inverts, cracked brains, worthless and depraved beings incapable of rehabilitation, dedicated in short to joining the ranks of tramps in *La Maub*'; or else parasitical toughs, hardened by suffering, who keep up their own special tradition. Cynics, but loyal to one another, such men preserve their 'emancipated' dignity with no illusions about either society or themselves. From this class professional criminals are recruited.

Truly wonderful was the struggle waged by some there, a pitiful minority, to preserve their capacity for living. I was very definitely one of these. For this purpose a considerable degree of a particular kind of will-power was necessary: passive to all appearance, yet artful and incorrigible. When we saw the 'new ones' arrive, we knew which of them, whether young or old, were not going to live. We were never wrong in these forecasts, but they had been wrong about me; I had appeared fated to die before long. A former budding lawyer of the Parisian bar, the victim of a shocking tragedy of middle-class life now serving a life sentence, had managed, with the aid of corruption, to found an efficiently concealed clandestine library of good scientific and philosophical works. His friendship and this precious food of the spirit was, I know, my salvation. In the poky, solitary cell in which each of us slept, whose window faced the sky, I was able to read only for a few moments in the morning, and for a few more in the evening. During my compulsory labour in the print-shop, I used to set up notes and comments in galley form for certain comrades to read. From the moment that thought and learning were possible for us, life was also possible, and worthwhile. The keen edge of this slow torture blunted itself against us, against myself especially. I was confident of beating the treadmill.

The outbreak of war was sudden, like an unexpected storm in a season of clear weather. We had not been able to observe its early symptoms, but knew of it through the unaccustomed panic which seized the warders (since many of them were liable to be called up). And this storm interpreted the world to us. For me, it heralded another, purifying tempest: the Russian Revolution. Revolutionaries knew quite well that the autocratic Empire, with its hangmen, its pogroms, its finery, its famines, its Siberian jails and ancient iniquity, could never survive the war. A gleam of light was at last visible: this would be the beginning of everything, the prodigious first day of Creation. An end to deadlock! This huge gateway would be open towards the future. No more problems now about the aims of the struggle or the rules of life, for the Russian Revolution was calling from the heart of the future.

For the time being, the sudden conversion to fratricidal patriotism of the German Social-Democrats and the French syndicalists, Socialists and anarchists, was incomprehensible to us. Did they then believe nothing of what they preached yesterday? Had we been right after all in refusing to trust them? Passionate singings of the 'Marseillaise', from crowds seeing troops off to the train, drifted across even to our jail. We could also hear shouts of '*To Berlin! To Berlin!*' This lunacy, which we could not explain, was the peak and climax of a permanent social crisis. At the risk of spending between sixty and eighty hours in the dungeons, with consequently almost certain death from tuberculosis, the half-dozen of us comrades who were scattered around the central prison carried on a feverish exchange of theses. Gustave Hervé, who a while before was proclaiming insurrection against war, was now demanding to be enlisted in the army; his *Guerre Sociale* changed its title to *La Victoire*. They were tricksters, nothing more: 'It's not the weathercock that's moving, it's the wind.' Fundamentally, the crowds were being swept along by an immense ignorance of the reality of modern war, whose existence had been forgotten since 1870. The infantrymen went off to the front line in their scarlet trousers, and the cadets of St. Cyr in their white gloves and plumed *képis*, just as though it were a parade. Over

the whole of Europe, the masses were letting their suppressed
energies run free. France forgot the disparity of forces whereby her
38,000,000 inhabitants, with a low birth-rate, engaged in mortal
struggle against a fecund Germany of 60,000,000.

Our opposition to the war was essentially a matter of human feeling. The two coalitions had practically the same social organization: republics based on high finance, more or less monarchical but
governed, with the sole exception of Russia, by bourgeois parliaments. On our side and on theirs, the same liberties equally stifled
by exploitation, the same slow progress that crushed human beings.
German militarism was a hideous peril, but we foresaw that an
Allied victory would establish over the Continent a French militarism whose capacity for reactionary idiocy was revealed in the
Dreyfus affair (not to mention General Galliffet, of bloody memory).[1] The invasion of Belgium was abominable, but the memory of
the obliteration of the two little South African Republics by British
arms was still fresh in our minds (1902). The recent conflicts over
Tripolitania and Morocco showed that butchery was being unleashed over Europe in the cause of a redivision of colonies. The
prospect of victory by either side appalled us. How was it that among
so many victims, no men were to be found brave enough to rush
across from either 'enemy' side and hail one another as brothers?
In asking each other that question we experienced a new despair.

Without our knowing anything of it, the line of invasion rolled
towards Paris. If we had been outside jail, I think that we would
have followed the stream and felt immediately that, despite all
theoretical considerations, a country under attack, unless it is at the
height of a social crisis, must defend itself; primitive reflexes,
infinitely stronger than principles, are at play; the sentiment of 'the
nation in danger' prevails.

The prison is situated on an island in the Seine, twenty-five
miles or so from the Marne. While the battle of the Marne was on,
the population of Melun began to flee. No one believed in victory
any longer, and Paris seemed lost. We learned that the prison would
not be evacuated and that the fighting would probably reach the
banks of the Seine. We would find ourselves cooped inside this cage,

[1] General Galliffet (1830–1909): noted for the pitiless severity with which he
suppressed the Paris Commune. Later (1899) appointed for a time as Minister of
War.

right in the middle of a battlefield. Warders and prisoners alike were sick with fear. I was not. On the contrary, I felt an ecstatic happiness at the thought that the cannonades would destroy this preposterous treadmill, even if we were entombed under the rubble as a result. The fighting moved away; everything went on exactly as before.

There were plenty of deaths in the jail. I saw young men gripped, three months before their release was due, with a kind of fever, losing their biological adaptation to the prison environment, awakening once more, eyes glittering, to some sort of life, and then suddenly dying in three days as though from an inner convulsion. I myself collapsed from undernourishment after six or eight months; I could no longer remain standing, and was admitted to the infirmary where broth and milk set me back on my feet within a fortnight. Then my sickness started again. On the first occasion I was afraid that I might be bound for the little reserved cemetery near by, thereby giving the convict in charge of grave-digging his little walk in the open air and his customary quart of wine (his rewarding position was a source of envy to us). Then I adapted myself, and made up my mind to survive. From beyond my conscious will I could feel another will, deeper and more powerful, asserting itself within me.

There came a certain winter dawn that arose over the Seine, over the tall poplars that I loved, over the sleeping, shabby little town where the only faces that passed by at this hour were humble, hardened and topped by helmets. I departed, alone, amazingly light-footed upon the ground, taking nothing with me, without any real joy, obsessed by the idea that, behind me, the treadmill was continuing endlessly to turn, crushing human beings. In the grey morning, I bought a cup of coffee in the station café. The proprietor came up to me with a kind of sympathy.

'Out of jail?'

'Yes.'

He wagged his head. Might he be interested in 'my crime', or my future? He leant over: 'You in a hurry? There's one hell of a brothel near here. . . .'

The first man I had met, in the mist of a gloomy bridge, had been a soldier with a mutilated face; this fat procurer was the second. Was it always to be the world-without-escape? What good was the war doing? Had the dance of death taught nothing to anyone?

Paris was leading a double life. Walking along, spellbound, I stopped in front of the lowly windows of the Belleville shops. The colours of the darning-wools were a wonder, the mother-of-pearl penknives enthralled me, and for several minutes I contemplated the picture-postcards of soldiers and their fiancées sending each other kisses through a messenger-dove, holding an envelope in its beak. Men and women passing by—how astonishingly real! A cat, sitting comfortably on the hot window-ledge of a bakery, with the smell of warm bread escaping outside! I smiled at it drunkenly. Belleville was the same, only sadder and poorer. 'Funerals in twenty-four hours, moderate prices, payment by instalments. . . .' A marble-cutter was displaying his enamel lockets; all of them represented young soldiers. Housewives in shawls were coming from the town hall, each bringing her sack of potatoes and her bucket of coal. The grey façades of the Rue Julien Lacroix oozed out their ancient misery in the cold.

People explained life to me: 'You know, it's almost a merry life. Every house has several dead, but the men have been away for so long that their wives are living with other men. There's no unemployment, there's a craze on for foreign labour, wages are high. . . . There's heaps of soldiers from every country in the world; some of them have money, the English and the Canadians, there's never been so much love-making in all the odd corners. Pigalle, Clichy, the Montmartre district, the fine boulevards, all those parasites are amusing themselves: after us, the deluge! The war's business, old chap. You'll see people are doing well out of it, nobody wants it to end any more. The troops are fed up, of course, but the lads home on leave are showing off. "Nothing to do about it, don't bother to try understanding it," that's what they say. Almereyda's running a daily paper in the smart end of town, he has two cars and a big house . . . Jules Guesde and Marcel Sembat[1] are in the Government; a Socialist is defending Jaurès' murderer—Maître Zévaès, you know him. Chose, the Illegalist, has won the Military Medal. Kropotkin has signed an appeal for the

---

[1] Marcel Sembat (1862–1922): revolutionary Socialist initially, then a leader of the French Socialist Party and member of the 'Cabinet of national defence' after 1914.

war-effort, along with Jean Grave. Machin is in the munitions business. . . . What's that you say? The Russian Revolution? Poor old chap, you're off the track. The Russians are solid, out there in the Carpathians and, believe me, all that's nowhere near changing. Only one thing to do: feather your own nest. It's a lot easier than before the war.'

That was the sort of talk I heard. I watched the skinny Algerians sluggishly sweeping the muck in the streets, and it never stopped, the muck actually grew. Shivering Indo-Chinese, in helmet and sheepskin, guarded the Préfecture and La Santé. The *Métro* was carting around its dense crowds, couple upon couple, convalescents lived out their boredom at hospital windows, a disfigured soldier hugged the waist of a working-girl under the bare trees of the Luxembourg Gardens, and the cafés were crowded. The outskirts rotted in deep darkness, but the centre of town, dotted with illuminations, throbbed on well into the night. 'Nowadays, see, there are only two poles to the world, love and money—and money comes first.'

I made inquiries about the Russians. The terrorist Savinkov[1] was recruiting for the Foreign Legion. A number of Bolsheviks had been killed at the front, as volunteers. Plekhanov was advocating the defence of the Empire. Trotsky, escorted to the Spanish frontier by two police inspectors, was about to be interned somewhere in America. Almereyda, in his combined office, flat and private empire in the smart boulevards, more elegant, more pushful than just lately, told me that he had given up trapping police-spies in the working-class movement, in case he did more harm than good: 'There are too many of them!' The war was leading nowhere; he was working for peace, whose supporters were growing and held the future in their hands. 'Poincaré and Joffre are finished. . . . Soon everything's going to change here.'

Certain people were harsh towards him: 'He's sold out to a bankers' clique; he's got the Chief of Police in his pocket.' Maître César Campinchi explained to me that France had been bled white, but would win in a year or two, with the Americans on her side. I went to see a performance of *The Bluebird*: in the theatre, couples,

<hr/>

[1] Boris V. Savinkov (1879–1925): Social-Revolutionary leader and terrorist, assassin of Grand Duke Sergei and Minister von Plehve. Later War Minister under Kerensky. Imprisoned for ten years in 1924 for conspiratorial work against Soviet Government. Died in prison, reportedly by his own hand.

couples and uniforms. . . . Everything reinforced the mad sensation that we were falling into the abyss.

Farewell, Paris! I took the Barcelona express. The trains and railway stations unveiled another face of the war: the soldiers. They were toughness itself, rough-hewn, stiff, and uncomplicated as a mass of stone: ravaged. Beyond the Pyrenees, vistas of peace and abundance opened anew, with no wounded invalids, no soldiers on leave counting up the hours, no funeral black, no frenzy for life on the eve of death. In the little villages of Catalonia the squares, lined with tall trees and fringed by little cafés under arcades, breathed an air of nonchalance. Barcelona was making merry, with its Ramblas[1] illuminated at night and luxuriously sunlit by day, full of birds and women. Here too the cornucopia of the war was gushing away. Both for the Allies and for the Central Powers, the factories were working full blast and the companies were positively coining gold. Zest for life shining at you from faces and shop-windows, oozing at you from banking-houses, smacking you on the back. Everything was going mad.

I underwent a phase of intense wretchedness. The treadmill that crushed human beings still revolved inside me. I found no happiness in awakening to life, free and privileged alone among my conscript generation, in this contented city. I felt a vague compunction at it all. Why was I there, in these cafés, on these golden sands, while so many others were bleeding in the trenches of a whole continent? How was I worth more than they? Why was I excluded from the common fate? I came across deserters who were happy to be beyond the frontier, safe at last. I admitted their right to safety, but inwardly I was horrified at the idea that people could fight so fiercely for their own lives when what was at stake was the life of everyone; a limitless suffering to be endured commonly, shared and drunk to the last drop. This feeling was in sharp opposition to my reasoned thought, but much stronger than it. I can see now that this need for sharing in the common fate has always held me, and has been one of my deepest sources of action. I worked in print-shops, went to bull-fights, resumed my reading, clambered up mountains, dallied in cafés to watch Castilian, Sevillan, Andalusian, or Catalan girls at their dancing, and I felt that it would be impossible for me to live like this. All I could think of was the men at war, who kept calling to me.

[1] Boulevard thoroughfares of Barcelona.

It is certain that I would have finally enlisted in some army or other, if certain long-awaited events had not at last been simultaneously set in motion.

In *Tierra y Libertad* I wrote my first article under the name of 'Victor Serge', in defence of Friedrich Adler,[1] who had just been condemned to death in Vienna: a few months before he had assassinated Count Stürgkh, one of the politicians responsible for the war. My next article was on the fall of the Russian autocracy. Then, awaited so keenly that we eventually wondered whether we should still believe in it, the Revolution appeared, and the improbable became reality. Reading the dispatches from Russia, we were transfigured; for the images that they conveyed were simple, concrete. A minute clarity was shed over things; the world was no longer impelled along by helpless lunacy. Certain French Individualists mocked me with their store of cynical stock phrases: 'Revolutions are useless. They will not change human nature. Afterwards reaction sets in and everything starts all over again. I've only got my own skin; I'm not marching for wars or for revolutions, thank you.'

'In fact', I would answer them, 'you people are no longer good for anything. You're at the end of your tether: you won't march for anything any more—because you yourselves are not worth marching for. . . . Your kind are the products of the degeneration of everything: of the bourgeoisie, of bourgeois ideas, of the working-class movement, of anarchism. . . .'

My break with these 'comrades', who were no more than the shadows of comrades, became complete: it was useless to argue, and difficult to endure one another. The Spaniards, even the workers on the shop floor beside me, who were no militants, instinctively understood the Petrograd days, since their imagination transposed those events to Madrid and Barcelona. The monarchy of Alfonso XIII was no more popular or stable than that of Nicholas II. The revolutionary tradition of Spain, like that of Russia, went back to the time of Bakunin. Similar social causes were operating in both countries: agrarian problems, retarded industrialization, a political

---

[1] Friedrich Adler (1879–1960): Austro-Marxist, son of the founder of the Austrian Socialist Party, Victor Adler; his death-sentence was later commuted to imprisonment. Released at the end of the war, he became President of the Workers' and Soldiers' Councils. Subsequently, General Secretary for many years of the Second International.

régime at least a century and a half behind Western Europe. The wartime industrial and commercial boom strengthened the bourgeoisie, especially that of Catalonia, which was hostile to the old land-owning aristocracy and to the utterly hidebound royal administration; it also expanded the energies and appetites of a young proletariat which had had no time to form a working-class aristocracy, that is, to become bourgeoisified. Knowledge of the war aroused a disposition towards violence, and the low wages (I earned four pesetas a day, about eighty American cents) stimulated the workers to press their immediate demands.

From one week to another the horizon became visibly clearer. Within three months the mood of the Barcelona working class was transformed. Their fighting spirit mounted. The C.N.T. gathered strength. I belonged to a tiny trade union in the print-shop. Without any increase in the number of activists (there must have been about thirty of us) its influence advanced to such an extent that the whole body of workers seemed to have woken up. Three months after the news of the Russian Revolution, the Comitè Obrero began to prepare a revolutionary general strike, entered negotiations for a political alliance with the Catalan liberal bourgeoisie, and calmly planned the overthrow of the monarchy. The Comitè Obrero's programme of demands, drawn up in June 1917 and published in *Solidaridad Obrera*, was borrowed from the accumulated experience of the Russian Soviets. I was soon to discover that in France too, the same, intensely alive electric current was crossing from the trenches to the factories, the same violent hopes were coming to birth.

At the Café Espagnol, on the Paralelo, that crowded thoroughfare with its blazing lights of evening, near the horrible *barrio chino* whose mouldering alleys were full of half-naked girls lurking in doorways that gaped into hell-holes—it was here that I met militants arming for the approaching battle. They spoke enthusiastically of those who would fall in that fight, they dealt out Browning revolvers, and baited, as we all did, the anxious spies at the neighbouring table. In a revolutionary side-street, with a *Guardia Civil* barracks on one side and poor tenements on the other, I found Barcelona's hero of the hour, the quickening spirit, the uncrowned leader, the fearless man of politics who distrusted politicians: Salvador Seguí, affectionately nicknamed '*Noy del Sucre*'.[1] We used

---

[1] i.e. 'Sugar boy'; so called because of his fondness for sugar as a child.

to dine together in the faint flicker of a paraffin lamp. The meal, set on the table of smooth wood, would consist of tomatoes, onions, coarse red wine, and a country-style soup. The child's underclothes would be hanging on a line of string and Teresita would be nursing the baby. The balcony was open on the menacing darkness, on the barracks packed with killers, on the red, starry halo of the Rambla. There, we examined the various problems: the Russian Revolution, the coming general strike, alliance with the Catalan liberals, the trade unions, the ingrained anarchist hostility to any fresh forms of organization. As to the Russian Revolution, I was certain only on one point: that it would not stop half-way. The avalanche would carry on rolling right to the end. What end? 'The peasants will seize the land, and the workers the factories. After that, I don't know.'

I wrote: 'After that, struggles devoid of any greatness will begin once again, but on a rejuvenated soil. Mankind will have made a great leap forward.' The Comitè Obrero did not ask itself any fundamental questions. It entered the battle without knowing its ultimate perspective or assessing the consequences of its action; and, of course, it could hardly do otherwise. The Committee was the expression of an expanding power which could not remain inactive; nor, any longer, could it be simply beaten down, even if it fought badly. The notion of seizing Barcelona was straightforward: it was studied in detail. But Madrid? The other regions? Liaison with the rest of Spain was weak. Would it lead to the overthrow of the monarchy? Some of the Republicans who hoped for this, including Lerroux (still popular, though already discredited on the Left), wanted to throw libertarian Barcelona into the front line, with the way open for themselves to retreat if Barcelona was defeated. The Catalan Republicans associated with Marcelino Domingo were leaning on the power of the workers only to wrest a degree of independence from the monarchy; these kept tantalizing the Government with the threat of disorders. Together with Seguí, I followed the negotiations between the Catalan liberal bourgeoisie and the Comitè Obrero. It was a dubious alliance, in which the partners feared, justifiably mistrusted and subtly outmanœuvred one another.

Seguí summed up the position: 'They would like to use us and then do us down. For the moment, we are useful in their game of political blackmail. Without us they can do nothing: we have the streets, the shock-troops, the brave hearts among the people. We know this, but we need them. They stand for money, trade, possible legality (at the beginning, anyway), the Press, public opinion, etc.'

'But', I would reply, 'unless we have a brilliant victory, which I don't believe, they are ready to desert us at the first obstacle. We are betrayed in advance.'

Seguí could see the dangers, but he was still optimistic: 'If we are beaten, they will be beaten with us—too late then to betray us. If we win, we, not they, will be the masters of the situation.' It was Salvador Seguí who gave me the inspiration for the character of Dario in *Naissance de Notre Force*. A worker, and usually dressed like a worker coming home from the job, cloth cap squashed down on his skull, shirt-neck unbuttoned under his cheap tie; tall, strapping, round-headed, his features rough, his eyes big, shrewd and sly under heavy lids, of an ordinary degree of ugliness, but intensely charming to meet and with his whole self displaying an energy that was lithe and dogged, practical, shrewd, and without the slightest affectation. To the Spanish working-class movement he brought a new role: that of the superb organizer. He was no anarchist, but rather a libertarian, quick to scoff at resolutions on 'harmonious life under the sun of liberty', 'the blossoming of the self', or 'the future society'; he presented instead the immediate problems of wages, organization, rents, and revolutionary power. The anarchists would not hear any talk of the seizure of power. They refused to see that if the Comitè Obrero was victorious, it would be the Catalan government of tomorrow. Seguí saw this, but, afraid of starting a clash of ideas that would have isolated him, dared not talk of it. And so we went into battle, as it were in the dark.

Our enthusiasm and strength were gathering for the great day, and the preparations for it were almost ready. Towards the middle of July, squads of blue-overalled militants patrolled the town, hands on their revolvers. I went on these patrols, and we used to pass the *Guardia Civil* on horseback with their black cocked hats and their bearded faces. They knew that we were tomorrow's insurgents, but they had orders not to engage with us. The authorities had lost their wits, or else anticipated what was going to happen: the defection of the Catalan Parliamentary democrats. The building of La Calle de las Egypciacias, where I happened to be one day with Seguí, was surrounded by the black-hats; we helped Seguí to escape over the flat roofs on the house-tops. I was arrested, and spent three hateful hours in a tiny police cell painted in red ochre. I could hear the roar of the riots on the Rambla near by, a roar so loud that a kindly old police officer released me with his apologies. The plain-clothes men at our heels, distressingly courteous, assured us of their sympathy and apologized for pursuing so disgraceful a trade to earn their children's bread.

I doubted if we would win, but I would gladly have fought for the future's sake. Much later, in a meditation on the conquest of power, I wrote:

'Very likely, Dario, at the end of all this trouble we shall be shot. I have doubts about today and about ourselves. You would laugh, Dario, if I told you this aloud. You would say, spreading out your great, shaggy, brotherly, strong hands: "Me, I feel able to win all the way. All the way." That is how we all feel, immortal, right up to the moment when we feel nothing any more. And life goes on after our little drop of water has flowed back into the ocean. In this sense my confidence is one with yours. Tomorrow is great. We will not have prepared this conquest in vain. This city will be won, if not by our hands, at least by hands like ours, only stronger: perhaps stronger by being better toughened through our very weakness. If we are beaten, other men, infinitely different from us, infinitely like us, will come down this Rambla on an evening like this, in ten years, twenty years, it matters not, planning this same conquest; perhaps they will be thinking of the blood we have shed. Even now I think I can see them. I am thinking of their blood, which will also flow. But they will win the city.'

I was right. Those others did win the city, on 19 July 1936. They were called Ascaso, Durruti, Germinal Vidal,[1] the C.N.T., the F.A.I., the P.O.U.M. But on 19 July 1917 we were beaten almost without a fight, since the Catalan liberals took fright at the last minute and refused to join the struggle. We fought alone, in a day of sunshine and shouting, of impetuous crowds and chases in the streets, while the cautious black-hats charged lazily and pursued us without enthusiasm: they were afraid.

[1] Ascaso and Durruti were outstanding figures of the Spanish anarchist movement whose destinies were linked in imprisonment, exile, and then battle in the Civil War, in which each died a heroic death. Germinal Vidal was the Youth Secretary of the independent Marxist party P.O.U.M., who also died fighting on the Republican side. Serge's prophecy is from *Naissance de Notre Force*, written in 1929–30.

The Comitè Obrero sounded the retreat. Around noon I joined the multitude of comrades in the cramped Conde del. Asalto hall. While we were awaiting instructions, the *Guardia Civil*, rifles raised, suddenly burst in from the Rambla and advanced on us, slowly herding us back. A small, sickly officer shouted that he would give the order to fire if we did not disperse. It was impossible for us to disperse, for behind us was another crowd—and we had no inclination to do so. A gap opened between us and this wall of men aiming at us with their rifles. Into it there suddenly leapt a young man in grey, his hand balancing a bomb wrapped in newspaper. He shouted, 'I am a free man! Sons of whores!' I rushed towards him and grabbed his wrists: 'Are you mad? You're going to start a useless slaughter.' We wrestled for a brief moment, while the police were motionless and hesitant; then some of the comrades surrounded us and dragged us away. . . . Isolated shots cracked out. In the opening of a door the young man, still shaking with exasperation, was wiping his forehead with his hand. 'You're the Russian, aren't you? Lucky I recognized you in time.'

In the evening, Seguí returned, worn out with fatigue. 'Cowards, cowards!' he kept whispering. I was never to see him again, for he went into hiding to organize the August rebellion. In 1921, when I was in Petrograd, I had a letter from him with the news that he was coming to Russia. He had become Barcelona's unchallenged tribune, and was returning from Minorca where he had been for some time under sentence of deportation. At the beginning of 1922 he was killed in the street, a few yards from the Rambla, by the *pistoleros* of the employers' agency *Sindicato Libre*.

The rebellion broke out in the August of 1917, resulted in a hundred-odd corpses on all sides, and was crushed, without, however, blocking the progress of the Barcelona working class. I was on my way to Russia. The defeat of 19 July had made up my mind for me: I had lost all hope of victory hereabouts, I was weary of discussions with militants who often seemed to me no more than great big children. The Russian Consul-General in Barcelona, a Prince K——, received me at once when my name was sent in: 'How can I be of service to you?' This gentleman had just given his allegiance to the Provisional Government. I had previously been a little afraid of him, for any Russian revolutionaries of whose presence in the city he became aware were arrested by the Commandant at his instigation. Now all was sweetness. I asked him only for a recruiting form, so that I could go and do my military service in liberated Russia. 'But of course, with pleasure! At once!' We each understood what the other left half-said.

Paris. The Russian military headquarters in the Avenue Rapp was full of dapper officers, quite at home in the new situation: republicans within the week, and good republicans of course. Exceedingly polite, they enumerated all the difficulties to me and other callers. Communications with Russia were clogged with all kinds of obstacles. Why not, they suggested, serve our rediscovered country in the Russian formation fighting in France? That would be easy to arrange. However, I continued my efforts, only to learn at last that, as it appeared, the British Admiralty was refusing transit to the group of returning revolutionaries of which I was a member. We kept sending telegrams to the Petrograd Soviet and Kerensky, which made a deplorable impression, and it was not concealed from us that, what with one censorship and another, it was by no means certain that our telegrams arrived. Meanwhile, a Russian division, demanding repatriation, mutinied at the La Courtine camp; it was crushed by cannon-fire. I had the idea of journeying via the Foreign Legion, which was promising incorporation in the Russian army to its Russian volunteers; but then I found that most of the comrades who had tried this route had met a hero's death in the front line, while their representatives, who were mandated to put their demands, were shot somewhat farther behind the trenches.

In the ante-rooms of the military mission I made the acquaintance of a Russian soldier, about thirty, lately from Transjordania where he had fought in the British forces. Like me he was trying to return, though for different reasons, and he got his way before I did. He defined his position right from our first conversation: 'I am a traditionalist, monarchist, imperialist, and pan-Slavist. Mine is the true Russian nature, just as it was formed by Orthodox Christianity. You also have the true Russian nature, but at its opposite extreme, that of spontaneous anarchy, primitive violence, and unruly beliefs. I love all of Russia, even what I want to fight in it, even what you represent. . . .'

On these subjects we had excellent discussions, in our walks up and down the esplanade of Les Invalides. At least he was frank, daring in thought, tremendously in love with adventure and battle, and from time to time he would recite verses with magical effect. He was rather lean and singularly ugly: his face too long, heavy lips and nose, conical forehead, weird eyes, bluish-green and over-large, like a fish or Oriental idol—and indeed, he was very fond of the priestly statues of Assyria, which everyone came to think he resembled. This was one of the greatest Russian poets of our generation, already famous: Nikolai Stepanovich Gumilev. We were destined to meet several times in Russia, antagonists but friends. In 1921 I was to struggle vainly for several days, trying to stop the Cheka from shooting him. But of this approaching future we had no foreknowledge.

The Russian officers usually called themselves Social-Revolutionaries, and the fact is that the S-R Party was visibly inflated, like the frog in the fable, with no doubts at all that it would have the majority in the forthcoming Constituent Assembly. I knew only very little about Bolshevism, the very mention of which set the splendid officers foaming at the mouth. Its strength was being proved in the July troubles in Petrograd. The critical question that was put to everyone, including myself, was, all the time: 'For or against Bolshevism? For or against the Constituent Assembly?' To this I would reply as I was wont, rashly and frankly: the Russian Revolution cannot confine itself to changing the political order; it is, and must be, of a social character. In other words, the peasants are bound to seize the land, and will take it from the landlords, with or without uprisings, with or without the permission of a Constituent Assembly; the workers will insist on the nationalization or at the very least the control of large-scale industry and the banks. They did not kick out the Romanovs just to go back to their workshops as powerless as yesterday or to help the cannon-kings grow rich. This, for me, was a self-evident truth, but I saw very soon that although I confined myself to proclaiming it within the Russian military emigration, I ran a grave risk of getting into trouble with the French authorities. Trouble was indeed coming, in no uncertain manner. Without knowing it, I was 'on the line' advocated by Lenin.

The strangest feature of all this was the indignation of these newly-discovered Social-Revolutionaries when anyone reminded them that the cardinal point of their programme was the demand for the nationalization of land, immediate expropriation of the large estates, without compensation, and the liquidation of the landed aristocracy. 'But there's the war!' they exclaimed, 'Let's win first!' It was easy to reply to them that the autocracy had led the Empire to defeat and invasion; and that, since then, a conservative republic, without understanding of the people's needs, had been managing only to accumulate further catastrophes, until the day of some terrible social crisis when it would go down in unforeseeable ruin.

I was working in a print-shop on the Boulevard Port-Royal. Here and elsewhere, I had many contacts with the workers. They, too, were evidently annoyed at the unexpected direction taken by the Russian Revolution. At first they had greeted it with heart-felt pleasure; then they had been sold on the idea that disturbances and so-called 'maximalist' demands were weakening the Russian army. I was always being told (since people would say it for my benefit as soon as I disclosed my Russian nationality): 'The Bolsheviks are rats, sold out to Germany', or 'The Russians are all yellow'. I was nearly brained in one *bistro* for opening a Russian newspaper. I kept telling myself that this people, already bled white, could not be expected to think calmly, still less to have a brotherly understanding of what another distant people, equally bled and overworked, was yearning for. I learnt that, through an outstanding coincidence of events, France had just passed through a submerged revolutionary crisis. March 1917: downfall of the Russian autocracy. April 1917: the mutinies in Champagne. These were actually more serious than has been made out since. A whole army practically disintegrated, and there was talk of its marching on Paris. Com-mander-in-Chief Nivelle, Joffre's successor, had in April tried to break through the German front at Craonne and Rheims, and paid so hard a price for a slight advance that he had to stop the offensive himself. At this point the mutinies broke out. They were quelled without excessive repression, which proved to be a most sensible move. Another supremely important psychological factor came to bear at just this moment to restore the army's morale; the entry of the United States into the war (6 April; the Nivelle offensive began on 9 April). Confidence was restored; from now on victory was possible; the Russian Revolution, which was complicating the situa-tion, became unpopular. A tiny working-class minority alone con-tinued to support it, together with the *Vie Ouvrière* group (Monatte and Rosmer),[1] a few Socialists like Jean Longuet and Rappoport,[2] and anarchist elements which were more numerous but also more muddled. Clemenceau came to power at apparently the most critical hour; actually the worst moment of the crisis was over, whichever way you looked at it. Psychological recovery had been achieved, the American troops were landing, the Battle of the Atlantic was turning in the Allies' favour (in April, the black month, Britain had only three weeks' supply of food, because of the U-boat campaign). He began by destroying the peace party from within; its semi-official leader was Joseph Caillaux, Deputy for La Sarthe and former Prime Minister, a cunning and reactionary financier whom I had recently called '*Caillot de sang*' ('blood-clot') in a newspaper headline.[3] The peace party was counting on the weariness of the masses, on the fear of a European revolution, on the vacillations of the Habsburgs and on the social crisis maturing in Germany, and it was encouraged in various ways by German agents. Almereyda, now editor of *Le Bonnet Rouge*, had become the factotum of this party; if it had won, he would have made a popular minister able, honestly but still treacherously, to exploit the feelings of the masses that were sympathetic to Socialism and anarchism. Like nearly all the other revolutionaries, I had stopped seeing him ever since he became involved in what we ironically called 'high politics' behind the scenes of high finance. Intoxicated with money and danger, he was

[1] Pierre Monatte (1881–1960): anarcho-syndicalist; strike-leader, union organizer, journalist; founder of the syndicalist weekly *La Vie Ouvrière*, important in the years before the First World War, then of *La Révolution Prolétarienne*, which was a platform for Serge over many years. Alfred Rosmer (1877–1964): internationalist in the First World War, delegate and Executive member of the Communist International (1920–1), and prominent in the French Communist Party until his expulsion as an oppositionist in 1924. Supporter of the Left Opposition abroad and friend of Trotsky and Serge in exile. Author of books on working-class and Communist history.

[2] Jean Longuet (1876–1938): lawyer, grandson of Karl Marx; editor of *L'Humanité* when it belonged to the Socialist Party, then a founder of *Le Populaire*. Deputy and author. Charles Rappoport (1865–1941): former Russian citizen and member of *Narodnaya Volya*; after settling in France (1887), active in the French Socialist movement, founder-member of the French Communist Party (1920); resigned from the C.P. after the show trials of Old Bolsheviks, many of whom he had known personally.

[3] Joseph Caillaux (1863–1941): Radical-Socialist Deputy and Minister, was arrested by Clemenceau's administration in December 1917, on a charge of 'dealings with the enemy', and found guilty in February 1920 of 'correspondence with the enemy'. Sentenced to three years' imprisonment, after his release he reentered politics and became Finance Minister (1925–6) and a Senator.

dissipating his life, a morphine addict now, surrounded by theatri-
cals, blackmailers, beautiful women and political touts of every
description. The graph of his destiny had started from the Paris
underworld, had mounted to a climax of revolutionary pugnacity,
and was now tailing off in corruption, among the money-bags.
When Clemenceau had him and his staff arrested,[1] I knew at once
that it would be impossible to try him; he would have been too
likely to put the war in the dock and thoroughly compromise the
men behind him. He would probably have been shot: but not alone.
A few days afterwards, he was found in his prison bunk, strangled
with a shoe-lace. The business was never cleared up.

That summer Paris lived merrily, as much out of determined
confidence as from recklessness. The American soldiers were bringing
in plenty of money. The Germans had been at Noyon, 100 or so
kilometres away, for so long that people had got used to them and felt
no unusual anxiety. At night the approach of the Gotha bombers set
off the reverberation of the warning sirens, everyone went down to the
cellars, and a few bombs would fall. Suspicion, betrayal and fears
were the rule everywhere; some poor wretches were arrested for a
word spoken in the street. I was enjoying my precarious freedom by
studying the history of art—what was there better to do while this
respite lasted? One day I was arrested in the street by two terrified
inspectors, who for some unknown reason were expecting me to resist
to the death. They were visibly gratified when I told them that I had
no arms and no intention of putting up a fight. Since there was
strictly nothing that could be held against me, except perhaps
'dangerous thoughts', to use the happy expression of the Japanese
legislator, I was conveyed by administrative decision to a concentration-camp at Précigné, in La Sarthe.

There I found a whole collection of revolutionaries, mainly
Russians and Jews, like me labelled 'Bolsheviks' without, of course,
being anything of the kind. At Précigné I quickly started a Russian
revolutionary grouping, consisting of about fifteen militants and
twenty or so sympathizers. It included only one Bolshevik, the
chemical engineer Krauterkrafft, whose constant antagonist I was,
since he advocated a merciless dictatorship, suppression of Press
freedom, authoritarian revolution, and education on Marxist lines.

---

[1] Actually it was Ribot who had them arrested, before Clemenceau's second
Cabinet came into being.

(Later on he refused to leave for Russia.) We desired a libertarian, democratic revolution, without the hypocrisy and flabbiness of the bourgeois democracies—egalitarian and tolerant towards ideas and people, which would employ terror if it was necessary but would abolish the death-penalty. From a theoretical point of view, we stated these problems very badly; certainly the Bolshevik put them better than we. From the human standpoint, we were infinitely nearer the truth than he was. We saw in the power of the Soviets the realization of our deepest hopes, as he did also. Our mutual understanding was based on deep misunderstanding, as well as on sheer necessity.

Guarded by weary Territorials, who never had an idea unless it was to re-sell us bottles of wine at a handsome profit, we would hold pro-Soviet meetings in the courtyard of this secularized monastery. Paul Fouchs, an impassioned old libertarian artlessly proud of his resemblance to Lafargue, used to take the platform with me. Belgians, Macedonians, and Alsatians, variegated 'suspects' (some of them genuinely, in fact horribly, suspect), would hear us out in silence, respectful but disapproving since we were 'in bad odour' with the authorities as well as throwing away any hope of release that we had; and then too, 'what has been will be, there's always been rich and poor, war is in man's blood, you won't change anything of that, you'd do better to get out of your own mess. . . .'

The Belgians and Alsatians were vaguely pro-German; the Macedonians, proud, destitute, and silent, were just Macedonians, ready to fight the whole world for their primitive mountain liberty. These lived as a community, all sharing the same misery, all lousy, hungry, and brotherly. Belgians and Alsatians were partitioned into the rich, the poor, and the corrupt middlemen, a miniature society, utterly self-contained and utterly divided, scorned by us and a little afraid of us.

The camp's regimen was reasonably fair and free. The only trouble was that we were hungry. Spanish influenza was rife and death was our perpetual companion. An infirmary improvised in a ground-floor room held the dying, with those of us who had volunteered as nurses sitting up by them. They were left to wheeze and go blue, or else spotty like a panther's skin, and then cold. . . . What could we do? For my part I spent the night in the open, near the doorway of this stinking mortuary, getting up now and then to give a drink to some dying man. Our group did not have a single death, although we had nearly all been infected; but our solidarity meant that we could eat better than the other poor devils. A quarter of the camp's population was carried off in a few weeks; however, not one rich prisoner died.

During the epidemic we continued to assemble and conduct our studies. During one of the meetings, which I was holding purposely on that particular evening to distract the guards' attention, one of our group tried to escape, under cover of a storm. He fell in the camp's perimeter, under the livid glare of searchlights: 'Twenty years old, and six bullets in his body,' it was remarked. On the following day we summoned the camp to revolt. The Starost, or Elder of the Macedonians, came and told us that they would support us. The Belgians and the Alsatians answered that this trifle was no business of theirs, that it would all come to grief, and as far as they were concerned, nothing doing. The local Prefect came, and promised us an inquiry. The commandant of the camp asked for a confidential interview with me. At it he disclosed that he knew of the plan of escape from a camp trader; that several internees were due to bolt (this was true) and that the guards had meant to kill another prisoner, a Rumanian scoundrel suspected of espionage, who was an informer into the bargain.

'On my word of honour, we did intend to let your comrade run off, and I am broken-hearted at what happened; a mistake, I assure you. . . .'

His information was correct, and the revolt subsided. We felt a physical revulsion for the spies. The reprieved informer continued to stroll up and down the yard, smoking his dirty-yellow cigarettes.

Civil war was breaking out in Russia. In consequence of the counter-revolutionary rising at Yaroslavl and Dora Kaplan's attempt against Lenin, the Cheka arrested Mr. Lockhart, the British Consul in Moscow, and the French military mission under General Lavergne. Negotiations were set in hand through the Danish Red Cross, with a view to an exchange of hostages. Chicherin, himself released from a British concentration-camp, demanded the liberation of Litvinov, who was imprisoned in London, and of the 'Bolsheviks' interned in France—us, that is. The negotiations were successful only after the general explosion of goodwill at the Armistice. The authorities offered us a choice between release, in the

near future, or leaving now for Russia as hostages, with the safety of
the French officers hanging over our heads. Five out of the fifteen
or so in our group joined me in insisting on departure. We set off with
our sacks over our shoulders, in the cold of the night, pursued by
shouts of mirth from the whole camp. Several of the worst inmates
had come to embrace us as we left, and we had no heart to push them
away. The frozen snow echoed sharply under our feet, and the stars
receded in front of us. The night was huge and buoyant.

We journeyed through bombarded towns, in countryside dotted
with wooden crosses on the railway embankments, until we came
into the territory of the 'Tommies'. One night, in a port whose
houses were shattered by bombs, the sick man in our party, some
police officers and I went into a tavern filled with British soldiers.
They noticed our unusual appearance. 'Who are you lot? Where
are you going?'

'Revolutionaries—we are going to Russia.' Thirty tanned faces
surrounded us eagerly, there were hearty exclamations all round us,
and we had to shake everybody's hand. Since the Armistice popular
feeling had changed once again; the Russian Revolution was once
more a distant beacon to men.

In the converted prison at Dunkirk another group of hostages
was waiting for us, led from another camp by a Dr. N——ko. The
exchange was being made man for man, and the Russians were
tricked: out of forty hostages, hardly ten were genuine militants,
and nearly twenty were children. Should we protest against this
trickery? Dr. N——ko, very tall, white-haired and narrow-eyed,
affirmed that 'a child at the breast is well worth any general'.
Connected with the Russian seamen's union, he had organized a
strike at Marseilles on ships loaded with munitions bound for the
Whites. He and I were elected as delegates by the whole group.

'Are these hostages too, these kids less than ten years old?' I
asked some of the officers, 'Do you think that is compatible with
military honour?' They spread out their hands, mortified: 'We can
do nothing about it.' Rather likeable men, they used to read
Romain Rolland's *Above the Battle* in their cabins.[1] This conversation
took place at sea, off the level shores of Denmark, on a milky sea
from which the mast-ends of sunken ships could sometimes be seen

---

[1] Rolland's *Above the Battle* (*Au-dessus de la Mêlée*) was a collection of articles,
originally published in the *Journal de Génève*, condemning the war.

emerging. Our remarks were apropos of a rumour then abroad that some French officers had perished in Russia; we were informed that we were in danger of reprisals.

It was a fine voyage, in first-class berths. A destroyer escorted our steamer, and now and then took long shots at floating mines. A dark gush would rise from the waves and the child-hostages applauded. From mist and sea there emerged the massive outline of Elsinore's grey stone castle, with its roofs of dull emerald. Weak Prince Hamlet, you faltered in that fog of crimes, but you put the question well. 'To be or not to be', for the men of our age, means free-will or servitude, and they have only to choose. We are leaving the void, and entering the kingdom of the will. This, perhaps, is the imaginary frontier. A land awaits us where life is beginning anew, where conscious will, intelligence, and an inexorable love of mankind are in action. Behind us, all Europe is ablaze, having choked almost to death in the fog of its own massacres. Barcelona's flame smoulders on. Germany is in the thick of revolution, Austro-Hungary is splitting into free nations. Italy is spread with red flags. . . . This is only the beginning. We are being born into violence; not only you and I, who are fairly unimportant, but all those to whom, unknown to themselves, we belong, down to this tin-hatted Senegalese, freezing under his fur on his dismal watch at the foot of the officers' gangway. Outbursts of idealism like this, if truth be known, kept getting mixed up with our heated discussions on points of doctrine. Then an amazing girl-child of twenty, whose big eyes held both smiles and a kind of suppressed fear, would come on deck to seek us out, telling us that tea was ready in the cabin, crammed with children, occupied by an old anarchist worker who was more enthusiastic even than we were. I called this girl-child 'Bluebird'; and it was she who brought me the news of the murder of Karl Liebknecht and Rosa Luxemburg.

From the Åland Isles onwards the Baltic was ice, studded with islands of white. A hundred yards ahead, a destroyer kept ramming the ice, and our steamer would advance slowly through the floe, by a narrow, gurgling channel. Enormous blocks of ice, torn away in some elemental struggle, floated round and round under our bows. We gazed at them till we were dizzy. There were moments of trance when I found this spectacle pregnant with meaning, and it was lovelier than all the enchantment of the countryside.

Finland received us as foes, for the White Terror was only just over. Hangö, a deserted port, under snow. We were caged in railway-carriages whose exits were guarded by silent blond giants, stony-eyed and cowled in white, with orders to shoot (as we were warned) at the first attempt to leave the train. I pressed my question: 'Please ask Monsieur the Finnish officer if this order applies to the child-hostages as well?'

Monsieur the officer was enraged: 'To everybody!'

'Please thank Monsieur the officer.'

The cold air was heavy with chilled violence. Without ever leaving the train, we crossed this huge land of sleepy woods, snow-covered lakes, tracts of whiteness, and pretty painted cottages lost in the wilderness. We went through towns so tidy and silent that they reminded us of children's toys. We had a moment of panic when, as evening fell, the train stopped in a clearing and soldiers lined up alongside the tracks: we were invited to get down. The women murmured, 'They're going to shoot us.' We refused to leave the train, but it was only to give us a breath of air while we waited for the carriages to be cleaned and the engine to be fuelled with wood. The sentries ignored their instructions and started to be pleasant to the children.

We crossed the Soviet frontier at dead of night, in the middle of a forest. Our progress was painful, blocked by the snow. The sharp cold bored through our thin Western clothing and our teeth chattered. The children, swaddled in bed-clothes, were crying. Men with lanterns, standing on a little white bridge in the misty moonlight, counted us as we passed. Choked with joy, we shouted 'Greetings, comrade!' to a Red sentry; he nodded, and then asked if we had any food. We had. Here, take it. The Revolution is hungry.

We gathered around a wood fire which lit us up with fantastic shadows. In the command-post of this dead sector of the front, a log hut unfurnished but equipped with telephones, we considered the strangeness of this first contact with our homeland, our Revolution. Two or three Red soldiers in worn greatcoats were busy at the telephones, without any sign of interest in us. Their faces were haggard and they did what they had to, rising above their prodigious fatigue. They livened up when we offered them some tinned food. 'What, aren't they hungry in France? Do they still have white bread over there?' We asked them for newspapers, but none were being delivered to them.

We never thought of sleep once we were in the goods-wagon. This was efficiently heated by an iron stove and pulled by an asthmatic locomotive that was taking us, through the pale, ideally pure dawn, to Petrograd. A wintry landscape, without trace of man. Brilliance of snow, borderland of emptiness. In a second forlorn little outpost, another soldier, indifferent to everything but hunger and food, found us a copy of *Severnaya Kommuna*, organ of the Petrograd Soviet. It was only a single, fairly large grey sheet, printed in pale ink. From it came our first shock. We had never thought that the idea of revolution could be separated from that of freedom. All we knew of the French Revolution, of the Paris Commune, of 1905 in Russia, showed us popular ferment, bubbling ideas, rivalry of clubs, parties, and publications—except during the Terror, under the 'Reign of the Supreme Being'; but the Terror of 1793 was simultaneously a climax and the beginning of a decline, the approach to Thermidor. In Petrograd we expected to breathe the air of a liberty that would doubtless be harsh and even cruel to its enemies, but was still generous and bracing. And in this paper we found a colourless article, signed 'G. Zinoviev', on 'The Monopoly of Power'. '*Our Party rules alone . . . it will not allow anyone. . . . The false democratic liberties demanded by the counter-revolution.*' I am quoting from memory, but such was certainly the sense of the piece. We tried to justify it by the state of siege and the mortal perils; however, such considerations could justify particular acts, acts of violence towards men and ideas, but not a theory based on the extinction of all freedom. I note the date of this article: January 1919. The desert of snow was still rolling on beneath our eyes. We were approaching Petrograd.

3

ANGUISH AND ENTHUSIASM

1919–1920

We were entering a world frozen to death. The Finland station, glittering with snow, was deserted. The square where Lenin had addressed a crowd from the top of an armoured car was no more than a white desert surrounded by dead houses. The broad, straight thoroughfares, the bridges astride the Neva, now a river of snowy ice, seemed to belong to an abandoned city; first a gaunt soldier in a grey greatcoat, then after a long time a woman freezing under her shawls, went past like phantoms in an oblivious silence.

Towards the city centre, gentle ghost-like hints of life began. Open sleds, pulled by starving horses, proceeded unhurriedly over the white expanse. There were practically no cars. The rare passers-by, eaten by cold and hunger, had faces of ghastly white. Squads of half-ragged soldiers, their rifles often hanging from their shoulders by a rope, tramped around under the red pennants of their units. Palaces drowsed at the end of spacious prospects, or in front of the frozen canals; others, more massive, lorded it over yesterday's parade-squares. The smart baroque façades of the Imperial family's residences were painted over in ox-blood red; the theatres, the military headquarters, the former ministries, all in Empire style, made a background of noble colonnades among huge stretches of emptiness. The high gilded dome of St. Isaac, upheld by mighty red granite pillars, hung over this wasting city like a symbol of past glories. We contemplated the low embrasures of the Peter-Paul Fortress and its golden spire, thinking of all the revolutionaries who, since Bakunin and Nechayev, had fought and now lay dead under those stones, that the world might belong to us.

It was the metropolis of Cold, of Hunger, of Hatred, and of Endurance. From about a million inhabitants its population had now fallen, in one year, to scarcely 700,000 souls.

At a reception centre we were issued with basic rations of black bread and dried fish. Never until now had any of us known such a horrid diet. Girls with red head-bands joined with young bespectacled agitators to give us a summary of the state of affairs: 'Famine, typhus and counter-revolution everywhere. But the world revolution is bound to save us.' They were surer of it than we were, and our doubts made them momentarily suspicious of us. All they asked us was whether Europe would soon be kindled: 'What is the French proletariat waiting for before it seizes power?'

The Bolshevik leaders that I saw spoke to me in more or less the same tones. Zinoviev's wife Lilina, People's Commissar for Social Planning in the Northern Commune, a small crop-haired, grey-eyed woman in a uniform jacket, sprightly and tough, asked me, 'Have you brought your families with you? I could put them up in palaces, which I know is very nice on some occasions, but it is impossible to heat them. You'd better go to Moscow. Here, we are besieged people in a besieged city. Hunger-riots may start, the Finns may swoop on us, the British may attack. Typhus has killed so many people that we can't manage to bury them; luckily they are frozen. If work is what you want, there's plenty of it!' And she told me passionately of the Soviet achievement: school-building, children's centres, relief for pensioners, free medical assistance, the theatres open to all. . . . 'We work on in spite of everything and we shall carry on working till our last hour!' Later I was to learn at first hand how hard she worked, never showing any sign of being worn down.

Shklovsky, People's Commissar for Foreign Affairs (in the Northern Commune), an intellectual with a black beard and a jaundiced complexion, met me in a room of what was lately the main military headquarters.

'What are they saying about us abroad?'

'They're saying that Bolshevism equals banditry.'

'There's something in that,' he replied calmly. 'You'll see for yourself, things are too much for us. In the Revolution the revolutionaries only amount to a very tiny percentage.' He outlined the situation to me, sparing nothing: a revolution dying, strangled by blockade, ready to collapse from inside into the chaos of counter-revolution. He was a man of bitterly clear vision. (He committed suicide around 1930.)

Zinoviev, the President of the Soviet, by contrast affected an extraordinary confidence. Clean-shaven, pale, his face a little puffy, he felt absolutely at home on the pinnacle of power, being the most long-standing of Lenin's collaborators in the Central Committee: all the same there was also an impression of flabbiness, almost of a lurking irresolution, emanating from his whole personality. Abroad, a frightful reputation for terror surrounded his name; I told him this.

'Of course', he answered, smiling, 'they don't like our plebeian methods of fighting.' And he alluded to the latest delegation from the Consular Corps, who were making representations to him in favour of the hostages taken from the bourgeoisie. He sent them about their business: 'If it was we who were being shot, these gentlemen would be quite happy, wouldn't they?'

Our conversation turned principally on the state of mass feeling in the Western countries. I kept saying that tremendous events were maturing, only the process was sluggish, halting, and blind; that in France, more particularly, no revolutionary upheaval was to be expected for a long time. Zinoviev smiled, with an air of kindly condescension. 'It is easy to tell that you are no Marxist. History cannot stop half-way.'

Maxim Gorky welcomed me affectionately. In the famished years of his youth, he had been acquainted with my mother's family at Nizhni-Novgorod. His apartment in the Kronversky Prospect, full of books and Chinese *objets d'art*, seemed as warm as a greenhouse. He himself was chilly even under his thick grey sweater, and coughed terribly, the result of his thirty years' struggle against tuberculosis. Tall, lean and bony, broad-shouldered and hollow-chested, he stooped a little as he walked. His frame, sturdily-built but anaemic, appeared essentially as a support for his head, an ordinary, Russian man-in-the-street's head, bony and pitted, really almost ugly with its jutting cheek-bones, great thin-lipped mouth and professional smeller's nose, broad and peaked. His complexion deathly, he was chewing away under his short, bristly moustache, full of dejection, or rather of anguish mingled with indignation. His bushy brows puckered readily, and his big, grey eyes held an extraordinary

wealth of expression. His whole being expressed hunger for knowledge and human understanding, determination to probe all inhuman doings to their depths, never stopping at mere appearances,
never tolerating any lies told to him, and never lying to himself. I saw him immediately as the supreme, the righteous, the
relentless witness of the Revolution, and it was as such that he talked
with me.

He spoke harshly about the Bolsheviks: they were 'drunk with
authority', 'cramping the violent, spontaneous anarchy of the
Russian people', and 'starting bloody despotism all over again'; all
the same they were 'facing chaos alone' with some incorruptible
men in their leadership. His observations always started from facts,
from chilling anecdotes upon which he would base his well-
considered generalizations.

The prostitutes were sending a delegation to him, demanding
the right to organize a trade union. The fate of the hostages in the
jails was nothing short of monstrous. Hunger was weakening the
masses, and distorting the cerebral processes of the whole country.
At present it was imperative to side with the revolutionary régime,
for fear of a rural counter-revolution which would be no less than an
outburst of savagery. Alexei Maximovich spoke to me of strange
tortures rediscovered for the benefit of 'Commissars' in remote
country districts; such as pulling out the intestines through an
incision in the abdomen and coiling them slowly around a tree.
He thought that the tradition of these tortures was kept up through
the reading of *The Golden Legend*.[1]

The non-Communist (i.e. anti-Bolshevik) intellectuals whom I
saw gave me more or less the same general picture. They thought
of Bolshevism as finished, consumed by famine and terror, opposed
by all the peasants of the countryside, all the intelligentsia, and the
great majority of the working class. The people who spoke thus to
me were Socialists who had been enthusiastic participants in the
March 1917 Revolution. The Jews among them were living in
terror of approaching pogroms. All of them expected chaos, replete
with massacres. The dissolution of the Constituent Assembly, and
certain crimes at the beginning of the Revolution, such as the execution (or murder) of the Hingleize brothers and the murder, in a hospital, of the Liberal deputies Shingarev and Kokoshkin, had left a

---

[1] *The Golden Legend*: a thirteenth-century 'Lives of the Saints'.

wake of enraged resentment. The violent acts of mob-agitators such as the Kronstadt sailors so offended the humane feelings of men of goodwill that they lost all their critical faculties. Against how many hangings, humiliations, ruthless repressions, threatened reprisals, did these excesses have to be set? If the other side won would it be any more merciful? Besides, what were the Whites doing in the areas where they ruled the roost? I moved among intellectuals who wept for their dream of an enlightened democracy, governed by a sagacious Parliament and inspired by an idealistic Press (their own, of course). Every conversation I had with them convinced me that, face to face with the ruthlessness of history, they were wrong. I saw that their cause of democracy had, at the end of the summer of 1917, stood between two fires, that is to say between two conspiracies, and it seemed obvious to me that, if the Bolshevik insurrection had not taken power at that point, the cabal of the old generals, supported by the officers' organizations, would have certainly done so instead. Russia would have avoided the Red Terror only to endure the White, and a proletarian dictatorship only to undergo a reactionary one. In consequence, the most outraged observations of the anti-Bolshevik intellectuals only revealed to me how necessary Bolshevism was.

Moscow, with its old Italian and Byzantine architecture, its innumerable churches, its snows, its human ant-heap, its great public Departments, its half-clandestine markets, wretched but colourful, taking up vast squares: Moscow seemed to live a little better than Petrograd. Here Committees were piled on top of Councils, and Managements on top of Commissions. Of this apparatus, which seemed to me to function largely in a void, wasting three-quarters of its time on unrealizable projects, I at once formed the worst possible impression. Already, in the midst of general misery, it was nurturing a multitude of bureaucrats who were responsible for more fuss than honest work. In the offices of Commissariats one came across elegant gentlemen, pretty and irreproachably powdered typists, chic uniforms weighed down with decorations; and everybody in this smart set, in such contrast with the famished populace in the strccts, kept sending you back and forth from office to office for the slightest matter and without the slightest result. I witnessed members of Government circles driven to telephoning Lenin to obtain a railway ticket or a room in the hotel, i.e. the 'House of the Soviets'. The Central Committee's secretariat gave me some tickets for lodgings, but I got none, because initiation into the racket was more necessary than any ticket.

I met the Menshevik leaders, and certain anarchists. Both sets denounced Bolshevik intolerance, the stubborn refusal to revolutionary dissenters of any right to exist, and the excesses of the Terror. Neither group, however, had any substantial alternative to suggest. The Mensheviks were publishing a daily paper, which was widely read; they had recently announced their allegiance to the régime and recovered their legality. They demanded the abolition of the Cheka and sang the praises of a return to Soviet democracy. One anarchist group canvassed the idea of a federation of free communes; others saw no future except in fresh insurrections, although realizing that famine was blocking all possible progress in the Revolution. I learnt that, around the autumn of 1918, the anarchist Black Guards had felt powerful enough for their leaders to discuss whether or not they should seize Moscow. Novomirsky and Borovoy had won the majority over to the virtues of abstention. 'We would not know what to do about the famine,' they said. 'Let it exhaust the Bolsheviks and lead the dictatorship of the Commissars to its grave. Then our hour will come!'

The Mensheviks seemed to me to be admirably intelligent, honest and devoted to Socialism, but completely overtaken by events. They stood for a sound principle, that of working-class democracy, but in a situation fraught with such mortal danger that the stage of siege did not permit any functioning of democratic institutions. And their bitterness, arising out of their brutal defeat as the party of compromise, disfigured their thinking; since they waited on the coming of some catastrophe, their declaration of support for the régime was only lip-service.

Of the Bolshevik leaders, on this occasion in Moscow I saw only Aveli Yenukidze, Secretary of the Executive Committee of the All-Union Soviets—actually the key post in the Republic's government. He was a fair-headed Georgian, with a kind, sturdy face lit up by blue eyes. His bearing was corpulent and grand, that of a mountain-dweller born and bred. He was affable, humorous and realistic, striking the same note as the Bolsheviks in Petrograd.

'Our bureaucracy's a scandal, no doubt about it. I think Petrograd is healthier. I even advise you to settle down there unless you are too scared of Petrograd's peculiar dangers. Here, we combine all the vices of the old Russia with those of the new. Petrograd is an outpost, the front line.'

Gorky offered me employment with him in the publishing-house 'Universal Literature', but the only people I met there were ageing or embittered intellectuals trying to escape from the present by re-translating Boccaccio, Knut Hamsun, or Balzac. My mind was made up: I was neither against the Bolsheviks nor neutral; I was with them, albeit independently, without renouncing thought or critical sense. Certainly on several essential points they were mistaken: in their intolerance, in their faith in statification, in their leaning towards centralism and administrative techniques. But, given that one had to counter them with freedom of the spirit and the spirit of freedom, it must be with them and among them. Possibly, after all, these evils had been impelled by civil war, blockade and famine, and if we managed to survive, the remedy would come of itself. I remember having written in one of my first letters from Russia that I was 'resolved to make no career out of the Revolution, and, once the mortal danger has passed, to join again with those who will fight the evils of the new régime. . . .'

I was on the staff of the *Severnaya Kommuna* (Northern Commune) the organ of the Petrograd Soviet, an instructor in the public education clubs, organizing inspector for schools in the Second District, lecturing assistant to the Petrograd militia, etc. People were in short supply, and I was overwhelmed with work. All this activity brought me the means of bare existence from one day to the next, in a chaos that was oddly organized. The militiamen to whom I gave evening classes in history and the first elements of 'political science' (or 'political grammar', as it was called) would offer me a cob of black bread and a herring if the lesson had been interesting. Happy to ask me endless questions, they would escort me after the lesson through the shadows of the city, right up to my lodgings, in case anyone should steal my precious little parcel; and we would all trip over the carcass of a horse, dead in the snow in front of the Opera House.

The Third International had just been founded in Moscow (it was now March 1919) and had appointed Zinoviev as President of its Executive (the proposal was actually Lenin's). The new Executive still possessed neither personnel nor offices. Although I was not a member of the Party, Zinoviev asked me to organize his administration. As my knowledge of Russian life was too limited, I was unwilling to assume such a responsibility by myself. After some days Zinoviev told me, 'I've found an excellent man, you'll get along with him really well. . . .'; and so it turned out. It was thus that I came to know Vladmir Ossipovich Mazin who, prompted by the same motives as myself, had just joined the Party.

Through its severely practical centralization of power, and its repugnance towards individualism and celebrity, the Russian Revolution has left in obscurity at least as many first-rate men as it has made famous. Of all these great but still practically unknown figures, Mazin seems to me to be one of the most remarkable. One day, in an enormous room in the Smolny Institute, furnished solely with a table and two chairs, we met face to face, both of us rigged out rather absurdly. I still wore a large sheepskin hat which had been a present from a Cossack and a short, shabby overcoat, the garb of the Western unemployed. Mazin wore an old blue uniform with worn-out elbows; he had a three days' growth of beard, his eyes were encircled by old-fashioned spectacles of white metal, his face was elongated, his brow lofty and his complexion pasty from starvation.

'Well,' he said to me, 'so we're the Executive of the new International. It's really ridiculous!' And upon that bare table we set about drawing rough sketches of seals, for a seal was required immediately for the President: the great seal of the World Revolution, no more, no less! We decided that the globe would be the emblem on it.

We were friends with the same points of concern, doubt, and confidence, spending any moments spared us from our grinding work in examining together the problems of authority, terror, centralization, Marxism, and heresy. We both had strong leanings towards heresy. I was beginning my initiation into Marxism. Mazin had arrived there through the path of personal experience in jail. With those convictions he combined an old-fashioned libertarian heart and an ascetic temperament.

As an adolescent in 1905 on the revolutionary day of 22 January, he had seen the St. Petersburg streets running with the blood of working-class petitioners, and at once decided, even while the Cossacks were clearing away the crowd with their stubby whips, to study the chemistry of explosives. He very soon became one of the chemists of the Maximalist group, who wanted a 'total' socialist revolution. He, Vladimir Ossipovich Lichtenstadt, son of a good liberal-bourgeois family, manufactured the bombs that went with three of his comrades who presented themselves, dressed as officers, on 12 August 1906, at a gala entertainment for the Prime Minister Stolypin, and who, in blowing up the house, blew themselves up too. Some time afterwards, the Maximalists attacked a Treasury van in the broad daylight of St. Petersburg. Lichtenstadt was condemned to death, then pardoned; he spent ten years in prison at Schlüsselburg,[1] much of it in the same cell as the Georgian Bolshevik Sergo Ordzhonikidze, who was to become one of the organizers of Soviet industrialization. In confinement Lichtenstadt wrote a work of scientific meditation which was later published (*Goethe and the Philosophy of Nature*), and studied Marx.

After another prisoner, a friend whom he admired, was killed, Lichtenstadt adopted the dead man's name and called himself Mazin, to remain faithful to his example. As a Marxist, he was at first a Menshevik, because of his zeal for democracy, and then entered the Bolshevik Party to be on the side of those who were the most active, the most creative and the most imperilled. He had a consuming interest in great books, a scholar's soul, a childlike frankness in the face of evil, and few basic wants. For eleven years he had been waiting to see his wife again; she was at present separated from him by the Southern front. 'The faults in the Revolution', he would say to me over and over again, 'must be fought in the realm of action.'

We spent our lives among telephones, trailing around the huge, dead city in wheezy motor-cars, commandeering print-shops, selecting staff, correcting proofs even in the trams, bargaining with the Board of Trade for string and with the State Bank's printers for paper, running to the Cheka or to distant suburban prisons whenever (which was every day) we were notified of some abomination, fatal mistake, or piece of cruelty, and conferring with Zinoviev in the evening. Since we were senior officials we lived in the Hotel Astoria, the foremost 'House of the Soviets', where the most responsible of the Party's militants resided under the protection of machineguns posted on the ground floor. Through the black market I came

---

[1] Schlüsselburg: (also known as Petrokrepost or 'Peter's Fortress'); a redoubtable prison for political prisoners about forty miles up the River Neva from Petrograd.

into possession of a fur-lined riding-jacket which, cleared of its fleas, made me look wonderful. In the former Austro-Hungarian Embassy we found some Habsburg officers' clothes, in excellent condition, for some of the comrades on our new staff. We were enormously privileged, although the bourgeoisie, dispossessed and now addicted to every imaginable form of speculation, lived much better than we did. Every day at the table reserved for the Northern Commune Executive, we found greasy soup and often a ration of slightly high but still delicious horse-meat. The customary diners there were Zinoviev, Yevdokimov from the Central Committee, Zorin from the Petrograd Committee, Bakayev, President of the Cheka, sometimes Helena Stassova, Secretary of the Central Committee, and sometimes Stalin, who was practically unknown. Zinoviev occupied an apartment on the first floor of the Astoria. As an extraordinary privilege, this hotel of dictators was kept almost warm, and was lit brightly at nightfall since work there never stopped; it thus formed an enormous vessel of light above the dark public squares. Rumour endowed us with incredible comfort and even detailed our alleged orgies, with actresses from the *corps de ballet*, naturally. All this time, Bakayev of the Cheka was going round with holes in his boots. In spite of my special rations as a Government official, I would have died of hunger without the sordid manipulations of the black market, where we traded the petty possessions we had brought in from France. The eldest son of my friend Yonov, Zinoviev's brother-in-law, an Executive member of the Soviet and founder and director of the State Library, died of hunger before our very eyes. All this while we were looking after considerable stocks, and even riches, but on the State's behalf and under rigorous control. Our salaries were limited to the 'Communist maximum', equal to the average wage of a skilled worker. During this period the old Lettish Bolshevik, Peter Stuchka,[1] a great figure now forgotten, instituted a strictly egalitarian régime in his Sovietized Latvia, in which the Party Committee was also the Government; its members were forbidden to enjoy

[1] Peter Ivanovich Stuchka (1865–1932) was a founder of the Latvian Marxist movement and later a prominent Soviet jurist. A Bolshevik since 1903, he became People's Commissar for Justice (1917–18), Chairman of the Latvian Soviet Government (1918–19), Deputy People's Commissar for Justice of the R.S.F.S.R. (1921), and from 1923 till his death Chairman of the Supreme Court of the R.S.F.S.R. He wrote a number of works on Soviet legal theory.

any material privileges at all. Vodka was banned, though the comrades obtained it clandestinely from peasants, who through home distilling extracted a terrifying alcohol from corn, eighty degrees proof.

The telephone became my personal enemy; perhaps it is for that reason that I still feel a stubborn aversion from it. At every hour it brought me voices of panic-stricken women who spoke of arrests, imminent executions, and injustice, and begged me to intervene at once, for the love of God! Since the first massacres of Red prisoners by the Whites, the murders of Volodarsky and Uritsky[1] and the attempt against Lenin (in the summer of 1918), the custom of arresting and, often, executing hostages had become generalized and legal. Already the Cheka (the Extraordinary Commission for Repression against counter-revolution, speculation, and desertion), which made mass arrests of suspects, was tending to settle their fate independently, under formal control by the Party, but in reality without anybody's knowledge. It was becoming a State within the State, protected by military secrecy and proceedings *in camera*. The Party endeavoured to head it with incorruptible men like the former convict Dzerzhinsky, a sincere idealist, ruthless but chivalrous, with the emaciated profile of an Inquisitor: tall forehead, bony nose, untidy goatee, and an expression of weariness and austerity. But the Party had few men of this stamp and many Chekas: these gradually came to select their personnel by virtue of their psychological inclinations. The only temperaments that devoted themselves willingly and tenaciously to this task of 'internal defence' were those characterized by suspicion, embitterment, harshness, and sadism. Long-standing social inferiority-complexes and memories of humiliations and suffering in the Tsar's jails rendered them intractable, and since professional degeneration has rapid effects, the Chekas inevitably consisted of perverted men tending to see conspiracy everywhere and to live in the midst of perpetual conspiracy themselves.

I believe that the formation of the Chekas was one of the gravest

[1] V. Volodarsky (1891–1918): Bolshevik orator and Petrograd Commissar of Press, Propaganda, and Agitation. Assassinated by a Social-Revolutionary terrorist in June 1918. Moisei S. Uritsky (1873–1918): Bolshevik since 1917 and member of the Revolutionary Military Committee which directed the October rising; 'Left Communist' in 1918; Chairman of the Petrograd Cheka at the time of his murder by a Social-Revolutionary.

and most impermissible errors that the Bolshevik leaders committed in 1918, when plots, blockades, and interventions made them lose their heads. All evidence indicates that revolutionary tribunals, functioning in the light of day (without excluding secret sessions in particular cases) and admitting the right of defence, would have attained the same efficiency with far less abuse and depravity. Was it so necessary to revert to the procedures of the Inquisition? By the beginning of 1919, the Chekas had little or no resistance against this psychological perversion and corruption. I know for a fact that Dzerzhinsky judged them to be 'half-rotten', and saw no solution to the evil except in shooting the worst Chekists and abolishing the death-penalty as quickly as possible. . . . Meanwhile, the Terror went on, since the whole Party was living in the sure inner knowledge that they would be massacred in the event of defeat; and defeat remained possible from one week to the next.

In every prison there were quarters reserved for Chekists, judges, police of all sorts, informers and executioners. The executioners, who used Nagan revolvers, generally ended by being executed themselves. They began to drink and to wander around firing unexpectedly at anybody. I was acquainted with several cases of this sort. I was also closely acquainted with the terrible Chudin case. Still young, though a revolutionary of 1905 vintage, Chudin, a tall curly-headed lad whose roguish stare was softened by his pince-nez, had fallen in love with a girl he had met at a class. She became his mistress. A number of swindlers exploited his sincerity by prevailing on him to intercede for some genuine speculators, more than mere suspects, whose release they thus obtained. Dzerzhinsky had Chudin and his girl and the swindlers all shot. No one doubted Chudin's honesty; there was bitter dismay all round. Years later, comrades said to me, 'On that day we shot the best man among us.' They never forgave themselves.

Fortunately, the democratic manners of the Party were still strong enough to enable militants to intercede fairly easily with the Cheka against certain blunders. It was all the easier for me to do this since the leaders of the Cheka lived at the Astoria, including Ivan Bakayev, President of the 'Extraordinary Commission'. Bakayev was a handsome fellow of about thirty, with the careless appearance of a Russian village accordion-player; indeed, he liked to wear a smock with an embroidered collar and coloured border, just like such a player. In the performance of his frightful duty he exercised an impartial will and a scrupulous vigilance. I saved several people, although once I failed, in circumstances that were both cruel and ridiculous. This concerned an officer named (I think) Nesterenko, a Frenchwoman's husband, who was arrested at Kronstadt in connexion with the Lindquist conspiracy. Bakayev promised me that he would personally review the dossier. When I met him again he smiled: 'It isn't serious, I'll soon have him released.' I took pleasure in disclosing this good news to the suspect's wife and daughter.

A few days later I met Bakayev passing from room to room in the Smolny, joking as he loved to. When he saw me, his face grew pale: 'Too late, Victor Lvovich! While I was away they shot the poor devil.' He went past to his next business, spreading his hands wide in a gesture of powerlessness.[1]

Shocks of this kind did not happen often, but the Terror was too much for us. I arranged the release of a distant relative, a subaltern confined as a hostage in the Peter-Paul Fortress. He came to me to tell me that they had failed to give him back his papers on his discharge. 'Go and ask for them back,' I said. Off he went, only to return thunderstruck. 'An official whispered me an answer, "Don't press for it, you've been reported shot for the last ten days." ' He gave up bothering about the matter.

Often at the Cheka I would meet the man whom I came to dub mentally as the 'great interceder', Maxim Gorky. His efforts tormented Zinoviev and Lenin, but he nearly always got his way. In cases that were difficult I approached him, and he never refused to intervene. But, although he was working for the journal *Communist International*, not without violent arguments with Zinoviev over some wording in every article he wrote, he once greeted me with a kind of roaring fury. On that day I was coming from a discussion with Zinoviev. Gorky shouted out, 'Don't talk to me of that beast ever again—tell him that his torturers are a disgrace to the human image!' Their quarrel lasted until Petrograd underwent its new phase of mortal peril.

[1] After his period as Chairman of the Petrograd Cheka, Bakayev went on (1920) to fill a similar post in south-east Russia. Later a prominent member of the Zinoviev Opposition, he was sentenced to death and shot as a result of the 1936 'Trial of the Sixteen'.

The spring of 1919 opened with events at once expected and surprising. At the beginning of April Munich acquired a Soviet régime. On 22 March Hungary quietly became a Soviet Republic through the abdication of Count Karolyi's bourgeois government. Bela Kun, who had been sent to Budapest by Lenin and Zinoviev, came out of jail to take power. The bad news from the Civil War fronts lost their importance. Even the fall of Munich, captured by General Hoffmann on 1 May, seemed rather unimportant by comparison with the revolutionary victories now expected to follow in Central Europe, Bohemia, Italy, and Bulgaria. (However, the massacres at Munich did reinforce the terrorist state of mind, and the atrocities committed at Ufa by Admiral Kolchak's troops, who burned Red prisoners alive, had lately enabled the Chekists to prevail against those Party members who hoped for a greater degree of humanity.)

The Executive of the International was in session at Moscow, with Angelica Balabanova in charge of the secretariat; actually its political control was managed from Petrograd, by Zinoviev, with whom Karl Radek and Bukharin used to come and confer. The Executive held a session also at Petrograd; this was attended by Finns (e.g. Sirola), Bulgarians, the ambassador from Soviet Hungary, Rudniansky, and the Volga German Klinger. I was present at these meetings, although I had still not joined the Party. I remember that the anarchist William Shatov, for a short while the military governor of the old capital, was also invited. There the superiority of the Russians, compared with the foreign revolutionaries, amazed me: it was immediately obvious. I found Zinoviev's optimism terrifying. He seemed to have no doubts at all: the European Revolution was on the way, and nothing would stop it. I can see him now, at the end of the session, his finger-tips playing with the little tassels of silken cord which he wore instead of a tie, wreathed in smiles, and saying about some resolution or other, 'Always provided that new revolutions do not come and upset our plans for the forthcoming weeks!' He was setting the tone.

We had white nights, and superb weather. Towards one in the morning a faint bluish light lay over the canals, the Neva, the golden spires of the palaces and the empty squares with their equestrian statues of dead emperors. I went to bed in guard-houses, and did my turn of sentry-duty in outlying railway stations, reading Alexander

Herzen. Quite a few of us sentries took books with us. I searched people's homes: house by house we sifted apartments, looking for arms and White agents. I could have easily avoided this unpleasant work, but I went off to it with a will, knowing that wherever I went no brutality, thefts, or stupid arrests would take place. I remember a weird exchange of shots on the roofs of high buildings overlooking a sky-blue canal. Men fled before us, firing their revolvers at us from behind the chimney-pots. I kept slipping on the sheet-iron roof and my heavy rifle dragged on me frightfully. The men we were after escaped, but I treasured an unforgettable vision of the city, seen at 3 a.m. in all its magical paleness.

The city was saved mainly through Grigori Yevdokimov, an old seafarer, vigorous and grey-haired, with a *mujik's* roughness. Loud of voice, fond of the bottle, he never seemed to admit that a situation was hopeless. When it seemed impossible for the Moscow–Petrograd railway to operate, since there was not more than two days' supply even of dry wood, I heard him exclaim, 'Well, they can chop down wood on the way! The journey will be done in twenty hours, no more!' He was the organizer of the city's second line of defence, where the gun-batteries were lined up by young girls from the Communist Party.

The actual operations leading to the sailors' capture of the fort of Krasnaya Gorka were directed by Bill Shatov. I was present at a private meeting in his room at the Astoria, which concerned the best method of using the crews of the Fleet. Shatov explained that these merry youngsters were the best fed in the garrison, the best accommodated, and the most appreciated by pretty girls, to whom they could now and then slip a tin of food; consequently none of them was agreeable to fighting for more than a few hours, being concerned to get a comfortable sleep on board ship. Someone suggested that once they were disembarked, the ships should be sent away on some plausible pretext. They would then have to hold the front for twenty-four hours, having no further means of retreat!

How did Bill Shatov manage to keep his rotundity and good humour? He was the only fat man among us, with a remarkable face, like an American businessman's, clean-shaven and fleshy. Working-class, converted to anarchism by exiles in Canada, a lively and decisive organizer, he was the real leader of the Tenth Red Army. Every time he returned from the front, he loaded us with anecdotes, such as the tale of a certain small-town mayor who, mistaking the Reds for the Whites, and Shatov himself for a colonel, had come to him in the thick of the gunfire to present a complimentary address, specially written for the occasion. Bill knocked him down on the spot. 'Just imagine, the idiot had his big medallion from the Tsar hung around his neck!' Later, in 1929 or so, Shatov became one of the builders of the Turkestan–Siberia railway.

For several months we experienced a lull. The summer brought us inexpressible relief. Even the famine was a little diminished. I made frequent journeys to Moscow. Its circular, leafy boulevards were filled in the evening with a buzzing, amorous crowd, dressed in bright colours; there was very little illumination at nightfall, and the hum of the crowd could be heard from far away in the twilight and afterwards in the darkness. Soldiers from the Civil War, girls from the old bourgeoisie who packed the Soviet offices during the day, refugees from the massacres in the Ukraine, where nationalist bands were systematically slaughtering the Jewish population, men wanted by the Cheka, plotting in broad daylight two steps from the torture-cellars, Imagist poets and Futurist painters; all of them could be seen scurrying to live.

In Tverskaya Street there were several poets' cafés; it was the time when Sergei Yesenin was becoming famous, sometimes writing his splendid poetry in chalk on the walls of the now secularized Monastery of the Passion. I met him in a seedy café. Over-powdered, over-painted women, leaning on the marble slabs, cigarettes between their fingers, drank coffee made from roasted oats; men clad in black leather, frowning and tight-lipped, with heavy revolvers at their belts, had their arms around the women's waists. These fellows knew what it was to live rough, knew the taste of blood, the odd, painful impact of a bullet in the flesh, and it all made them appreciative of the poems, incanted and almost sung, whose violent images jostled each other as though in a fight.

When I saw Yesenin for the first time, I disliked him. Twenty-four years old, he mixed with the women, ruffians, and ragamuffins from the dark corners of Moscow. A drinker, his voice was hoarse, his eyes worn, his handsome young face puffed and polished, his golden-blond hair flowing in waves around his temples. He was surrounded by sheer glory: the old Symbolist poets recognized him as an equal, the intelligentsia acclaimed his slim volumes, and the folk of the street sang his poems! He deserved all of it. Dressed in a white silk smock, he would mount the stage and begin to declaim. The affectation, the calculated elegance, the alcoholic's voice, the puffy face, everything prejudiced me against him; and the atmosphere of a decomposing Bohemianism, entangling its homosexuals and exotics with our militants, all but disgusted me. Yet, like everyone else, I yielded in a single instant to the positive sorcery of that ruined voice, of a poetry which came from the inmost depths of the man and the age.

Coming from there, I used to stop in front of the glass cases, some of them with long cracks from last year's bullets, where Mayakovsky was sticking his agitational posters against the Entente, The Flea,[1] the White generals, Lloyd George, Clemenceau, and capitalism, this last being symbolized by a pot-bellied character in a top hat, smoking an enormous cigar. A small volume by Ehrenburg (now on the run) was in circulation: it was a *Prayer for Russia*, so ravished and crucified by the Revolution. Lunacharsky, People's Commissar for Public Education, had given the Futurist painters a free hand in the decoration of Moscow; they had transformed the stalls in one of the markets into gigantic flowers. The great lyric tradition, hitherto confined to literary circles, was seeking fresh outlets in the public squares. The poets were learning to declaim or chant their work before huge audiences from the streets; by this approach their personal tone was regenerated and their preciosity gave way to power and fervour.

As autumn approached we in Petrograd, the front-line city, sensed the return of danger, this time perhaps mortal. True enough, we were accustomed to it. In Tallinn (Reval), Estonia, a British general was setting up a provisional government for Russia, at whose head he placed a certain Mr. Liasoñov, a big oil-capitalist. That at any rate was not dangerous. In Helsinki, the exiles had a White Stock Exchange where they still quoted bank-notes bearing the Tsars' effigy. (This was pretty good, since we used to print them specially for the poor fools.) Here, too, they sold the real estate of Soviet towns and the shares of socialized enterprises; a ghost-capitalism was struggling to survive over there. That was not dangerous either. What was really dangerous was typhus and famine. The

[1] Mayakovsky's parody of Moussorgsky's famous song. In Mayakovsky's version the Flea is Denikin.

Red divisions on the Estonian front, exposed to lice and hunger, were demoralized. In the shattered trenches I saw emaciated, dejected soldiers, absolutely incapable of any further effort. The cold rains of autumn came, and the war went by dismally for those poor fellows, without hope, or victories, or boots, or provisions; for a number of them it was the sixth year of war, and they had made the Revolution to gain peace! They felt as though they were in one of the rings of Hell. Vainly the *ABC of Communism* explained that they would have land, justice, peace, and equality, when in the near future the world revolution was achieved. Our divisions were slowly melting away under the ghastly sun of misery.

A most mischievous movement had grown up inside the armies engaged in the Civil War, White, Red, and the rest: that of the Greens. These borrowed their title from the forests in which they took refuge, uniting deserters from all the armies that were now unwilling to fight for anyone, whether Generals or Commissars: these would fight now only for themselves, simply to stay out of the civil war. The movement existed over the whole of Russia. We knew that in the forests of the Pskov region, the Greens' effective forces were on the increase, numbering several tens of thousands. Well organized, complete with their own general staff, and supported by the peasants, they were eating the Red Army away. Cases of desertion to the enemy had also been multiplying ever since it became known that the generals were giving white bread to their troops. Fortunately, the caste-outlook of the officers of the old régime neutralized the trouble; they persisted in wearing epaulettes, demanding the military salute, and being compulsorily addressed as 'Your Honour', thus exhaling such a stench of the past that our deserters, once they had fed themselves, deserted again and came back to receive a pardon, if they did not join the Greens. On both sides of the front line numbers fluctuated constantly.

On 11 October the White army under General Yudenich captured Yamburg, on the Estonian border; in fact it encountered hardly any resistance. Our skeletons of soldiery (or, to be exact, all that was left of them) broke and fled. It was a nasty moment. General Denikin's National Army was now occupying the whole of the Ukraine and on the way to capturing Orel. Admiral Kolchak, the 'Supreme Head' of the counter-revolution, was in control of all Siberia and now threatened the Urals. The British occupied Archangel, where one of the oldest Russian revolutionaries, Chaikovsky, a former friend of my father, presided over a 'democratic' government which shot the Reds without quarter. The French and Rumanians had just been chased out of Odessa by a Black (anarchist) army, but a French fleet was in the Black Sea. Soviet Hungary had perished. In short, when we drew up the balance-sheet it seemed most probable that the Revolution was approaching its death-agony, that a White military dictatorship would soon prevail and that we should be all hanged or shot. This frank conviction, far from spreading discouragement, galvanized our spirit of resistance.

My friend Mazin (Lichtenstadt) went off to the front, after a talk we both had with Zinoviev. 'The front line is everywhere,' we told him. 'Out in the scrubland or the marshes you will die soon and without achieving anything. Men better fitted for war than you are needed for that, and there is no shortage of them.' But he insisted. He told me afterwards that since we were facing utter ruin, and were probably doomed, he saw no point in gaining a mere few month's reprieve for his own life, doing jobs of organization, publishing, etc., which were fruitless from now on; and that, at an hour when so many men were dying quite uselessly out in the wilds, he felt a horror of Smolny offices, committees, printed matter, and the Hotel Astoria. I imagined that the war-service of this myopic intellectual, absent-minded over the smallest things, was destined to last a fortnight at the most. Mazin-Lichtenstadt departed, and made war for a little longer than that. Zinoviev, doubtless wishing to save him, had him appointed political commissar to the Sixth Division, which was barring Yudenich's path. The Sixth Division broke under fire and was overwhelmed; its remnants fled in disarray over the sodden roads. Bill Shatov, scandalized, showed me a letter from Mazin which said: 'The Sixth Division no longer exists; there is only a fleeing mob over which I have no more control. The command no longer exists. I demand to be relieved of my political functions and given a private's rifle.'

'He is mad!' Shatov exclaimed, 'If all our commissars were so romantic, a fine state we should be in! I'm giving him a dressing-down by telegram and I won't mince my words, I assure you!'

Vladimir Ossipovich Mazin did as he had written: he renounced his command, picked up a rifle, collected a little band of Communists and tried to stop the rout and the enemy simultaneously. There

were four of these determined comrades on the outskirts of a forest;
one of the four was his orderly, who had refused to desert him. These
four engaged in combat alone against the White cavalry, and were
killed. Much later, some peasants pointed out to us the spot where
the commissar had fired his last bullets before falling. They had
buried him there. Four corpses, calcined by the earth, were taken
back to Petrograd; one of them, a little soldier beaten to death with a
rifle-butt, his skull battered in, was still making to protect his face
with his stiffened arm. I identified Mazin by his fine finger-nails,
a former prisoner from Schlüsselburg identified him by his teeth.
We laid him in his grave in the Field of Mars. (This was after our
victory, a victory in which I think none of us then believed.)

Naturally, like all the comrades, I performed a host of functions.
I ran the Romance-language section and publications of the International, I met the foreign delegates who kept arriving by adventurous routes through the blockade's barbed-wire barrier. I
carried out a Commissar's duties over the archives of the old
Ministry of the Interior, i.e. the Okhrana; I was at the same time a
trooper in the Communist battalion of the Second District, and a
member of the Defence staff, where I was engaged in smuggling
between Russia and Finland. From honest dealers in Helsinki we
would buy excellent weapons, Mauser pistols in wooden cases which
were delivered to us on a 'quiet sector' of the front (quiet because of
this minor traffic) fifty or so kilometres from Leningrad. To pay for
these useful commodities, we printed whole casefuls of beautiful 500
rouble notes, watery in appearance, with the image of Catherine
the Great and the signature of a bank-director as dead as his bank,
his social order and the Empress Catherine. Case for case, the
exchange was made silently in a wood of sombre firs—it was really
the maddest commercial transaction imaginable. Obviously the
recipients of the Imperial bank-notes were taking out a mortgage on
our deaths, at the same time furnishing us with the means for our
defence.

The archives of the Okhrana, the late political police of the
autocracy, presented a serious problem. In no event were they
to be allowed to fall again into reactionary hands. They contained
biographies and even excellent historical dissertations on the revolutionary parties; if we were to undergo a defeat, followed by White
terror and illegal resistance (for which we were making preparation),

the whole collection would provide precious weapons for tomorrow's hangmen and firing-squads. To add another relatively minor inconvenience, some scholarly and sympathetic archivists, who also anticipated our coming end, were surreptitiously pilfering these stirring old documents, out of an entirely admirable concern to see that they were not destroyed. There were no railway trucks to convey them to Moscow, and no time either, since Petrograd might fall any week now. While barricades were being raised at street-corners, I saw to the packing of those boxes considered the most interesting, so that I could try to get them out at the last moment; and I ordered arrangements to be made whereby, either in the Senate building or at the station itself, everything would be burnt and blown up by a squad of trusted comrades at the moment when any alternative course would cease to be possible. The archivists (from whom I concealed this plan) suspected that something was afoot and were sick with fear and vexation. Leonid Borisovich Krassin came on behalf of the Central Committee to inquire about the measures that were being taken to save or destroy the police-archives, in which he was a figure of perceptible importance. A perfect gentleman, dressed in bourgeois style with a genuine concern for correctness and elegance, he passed through our headquarters, which were full of workers in cloth caps and overcoats with cartridge-belts. A handsome man, with a beard neatly trimmed to a broad point, an intellectual in the grand style, he was at the time of our snatched conversation so tired that I thought he was sometimes asleep on his feet.

On 7 October Yudenich captured Gatchina, about twenty-five miles from Petrograd. Two days later his advance forces entered Ligovo, on the city's outskirts, about nine miles away. Bill Shatov stormed away: 'The principles of military science, which my experts never stop reminding me of, require Divisional Headquarters to be such-and-such many miles from the firing-line. Here we are, 200 yards away! I told them, "To hell with your scientific principles!" '

It seemed quite plainly to be our death-agony. There were no trains and no fuel for evacuation, and scarcely a few dozen cars. We had sent the children of known militants off to the Urals; they were travelling there now in the first snows, from one famished village to the next, not knowing where to halt. We arranged new identities for ourselves, trying to 'change our faces'. It was relatively easy for those with beards, who only had to shave, but as for the others. . . . An efficient girl-comrade, lively and affable as a child, was setting up secret arms-depots. I no longer slept at the Astoria, whose ground floor was lined with sandbags and machine-guns against a siege; I spent my nights with the Communist troops in the outer defences. My wife, who was pregnant, resorted to sleeping in an ambulance in the rear, with a case holding a little linen and our most precious possessions, so that we might be reunited during the battle and fight together in the retreat along the Neva.

The plan for the city's internal defence envisaged fighting along the canals dividing the town, a stubborn defence of the bridges, and a final retreat that was quite impracticable. The huge solemn spaces of Petrograd, in their pale autumn melancholy, fitted this atmosphere of inescapable defeat. So deserted was the city that riders could gallop at full speed along the central thoroughfares. The Smolny Institute (once an educational establishment for young ladies of the aristocracy) now the office of the Executive of the Soviet and the Party Committee, presented a stern picture with its show of cannon at the entrance. It is made up of two masses of buildings surrounded by gardens, standing between vast streets and the equally vast turbulence of the Neva, which is straddled not far from there by an iron bridge. There is a former convent, whose Baroque architecture is charmingly ornate, standing with its church, a rather lofty building with figured belfry-turrets; the whole is painted in a bright blue. Next to it is the Institute proper, with pediments and columns on all four sides, a two-floor barracks built by architects who knew of nothing but straight lines, rectangle upon rectangle. The convent housed the Workers' Guards. The great square office-rooms, whose windows overlooked the waste-lands of the dying city, were practically empty. A pale, puffy Zinoviev, round-shouldered and quiet-spoken, lived there amidst telephones, in constant communication with Lenin. He pleaded for resistance, but his voice was weakening. The most competent experts, engineers, and former pupils of the Military School (no less), considered resistance to be quite impossible and made constant reference to the massacres it would entail, just as though the city's surrender or abandonment were not bound to entail a massacre of a more demoralizing character.

The news from the other fronts was so bad that Lenin was reluctant to sacrifice the last available forces in the defence of a doomed city. Trotsky thought otherwise; the Politbureau entrusted him with the final initiative. He arrived at almost the last moment and his presence instantly changed the atmosphere at Smolny, as it did when he visited headquarters and the Peter-Paul Fortress.

Trotsky arrived with a train, that famous train which had been speeding to and fro along the different fronts since the day in the previous year when its engine-men, orderlies, typists and military experts had, together with Trotsky, Ivan Smirnov, and Rosengoltz, retrieved a hopeless situation by winning the battle of Sviazhsk. The train of the Revolutionary War Council's President contained excellent motor-cars, a liaison staff, a court of justice, a printshop for propaganda, sanitary squads, and specialists in engineering, provisioning, street-fighting, and artillery, all of them men picked in battle, all self-confident, all bound together by friendship and trust, all kept to a strict, vigorous discipline by a leader they admired, all dressed in black leather, red stars on their peaked caps, all exhaling energy. It was a nucleus of resolute and efficiently serviced organizers, who hastened wherever danger demanded their presence.

They took everything in hand, meticulously and passionately. It was magical. Trotsky kept saying, 'It is impossible for a little army of 15,000 ex-officers to master a working-class capital of 700,000 inhabitants.' He had posters put up proclaiming that the city would 'defend itself on its own ground', that from now on this was the best strategic method, that the small White army would be lost in the labyrinth of fortified streets and there meet its grave. In contrast to this determination to win, a French Communist, René Marchand, who had just seen Lenin, told me of Vladimir Ilyich's remark, matter-of-fact and mischievous as usual: 'Oh well, we shall have to go underground all over again!' Or was this really so much of a contrast?

I caught only a glimpse of Trotsky in the street, then at a packed meeting of the Soviet, where he announced the arrival of a division of Bashkirian cavalry which we would launch relentlessly against Finland if Finland budged an inch! (It depended on Finland to deal us the death-blow.) This was an extremely skilful threat, which caused a chill of terror to pass over Helsinki. This session of the

Soviet took place beneath the lofty white columns of the Tauride Palace, in the amphitheatre of the old Imperial Duma. Trotsky was all tension and energy: he was, besides, an orator of unique quality, whose metallic voice projected a great distance, ejaculating its short sentences that were often sardonic and always infused with a truly spontaneous passion. The decision to fight to the death was taken enthusiastically, and the whole amphitheatre raised a song of immense power. I reflected that the psalms sung by Cromwell's Roundheads before their decisive battles must have sounded no different a tone.

Capable regiments of infantry, recalled from the Polish front, now marched through the city to take up their positions in the suburbs. The Bashkirian cavalry, mounted on small, long-haired horses from the steppes, rode in line along the streets. These horsemen, figures from a distant past, swarthy and wearing black sheepskin caps, sang their old songs in guttural voices to an accompaniment of shrill whistling. Sometimes a thin, bespectacled intellectual would ride at their head: he was destined to become the author Konstantin Fedin. They fought rarely and deplorably, but that was unimportant. Convoys of provisions, extorted God knows how from God knows where, were arriving too: this was the most efficient weapon. It was rumoured that the Whites had tanks. Trotsky had it proclaimed that the infantry was well able to knock tanks out. Certain mysterious but ingenious agitators spread the rumour, which may even have been true, that Yudenich's tanks were made of painted wood. The city was dotted with veritable fortresses; lines of cannon occupied the streets. Material from the underground drainage-system was used to build these fortifications, the big pipes from the sewers being particularly handy.

The anarchists were mobilized for the work of defence. Kolabushkin, once a prisoner at Schlüsselburg, was their leading light. The Party gave them arms, and they had a 'Black headquarters' in a devastated apartment belonging to a dentist who had fled. There, disorder and comradeship presided above all. There also presided the smile of a fair-haired and intensely charming girl, who came from the Ukraine with reports of frightful massacres and the latest news of Makhno. Tsvetkova was to die shortly of typhus. She brought a real beam of sunshine into that group of inflamed and embittered men. It was they who, on the night of the worst danger, occupied the printing-works of *Pravda*, the Bolshevik paper that they hated, ready to defend it to the death. They discovered two Whites in their midst, armed with hand-grenades and about to blow them up. What were they to do? They locked them in a room and looked at each other in embarrassment: 'We are jailers, just like the Cheka!' They despised the Cheka with all their hearts. A proposal to shoot these enemy spies was rejected with horror. 'What, us to be executioners!'

Finally, my friend Kolabushkin, the ex-convict, at the time one of the organizers of the Republic's fuel-supply, was charged with taking them to the Peter-Paul Fortress. This was a poor compromise, since there the Cheka would shoot them within the hour. Once in the Black Guard's motor-car, Kolabushkin, who in the past had made this very same journey himself between a couple of Tsarist gendarmes, saw their trapped faces and remembered the days of his youth. He stopped the car and impulsively told them, 'Hop it, you bastards!' Afterwards he came, relieved but vexed, to tell me about those unbearable moments. 'I was a fool, wasn't I?' he asked me. 'But you know, all the same, I'm glad of it.'

Petrograd was saved on 21 October at the battle of the Pulkovo heights, some ten miles south of the half-encircled city. Defeat was transformed into a victory so complete that Yudenich's troops rolled back in disorder towards the Estonian frontier. There the Estonians blocked their path. The White army that had failed to capture Petrograd perished miserably. About 300 workers who had hastened from Schlüsselburg had also blocked the Whites at one critical moment, before being mown down by a body of officers who marched into the fray as though on parade.

Mazin-Lichtenstadt's last message reached me after the battle. It was a letter that he asked me to send on to his wife. It said, 'He who sends men to their deaths must see that he himself gets killed.'

It was an extraordinary fact, and one that proves how deep-rooted in its causes, both social and psychological (they amount to the same), our resilience was: but the same apparent miracle was achieved simultaneously on all the fronts of the Civil War, although at the end of October and the beginning of November the situation seemed equally hopeless everywhere. During the battle near Pulkovo, the White army of General Denikin was beaten not far from Voronezh by the Red cavalry, hastily assembled by Trotsky and commanded by a former N.C.O. named Budyenny. On 14 November Admiral Kolchak, the 'Supreme Head', lost Omsk, his capital in western Siberia. Salvation had come.

The White disaster was the result of two cardinal errors: their failure to have the intelligence and courage to carry out agrarian reform in the territories they wrested from the Revolution, and their reinstatement everywhere of the ancient trinity of generals, high clergy, and landlords. A boundless confidence returned to us. I remembered what Mazin said, in the worst days of our famine when we saw old folk collapsing in the street, some holding out a little tin saucepan in their emaciated fingers. 'All the same' he told me, we are the greatest power in the world. Alone, we are bringing the world a new principle of justice and the rational organization of work. Alone, in all this war-sick Europe where nobody wants to fight any more, we are able to form new armies, and tomorrow we shall be able to wage wars that are truly just. Their house of cards must fall; the longer it lasts, the more misery and bloodshed it will cost.' By 'the house of cards' we meant the Versailles Treaty which, in June 1919, had just been signed.

Together with Maxim Gorky, P. E. Shchegolev, the historian, and Novorusky, the veteran of the *People's Will* Party, we founded the first Museum of the Revolution. Zinoviev had a large part of the Winter Palace allotted to us. Like most of the Party leaders, he really wanted to make it a museum for Bolshevik propaganda but, anxious to have the support of the revolutionary intellectuals, and at least the appearance of a scientific concern, he allowed us to make an honest beginning. I continued to investigate the Okhrana archives. The frightful mass of documents that I found there afforded a unique kind of psychological interest; but the practical bearing of my research was perhaps even greater. For the first time the entire mechanism of an authoritarian empire's police-repression had fallen into the hands of revolutionaries. Thorough study of this material could furnish the militants of other countries with useful clues. Despite our enthusiasm and our sense of right, we were not certain that one day reaction would not drive us back. We were, indeed, more or less convinced to the contrary: it was a generally accepted thesis, which Lenin stated several times, that Russia, agricultural and backward (from an industrial standpoint) as it was, could not create a lasting Socialist system for itself by its own efforts, and that consequently we should be overcome sooner or later unless the European revolution, or at the very least the Socialist revolution in Central Europe, assured Socialism of a broader and more viable base. Finally, we knew that former police-spies were at work among us, most of them ready to resume their services to the counter-revolution; this implied grave danger for us.

In the first days of the March 1917 Revolution, the Petrograd Palace of Justice had gone up in flames. We knew that the destruction of its archives, its anthropometric cards and collection of secrets had been the work both of the criminal underworld, which was interested in destroying these documents, and of police agents. At Kronstadt a 'revolutionary' who was also a police-spy had carried off the Security archives and burnt them. The Okhrana's secret collection contained between 30,000 and 40,000 records of *agents-provocateurs* active over the last twenty years. By devoting ourselves to a simple calculation of the probabilities of decease, and various other eliminations, and taking account of the 3,000 or so that had been unmasked through the patient work of the archivists, we estimated that several thousand former secret agents were still active in the Revolution; at least 5,000, according to the historian Shchegolev, who told me of the following incident which happened in a town on the Volga.

A commission, composed of known members of the different parties of the extreme Left and the Left in general, was interrogating the leading officials of the Imperial police on this question of provocation. The head of the political police apologized for not being able to name two of his ex-agents since they were members of this very commission; he would rather that these gentlemen obeyed the voice of their conscience and identified themselves! And two of the 'revolutionaries' stood up in confusion.

The old secret agents, all of them initiates into the political life, could pretend to be seasoned revolutionaries; since they were not at all troubled by scruples, they found it to their own advantage to rally to the ruling party, in which it was easy for them to obtain good positions. Consequently they played a certain role in the system: we guessed that some of them were under orders to select and follow the worst possible policies, engineering excesses and sowing discredit. It was extremely hard to unmask them. As a rule the records were classified under pseudonyms, and assiduous cross-checking was necessary before an identification could be established. For example, in 1912 there were in the revolutionary organizations of Moscow (which were by no means mass organizations) fifty-five police agents: seventeen Social-Revolutionaries, twenty Menshevik or Bolshevik Social-Democrats, three anarchists, eleven students, and several Liberals. In the same period the leader of the Bolshevik fraction in the Duma, and spokesman for Lenin, was a police-spy, Malinovsky. The head of the Social-Revolutionary Party's terrorist organization, a member of its Central Committee, was an Okhrana agent, Evno Azev; this from 1903 to 1908, at the time of the most sensational assassinations. Somewhere around 1930, to cut a long story short, several former police agents were finally unmasked among the Leningrad leadership! I found an extraordinary file, one in need of no deciphering, No. 378: Julia Orestovna Serova, wife of a Bolshevik deputy in the Second Imperial Duma; he was a fine militant who had been shot in 1918 at Chita. The catalogue of Serova's services, listed in a report to the Minister, revealed that she had betrayed caches of arms and literature, had Rykov, Kamenev and many others arrested, and spied for a great length of time on the Party committees. Having at last fallen under suspicion and been sent packing she wrote, in February 1917, a few weeks before the fall of the autocracy, to the head of the secret police asking to be re-employed 'in view of the great events that are drawing near'. She got married again, to a Bolshevik worker, and so was once again in a position to carry on her activities. The letters revealed a woman of practical intelligence, zealous, greedy for money, and perhaps hysterical. One evening, in a circle of friends having tea, we discussed this particular psychological case. An old woman-militant stood up flabbergasted: 'Serova? But I just met her in town! She's actually married again, to a comrade in the Vyborg district!' Serova was arrested and shot.

The psychology of the police-spy was usually double-natured. Gorky showed me a letter which one of them, still at large, had written to him. The gist of it ran: 'I hated myself, but I knew that my little betrayals would not stop the Revolution from marching on.' The Okhrana's instructions advised its minions to seek out those revolutionaries who were fainthearted, embittered or disappointed, to make use of personal rivalries, and to assist the advancement of skilful agents by eliminating the most talented militants. The old barrister Kozlovsky, who had been the first People's Commissar for Justice, told me his impressions of Malinovsky. The former Bolshevik leader in the Duma returned to Russia from Germany in 1918, even after his unmasking and, presenting himself at Smolny, asked to be arrested. 'Malinovsky? Don't know the name!' replied the commandant of the guard, 'Go and explain yourself to the Party Committee!' Kozlovsky interrogated him; Malinovsky said that he could not live outside the Revolution: 'I have been a double-dealer despite my own best feelings. I want to be shot!' He maintained this attitude in front of the revolutionary tribunal. Krylenko ruthlessly demanded sentence ('The adventurer is playing his last card!'), and Malinovsky was shot in the gardens of the Kremlin. Many indications led me to believe that he was absolutely sincere and that if he had been allowed to live, he would have served as faithfully as the others. But what confidence could the others have in him?

Gorky tried to save the lives of the police-spies, who in his eyes were the repositories of a unique social and psychological experience. 'These men are a sort of monster, worthy of preservation for research.' He used the same arguments to defend the lives of high officials in the Tsarist political police. I remember a conversation on these matters which wandered on to the question of the necessity for applying the death-penalty to children. The Soviet leaders were concerned at the scale of juvenile crime. Certain children, more or less abandoned, formed actual gangs. These were put into children's homes, where they still starved; then they would abscond and resume a life of crime. Olga, a pretty little girl of fourteen, had several child murders and several absconsions on her record. She organized burglaries in apartments where a child had been left alone by the parents. She would talk to it through the door, win its confidence, and get it to open the door to her. . . . What could be done with her? Gorky argued for the establishment of colonies for child-criminals in the North, where life is rough and adventure always at hand. I do not know what became of the idea.

The Civil War seemed about to end. General Denikin's National Army was in flight across the Ukraine. In Siberia Admiral Kolchak's forces, encircled by the Red partisans, were in retreat. The idea of a normalization of life was exerting increasing pressure within the Party. Riazanov tirelessly demanded the abolition of the death-penalty. The Cheka was unpopular. In the middle of January 1920

Dzerzhinsky, with the approval of Lenin and Trotsky, recommended the abolition of the death-sentence throughout the country, except in districts where there were military operations.

On 17 January the decree was passed by the Government and signed by Lenin as President of the Council of People's Commissars. For several days the prisons, crammed with suspects, had been living in tense expectation. They knew immediately of the tremendous good news, the end of the Terror; the decree had still not appeared in the newspapers. On the 18th or the 19th some of the comrades at Smolny told me in hushed voices of the tragedy of the preceding night—no one mentioned it openly. While the newspapers were printing the decree, the Petrograd Chekas were liquidating their stock! Cartload after cartload of suspects had been driven outside the city during the night, and then shot, heap upon heap. How many? In Petrograd between 150 and 200; in Moscow, it was said, between 200 and 300. In the dawn of the days that followed, the families of the massacred victims came to search that ghastly, freshly-dug ground, looking for any relics, such as buttons or scraps of stocking, that could be gathered there.

The Chekists had presented the Government with a *fait accompli*. Much later I became personally acquainted with one of those responsible for the Petrograd massacre: I will call him Leonidov. 'We thought', he told me 'that if the People's Commissars were getting converted to humanitarianism, that was their business. Our business was to crush the counter-revolution for ever, and they could shoot us afterwards if they felt like it!' It was a frightful and tragic example of occupational psychosis. Leonidov, when I knew him, was in any case definitely half insane. In all likelihood the incorrigible counter-revolutionaries were only a very minute percentage of the victims. A few months later, during my wife's confinement, I had a conversation with a sick woman who had just given birth to a stillborn child. Her husband, the engineer Trotsky or Troytsky, had been shot during that abominable night. He was a former Social-Revolutionary who had taken part in the 1905 Revolution, and had been imprisoned for 'speculation', that is, for a single purchase of sugar on the black market.

Even at Smolny, this drama was shrouded in utter mystery. However, it redounded to the régime's profound discredit. It was becoming clear, to me and to others, that the suppression of the

Cheka and the reintroduction of regular tribunals and rights of defence were from now on pre-conditions for the Revolution's own safety. But we could do absolutely nothing. The Politbureau, then composed (if I am not mistaken) of Lenin, Trotsky, Zinoviev, Kamenev, Rykov, and Bukharin, deliberated the question without daring to answer it, being itself, I have no doubt, the victim of a certain psychosis born of fear and ruthless authority. Against the Party the anarchists were right when they inscribed on their black banners, 'There is no worse poison than power'—meaning absolute power. From now on the psychosis of absolute power was to captivate the great majority of the leadership, especially at the lower levels. I know the greatness of these men; but they, who belonged to the future, were in this respect the prisoners of the past.

The spring of 1920 opened with a victory—the capture of Archangel, now evacuated by the British—and then, all at once, changed its aspect. Again there was peril, immediate and mortal: the Polish invasion. In the files of the Okhrana I had photographs of Pilsudski, condemned years ago for plotting against the Tsar's life. I met a doctor who had attended Pilsudski in a St. Petersburg hospital where he had pretended to be mad, with a rare perfection, in order to get away. Himself a revolutionary and a terrorist, he was now hurling his legions against us. A wave of anger and enthusiasm rose against him. Brussilov and Polivanov, old Tsarist generals, volunteered for the fight in response to an appeal by Trotsky. I could see Gorky burst into tears on a balcony in the Nevsky Prospect, haranguing a battalion off to the front. 'When will we stop all this killing and bleeding?' he would mutter under his bristling moustache.

The death-penalty was reintroduced and, under the stimulus of defeat, the Chekas were given enlarged powers. The Poles were entering Kiev. Zinoviev kept saying, 'Our salvation lies in the International,' and Lenin agreed with him. At the height of the war the Second Congress of the Communist International was hastily summoned. I worked literally day and night to prepare for it since, thanks to my knowledge of languages and the Western world, I was practically the only person available to perform a whole host of duties. I met Lansbury[1] and John Reed on their arrival. I hid a

[1] George Lansbury did visit Russia in February 1920, but not for the Comintern Congress.

delegation of Hungarian Left Communists, who were in opposition to Bela Kun and in some kind of liaison with Rakovsky. We published the International's periodical in four languages. We sent innumerable secret messages abroad by various adventurous routes. I translated Lenin's messages, and also the book that Trotsky had just written in his military train, *Terrorism and Communism*, which emphasized the necessity for a long dictatorship 'In the period of transition to socialism', for several decades at least. Trotsky's rigid ideas, with their schematism and voluntarism, disturbed me a little. Everything was scarce: staff, paper, ink, even bread, as well as facilities for communication. All we received in the way of foreign newspapers were a few copies bought in Helsinki by smugglers who crossed the front lines specially for the purpose. I paid them 100 roubles per copy. On occasions when one of their number had been killed they came to ask for extra money, at which we did not demur. In Moscow, organizational activity was proceeding at an equally feverish pace under the supervision of Angelica Balabanova and Bukharin.

I met Lenin when he came to Petrograd for the first session of the Congress. We had tea together in a small entertainment-room in the Smolny; Yevdokimov and Angel Pestaña, the delegate from the Spanish C.N.T., were with me when Lenin came in. He beamed, shaking the hands that were outstretched to him, passing from one salutation to the next. Yevdokimov and he embraced one another gaily, gazing straight into each other's eyes, happy like over-grown children. Vladimir Ilyich was wearing one of his old jackets dating back to the emigration, perhaps brought back from Zurich; I saw it on him in all seasons. Practically bald, his cranium high and bulging, his forehead strong, he had commonplace features: an amazingly fresh and pink face, a little reddish beard, slightly jutting cheek-bones, eyes horizontal but apparently slanted because of the laughter-lines, a grey-green gaze at people, and a surpassing air of geniality and cheerful malice.

In the Kremlin he still occupied a small apartment built for a palace servant. In the recent winter he, like everyone else, had had no heating. When he went to the barber's he took his turn, thinking it unseemly for anyone to give way to him. An old housekeeper looked after his rooms and did his mending. He knew that he was the Party's foremost brain and recently, in a grave situation, had used no threat worse than that of resigning from the Central Committee so as to appeal to the rank and file! He craved a tribune's popularity, stamped with the seal of the masses' approval, devoid of any show or ceremony. His manners and behaviour betrayed not the slightest inkling of any taste for authority; what showed through was only the urgency of the devoted technician who wants the work to be done, and done quickly and well. Also in evidence was his forthright resolve that the new institutions, weak though they might be to the point of a merely symbolic existence, must nevertheless be respected.

On that day, or perhaps the following one, he spoke for several hours at the first formal session of the Congress, under the white colonnade of the Tauride Palace. His report dealt with the historical situation consequent upon the Versailles Treaty. Quoting abundantly from Maynard Keynes, Lenin established the insolvency of a Europe carved up arbitrarily by victorious imperialisms, and the impossibility of any lengthy endurance by Germany of the burdens that had been so idiotically imposed upon her; he concluded that a new European revolution, which was destined also to involve the colonial peoples of Asia, must be inevitable.

He was neither a great orator nor a first-rate lecturer. He employed no rhetoric and sought no demagogical effects. His vocabulary was that of a newspaper-article, and his technique included diverse forms of repetition, all with the aim of a driving in ideas thoroughly, as one drives in a nail. He was never boring, on account of his mimic's liveliness and the reasoned conviction which drove him. His customary gestures consisted of raising his hand to underline the importance of what he had said, and then bending towards the audience, smiling and earnest, his palms spread out in an act of demonstration: 'It is obvious, isn't it?' Here was a man of a basic simplicity, talking to you honestly with the sole purpose of convincing you, appealing exclusively to your judgement, to facts and sheer necessity. 'Facts have hard heads,' he was fond of saying. He was the embodiment of plain common sense, so much so that he disappointed the French delegates, who were used to impressive Parliamentary joustings. 'When you see Lenin at close quarters, he loses much of his glamour,' I was told by one French deputy, an eloquent sceptic positively stuffed with witty epigrams.

The Comintern's Second Congress took up the rest of its work in Moscow. The Congress staff and the foreign delegates lived in the Hotel *Delovoy Dvor*, centrally situated at the end of a wide boulevard, one side of which was lined by the white embattled rampart of Kitay-Gorod. Medieval gateways topped by an ancient turret formed the approach to the nearby Varvarka, where the first of the Romanovs had lived. From there we came out into the Kremlin, a city within a city, every entrance guarded by sentries who checked our passes. There, in the palaces of the old autocracy, in the midst of ancient Byzantine churches, lay the headquarters of the Revolution's double arm, the Soviet Government and the International. The only city the foreign delegates never got to know (and their incuriosity in this respect disturbed me) was the real, living Moscow, with its starvation-rations, its arrests, its sordid prison-episodes, its backstage racketeering. Sumptuously fed amidst universal misery (although, it is true, too many rotten eggs turned up at meal-times), shepherded from museums to model nurseries, the representatives of international Socialism seemed to react like holiday-makers or tourists within our poor Republic, flayed and bleeding with the siege. I discovered a novel variety of insensitivity: Marxist insensitivity. Paul Levi, a leading figure in the German Communist Party, an athletic and self-confident figure, told me outright that 'for a Marxist, the internal contradictions of the Russian Revolution were nothing to be surprised at'; this was doubtless true, except that he was using this general truth as a screen to shut away the sight of immediate fact, which has an importance all of its own. Most of the Marxist Left, now Bolshevized, adopted this complacent attitude. The words 'dictatorship of the proletariat' functioned as a magical explanation for them, without it ever occurring to them to ask where this dictator of a proletariat was, what it thought, felt, and did.

The Social-Democrats, by contrast, were notable for their critical spirit and for their incomprehension. Among the best of them (I am thinking of the Germans Daümig, Crispien, and Dittmann), their peaceful, bourgeoisified socialist humanism was so offended by the Revolution's harsh climate that they were incapable of thinking straight.[1] The anarchist delegates, with whom I held many discussions, had a healthy revulsion from 'official truths' and the

[1] Arthur Crispien (1875–1946) and Wilhelm Dittmann (1874–1954) both opposed the '21 Conditions' for affiliation to the Communist International, and broke with it after this Congress; Ernst Daümig (1866–1922), an experienced shock-fighter and underground worker, who had led the Revolutionary Shop Stewards' movement in 1918, supported and joined the International at this juncture, but sided with Paul Levi after the latter's expulsion from the Comintern in 1921.

E

trappings of power, and a passionate interest in actual life; but, as the adherents of an essentially emotional approach to theory, who were ignorant of political economy and had never faced the problem of power, they found it practically impossible to achieve any theoretical understanding of what was going on. They were excellent comrades, more or less at the stage of the romantic arguments for the 'universal revolution' that the libertarian artisans had managed to frame between 1848 and 1860, before the growth of modern industry and its proletariat. Among them were: Angel Pestaña of the Barcelona C.N.T., a watchmaker and a brave popular leader, slender in build, with beautiful dark eyes and a small moustache of the same hue; Armando Borghi, of the Italian *Unione Sindicale*, with his fine face, bearded, young and Mazzini-like, and his fervent but velvety voice; Augustin Souchy, red-haired and with an old trooper's face, the delegate from the Swedish and German syndicalists; Lepetit, a sturdy navvy from the French C.G.T. and *Le Libertaire*, merry but mistrustful and questioning, who suddenly swore that 'in France the revolution would be made quite differently!' Lenin was very anxious to have the support of 'the best of the anarchists'.

To tell the truth, outside Russia and perhaps Bulgaria, there were no real Communists anywhere in the world. The old schools of revolution, and the younger generation that had emerged from the war, were both at an infinite distance from the Bolshevik mentality. The bulk of these men were symptomatic of obsolete movements which had been quite outrun by events, combining an abundance of good intentions with a scarcity of talent. The French Socialist Party was represented by Marcel Cachin and L.-O. Frossard, both of them highly Parliamentary in their approach. Cachin was, as usual, sniffing out the direction of the prevailing wind. Ever mindful of his personal popularity, he was shifting to the Left, after having been a supporter of the 'Sacred Union' during the war and a backer, on behalf of the French Government, of Mussolini's jingoist campaigns in Italy: this was in 1916. The Paris Committee of the Third International had sent Alfred Rosmer; he of the Ibsenesque surname was a syndicalist, a devoted internationalist, and an old personal friend of Trotsky. Beneath his half-smile Rosmer incarnated the qualities of vigilance, discretion, silence, and dedication. His colleague from the same Committee was Raymond Lefebvre, a tall sharp-featured young man who had carried stretchers at Verdun. A poet and novelist, he had just written his confession of faith as a man home from the trenches, in a luxuriantly poetic style. It was entitled *Revolution or Death!* He spoke for the survivors of a generation now lying buried in communal graves. We quickly became friends.

Of the Italians, I remember the veteran Lazzari, an upright old man whose feverish voice burned with an undying enthusiasm; Serrati's bearded, myopic, and professorial face; Terracini, a young theoretician with a tall, ascetic forehead, who was fated to spend the best years of his life in jail, after giving the world a few pages of his keen intellect; Bordiga, exuberant and energetic, features blunt, hair thick, black and bristly, a man quivering under his encumbrance of ideas, experiences, and dark forecasts.[1]

There was Angelica Balabanova, a slender woman whose delicate, already motherly face was framed in a double braid of black hair. An air of extreme gracefulness compassed her about. Perpetually active, she still hoped for an International that was unconfined, open-hearted, and rather romantic. Rosa Luxemburg's lawyer, Paul Levi, represented the German Communists; Daümig, Crispien, Dittmann, and another represented Germany's Independent Social-Democratic Party, four likeable, rather helpless middlemen, good beer-drinkers, one could be sure, and conscientious officials in stodgy, established working-class organizations. It was obvious at first glance that here were no insurgent souls. Of the British, I met only Gallacher, who looked like a stocky prize-fighter. From the United States came Fraina, later to fall under grave suspicion,[2] and

[1] Of these Italian delegates, Giacinto Serrati (1872–1926), a Socialist Party leader, hesitated for a time over the break with the 'reformists' demanded by the '21 Conditions', but later joined the Communist Party. Constantino Lazzari (1857–1927) was similarly inclined, but stayed with the Socialist Party. Umberto Terracini (1895–) became a leading Communist, was imprisoned by Mussolini from 1926 to 1943, and after the Liberation was President of the National Assembly (1947); now Chairman of the Communist group in the Senate, occupying an 'orthodox' position in the post-1956 internal debates on Stalinism. Amadeo Bordiga (1889–1970) was for a few years the main leader of Italian Communism, but was eventually displaced by the more pliant Togliatti, and went into the libertarian and sectarian wilderness.

[2] Louis Fraina (1894–1953) broke with the Comintern in late 1922; the 'grave suspicion' Serge mentions could refer either to a much-inflated story of embezzlement or to an earlier charge of being a police-spy, of which he was cleared at the time. After his break with Communism, Fraina made a reputation as an economist under the name of Lewis Corey, but still suffered for his past under McCarthy's witch-hunt.

John Reed, the eye-witness of the 1917 Bolshevik uprising, whose book on the Revolution was already considered authoritative. I had met Reed in Petrograd, whence we had organized his clandestine depature through Finland: the Finns had been sorely tempted to finish him off and had confined him for a while in a death-trap of a jail. He had just visited some small townships in the Moscow outskirts, and reported what he had seen: a ghost-country where only famine was real. He was amazed that Soviet production continued despite everything. Reed was tall, forceful, and matter-of-fact, with a cool idealism and a lively intelligence tinged by humour. Once again I saw Rakovsky, the head of the Soviet Government in a Ukraine that was now prey to hundreds of roving bands: White, Nationalist, Black (or anarchist), Green, and Red. Bearded and dressed in a soldier's worn uniform, he broke into perfect French while he was on the rostrum.

From Bulgaria Kolarov[1] arrived, huge and somewhat pot-bellied, whose noble and commanding face bore the stamp of assurance: he blurted out a promise to the Congress that he would take power at home as soon as the International asked him! From Holland there came Wijnkoop,[2] among others: dark-bearded and long-jawed, apparently aggressive, but destined as it turned out to a career of limitless servility. From India, by way of Mexico, we had the pockmarked Manabendra Nath Roy: very tall, very handsome, very dark, with very wavy hair, he was accompanied by a statues-que Anglo-Saxon woman who appeared to be naked beneath her flimsy dress. We did not know that in Mexico he had been the target of some unpleasant suspicions; he was fated to become the guiding spirit of the tiny Indian Communist Party, to spend several years in prison, to start activity again, to slander the Opposition with nonsensical insults, to be expelled himself, and then to return to grace—but this was all in the distant future.[3]

[1] Vasil Kolarov (1877–1950): became a leading Comintern emissary to West European parties, Secretary to the Comintern Executive (1922–4), and Prime Minister of Bulgaria after Dimitrov's death in 1949.

[2] David Wijnkoop (1876–1941): Dutch 'Tribunist' (one of the founders of the left-wing paper *De Tribune*, 1907), then Left Social-Democrat and Communist. Tried to set up an abortive semi-autonomous Communist centre in Amsterdam (1920); formed an opposition outside the party 1926–1931; then returned to orthodoxy.

[3] Serge is not altogether accurate on Roy's career. For example, Roy was expelled in 1929 as the result of his support for the Brandler group in Germany, and

The Russians led the dance, and their superiority was so obvious that this was quite legitimate. The only figure in Western Socialism that was capable of equalling them, or even perhaps of surpassing them so far as intelligence and the spirit of freedom were concerned, was Rosa Luxemburg, and she had been battered to death with a revolver-butt in January 1919 by German officers. Apart from Lenin, the Russians consisted of Zinoviev, Bukharin, Rakovsky (who, though Rumanian by origin, was as much Russified as he was Frenchified), and Karl Radek, recently released from a Berlin prison in which he had courted death and where Leo Jogiches[1] had been murdered at his side. Trotsky, if he indeed came to the Congress, must have made only rare appearances, for I do not remember having seen him there. He was principally occupied with the state of the fronts, and the Polish front was still ablaze.

The work of the Congress centred upon three issues, and also a fourth which, though even more important, was not touched upon in open session. Lenin was bending every effort to convince the 'Left Communists'—Dutch, German, or (like Bordiga) Italian—of the necessity for compromise and participation in electoral and Parliamentary politics; he warned of the danger of their becoming revolutionary sects. In his discussion of the 'national and colonial question', Lenin emphasized the possibility, and even necessity, of inspiring Soviet-type revolutions in the Asiatic colonial countries. The experience of Russian Turkestan seemed to lend support to his arguments. He was aiming primarily at India and China; he thought that the blow must be directed to these countries in order to weaken British imperialism, which then appeared as the inveterate foe of the Soviet Republic. The Russians had no further hopes for the traditional Socialist parties of Europe. They judged that the only possible course was to work for splits that would break with the old reformist and Parliamentary leaderships, thereby

---

never again achieved any prominence in the Indian Communist Party. He did, however, think highly of Stalin even in later years. Roy died in 1954, editor by then of his magazine *The Radical Humanist*. The 'unpleasant suspicions' mentioned by Serge probably arose from Roy's campaigning for Indian independence on German subsidies.

[1] Leo Jogiches (Tyszko) (1867–1919): founder of Polish Social-Democracy and later of German Communism; during the war organized the first *Spartakus* group along with Karl Liebknecht; after the assassination of Liebknecht and Rosa Luxemburg continued revolutionary activity and was murdered in prison in March 1919.

creating new parties, disciplined and controlled by the Executive in Moscow, which would proceed efficiently to the conquest of power.

Serrati raised serious objections to the Bolshevik tactic of support for the colonial nationalist movements, demonstrating the reactionary and disturbing elements in these movements which might emerge in the future. It was naturally out of the question to listen to him. Bordiga opposed Lenin on questions of organization and general perspective. Without daring to say so, he was afraid of the influence of the Soviet State on the Communist Parties, and the temptations of compromise, demagogy, and corruption. Above all, he did not believe that a peasant Russia was capable of guiding the international working-class movement. Beyond doubt, his was one of the most penetrating intellects at the Congress, but only a very tiny group supported him.

The Congress made ready for the splitting of the French Party (at Tours) and the Italian Party (at Leghorn) by laying down twenty-one stringent conditions for the affiliates of the International, or rather twenty-two: the twenty-second, which is not at all well known, excluded Freemasons. The fourth problem was not on the agenda and no trace of it will ever be found in the published accounts; but I saw it discussed with considerable heat by Lenin, in a gathering of foreign delegates in a small room just off the grand, gold-panelled hall of the Imperial Palace. A throne had been bundled away here, and next to this useless piece of furniture a map of the Polish front was displayed on the wall. The rattle of typewriters filled the air. Lenin, jacketed, briefcase under arm, delegates and typists all round him, was giving his views on the march of Tukhachevsky's army on Warsaw. He was in excellent spirits, and confident of victory. Karl Radek, thin, monkey-like, sardonic and droll, hitched up his oversize trousers (which were always slipping down over his hips), and added, 'We shall be ripping up the Versailles Treaty with our bayonets!'

A little later, we were to discover that Tukhachevsky was complaining about the exhaustion of his troops and the lengthening of his lines of communication; that Trotsky considered the offensive to be too rushed and risky in those circumstances; that Lenin had forced the attack to a certain extent by sending Rakovsky and Smilga as political commissars to accompany Tukhachevsky; and that it would, despite everything, probably have succeeded if Stalin and Budyenny had provided support instead of marching on Lvov to assure themselves of a personal victory.

Defeat came at Warsaw, quite suddenly, just at the moment when the fall of the Polish capital was actually being announced. Apart from some students and a very few workers, the peasantry and proletariat of Poland had not welcomed the Red Army. I remained convinced that the Russians had made a psychological error by including Dzerzhinsky, the man of the Terror, side by side with Marchlewski on the Revolutionary Committee that was to govern Poland. I declared that, far from firing the popular enthusiasm, the name of Dzerzhinsky would freeze it altogether. That is just what happened. Once more, the westward expansion of the revolution had failed. There was no alternative for the Bolsheviks but to turn east.

Hastily, the Congress of the Oppressed Nationalities of the East was convened at Baku. As soon as the Comintern Congress was over, Zinoviev, Radek, Rosmer, John Reed, and Bela Kun went off to Baku in a special train, whose defence (since they were to pass through perilous country) and command were entrusted to Yakov Blumkin, a friend of mine. I shall say more of Blumkin later, apropos of his frightful death. At Baku, Enver Pasha put in a sensational appearance.[1] A whole hall full of Orientals broke into shouts, with scimitars and yataghans brandished aloft: '*Death to imperialism!*' All the same, genuine understanding with the Islamic world, swept as it was by its own national and religious aspirations, was still difficult. Enver Pasha aimed at the creation of an Islamic state in Central Asia; he was to be killed in a battle against the Red cavalry two years later. Returning home from this remarkable trip, John Reed took a great bite out of a water-melon he had bought in a picturesque Daghestan market. As a result he died, from typhoid.

The Moscow Congress is associated for me with more than one such loss. Before I write of these deaths, I would like to say more of the circumstances of the time. My own experience was probably unique, since in this period I maintained a staunch openness in my approach, being in daily contact with official circles, ordinary folk and the Revolution's persecuted dissenters. Throughout the Petrograd celebrations, I was concerned with the fate of Voline, though some friends and myself had managed to save his life for the time

[1] Enver Pasha (1881–1922): Turkish Minister of War in 1913; opposed the Kemalist revolution and fled to Russia in 1918.

being. Voline, whose real name was Boris Eichenbaum, was a working-class intellectual who had been one of the founders of the 1905 St. Petersburg Soviet. He had returned from America in 1917 to lead the Russian anarchist movement. He had joined Makhno's 'Ukrainian Army of Insurgent Peasants', fought the Whites, resisted the Reds, and tried to organize a free peasants' federation in the region of Gulyai-Polye. After he had caught typhus, he was captured by the Red Army in the course of a Black retreat. We were afraid that he might be shot out of hand. We succeeded in preventing this extremity by dispatching a Petrograd comrade straight to the spot; he had the prisoner transferred to Moscow. Now I had no sure news of him: I was at the time, together with the Comintern delegates, watching the performance of an authentic Soviet mystery-play in the court inside the old Exchange. We saw the Paris Commune raise its red banners, then perish; we saw Jaurès assassinated, and the audience cried out in grief; we saw, at last, the joyful and victorious Revolution in triumph over the world.

In Moscow, I learned that Lenin and Kamenev had promised to see that Voline, now in a Cheka prison, would not die. Here we were with our discussions in the Imperial halls of the Kremlin, while this model revolutionary was in a cell awaiting an uncertain end.

After I left the Kremlin I would visit another dissident, this time a Marxist, whose honesty and brilliance were of the first order: Yuri Ossipovich Martov, co-founder, with Plekhanov and Lenin, of Russian Social-Democracy, and the leader of Menshevism. He was campaigning for working-class democracy, denouncing the excesses of the Cheka and the Lenin-Trotsky 'mania for authority'. He kept saying, 'Just as though Socialism could be instituted by decree, and by shooting people in cellars!' Lenin, who was fond of him, protected him against the Cheka, though he quailed before Martov's sharp criticism. When I saw Martov he was living on the brink of utter destitution in a little room. He struck me at the very first glance as being aware of his absolute incompatibility with the Bolsheviks, although like them he was a Marxist, highly cultured, uncompromising and exceedingly brave. Puny, ailing, and limping a little, he had a slightly asymmetrical face, a high forehead, a mild and subtle gaze behind his spectacles, a fine mouth, a straggly beard and an expression of gentle intelligence. Here was a man of scruple and scholarship, lacking the tough and robust revolutionary will that sweeps obstacles aside. His criticisms were apposite, but his general solutions verged on the Utopian. 'Unless it returns to democracy, the Revolution is lost': but how return to democracy and what sort of democracy? All the same I felt it to be quite unforgivable that a man of this calibre should be put into a position where it was impossible for him to give the Revolution the whole wealth available in his thinking. 'You'll see, you'll see,' he would tell me, 'Free co-operation with the Bolsheviks is never possible.'

Just after I had returned to Petrograd, along with Raymond Lefebvre, Lepetit, Vergeat (a French syndicalist), and Sasha Tubin, a frightful drama took place there, which confirmed Martov's worst fears. I will summarize what happened, though the affair was shrouded in obscurity. The recently founded Finnish Communist Party emerged resentful and divided from a bloody defeat in 1918. Of its leaders, I knew Sirola and Kuusinen, who did not seem particularly competent and had indeed acknowledged the commission of many errors. I had just published a little book by Kuusinen on the whole business; he was a timid little man, circumspect and industrious. An opposition had been formed within the Party, in revulsion from the old Parliamentary leadership which had been responsible for the defeat and which nowadays adhered to the Communist International. A Party Congress at Petrograd resulted in an oppositional majority against the Central Committee, which was supported by Zinoviev. The Comintern President had the Congress proceedings stopped. One evening a little later, some young Finnish students at a military school went along to a Central Committee meeting and shot the eight members present. The Press printed shameless lies blaming the assassination on the Whites. The accused openly justified their action, accusing the Central Committee of treason, and demanded to be sent to the front. A committee of three including Rosmer and the Bulgarian Shablin was set up by the International to examine the affair; I doubt if it ever met. The case was tried later in secret session by the Moscow revolutionary tribunal, Krylenko being the prosecutor. Its upshot was in some ways reasonable, in others monstrous. The guilty ones were formally condemned, but authorized to go off to the front (I do not know what actually happened to them). However, the leader of the Opposition, Voyto Eloranta, who was considered as 'politically responsible', was first condemned to a period of imprisonment, and then, in 1921, shot.

Travelling with Raymond Lefebvre, Lepetit, and Vergeat was a late friend of mine whom I had never actually met, Sasha Tubin. During my confinement in France he had given me patient assistance in keeping up my clandestine mail. Now while we were passing through Petrograd, I saw him, itching to go and obsessed by sombre forebodings. The four set off from Murmansk, on a difficult route over the Arctic Sea which was designed to break the naval blockade. Our International Relations Section had worked out this perilous itinerary: embark in a fishing-boat, sail well past the tip of the Finnish coast, and land at Vardoe in Norway, on ground that was free and safe. The four started on this route. In a hurry to attend a C.G.T. congress, they set out on a day of stormy weather, and disappeared at sea. Possibly they were engulfed in the storm, or perhaps a Finnish motor-boat intercepted them and mowed them down; I knew that in Petrograd spies had trailed our every step. Every day for a fortnight Zinoviev asked me, with mounting anxiety, 'Have you any news of the French comrades?' Around this disaster unworthy legends were to grow: they are all lies.[1] (This would be in August or September, 1920.)

I end this chapter in the aftermath of the Second Congress of the International, in the September and October of 1920. I have the feeling that this point marked a kind of boundary for us. The failure of the attack on Warsaw meant the defeat of the Russian Revolution in Central Europe, although no one saw it as such. At home, new dangers were waxing and we were on the road to catastrophes of which we had only a faint foreboding. (By 'we', I mean the shrewdest comrades; the majority of the Party was already blindly dependent on the schematism of official thinking.) From October onwards significant events, fated to pass unnoticed in the country at large, were to gather with the gentleness of a massing avalanche. I began to feel, acutely I am bound to say, this sense of a danger from inside, a danger within ourselves, in the very temper and character of victorious Bolshevism. I was continually racked by the contrast between the stated theory and the reality, by the growth of intolerance and servility among many officials and their drive towards

---

[1] i.e. as retailed in the bourgeois press, to the effect that the deaths were the deliberate result of Communist policy.

privilege. I remember a conversation I had with the People's Commissar for Food, Tsiuriupa, a man with a splendid white beard and candid eyes. I had brought some French and Spanish comrades to him so that he could explain for our benefit the Soviet system of rationing and supply. He showed us beautifully-drawn diagrams from which the ghastly famine and the immense black market had vanished without trace.

'What about the black market?' I asked him.

'It is of no importance at all,' the old man replied. No doubt he was sincere, but he was a prisoner of his scheme, a captive within offices whose occupants had obviously all primed him with lies. I was astounded. So this was how Zinoviev could believe in the imminence of proletarian revolution in Western Europe. Was this perhaps how Lenin could believe in the prospects of insurrection among the Eastern peoples? The wonderful lucidity of these great Marxists was beginning to be fuddled with a theoretical intoxication bordering on delusion; and they began to be enclosed within all the tricks and tomfooleries of servility. At meetings on the Petrograd front, I saw Zinoviev blush and bow his head in embarrassment at the imbecile flattery thrown in his face by young military careerists in their fresh shiny leather outfits. One of them kept shouting, 'We will win because we are under the command of our glorious leader, Comrade Zinoviev!' A comrade who was a former convict had a sumptuously coloured cover designed by one of the greatest Russian artists, which was intended to adorn one of Zinoviev's pamphlets. The artist and the ex-convict had combined to produce a masterpiece of obsequiousness, in which Zinoviev's Roman profile stood out like a proconsul in a cameo bordered by emblems. They brought it to the President of the International, who thanked them cordially and, as soon as they were gone, called me to his side.

'It is the height of bad taste', Zinoviev told me in embarrassment, 'but I didn't want to hurt their feelings. Have a very small number printed, and get a very simple cover designed instead.'

On another day he showed me a letter from Lenin which touched on the new bureaucracy, calling them 'all that Soviet riff-raff'. This atmosphere was often sharpened, because of the perpetuation of the Terror, by an element of intolerable inhumanity.

A notable saying of Lenin kept rising in my mind: 'It is a terrible misfortune that the honour of beginning the first Socialist revolution should have befallen the most backward people in Europe.' (I quote from memory; Lenin said it on several occasions.) Nevertheless, within the current situation of Europe, bloodstained, devastated, and in profound stupor, Bolshevism was, in my eyes, tremendously and visibly right. It marked a new point of departure in history.

World capitalism, after its first suicidal war, was now clearly incapable either of organizing a positive peace, or (what was equally evident) of deploying its fantastic technical progress to increase the prosperity, liberty, safety, and dignity of mankind. The Revolution was therefore right, as against capitalism; and we saw that the spectre of future war would raise a question-mark over the existence of civilization itself, unless the social system of Europe was speedily transformed. The fearful Jacobinism of the Russian Revolution seemed to me to be quite unavoidable; as was the institution of a new revolutionary State, now in the process of disowning all its early promises. In this I saw an immense danger: the State seemed to me to be properly a weapon of war, not a means of organizing production. Over all our achievements there hung a death-sentence; since for all of us, for our ideals, for the new justice that was proclaimed, for our new collective economy, still in its infancy, defeat would have brought a peremptory death and after that, who knows what? I thought of the Revolution as a tremendous sacrifice that was required for the future's sake; and nothing seemed to me more essential than to sustain, or rescue, the spirit of liberty within it.

In penning the above lines, I am no more than recapitulating my own writings of that period.

4

DANGER FROM WITHIN
1920—1921

The social system in these years was later called 'War Communism'. At the time it was called simply 'Communism', and any one who, like myself, went so far as to consider it purely temporary was looked upon with disdain. Trotsky had just written that this system would last over several decades if the transition to a genuine, unfettered Socialism was to be assured. Bukharin was writing his work on *The Economy In the Period of Transition*, whose schematic Marxism aroused Lenin's ire. He considered the present mode of organization to be final. And yet, all the time it was becoming simply impossible to live within it: impossible, not of course for the administrators, but for the mass of the population. In fact, in order to eat it was necessary to resort, daily and without interruption, to the black market; the Communists did it like everyone else. Bank-notes were no longer worth anything, and ingenious theoreticians spoke of the coming abolition of money. There was no paper or coloured ink to print stamps, so a decree was issued abolishing postal charges: 'a new step in the realization of Socialism'. Tram-fares were abolished, with disastrous effects, since the overloaded stock deteriorated day by day.

The rations issued by the State co-operatives were minute: black bread (or sometimes a few cupfuls of oats instead); a few herrings each month, a very small quantity of sugar for people in the 'first category' (workers and soldiers), and none at all for the third category (non-workers). The words of St. Paul that were posted up everywhere, '*He that doth not work, neither shall he eat!*' became ironical, because if you wanted any food you really had to resort to the black market instead of working. In the dead factories, the workers spent their time making pen-knives out of bits of machinery, or shoe-soles out of the conveyor-belts, to barter them on the underground market. The total of industrial production had fallen to less than 30 per cent. of the 1913 figure. If you wished to procure a little flour, butter, or meat from the peasants who brought these things illicitly into town, you had to have cloth or articles of some kind to exchange. Fortunately the town residences of the late bourgeoisie contained quite a lot in the way of carpets, tapestries, linen, and plate. From the leather upholstery of sofas one could make passable shoes; from the tapestries, clothing.

Winter was a torture (there is no other word for it) for the towns-people: no heating, no lighting, and the ravages of famine. Children and feeble old folk died in their thousands. Typhus was carried everywhere by lice, and took its frightful toll. All this I saw and lived through, for a great while indeed. Inside Petrograd's grand apartments, now abandoned, people were crowded in one room, living on top of one another around a little stove of brick or cast-iron which would be standing on the floor, its flue belching smoke through an opening in the window. Fuel for it would come from the floor-boards of rooms near by, from the last stick of furniture available, or else from books. Entire libraries disappeared in this way. I myself burned the collected *Laws of the Empire* as fuel for a neigh-bouring family, a task which gave me considerable satisfaction. People dined on a pittance of oatmeal or half-rotten horsemeat, a lump of sugar would be divided in tiny fragments among a family, and a single mouthful taken out of turn would start angry scenes. The local Commune did everything it could to keep the children fed, but what it managed was pitiful.

The co-operative provisioning system had to be maintained, since it catered primarily for the starved and battered proletariat, the army, the fleet and the Party activists. And so requisitioning detach-ments were sent out into the outlying countryside, only to be driven away, as likely as not, or sometimes even massacred by *mujiks* wielding pitchforks. Savage peasants would slit open a commissar's belly, pack it with grain and leave him by the roadside as a lesson for all. This was how one of my own comrades died, a printing worker. It took place not far from Dno, and I went there afterwards to explain to the desperate villagers that it was all the fault of the imperialist blockade. This was true, but all the same the peasants continued, not unreasonably, to demand both the abolition of requisitioning and the legalization of the market.

'War Communism' could be defined as follows: firstly, requisitioning in the countryside; secondly, strict rationing for the town population, who were classified into categories; thirdly, complete 'socialization' of production and labour; fourthly, an extremely complicated and chit-ridden system of distribution for the remaining stocks of manufactured goods; fifthly, a monopoly of power tending towards the single Party and the suppression of all dissent; sixthly, a state of siege, and the Cheka. This system had been approved by the Ninth Congress of the Communist Party in the March and April of 1920. No one dared to admit that it would not work, and the Party did not know that in February of that year Trotsky had asked the Central Committee to abolish requisitioning. Rozhkov, the Marxist historian, wrote to Lenin saying that we were heading for catastrophe; there must be an immediate change in economic relations with the countryside. The Central Committee ordered him off to Pskov, where he was obliged to live, and Lenin replied to him that he had no intention of entering on a policy of surrender before the rural counter-revolution.

The winter of 1920–1 was hideous. Searching for houses fit for our staff to occupy, I visited several buildings in the heart of Petrograd. In a mansion that had once belonged to the society beauty Morskaya, not far from our main military headquarters and the triumphal gateway that opens into the court of the Winter Palace, I found whole rooms plastered with frozen excrement. The w.c.'s would not flush and the soldiers billeted there had installed field latrines on the floor-boards. Many houses were in a similar condition; when spring came and the excrement began to run all over the floors, anything might happen to the city. Compulsory clearance-squads were organized hastily.

I remember what happened one day when I was tramping through the snow with one of the regional military commanders, Mikhail Lashevich, an old revolutionary for the last thirty-five years, one of the architects of the seizure of power and a fearless warrior. I talked to him of the changes that had to be made. Lashevich was a stocky, thick-set man whose face was fleshy and creased with wrinkles. The only solution he could envisage for any problem was a resort to force. Speculation? We'll put a stop to that! 'I shall have the covered markets pulled down and the crowds dispersed! There you are!' He did it too, which only made matters worse.

Political life was pursuing the same line of development; indeed, it could hardly do otherwise. The tendency to override economic difficulties by compulsion and violence led to the growth of general discontent; any free (i.e. critical) expression of opinion became dangerous and consequently had to be treated as enemy activity. I was exceptionally well placed to follow the progress of this evil: I belonged to the governing circles in Petrograd, and was on terms of confidence with various oppositional forces, anarchists, Mensheviks, Left Social-Revolutionaries, and even Communists—those of the 'Workers' Opposition', which was already castigating the growing bureaucracy of the régime and the wretched condition of the ordinary worker: wretched not only in material circumstance but (what was much worse) in point of law, since the administration denied him any possibility of speaking out.

Except for the 'Workers' Opposition' these dissenters, who were always falling out among themselves, had become politically bankrupt, in different ways. The Mensheviks were outright opponents of the seizure of power by the Soviets; in other words, they stood for the continuation of a bourgeois democracy that was quite unworkable and, in the case of some of their leaders, for the vigorous suppression of Bolshevism. The Left Social-Revolutionaries, led by Maria Spiridonova and Kamkov, had first boycotted the Bolshevik authorities, then collaborated with them, and then, in July 1918, raised an insurrection against them, proclaiming their intention to govern alone. The anarchists were chaotically subdivided into pro-Soviet, anti-Soviet, and intermediate tendencies. In 1919 the anti-Soviet anarchists had thrown a bomb into a plenary session of the Communist Party's Moscow Committee, with a total of fifteen victims.

However, these impassioned dissidents of the Revolution, crushed and persecuted as they might be, were still right on many points, above all in their demand, on their own behalf and that of the Russian people, for freedom of expression and the restoration of liberty in the Soviets. The Soviets indeed, which had been so lively in 1918, were now no more than auxiliary organs of the Party; they possessed no initiative, exercised no control and in practice represented nothing but the local Party Committees. But as long as the economic system remained intolerable for nine-tenths or so of the population, there could be no question of recognizing freedom of speech for any Tom, Dick, or Harry, whether in the Soviets or elsewhere. The state of siege had now entered the Party itself, which was increasingly run from the top, by the Secretaries. We were at a loss to find a remedy for this bureaucratization: we knew that the Party had been invaded by careerist, adventurist, and mercenary elements who came over in swarms to the side that had the power. Within the Party the sole remedy to this evil had to be, and in fact was, the discreet dictatorship of the old, honest, and incorruptible members, in other words the Old Guard.

It was with particular intimacy that I followed the unfolding drama of anarchism, which was to achieve historic significance with the Kronstadt uprising. During the Second Congress of the Communist International, I had observed the negotiations between Lenin and Benjamin Markovich Aleynnikov, an intelligent anarchist whose career had included exile, mathematics, and work as a 'Soviet businessman' in Holland. The discussion concerned co-operation with the anarchists. Lenin indicated his agreement with the idea. He had recently given a friendly reception to Nestor Makhno; Trotsky was, much later (in 1938, I think), to recount that Lenin and he had thought of recognizing an autonomous region for the anarchist peasants of the Ukraine, whose military leader Makhno was. That arrangement would have been both just and diplomatic, and perhaps an outlook as generous as this would have spared the Revolution from the tragedy towards which we were drifting. Two pro-Soviet anarchists, energetic and capable men, were working with Chicherin in the Commissariat of Foreign Affairs: Herman Sandomirsky, a young scholar who had once been condemned to death in Warsaw and had known the inside of a prison, and Alexander Shapiro, a man of critical and moderate temper.

Kamenev, the President of the Moscow Soviet, offered the anarchists the legalization of their movement, complete with its own press, clubs, and bookshops, on condition that they should draw up a register of themselves and conduct a purge of their favourite haunts, which were crawling with malcontents, uncontrollables, semi-lunatics, and a few ill-disguised genuine counter-revolutionaries. The majority of the anarchists gave a horrified refusal to this suggestion of organization and enrolment: 'What, are we to form a kind of Party—even us?' Rather than that they would disappear, and have their press and premises taken off them.

Of the anarchist leaders from that tempestuous year of 1918, one was now constructing a new universal language, entirely in mono-syllables, called 'Ao'. Another, Yarchuk, a notable figure among the Kronstadt sailors, was in the Butyrki prison, suffering the pains of scurvy. A third, Nikolai Rogdayev, was in charge of Soviet propaganda in Turkestan. A fourth, Novomirsky, a former terrorist and convict, had joined the Party and was now working with me in Zinoviev's service and displaying the bizarre passion of the newly initiated. A fifth, Grossman-Roschin, who in the old days of 1906 had been the theoretician of 'motiveless terror' (which was intended to strike the old régime anywhere, at any time), became a syndicalist and a friend of Lenin and Lunacharsky; he was developing a libertarian theory of the dictatorship of the proletariat. Finally, there was my old friend Appolon Karelin, a splendid old man I had known in Paris, studying co-operative problems in a little room on the Rue d'Ulm. He was now a member of the All-Russian Executive of Soviets, still living with his white-haired wife in a little room at the National Hotel (one of the Houses of the Soviets). There, broken by old age, his sight failing, his beard white and expansive, he would type, with one finger on an antique machine, his huge book, *Against the Death Penalty*, and expatiate upon the virtues of a federation of free communes.

The group that was almost an ally of Communism, that of Askarov, was devising a 'universalist anarchism'. Another, the Kropotkinist formation under Atabekian, saw free co-operatives as the only remedy. Boris Voline, still in jail, refused to take up the post as director of education in the Ukraine which was offered him by the Bolshevik leaders. He replied, 'I will never treat with the autocracy of the commissars.' It was, altogether, a lamentable chaos of sectarian good intentions. Anarchism was basically a doctrine of far more emotive power than intellectual. When these men met together it was only to proclaim that '*We fight for the obliteration of all State frontiers and boundaries. We proclaim that the whole earth belongs to all peoples!*' (conference of the Moscow Anarchist Union, December 1919). Would it have endangered the Soviet régime if they had been granted freedom of thought and expression? It would be lunatic to think so. It was merely that the majority of Bolsheviks, true to the

Marxist tradition, regarded them as 'petty-bourgeois Utopians' whose existence was incompatible with the extension of 'scientific socialism'. Inside the brains of the Chekists and of certain bureaucrats who had fallen prey to the psychoses of authority, these 'petty-bourgeois' types were fast growing into a rabble of objective counter-revolutionaries who had to be put down once for all.

As Gorky often said, the character of the Russian people, moulded both by resistance to despotism and submission to it, engenders an 'anti-authoritarian complex', that is to say a potent element of spontaneous anarchism which has generated periodic explosions throughout history. Among the peasants of the Ukraine, their spirit of rebellion, their capacity for self-organization, their love for local autonomy, the necessity of relying on nobody but themselves as defence against the Whites, the Germans, the Yellow-and-Blue nationalists, and often against harsh and ignorant commissars from Moscow, heralds of endless requisitioning—all these factors gave rise to an extraordinarily vital and powerful movement: the 'Insurgent Peasant Armies' assembled in the regions of Gulyai-Polye by an anarchist schoolmaster and ex-convict, Nestor Makhno. Under the inspiration of Boris Voline and Aaron Baron, the anarchist *Nabat* (or 'Alarm') Federation provided this movement both with an ideology, that of the Third (libertarian) Revolution, and with a banner, the black flag. These peasants displayed a truly epic capacity for organization and battle. Nestor Makhno, boozing, swashbuckling, disorderly and idealistic, proved himself to be a born strategist of unsurpassed ability. The number of soldiers under his command ran at times into several tens of thousands. His arms he took from the enemy. Sometimes his insurgents marched into battle with one rifle for every two or three men: a rifle which, if any soldier fell, would pass at once from his still-dying hands into those of his alive and waiting neighbour.

Makhno invented a form of infantry mounted in carts, which gave him enormous mobility. He also invented the procedure of burying his weapons and disbanding his forces for a while. His men would pass, unarmed, through the front lines, unearth a new supply of machine-guns from another spot, and spring up again in an unexpected quarter. In September 1919, at Uman, he inflicted a defeat on General Denikin from which the latter was never to recover. Makhno was known as *'Batko'* (little father, or master).

When the railwaymen of Yekaterinoslav (later Dniepropetrovsk) asked him for money to pay their wages, he replied, 'Get organized and run the railway yourselves. I don't need them.' His popular reputation through the whole of Russia was very considerable, and remained so despite a number of atrocities committed by his bands; despite, also, the strenuous calumnies put out by the Communist Party, which went so far as to accuse him of signing pacts with the Whites at the very moment when he was engaged in a life-and-death struggle against them.

In October 1920, when Baron Wrangel still held the Crimea, a Treaty of Alliance was signed between the Black army and the Red Army. Bela Kun, Frunze and Gusev were the signatories for the Reds. This treaty was to be a preliminary to an all-Russian amnesty for the anarchists, the legalization of their movement and the convention of an anarchist Congress at Kharkhov. The Black cavalry broke through the White lines and penetrated into the Crimea; this victory, coinciding with that of Frunze and Blücher at Perekop, was the decisive blow against the White Crimean régime, which had recently received recognition from Britain and France.

In Petrograd and Moscow the anarchists were making ready for their Congress. But no sooner had this joint victory been won than they were suddenly (in November 1920) arrested *en masse* by the Cheka. The Black victors of the Crimea, Karetnik, Gavrilenko, and others, were betrayed, arrested and shot. Makhno, surrounded at Gulyai-Polye, resisted like a madman. He cut a way out for his troops and kept fighting right up to August 1921. (Later he was to be interned in Rumania, Poland, and Danzig, and end his days as a factory worker in Paris.)

This fantastic attitude of the Bolshevik authorities, who tore up the pledges they themselves had given to this endlessly daring revolutionary peasant minority, had a terribly demoralizing effect; in it I see one of the basic causes of the Kronstadt rising. The Civil War was winding to its close, and the peasantry, incensed by the constant requisitioning, was drawing the conclusion that it was impossible to come to any understanding with 'the commissars'.

Equally serious was the fact that many workers, including quite a few Communist workers, were pretty near the same opinion. The 'Workers' Opposition', led by Shliapnikov, Alexandra Kollontai, and Medvedev, believed that the revolution was doomed if the Party failed to introduce radical changes in the organization of work, restore genuine freedom and authority to the trade unions, and make an immediate turn towards establishing a true Soviet democracy. I had long discussions on this question with Shliapnikov. A former metalworker, one of the very few Bolsheviks who had taken part in the Petrograd revolution of February–March 1917, he kept about him, even when in power, the mentality, the prejudices, and even the old clothes he had possessed as a worker. He distrusted the officials ('that multitude of scavengers') and was sceptical about the Comintern, seeing too many parasites in it who were only hungry for money. Corpulent and unwieldy, with a large, round, moustachioed face, he was a very bitter man when I met him. The discussion on the trade unions, in which he was a passionate participant, yielded little result. Trotsky advocated the fusion of the trade unions with the State. Lenin stood for the principles of trade-union autonomy and the right to strike, but with the complete subordination of the unions to the Party. The Party steamroller was at work. I took part in the discussion in one of the districts of Petrograd, and was horrified to see the voting rigged for Lenin's and Zinoviev's 'majority'. That way would resolve nothing: every day in Smolny the only talk was of factory incidents, strikes, and booing at Party agitators. This was in November and December of 1920.

In February, old Kropotkin died at Dimitrovo, near Moscow. I had made no effort to see him, fearing that any conversation between us would be painful; he still believed that the Bolsheviks had received German money, etc. My friends and I had known that he was living in cold and darkness, working on his *Ethics* and playing the piano a little for recreation, and so we had sent him a luxurious parcel of wax candles. I knew the contents of his letters to Lenin about Bolshevik intolerance and the nationalization of the book trade. If they are ever published, the acuteness with which Kropotkin denounced the perils of directed thought will be plainly evident. I went up to Moscow for his funeral. These were heartbreaking days: the great frost in the midst of the great hunger. I was the only member of the Party to be accepted as a comrade in anarchist circles. Around the corpse of the great old man, exposed to view in the Hall of Columns of the House of Trade Unions, untoward incidents multiplied despite all Kamenev's tact and good intentions.

The shadow of the Cheka fell everywhere, but a packed and passionate multitude thronged around the bier, making this funeral ceremony into a demonstration of unmistakable significance.

Kamenev had promised to release all the imprisoned anarchists for the day; so it was that Aaron Baron and Yarchuk stood on guard beside the dead man's remains. Frozen face, high, graceful forehead, narrow nose, beard like snow: Kropotkin lay there like a sleeping wizard, while around him angry voices were whispering that the Cheka was violating Kamenev's promise, that a hunger-strike had been voted in the jails: that so-and-so and so-and-so had just been arrested; that the shootings in the Ukraine were still going on. . . .

The lengthy negotiations to get permission for a black flag and a burial oration sent a wave of anger through the crowd. The long procession, surrounded by students making a chain of linked hands, set off to the cemetery of Novo-Devichy, accompanied by singing choirs who walked behind black flags bearing inscriptions in denunciation of all tyranny. At the cemetery, in the transparent sunlight of winter, a grave had been opened under a silvery birch. Mostovenko, the delegate from the Bolshevik Central Committee, and Alfred Rosmer, from the Executive of the International, spoke in conciliatory terms. Then Aaron Baron, arrested in the Ukraine, due to return that evening to a prison from which he would never again emerge, lifted his emaciated, bearded, gold-spectacled profile to cry relentless protests against the new despotism: the butchers at work in their cellars, the dishonour shed upon Socialism, the official violence that was trampling the Revolution underfoot. Fearless and impetuous, he seemed to be sowing the seeds of new tempests. The Government founded a Kropotkin Museum, endowed a number of schools with Kropotkin's name, and promised to publish his works . . . (10 February 1921).[1]

Eighteen days elapsed. On the night of 28–29 February I was awoken by the ringing of a telephone in a room at the Astoria next to my own. An agitated voice told me: 'Kronstadt is in the hands of the Whites. We are all under orders.'

The man who announced this frightful news to me (frightful, because it meant the fall of Petrograd at any minute) was Ilya Yonov,

[1] After the death of Kropotkin's widow in 1938, the Kropotkin Museum was suppressed and its contents dispersed.

Zinoviev's brother-in-law. 'What Whites? Where did they come from? It's incredible!'

'A General Kozlovsky.'

'But our sailors? The Soviet? The Cheka? The workers at the Arsenal?'

'That's all I know.'

Zinoviev was in conference with the Revolutionary Council of the Army. I ran to the premises of the Second District Committee, which I found full of gloomy faces. 'It's unbelievable, but it's true all the same.'

'Well', I said, 'everybody must be mobilized immediately!' I was given the evasive reply that this would be done, but that we were awaiting instructions from the Petrograd Committee.

I spent the rest of the night studying the map of the Gulf of Finland, along with some of the comrades. We gathered that a considerable number of small strikes were now spreading in the working-class suburbs: the Whites in front of us, famine and strikes at our backs! When I came away at dawn, I saw an old maid from the hotel staff, quietly making her way out with several parcels.

'Where are you off to like this, so early in the morning, grandmother?'

'There's a smell of trouble about the town. They're going to cut all your throats, my poor little ones, they're going to be looting everything, all over again. So, I'm taking my things away.'

Small posters stuck on the walls in the still empty streets proclaimed that the counter-revolutionary General Kozlovsky had seized Kronstadt through conspiracy and treason; the proletariat were summoned to arms. But even before I went to the District Committee I met comrades, rushing out with their revolvers, who told me that it was an atrocious lie: the sailors had mutinied, it was a naval revolt led by the Soviet. This was perhaps not less serious than the other story: quite the reverse. The worst of it all was that we were paralysed by the official falsehoods. It had never happened before that our Party should lie to us like this. 'It's necessary for the benefit of the public,' said some, who were none the less horror-stricken at it all. The strike was now practically general. No one knew whether the trams would run.

That same day I met my friends of the French-speaking Communist group (I remember that Marcel Body and Georges Hellfer were present). We resolved not to take up arms or to fight, either against famished strikers or against sailors pushed to the limits of their patience. At Vassili-Ostrov I saw a crowd, composed overwhelmingly of women, standing in the snow-white street, obstructing and slowly pushing back the cadets from the military schools who had been sent to clear the approaches to the factories. It was a quiet, sad-looking crowd; they told the soldiers of their misery, called them brothers and asked for their help. The cadets took bread from their pockets and shared it out. The organization of the general strike was being attributed to the Mensheviks and Social-Revolutionaries.

Pamphlets distributed in the working-class districts put out the demands of the Kronstadt Soviet. It was a programme for the renewal of the Revolution. I will summarize it: re-election of the Soviets by secret ballot; freedom of the spoken and printed word for all revolutionary parties and groupings; freedom for the trade unions; the release of revolutionary political prisoners; abolition of official propaganda; an end to requisitioning in the countryside; freedom for the artisan class; immediate suppression of the barrier-squads that were stopping the people from getting their food as they pleased. The Soviet, the Kronstadt garrison, and the crews of the First and Second Naval Squadrons were now in rebellion to ensure the triumph of this programme.

The truth seeped through little by little, past the smokescreen put out by the Press, which was positively beserk with lies. And this was our own Press, the Press of our revolution, the first Socialist Press, and hence the first incorruptible and unbiased Press in the world! Before now it had employed a certain amount of demagogy, which was, however, passionately sincere, and some violent tactics towards its adversaries. That might be fair enough and at any rate was understandable. Now, it lied systematically. The Leningrad *Pravda* stated that Kuzmin, the commissar in charge of the fleet and army, had been brutally handled during his captivity at Kronstadt and had only just escaped summary execution, which had been ordered for him in writing by the counter-revolutionaries. I knew Kuzmin, an expert in his particular line, a forceful and industrious soldier, grey from head to foot, from his uniform to his wrinkled face. He 'escaped' from Kronstadt and came back to Smolny. I told him, 'I can scarcely believe that they wanted to shoot you. Did you really see the order?'

He hesitated, in some embarrassment: 'Oh, you always get these exaggerations. There was some little sheet written in threatening terms.' In short, he had had a warm time of it, nothing more. The Kronstadt insurrection had shed no single drop of blood, and merely arrested a few Communist officials, who were treated absolutely correctly; the great majority of Communists, numbering several hundreds, had rallied to the uprising (a clear proof of the Party's instability at its base). All the same, a legend of narrowly-averted executions was put around. Throughout this tragedy, rumour played a fatal part. Since the official Press concealed everything that was not a eulogy of the régime's achievements, and the Cheka's doings were shrouded in utter mystery, disastrous rumours were generated every minute. The Kronstadt mutiny began as a movement of solidarity with the Petrograd strikes, and also as the result of rumours, which were overwhelmingly false, about their repression.

The real culprits, whose brutal bungling provoked the rebellion, were Kalinin and Kuzmin. Kalinin, the President of the Republic's Executive, was met by the Kronstadt garrison with music and welcoming salutes; once informed of the sailors' demands, he treated them as rogues and traitors merely out for themselves, and threatened them with merciless reprisals. Kuzmin shouted that indiscipline and treason would be smashed by the iron hand of the proletariat. They were chased away to a chorus of booing; the break was now final. It was probably Kalinin who, on his return to Petrograd, invented 'the White General Kozlovsky'. Thus, right from the first moment, at a time when it was easy to mitigate the conflict, the Bolshevik leaders had no intention of using anything but forcible methods. Later, we discovered that the whole of the delegation sent by Kronstadt to explain the issues to the Petrograd Soviet and people was in the prisons of the Cheka.

The idea of mediation arose during the discussions I had every evening with some American anarchists who had arrived recently: Emma Goldman, Alexander Berkman, and Perkus, the young Secretary of the Russian Workers' Union in the United States. I spoke of the matter to some comrades from the Party. They answered, 'It will all be quite useless. We are bound by Party discipline, and so are you.'

I flared up: 'One can leave a Party!'

They replied, cold and serious: 'A Bolshevik does not leave his

Party. And anyway, where would you go? You have to face it, there is no one but us.'

The anarchist mediating group met at the house of my father-in-law, Alexander Russakov. I was not present at this meeting since it had been decided that only the anarchists would undertake this initiative (in view of the influence they exerted within the Kronstadt Soviet) and that, as far as the Soviet Government was concerned, the American anarchists would take sole responsibility for the attempt. Emma Goldman and Alexander Berkman were received warmly by Zinoviev, since they were able to speak with authority, in the name of a still important section of the international working class. Their mediation was a complete failure. As a consolation, Zinoviev offered them every facility for touring the whole of Russia in a special train: 'Observe, and you will understand.' Most of the Russian 'mediators' were arrested, apart from myself. I owe this forbearance to the kindness of Zinoviev, Zorin, and others, as well as to my qualifications as a militant from the French working-class-movement.

After many hesitations, and with unutterable anguish, my Communist friends and I finally declared ourselves on the side of the Party. This is why. Kronstadt had right on its side. Kronstadt was the beginning of a fresh, liberating revolution for popular democracy: 'The Third Revolution!' it was called by certain anarchists whose heads were stuffed with infantile illusions. However, the country was absolutely exhausted, and production practically at a standstill; there were no reserves of any kind, not even reserves of stamina in the hearts of the masses. The working-class *élite* that had been moulded in the struggle against the old régime was literally decimated. The Party, swollen by the influx of power-seekers, inspired little confidence. Of the other parties, only minute nuclei existed, whose character was highly questionable. It seemed clear that these groupings could come back to life in a matter of weeks, but only by incorporating embittered, malcontent and inflammatory elements in their thousands, no longer, as in 1917, enthusiasts for the young revolution. Soviet democracy lacked leadership, institutions and inspiration; at its back there were only masses of starving and desperate men.

The popular counter-revolution translated the demand for freely-elected Soviets into one for 'Soviets without Communists'.

If the Bolshevik dictatorship fell, it was only a short step to chaos, and through chaos to a peasant rising, the massacre of the Communists, the return of the *émigrés*, and in the end, through the sheer force of events, another dictatorship, this time anti-proletarian. Dispatches from Stockholm and Tallinn testified that the *émigrés* had these very perspectives in mind; dispatches which, incidentally, strengthened the Bolshevik leaders' intention of subduing Kronstadt speedily and at whatever cost. We were not reasoning in the abstract. We knew that in European Russia alone there were at least fifty centres of peasant insurrection. To the south of Moscow, in the region of Tambov, Antonov, the Right Social-Revolutionary school-teacher, who proclaimed the abolition of the Soviet system and the re-establishment of the Constituent Assembly, had under his command a superbly organized peasant army, numbering several tens of thousands. He had conducted negotiations with the Whites. (Tukhachevsky suppressed this *Vendée* around the middle of 1921.)

In these circumstances it was the Party's duty to make concessions, recognizing that the economic régime was intolerable, but not to abdicate from power. 'Despite its mistakes and abuses', I wrote, 'the Bolshevik Party is at present the supremely organized, intelligent and stable force which, despite everything, deserves our confidence. The Revolution has no other mainstay, and is no longer capable of any thoroughgoing regeneration.'

The Politbureau decided to negotiate with Kronstadt, then to present an ultimatum and in the last resort to order an attack on the fort and the battleships, which were now immobilized in the ice. In fact, no negotiations took place. An ultimatum was published, signed by Lenin and Trotsky and worded in disgusting terms: 'Surrender, or you will be shot down like rabbits.' Trotsky did not come to Petrograd, and acted only within the Politbureau.

At the end of the autumn or the beginning of winter, simultaneously with the outlawing of the anarchists on the morrow of the victory that had been won with their aid, the Cheka had outlawed the Menshevik Social-Democrats. In a quite frightening official document they charged the Mensheviks with 'conspiracy with the enemy, organization of railway-wrecking' and other enormities in equally odious terms. The Bolshevik leaders themselves blushed at it all. They shrugged their shoulders ('The Cheka is mad!') but did nothing to set matters right; the most they would do was to promise the Mensheviks that there would be no arrests and that everything would sort itself out. Theodore Dan and Abramovich,[1] the leaders of Menshevism, were arrested in Petrograd. The Cheka, which at the time, if my memory is not at fault, was run by Semionov, a red-headed little worker, rude and cruel, wanted to shoot them as the leaders of the strike, which was now almost of a general character. This was most probably untrue since the strike was three-quarters spontaneous. I had just had a row with Semionov on the subject of two students who had been kept in freezing cells and manhandled. I appealed to Gorky; at that very moment he was intervening with Lenin to save the lives of the Menshevik leaders. Once Lenin was alerted they were absolutely safe. But for several nights we trembled in our shoes for them.

At the beginning of March, the Red Army began its attack, over the ice, against Kronstadt and the fleet. The artillery from the ships and forts opened fire on the attackers. In several places the ice cracked open under the feet of the infantry as it advanced, wave after wave, clad in white sheets. Huge ice-floes rolled over, bearing their human cargo down into the black torrent. It was the beginning of a ghastly fratricide.

The Tenth Congress of the Party, which was meanwhile in session at Moscow, was now, on Lenin's proposal, abolishing the system of requisitions, or in other words 'War Communism', and proclaiming the 'New Economic Policy'; all the economic demands of Kronstadt were being satisfied! At the same time the Congress gave a rough time to the various oppositions. The Workers' Opposition was classified as 'an anarcho-syndicalist deviation incompatible with the Party', although it had absolutely nothing in common with anarchism and merely demanded the management of production by the unions (which would have been a great step towards democracy for the working class). The Congress mobilized all present, including many Oppositionists, for the battle against Kronstadt. Dybenko, a former Kronstadt sailor himself and an extreme Left Communist, and Bubnov, the writer, soldier and

[1] Theodore Dan (1871–1947): Right Menshevik; during the First World War a moderate internationalist; emigrated in 1922; published a review of rather pro-Soviet inclinations in New York, where he died. Rafail Abramovich (1880–1963): Bundist and then a Menshevik-Internationalist in the War; after leaving Russia became a leading figure in the Second International and editor of the journal *Sotsialistichesky Vestnik* from 1921 until his death.

leader of the 'Democratic Centralism' group, went out to join battle on the ice against rebels who they knew in their hearts were right. Tukhachevsky prepared the final assault. In these dark days, Lenin said in so many words to one of my friends: 'This is Thermidor. But we shan't let ourselves be guillotined. We shall make a Thermidor ourselves.'

The Oranienbaum incident, which has not been related by anyone, as far as I know, brought Kronstadt within an inch of a victory undesired by its revolutionary sailors, and Petrograd within an inch of ruin. A whole regiment was on the point of wheeling round in solidarity with Kronstadt and summoning the army to revolt. At that moment Zorin reinforced it with trusty men, doubled the strength of the outposts and sentries, and arrested the regimental commander. The latter, a former officer in the Imperial army, was brutally frank: 'I waited years for this moment. Murderers of Russia, I hate you. I have lost the game, and now life means nothing to me!' He was shot, along with a good many others. It was a regiment that had been recalled from the Polish front.

The business had to be got over before the thaw began. The final assault was unleashed by Tukhachevsky on 17 March, and culminated in a daring victory over the impediment of the ice. Lacking any qualified officers, the Kronstadt sailors did not know how to employ their artillery; there was, it is true, a former officer named Kozlovsky among them, but he did little and exercised no authority. Some of the rebels managed to reach Finland. Others put up a furious resistance, fort to fort and street to street; they stood and were shot crying 'Long live the world revolution!' There were some of them who died shouting, 'Long live the Communist International!' Hundreds of prisoners were taken away to Petrograd and handed to the Cheka; months later they were still being shot in small batches, a senseless and criminal agony. Those defeated sailors belonged body and soul to the Revolution; they had voiced the suffering and the will of the Russian people; the N.E.P. had proved that they were right; and, finally, they were prisoners of war, civil war, and the Government had for a long time promised an amnesty to its opponents on condition that they offered their support. This protracted massacre was either supervised or permitted by Dzerzhinsky.

The leaders of the Kronstadt rising were hitherto unknown men, thrown up from the ranks. One of them, Petrichenko, is perhaps still alive; he reached sanctuary quickly enough in Finland.[1] Another, Perepelkin, happened to be in jail with a friend of mine whom I used to visit, in the old House of Arrest on Shpalernaya Street, through which so many revolutionaries, including Lenin and Trotsky, had passed in the old days. From the depths of his cell Perepelkin gave us an account of what had happened. Then he disappeared for ever.

18 March was a sombre day. The morning papers had come out with flamboyant headlines commemorating a working-class anniversary, that of the Paris Commune. Meanwhile the muffled thunder of the guns over Kronstadt kept shaking the windows. A guilty unease settled over the offices in Smolny. People avoided talking except with their closest friends, and among close friends, what was said was full of bitterness. By a remarkable historical coincidence on this same day, 18 March, a Communist rising in Berlin collapsed; its failure marked a new turn in the tactics of the International, which was now to proceed from the offensive to the defensive.

Within the Party, Kronstadt opened a period of dismay and doubt. In Moscow Paniushkin, a Bolshevik with a distinguished record in the Civil War, resigned demonstratively from the Party to found a new political organization: I think it was called the 'Soviet Party'. He opened a club in a working-class street; he was tolerated for a brief while, then arrested. Some comrades came and asked me to intercede for his wife and child, who had been evicted from their apartment and were now living in a corridor. I could do nothing for them. Another old Bolshevik, a worker named Miasnikov, who had taken part in the 1905 Upper Volga rising and knew Lenin personally, demanded freedom of the Press 'for everybody from the anarchists to the monarchists'. He broke off relations with Lenin after a sharp exchange of correspondence, and was soon to be deported to Erivan in Armenia. From there he escaped to Turkey. (I was to meet him twenty or so years later, in Paris.) The 'Workers' Opposition' appeared to be heading towards a break with the Party.

The truth was that emergent totalitarianism had already gone half-way to crushing us. 'Totalitarianism' did not yet exist as a word;

[1] In Finland Petrichenko joined pro-Soviet *émigré* groups, and got into trouble with the authorities during the Second World War on account of these sympathies. He was repatriated to Russia in 1945 and immediately imprisoned there. He died in jail in 1946.

as an actuality it began to press hard on us, even without our being aware of it. I belonged to that pitifully small minority that realized what was going on. Most of the Party leadership and activists, in reviewing their ideas about War Communism, came to the conclusion that it was an economic expedient analogous to the centralized régimes set up during the war in Germany, France, and Britain, which they termed 'war capitalism'. They hoped that, once peace came, the state of siege would fall away spontaneously and some sort of Soviet democracy, of which nobody had any clear conception, would return. The great ideas of 1917, which had enabled the Bolshevik Party to win over the peasant masses, the army, the working class, and the Marxist intelligentsia, were quite clearly dead. Did not Lenin, in 1917, suggest a Soviet form of free Press, whereby any group with the support of 10,000 votes could publish its own organ at the public expense? He had written that within the Soviets power could be passed from one party to another without any necessity for bitter conflicts. His theory of the Soviet State promised a state structure totally different from that of the old bourgeois states, 'without officials or a police-force distinct from the people', in which the workers would exercise power directly through their elected Councils, and keep order themselves through a militia system.

What with the political monopoly, the Cheka and the Red Army, all that now existed of the 'Commune-State' of our dreams was a theoretical myth. The war, the internal measures against counter-revolution, and the famine (which had created a bureaucratic rationing-apparatus) had killed off Soviet democracy. How could it revive, and when? The Party lived in the certain knowledge that the slightest relaxation of its authority would give the day to reaction.

To these historical features, certain important psychological factors must be added. Capitalist industrial society tends to encompass the whole of the world, fashioning all aspects of life to its design. Consequently, ever since the beginning of the twentieth century, Marxism has aimed to renew and transform everything: the property system, the organization of work, the map of the world (through the abolition of frontiers), and even the inner life of man (through the extinction of the religious mode of thought). Aspiring to a total transformation, it has consequently been, in the etymological sense of the word, totalitarian. It presents the two faces of the ascendant society, simultaneously democratic and authoritarian. The greatest Marxist party, from 1880 to 1920, the Social-Democratic Party of Germany, is bureaucratically organized on the lines of a State, and functions as a means of achieving power within the State. Bolshevik thinking is grounded in the possession of the truth. The Party is the repository of truth, and any form of thinking which differs from it is a dangerous or reactionary error. Here lies the spiritual source of its intolerance. The absolute conviction of its lofty mission assures it of a moral energy quite astonishing in its intensity—and, at the same time, a clerical mentality which is quick to become Inquisitorial. Lenin's 'proletarian Jacobinism' with its detachment and discipline both in thought and action is eventually grafted upon the pre-existing temperament of activists moulded by the old régime, that is by the struggle against despotism; I am quite convinced that a sort of natural selection of authoritarian temperaments is the result.

For all these reasons, even the great popular leaders themselves flounder within inextricable contradictions which dialectics allows them to surmount verbally, sometimes even demagogically. Twenty or maybe a hundred times, Lenin sings the praises of democracy and stresses that the dictatorship of the proletariat is a dictatorship against 'the expropriated possessing classes', and at the same time, 'the broadest possible workers' democracy'. He believes and wants it to be so. He goes to give an account of himself before the factories; he asks for merciless criticism from the workers. He also writes, in 1918, that the dictatorship of the proletariat is not at all incompatible with personal power; thereby justifying, in advance, some variety of Bonapartism. He has Bogdanov, his old friend and comrade, jailed because this outstanding intellectual confronts him with embarrassing objections. He outlaws the Mensheviks because these 'petty-bourgeois' Socialists are guilty of errors which happen to be awkward. He welcomes the anarchist partisan Makhno with real affection, and tries to prove to him that Marxism is right; but he either permits or engineers the outlawing of anarchism. He promises peace to religious believers and orders that the churches are to be respected; but he keeps saying that 'religion is the opium of the people'. We are proceeding towards a classless society of free men; but the Party has posters stuck up nearly everywhere announcing that 'the rule of the workers will never cease'. Over whom then will they rule? And what is the meaning of this word *rule*? Totalitarianism is within us.

At the end of spring in 1921, Lenin wrote a long article defining what the N.E.P. would be: an end to requisitions and taxes in kind from the peasants; freedom of trade; freedom for production by craftsmen; concessions on attractive terms to foreign capital; freedom of enterprise (within certain limits, of course) for Soviet citizens themselves. It amounted to a partial restoration of capitalism: Lenin admitted this in so many words. At the same time he refused to grant the country any political freedom at all: 'The Mensheviks will stay in jail!' And he proclaimed a purge of the Party, aimed against those revolutionaries who had come in from other parties—i.e. those who were not saturated with the Bolshevik mentality. This meant the establishment within the Party of a dictatorship of the old Bolsheviks, and the direction of disciplinary measures, not against the unprincipled careerists and conformist late-comers, but against those sections with a critical outlook.

A little while afterwards, during the Third Congress of the International, I was present at an address which Bukharin gave to the foreign delegates. He justified N.E.P. in terms of 'the impossibility of breaking the rural petty-bourgeoisie (the peasants, with their attachment to small private property) by means of a single blood-letting—an impossibility which stems from the isolation of the Russian Revolution'. If the German Revolution, with Germany's industrial resources behind it, had come to our assistance, we would have persisted in travelling the path of total Communism, even if it had required bloodshed. I do not have the text of this speech before me, but I was responsible for printing it, and am sure that this is an accurate summary. It amazed me all the more since I had chanced to meet Bukharin several times at Zinoviev's, and genuinely admired him.

Lenin, Trotsky, Karl Radek, and Bukharin had, beyond any doubt, become the brains of the Revolution. They spoke the same Marxist language, and had the same background of experience with the Socialism of Europe and America. Consequently they understood one another so well, by the merest hints, that they seemed to think collectively. (And it is a fact that the Party drew its strength from collective thinking.) Compared with them, Lunacharsky, the People's Commissar for Education, seemed a dilettante: he was a

F

playwright, a poet and a first-rate speaker, with a touch of vanity, who had translated Hölderlin and acted as the protector of Futurist painters. Beside them, Zinoviev was simply a demagogue, a popularizer of ideas worked out by Lenin; Chicherin, the foreign-affairs specialist, never emerged from his archives; Kalinin was no more than a wily figurehead, chosen for the post because of his splendid peasant face and his keen nose for the state of popular feeling. There were other outstanding figures, men of proven ability, but these were secondary characters, concerned purely with practical tasks: Krassin, Piatakov, Sokolnikov, Smilga, Rakovsky, Preobrazhensky, Joffe, Ordzhonikidze, Dzerzhinsky.

Nikolai Ivanovich Bukharin was thirty-three years old; for fifteen of those years he had been a militant. He had lived through a phase of exile in Onega, spent some time with Lenin in Cracow, and worked for the Party in Vienna, Switzerland, and New York. His devotion to theoretical economics was quite tireless. He had anticipated Lenin in elaborating a theory of the complete overthrow of the capitalist state. His mind was effervescent, always alert and active, but rigorously disciplined. The high forehead, balding at the temples, the thin hair, slightly turned-up nose, chestnut-brown moustache and small beard—all made him look just like the average Russian, and his careless manner of dress completed the picture. He dressed all anyhow, as if he had never found time to get a suit that fitted him properly. His usual expression was jovial; even when he was silent the look in his eye, sharpened by a humorous twinkle, was so lively that he always seemed to be just about to come out with some witticism or other. The manner in which he spoke of others savoured of a good-natured cynicism. He devoured books in several languages and had a playful touch in dealing with the most serious subjects. It was immediately obvious that what he most enjoyed was just thinking. He was habitually surrounded by crowds of smiling young listeners, who drank in all his incisive observations. He was bitingly contemptuous of the trade-union and Parliamentary politicians of the West.

Karl Bernardovich Radek (thirty-five years old) could, as we used to say, only speak his own language—the accent he used to express himself in all the others was so incredibly bad. A Galician Jew, he had grown up in the Socialist movements of Galicia, Poland, Germany, and Russia, all at the same time. He was a sparkling writer, with an equal flair for synthesis and for sarcasm. Thin, rather small, nervous, full of anecdotes which often had a savage side to them, realistic to the point of cruelty, he had a beard growing in a fringe around his clean-shaven face, just like an old-time pirate. His features were irregular, and thick tortoise-shell spectacles ringed his myopic eyes. His walk, staccato gestures, prominent lips, and screwed-up face, every part of which was continually expressive, all had something monkey-like and comical about them.

In 1918, when Lenin was thinking in terms of a mixed economy, Radek and Bukharin had been the first to demand the nationalization of large-scale industry. In the same year, during the Brest-Litovsk negotiations, they had accused Lenin, some fifteen years their senior, of opportunism, and advocated a romantic war of all-out resistance against the German Empire, even if it meant suicide for the Soviet Republic. In 1919 Radek had put his daring and common sense into an attempt to lead the German Spartakist movement, and was lucky to escape being murdered with his friends Rosa Luxemburg, Karl Liebknecht, and Leo Tyszko (Jogiches). I had seen him using his scornful dialectic to harry the German moderates. I can see him now, hitching up his trousers (which were always too big for him), as he stood on the rostrum and, demonstrating, after a grating '*Parteigenossen!*' that the collapse of the old order in Europe was shortly due. Although more of an extemporizer than a theoretician, he was also a scholar, and read every conceivable serious journal. He was now being called a Rightist because he did not mince his words about the German Communist Party, and believed that, for the time being, the period of insurrection and offensive in Central Europe was over.

The Third Congress of the Communist International met at Moscow, in an atmosphere much the same as that of the previous Congress, except that the attendance was larger and the proceedings were more relaxed. With the coming of the N.E.P., the famine was getting a little less severe, and people anxiously expected a policy of appeasement to follow. The foreign delegates showed no interest in the tragedy of Kronstadt and, except for a few, deliberately closed their minds to any understanding of it. They sat in commission to condemn the Workers' Opposition; this they did with enthusiasm, without giving it a hearing. They considered N.E.P., amenably enough, to be (as one of the French delegates put it to me) 'an inspired turn to the Right' that had saved the Revolution. It was hardly inspiration to yield to a famine after the situation had become quite insupportable. But the majesty of the Russian Revolution disarmed its supporters of all critical sense; they seemed to believe that approval of it entailed the abdication of the right to think.

At the Kremlin, in the great throne-room of the Imperial Palace, Lenin defended the New Economic Policy. As he spoke, he stood beneath tall, extravagantly gilded columns, under a canopy of scarlet velvet bearing the insignia of the Soviets. Dealing with international strategy, he argued for an armistice and a real effort to win over the masses. He was warm, friendly, genial, talking as simply as he could; it was as if he was determined to emphasize with every gesture that the head of the Soviet Government and the Russian Communist Party was still just another comrade—the leading one, of course, through his acknowledged intellectual and moral authority, but no more than this, and one who would never become just another statesman or just another dictator. He was obviously concerned to steer the International by persuasion. While some of the speeches were going on he would come down from the platform and sit on the steps, near the shorthand reporters, with his note-pad on his knee. From this position he would interrupt now and then with a little caustic comment that made everybody laugh, and a mischievous smile would light up his face. Or he would buttonhole foreign delegates, people who were almost unknown and practically insignificant, and take them into a corner of the hall to carry on, face to face, with the argument he had put forward. The Party must go to the masses! Yes, the masses! And not turn into a sect! And the N.E.P. was not nearly so dangerous as it looked from outside, because we still kept all the fullness of power.

Several times I saw him coming away from the Congress, wearing his cap and jacket, quite alone, walking along at a smart pace with the old cathedrals of the Kremlin on either side of him. I saw him batter Bela Kun with a speech of merciless invective, genial as ever, his face bursting with health and good spirits. This was at a meeting of the Executive Committee of the International, held during the Congress in a banqueting-room of a hotel on Theatre Square below the Kremlin, the *Continental*, I think. This speech marked a real turning-point in Communist policy.

I had some personal knowledge of Bela Kun, whom I found a

wholly unattractive personality. We had been most anxious on his behalf when, after the defeat of the Hungarian Soviets, he had been interned in a Vienna mental asylum, where the Austrian Social-Democrats actually lavished attention on him. A Socialist who in the course of military service had been taken prisoner in Russia, he had begun his revolutionary career in Siberia with the Tomsk Bolsheviks. At the time of the Left Social-Revolutionary uprising of 1918 in Moscow, he had won some distinction by his creation of an international brigade in support of the Party of Lenin and Trotsky. He was jailed at home and came out to become Chairman of the Council of People's Commissars of Hungary and leader of the Hungarian Communist Party. In these posts he had been responsible for a succession of faults and vacillations; he riddled his own Party with backstage repression and allowed a military conspiracy to gain control over practically the whole country. His personal role during the defeat of the Hungarian Soviets had been pathetic (though this was hardly ever mentioned, since a popular legend was being allowed to grow around his name). After some reverses the small Red Armies of Hungary regained the initiative. They beat the Rumanians and advanced into Czechoslovakia, where the popular movement gave them a sympathetic welcome. Clemenceau, alarmed by this recovery, sent a telegram to Bela Kun, asking him to call off the offensive and hinting that, if this were done, the Entente would negotiate with Red Hungary. Kun was taken in by this trick and halted the offensive; the Rumanians rallied their forces and counter-attacked. That was the end.

I cannot help thinking that for the rest of his life Bela Kun was dominated by his sense of failure, and never stopped trying to compensate for it. During his mission in Germany he had, on 18 March of the previous year (1921), instigated an uprising in Berlin which was both bloody and, given the undeniable weakness of the Communist Party, doomed to failure from the beginning. The Party emerged from the incident weakened, and divided by the expulsion of Paul Levi who strongly opposed such 'insurrectionary adventures'.[1] After his return from Germany in the disgrace of

[1] Paul Levi (1883–1930): Rosa Luxemburg's lawyer and a former leader of the Independent Social-Democrats; co-founder of the Spartakusbund and later a leader of the early German Communist Party; supported Serrati's objections to the '21 Conditions'; after 1921, founded a small independent group, then joined the Left wing of the Social Democrats; apparently committed suicide.

another failure, Bela Kun had gone off to win glory in the Crimea.

At a meeting of the Executive of the International Lenin made a lengthy analysis of the Berlin affair, this *putsch* initiated without mass support, serious political calculation, or any possible outcome but defeat. There were few present, because of the confidential nature of the discussion. Bela Kun kept his big, round, puffy face well lowered; his sickly smile gradually faded away. Lenin spoke in French, briskly and harshly. Ten or more times, he used the phrase '*les bêtises de Bela Kun*': little words that turned his listeners to stone. My wife took down the speech in shorthand, and afterwards we had to edit it somewhat: after all it was out of the question for the symbolic figure of the Hungarian Revolution to be called an imbecile ten times over in a written record!

Actually, Lenin's polemic marked the end of the International's tactics of outright offensive. The failure of this approach had to be clearly stated, and besides Russia was now entering a period of internal appeasement; of these two considerations, of unequal worth, I am not sure which was the more influential. In its official resolution the Congress still praised the fighting spirit of the German Communist Party, and Bela Kun was not removed from the Executive.

If the Revolution had not been in such a parlous condition at the time, Kun would have had to face questioning about two other crimes. He had been a signatory to the treaty of alliance with Makhno's Black army; he had also been one of those who tore it up as soon as the joint victory had been achieved. Then too, he had been a member of the Revolutionary Council of the Red Army, which in November 1920 had forced Baron Wrangel out of the Crimea. In this capacity Bela Kun had negotiated the surrender of the remnants of the White army. To this assortment of former Monarchist officers he promised an amnesty and the right to resume civilian work; later he ordered them to be massacred. Thousands of war prisoners were thus treacherously exterminated, in the name of 'purging the country'.

Trotsky came to the Congress many times. No one ever wore a great destiny with more style. He was forty-one and at the apex of power, popularity and fame—leader of the Petrograd masses in two revolutions; creator of the Red Army, which (as Lenin had said to Gorky) he had literally 'conjured out of nothing'; personally the victor of several decisive battles, at Sviazhsk, Kazan, and Pulkovo; the acknowledged organizer of victory in the Civil War—'Our Carnot!' as Radek called him. He outshone Lenin through his great oratorical talent, through his organizing ability, first with the army, then on the railways, and by his brilliant gifts as a theoretician. As against all this Lenin possessed only the pre-eminence, which was truly quite immense, of having, even from before the Revolution, been the uncontested head of the tiny Bolshevik Party which constituted the real backbone of the State, and whose sectarian temper mistrusted the over-rich, over-fluid mind of the Chairman of the Supreme War Council. For a short time there was some talk, in various small groups at the Congress, of elevating Trotsky to the chairmanship of the International. Zinoviev must have been outraged by these pressure-groups, and doubtless Lenin preferred to keep his own spokesman at the top of the 'World Party'. Trotsky himself intended to give his attention to the Soviet economy.

He made his appearance dressed in some kind of white uniform, bare of any insignia, with a broad, flat military cap, also in white, for headgear; his bearing was superbly martial, with his powerful chest, jet-black beard and hair, and flashing eye-glasses. His attitude was less homely than Lenin's, with something authoritarian about it. That, maybe, is how my friends and I saw him, we critical Communists; we had much admiration for him, but no real love. His sternness, his insistence on punctuality in work and battle, the inflexible correctness of his demeanour in a period of general slackness, all imparted a certain demagogic malice to the insidious attacks that were made against him. I was hardly influenced by these considerations, but the political solutions prescribed by him for current difficulties struck me as proceeding from a character that was basically dictatorial. Had he not proposed the fusion of the trade unions with the State—while Lenin quite rightly wanted the unions to keep some of their independence? We did not grasp that the trade-union influence might have actually worked upon the structure of the State, modifying it more effectively in a working-class direction. Had he not set up labour armies? And suggested the militarization of industry as a remedy for its incredible state of chaos? We did not know that earlier, in the Central Committee, he had unsuccessfully proposed an end to the requisitioning system. Labour armies were a good enough expedient in the phase of demobilization. Had he not put his signature to a repulsively threatening manifesto against Kronstadt? The fact was that he had been in the thick of everything, acting with a self-confident energy which tried out directly opposite solutions by turns.

During one session, he came down straight from the platform and stood in the middle of our French group to give a translation of his own speech. He spoke passionately, in slightly incorrect but fluent French. He replied sharply when he was heckled—about the Terror, about violence, about Party discipline. Our little group appeared to irritate him. Vaillant-Couturier, André Morizet, André Julien, Fernand Loriot, Jacques and Clara Mesnil, and Boris Souvarine were all there. Trotsky was easy and cordial, but imperious in argument. On another occasion he flew at the Spanish delegate, Orlandis, who was attacking the persecution of the anarchists. Trotsky seized him violently by the coat-lapels and almost shouted, 'I should certainly like to see that happening to you, petty-bourgeois that you people are!'

During this summer of 1921 I formed, among the comrades from abroad, a number of lasting and even life-long friendships. I resorted to those who came to Moscow with more concern for truth than orthodoxy, more anxiety for the future of the Revolution than admiration for the proletarian dictatorship. Our relationships were always initiated by conversations of an absolute frankness in which I set myself the responsibility of disclosing all the evils, dangers, difficulties, and uncertain prospects. In an era of fanatical conformism this was, as I still believe, a meritorious thing to do, demanding some courage. I gravitated towards people of a free spirit, those who were fired by a desire to serve the Revolution without closing their eyes. Already an 'official truth' was growing up, which seemed to me the most disastrous thing imaginable. I became acquainted with Henriette Roland-Holst, a Dutch Marxist and a notable poet. Lank, scrawny and grey-haired, her neck disfigured by a goitre, she had a delicately sculptured face with an expression of gentleness and intellectual austerity.[1] The questions she raised with me were symptomatic of a most scrupulous anxiety.

---

[1] Henriette Roland-Holst (1869-1952): Dutch 'Tribunist' and then Communist; founded a short-lived Independent Communist Party in 1924; later became a Christian Socialist, pacifist, and opponent of colonialism; *doyenne* of Dutch literature over many years.

Two young men from the Spanish delegation gave us pledges for the future which they were destined to fulfil at tremendous cost: Joaquín Maurín and Andreu Nin. I have always believed that human qualities find their physical expression in a man's personal appearance. A single glance was enough to tell the calibre of Maurín, the teacher from Lérida, and Nin, the teacher from Barcelona. Maurín had the bearing of a young Cavalier from a pre-Raphaelite painting; Nin, behind his gold-rimmed spectacles, wore an expression of concentration which was softened by his evident enjoyment of life. Both of them gave their lives to the cause: Maurín destined to an unending succession of jails; Nin to a horrible death during the Spanish Revolution. At this time the overwhelming impression they conveyed was one of idealism and the thirst for understanding.

The French, more sophisticated and more sceptical characters, were generally of a different stuff. André Morizet, the mayor of Boulogne, paraded his admirably sound and practical face and his drinking-songs for the benefit of us all. (Even now, at Suresnes, in occupied France, he is still fighting to keep his office as Labour mayor; he has returned, after a long interval, to traditional Socialism.) André Julien was piling up countless annotations for a work so compendious that he was never to write it. (In 1936 and 1937, he was to be one of the Socialist stalwarts of the Popular Front.)

Paul Vaillant-Couturier, a tank officer during the war, a poet, popular orator and ex-servicemen's leader, was a tall, chubby young man of extraordinary talents, but fated to become a great disappointment to me. He understood everything that was going on; but in the future he was to acquiesce in his own corruption, to become increasingly entangled with all the villainies of Bolshevism's degeneration, and to die, in working-class Paris, enviably popular.

Boris Souvarine, a Russian Jew by origin but a naturalized Frenchman, had no Socialist background; he came to us, at the age of twenty-five, from the world of left-wing journalism rather than from the working-class movement, with an amazing zest for knowledge and action. Slight and short, his eyes masked by lenses of unusual thickness, speech lisping slightly, manner aggressive and often quick both to offend and to take offence, he had a habit of coming out suddenly with awkward questions; he would deliver mercilessly realistic verdicts on French personalities and events, and amuse himself by deflating swollen heads by smart pinpricks of his own devising. His stock was then very high, even though his first request on arrival was for a tour of the prisons. All the time he showed a magnificent facility for analysis, a lively grasp of realities, and an aptitude for polemic that was designed to leave a trail of indignation wherever he went. He became one of the leaders of the International and a member of its Executive Committee. Souvarine, despite his expulsion from the Comintern in 1924, was for some ten years to be one of the most trenchant and perceptive brains of European Communism.

I was on very close terms with both the French Communist groups in Russia, and was more or less the leader of the one in Petrograd. These groups formed striking instances of the law whereby mass-movements transform individuals, impel them into unpredictable courses of development, and mould their convictions. They also illustrated the law that the ebb-tide of events carries men away just as surely as the flood-tide brings them in. Although their ranks included several former French Socialists (whose inclinations had been quite alien to Bolshevism), these zealous Communists, who for the most part were perfectly sincere, came from all points of the political horizon only to make a speedy departure once again in equally variegated directions. The Moscow group was a little nest of vipers, although it was led by Pierre Pascal, a man of exemplary character. The quarrels, grudges, denunciations, and counter-denunciations of its two leading figures at the time, Henri Guilbeaux and Jacques Sadoul, completely demoralized it and finally earned the attentions of the Cheka. Guilbeaux's whole life was a perfect example of the failure who, despite all his efforts, skirts the edge of success without ever managing to achieve it. He wrote cacophonous poetry, kept a card-index full of gossip about his comrades, and plagued the Cheka with confidential notes. He wore green shirts and pea-green ties with greenish suits; everything about him, including his crooked face and his eyes, seemed to have a touch of mould. (He died in Paris, about 1938, by then an anti-Semite, having published two books proving Mussolini to be the only true successor of Lenin.)

Jacques Sadoul was quite different: a Paris lawyer, an army captain, an information-officer in Russia on behalf of Albert

Thomas,[1] a member of the Comintern Executive, a flatterer of Lenin and Trotsky, a great charmer, a splendid raconteur, a sybarite, and a cool careerist to boot. However, he had produced a volume of *Letters* on the Revolution which is still a document of the first importance. He had been condemned to death in France for crossing over to the Bolshevik side, but was one day to return home, times having changed, with an acquittal. After that he trailed alongside the full course of Stalinism, both as a lawyer acting for Soviet interests and as an agent in Parliamentary circles, though at heart he did not entertain the slightest illusion about Russia. The bread of bitterness tasted by revolutionaries held no temptations for him.

René Marchand, once the Petrograd correspondent for the Catholic-reactionary *Figaro*, was a fresh convert troubled by perpetual crises of conscience. He was soon to go off to Turkey, there to renounce Bolshevism and become an apologist, doubtless a sincere one, for Kemal Ataturk.

The outstanding figure in the Moscow French Communist group was Pierre Pascal, probably a distant descendant of Blaise Pascal, of whom he reminded me. I had met him in Moscow in 1919. There, his head shaven Russian-style, sporting a big Cossack moustache and smiling perpetually with his bright eyes, he would walk through the city barefoot and clad in a peasant tunic to the Commissariat of Foreign Affairs, where he used to draft messages for Chicherin. A loyal and circumspect Catholic, he used St. Thomas's *Summa* to justify his adherence to Bolshevism and even his approval of the Terror. (The texts of the learned saint lent themselves admirably to this task.) Pascal led an ascetic life, sympathizing with the Workers' Opposition and hobnobbing with the anarchists. He had been a lieutenant with the French Military Mission, in charge of coding; he had crossed over to the Revolution in the middle of the intervention, to dedicate himself to it body and soul. He discussed its mystical significance with Berdyaev and translated Blok's poems. He was to suffer terribly as the birth of totalitarianism progressed. I met him again in Paris in 1936. He was now a professor at the Sorbonne, the author of a solid biography of the Archpriest

---

[1] Albert Thomas (1878-1932) was Minister of Munitions in the First World War and visited Russia after the February Revolution of 1917 in an attempt to arouse enthusiasm for the Allies.

Avvakum, and more or less a Conservative. We, who had almost been brothers, could not talk together about the battle of Madrid. . . .

The Executive had decided, on Russian initiative of course, to set up a trade-union International affiliated to the Comintern. Salomon Abramovich Lozovsky[1] (or Dridzo), an ex-Menshevik of recent vintage and an inexhaustible orator, was in charge of the new organization. He had the air of a slightly fastidious schoolmaster amidst his world-wide assortment of trade-union militants whose political horizons did not extend very far beyond their own working-class districts at home. Not far from him, a one-eyed giant would pass through the crowd, downcast and solitary, but now and then distributing vigorous thumps on the shoulders of his mates. This was Bill Haywood, a former timberman, organizer of the I.W.W.,[2] who had come to end his days in the stuffy rooms of the Lux Hotel, among Marxists not one of whom tried to understand him and whom he scarcely understood himself. Still, he got a big thrill out of the red flags in the public squares.

Here too I met a Russian militant who had been in a British prison and was now home from Latin America: Dr. Alexandrov, I think. He was thirty-five, with a swarthy commonplace face, dark hair, and black moustache; very well-informed on all the happenings in the great world outside. He was later to become Comrade Borodin, the Russian political adviser to the Kuomintang at Canton.[3]

On the whole, the foreign delegates were a rather disappointing crowd, charmed at enjoying appreciable privileges in a starving country, quick to adulate and reluctant to think. Few workers could be seen among them, but plenty of politicians. 'How pleased they are', Jacques Mesnil remarked to me, 'to be able to watch parades, at long last, from the official platform!' The influence of the International was expanded only at the expense of quality. We began to ask ourselves whether it had not been a grave error to split the Socialist movement to form new little parties, incapable of

---

[1] Lozovsky afterwards became Deputy Commissar for Foreign Affairs and then head of the Soviet Information Office; he was shot in 1952 at the age of 74.

[2] I.W.W.: Industrial Workers of the World. United States working-class movement of militant syndicalist complexion, founded in 1905 and achieving its prime between 1910 and 1920.

[3] Later still Borodin edited the *Moscow News*, an English-language newspaper produced, at first, largely for foreign technicians working in the Soviet Union. In 1949 he was arrested with most of his staff, and deported to Siberia, where he died early in 1953. Chinese intervention is said to have saved him from execution.

effective action, fed with ideas and money by the Executive's emissaries, and fated to become propaganda factories for the Soviet Government. We were already putting these problems to ourselves, but were reassured by the instability of Western Europe and the wave of enthusiasm which still held us. All the same, I did conclude that, in the International as well, the danger lay in ourselves.

The New Economic Policy was, in the space of a few months, already giving marvellous results. From one week to the next, the famine and the speculation were diminishing perceptibly. Restaurants were opening again and, wonder of wonders, pastries which were actually edible were on sale at a rouble apiece. The public was beginning to recover its breath, and people were apt to talk about the return of capitalism, which was synonymous with prosperity. On the other hand, the confusion among the Party rank-and-file was staggering. For what did we fight, spill so much blood, agree to so many sacrifices? asked the Civil War veterans bitterly. Usually these men lacked all the necessities: clothes, decent homes, money; and now everything was turning back into market-value. They felt that money, the vanquished foe, would soon come into its kingdom once again.

I personally was less pessimistic. I was glad that the change had taken place, though its reactionary side—the outright obliteration of every trace of democracy—worried and even distressed me. Would any other resolution of the drama of War Communism have been possible? This was by now a problem of only theoretical interest, but one worthy of some reflection. On this I developed some ideas, which I remember expounding on one occasion particularly, at a confidential meeting I had at the Lux Hotel with two Spanish Socialists. Fernando de los Ríos was one of them.[1] They ran as follows:

Through its intolerance and its arrogation of an absolute monopoly of power and initiative in all fields, the Bolshevik régime was floundering in its own toils. The big concessions to the peasantry were unavoidable, but small-scale manufacture, medium-scale trading, and certain industries could have been revived merely by

[1] Fernando de los Ríos (1879–1949): Professor of Ethics at Granada University, Minister of Justice and of Education in the first Spanish Republican Government, and Ambassador to Washington during the Civil War.

appealing to the initiative of groups of producers and consumers. By freeing the State-strangled co-operatives, and inviting various associations to take over the management of different branches of economic activity, an enormous degree of recovery could have been achieved straight away. The country was short of both shoes and leather; but the rural areas had leather, and shoe-makers' co-operatives would have easily got hold of it and, once left to themselves, would have sprung into action at once. Of necessity they would have charged relatively high prices, but the State could, in the process of assisting their operations, have exercised a downward pressure upon their prices, which in any case would have been lower than those demanded by the black market. In Petrograd I could see what was happening to the book trade; the stocks of the bookshops, which had been confiscated, were rotting away in cellars which as often as not became flooded with water in the spring. We were most thankful to the thieves who salvaged a goodly number of books and put them back, clandestinely, into circulation. The book trade could, if it had been turned over to associations of book-lovers, have speedily recovered its health. In a word, I was arguing for a 'Communism of associations'—in contrast to Communism of the State variety. The competition inherent in such a system and the disorder inevitable in all beginnings would have caused less inconvenience than did our stringently bureaucratic centralization, with its muddle and paralysis. I thought of the total plan not as something to be dictated by the State from on high, but rather as resulting from the harmonizing, by congresses and specialized assemblies, of initiatives from below. However, since the Bolshevik mind had already ordained other solutions, it was a vision confined to the realms of pure theory.

Ever since Kronstadt some of my friends and I had been asking ourselves what jobs we were going to do. We had not the slightest desire to enter the ruling bureaucracy and become heads of offices or secretaries of institutions. I was offered entry into a diplomatic career, in the Orient at first. I was attracted by the prospect of the Orient, but not by diplomacy. We thought we had found a way out. We would found an agricultural colony in the heart of the Russian countryside; while the N.E.P. reinstated bourgeois habits in the towns and furnished the new rulers with sinecures and easy careers, we would live close to the earth, in the wilds. The earth of Russia, with its sad and calm expanses, is endlessly fascinating. Without much ado we found a large, abandoned estate north of Petrograd, not far from Lake Ladoga, comprising some hundreds of acres of woodland and waste field, thirty head of cattle, and a landlord's residence. There, together with French Communists, Hungarian prisoners-of-war, a Tolstoyan doctor and my father-in-law Russakov, we founded 'the French Commune of Novaya-Ladoga'.

We made a valiant beginning to this experiment, which turned out to be very hard going. The estate had been abandoned because the peasants would not agree to exploit it collectively; they demanded that it be shared out among them. Two chairmen of short-lived communes there had been murdered in the space of eighteen months. The village nearby boycotted us, although the children came at all hours to stare at the extraordinary creatures that we were. At the same time they spied everywhere, and if you forgot a shovel it disappeared at once. One night our entire stock of corn, which was to last for both food and seed until harvest-time, was stolen from us. It was a real state of famine and siege. Every night we waited up in case anyone tried to set the house on fire. We knew who was hiding our corn, but we did not, as they expected, go out with our revolvers to search for it, which only increased the suspicion and hatred surrounding us. The peasants had all the necessities, but refused to sell anything to the 'Jews' and 'Anti-Christs' that we were.

We decided to break this blockade; I went off to the village with Dr. N——, an old believer and Tolstoyan whose musical voice and benign solemnity would, we hoped, have some effect. A peasant woman curtly refused us everything we asked for. The doctor opened the neck of his blouse and brought out the little golden cross that he wore over his breast. 'We are Christians too, little sister!' Their faces lit up and we were given eggs! And little girls made so bold as to come to see us in the evenings, when we would all sing French songs together. . . . However, it could not last; in three months hunger and weariness forced us to abandon the project.

Since Kronstadt there had been a revival of the Terror in Petrograd. The Cheka had just 'liquidated' the Tagantsev conspiracy by executing some thirty people. I had known Professor Tagantsev a little: a skinny little old man with white side-whiskers, a jurist and one of the longest-established university teachers in the former capital. With him they shot a lawyer named Bak to whom I used to send translation jobs and who had never concealed his counter-revolutionary opinions from me.[1] At the same time they executed the splendid poet Nikolai Stepanovich Gumilev, my comrade and adversary back in Paris. I called on his home at the Moyka Art House, where he had a room with his very young wife, a tall girl with a slender neck and the eyes of a terrified gazelle. It was a huge room, with murals showing swans and lotuses—it had once been the bathroom of a merchant who had a taste for poetry with this sort of imagery. Gumilev's young wife said to me in a low voice, 'Haven't you heard? They took him away three days ago.'

The comrades at the Soviet Executive gave me news which was both reassuring and disturbing: Gumilev was being very well treated at the Cheka, he had spent some nights there reciting his poems—poems overflowing with stately energy—to the Chekists there; but he had admitted to having drafted certain political documents for the counter-revolutionary group. All this seemed likely enough. Gumilev had never concealed his ideas. During the Kronstadt revolt the circle at the university must have believed that the régime was about to fall, and had thought to assist in its liquidation. The 'conspiracy' could have gone no further than that. The Cheka made ready to shoot all of them: 'This isn't the time to go soft!' One comrade travelled to Moscow to ask Dzerzhinsky a question: 'Were we entitled to shoot one of Russia's two or three poets of the first order?' Dzerzhinsky answered, 'Are we entitled to make an exception of a poet and still shoot the others?' It was dawn, at the edge of a forest, when Gumilev fell, his cap pulled down over his eyes, a cigarette hanging from his lips, showing the same calm he had expressed in one of the poems he brought back from Ethiopia: '*And fearless I shall appear before the Lord God.*' That, at least, is the tale as it was told to me. Over and over again, with mingled admiration and horror, I read the verses which he had entitled 'The Worker', where he describes a gentle, grey-eyed man who, before going to bed, finishes making '*the bullet that is going to kill me. . . .*'

[1] 'Monsieur Bak, a former businessman and journalist for an Iron and Steel Board in the days of the Empire, a small, smooth-faced gentleman, appallingly refined and nice, was agreeable to translating articles on theory, but not revolutionary appeals. "Pardon me, citizen," he would remark, "my conscience. . . ." Naturally, I respected his conscience. . . .' Serge, *Deux Rencontres*.

The faces of Nikolai and Olga Gumilev were to haunt me for years afterwards.

At the same time another of our greatest poets was dying of debility, which was the same thing as starvation: Alexander Blok, at the age of forty-one. I knew him only slightly, but admired him boundlessly. Together with Andrei Bely and Sergei Yesenin he had inspired the mystical vision of the Revolution: 'the Christ crowned with roses' who, 'invisible and silent', walks in the snow-storm before the Twelve Red Guards, soldiers in peak-caps whose rifles are aimed at the city's shadows. He had told me of his rebellions against the Revolution's new absolutism, and I had heard him reading his last great work. His two poems, 'The Twelve', and 'The Scythians', were being translated into many languages, and they remain spiritual monuments of that era. The first proclaimed the Messianic character of the Revolution; the second revealed its ancient, Asiatic face. Contradictory, but so was reality. Blok was a gentlemanly Westerner, rather like an Englishman, blue-eyed and with a long, serious face that hardly ever smiled. He was restrained in his gestures, with a fine dignity about him. Ever since the rise of Symbolism, fifteen years ago, he had been the foremost Russian poet. I followed his corpse to the Vassili-Ostrov cemetery at the moment when the Cheka was passing sentence on Gumilev.

I belonged to the last surviving free-thought society; in all probability I was the only Communist member. This was the Free Philosophic Society, or *Volfila*, whose real guiding spirit was another brilliant poet, Andrei Bely. We organized big public debates, in which one of the speakers was often a shabby, squinting little man, wretchedly dressed, whose face was scored with perpendicular wrinkles. He was Ivanov-Razumnik, the historian and philosopher, still one of the finest representatives of the old revolutionary intelligentsia of Russia. Sometimes the discussion would dissolve into grand lyrical effusions on the problems of existence, consciousness, and the Cosmos. Like Blok, both Bely and Ivanov-Razumnik were somewhat attracted, by reason of their revolutionary romanticism, to the persecuted and silenced Left Social-Revolutionary Party. On account of this sympathy, and because the philosophical flights of the two poets trespassed beyond the bounds of Marxism, the Cheka and the Party had their eye on the *Volfila*. Its organizers wondered every day whether they were going to be arrested. We held our private meetings at Andrei Bely's. At the time he was living in a huge room of the old military headquarters opposite the Winter Palace, just above the offices of the police-militia. There we would ask one another how we could preserve liberty of thought as a principle, and prove that it was not a counter-revolutionary principle. Bely suggested convening a World Congress of Free Thought in Moscow, and inviting to it Romain Rolland, Henri Barbusse, and Gandhi. A chorus of voices cried back: 'It'll never be allowed!' I told them that if they appealed to intellectuals abroad, who were certainly incapable of any real understanding of revolutionary Russia, the Russian intellectuals ran a risk of discrediting the Revolution, which was already the object of indiscriminate attacks by the *émigrés*.

Andrei Bely, a daring stylist, a splendid writer of poetry and prose, and a theosophist (or anthroposophist, as he himself termed it) was just over forty. He was embarrassed at being bald, and so always wore a black skull-cap beneath which his great seer's eyes, of a stony greenish-blue, gave out a continual glitter. The vitality and variety of his mind was prodigious. His whole behaviour reflected spiritual idealism, with sometimes the postures of a visionary, sometimes the frank outbursts of a child. In the aftermath of the 1905 Revolution, he had won fame through a psychological novel about the period, a mystical, revolutionary work impregnated with German and Latin culture. Now he was beginning to feel that his great energies were bankrupt.

'What can I do now in this life?' he asked me despondently one evening. 'I cannot live outside this Russia of ours and I cannot breathe within it!'

I answered that the state of siege was sure to end, and that Western Socialism would open out vast prospects for Russia. 'Do you think so?' he said thoughtfully. However, at the beginning of the autumn of 1921, as the carnage of the Terror was filling us with horror, we saw even the *Volfila* disintegrate.

I am well aware that terror has been necessary up till now in all great revolutions, which do not happen according to the taste of well-intentioned men, but spontaneously, with the violence of tempests; and that it is our duty to employ the only weapons that history affords us if we are not to be overwhelmed through our own folly. But at the same time I saw that the perpetuation of terror, after the end of the Civil War and the transition to a period of economic freedom, was an immense and demoralizing blunder. I was and still am convinced that the new régime would have felt a hundred times more secure if it had henceforth proclaimed its reverence, as a Socialist government, for human life and the rights of all individuals without exception.

The tragedies continued. From Odessa we had monstrous news: the Cheka had just shot Fanny Baron (the wife of Aaron Baron) and Lev Chorny, one of the theoreticians of Russian anarchism. Lev Chorny had been well known to me in Paris twelve years earlier. A figure straight out of a Byzantine icon, with a waxy complexion and eyes that flashed from hollow sockets, he lived in the Latin Quarter, cleaning restaurant windows and then going off to write his *Sociometry* beneath the trees of the Luxembourg Gardens. His death incensed Emma Goldman and Alexander Berkman. During the Third Congress of the International Emma Goldman had thought of making a scene, after the manner of the English suffragettes, by chaining herself to a bench on one of the public balconies and shouting out her protest to the Congress. The Russian anarchists had persuaded her to change her mind. In the country of the Scythians such demonstrations had little value; far better to keep on nagging at Lenin and Zinoviev.

Meanwhile, our persistent campaign for the release of the victimized prisoners had met with some success: ten anarchist prisoners, including the syndicalist Maximov and Boris Voline, were authorized to leave Russia, and others were freed. Kamenev promised that Aaron Baron would be banished; a promise that was not fulfilled, since the Cheka was to oppose it.[1] Certain Mensheviks, notably Martov, also obtained passports to travel abroad.

What with Kronstadt, these tragedies, and the influence of Emma Goldman and Alexander Berkman on the working-class movement in the Old World and the New, an unbridgeable gap was now to open between Marxists and libertarians. Later in history, this division would play a fatal part: it was one of the causes of the intellectual confusion and final defeat of the Spanish Revolution. In this respect, my worst forebodings were fulfilled.

The American background of Emma Goldman and Alexander

[1] Aaron Baron was later deported to the north; but he was arrested during the purges of 1937 and never heard of again.

Berkman estranged them from the Russians, and turned them into representatives of an idealistic generation that had completely vanished in Russia. (I have no doubt that they were just as disconcerted and indignant over a good deal of what happened in Makhno's movement.) They embodied the humanistic rebellion of the turn of the century: Emma Goldman with her organizing flair and practical disposition, her narrow but generous prejudices, and her self-importance, typical of American women devoted to social work; Berkman with the inward tension that sprang from his idealism in years long past. His eighteen years in an American prison had frozen him in the attitudes of his youth when, as an act of solidarity with a strike, he had offered up his life by shooting at one of the steel barons. When his tension relaxed he became dejected, and I could not help thinking that he was often troubled by ideas of suicide. In fact, it was only much later that he was to end his life, in 1936, on the Côte d'Azur.

The winds of an immeasurable calamity swept upon us from the parched plains of the Volga. The Civil War had crossed these regions, and now drought had destroyed them. Millions, starved of all necessities, fled from the famine. I saw them coming up even as far as Petrograd, on foot or in carts. Not everyone had the strength or the means to flee; these were all to die in millions on the spot. This scourge, which struck at both the Ukraine and the Crimea, devastated areas populated by 23,000,000 inhabitants. The blow was so severe that authority tottered. Could the Bolshevik dictatorship overcome the ghastly spectre of death? I met Maxim Gorky, bony, grey, and frowning as never before; he told me of the formation of a committee of leading intellectuals and non-Communist technicians, which was to appeal to all the latent energies of the country, and might well be the germ of tomorrow's democratic government. (The Government at first recognized this committee, which was headed by the Marxist-revisionist economist Prokopovich and the Liberal publicist, Ekaterina Kusskova; then it had these two arrested and expelled from the country.)[1]

[1] S. N. Prokopovich (1871–1955) and his wife Ekaterina Kusskova (1869–1958) were prominent on the Liberal (and subsequently the 'revisionist') wing of the Russian Labour and co-operative movement. Prokopovich served as a Minister under Kerensky and wrote in exile important works on the Soviet economy. Kusskova was a leading figure in the group of *émigrés* who believed in the eventual liberalization of the Soviet régime.

I did not share Gorky's opinion; the revolutionary régime seemed to me already encased in so impenetrable an armour that the skeleton hand of famine could not manage to dislodge it from power. And, despite everything, I was very definitely committed to the régime's survival; I had faith in its future and I knew that for some years Russia would be incapable of any fresh thrust forward from her present condition.

The two groups of friends whose company I kept, the French and the Russian, both suffered from a similar distress. Most of my comrades decided to abandon either political life or the Party. Novomirsky, a high official in the International, an ex-terrorist from 1905, an ex-convict and former anarchist who had been won for Bolshevism by Lenin's goodwill, now sent his membership card back to the Central Committee on account of his fundamental disagreements. He devoted himself to scientific work, and nobody thought of bearing him any grudge. (All the same, he was to be remembered in 1937 when he disappeared, along with his wife, into the concentration-camps.) Marcel Body, a Socialist worker, arranged to be sent to the Soviet Embassy in Oslo. Another got sent to Turkey. Another went to manage a sawmill in the heart of the Far East. Pierre Pascal quietly withdrew from the Party and earned his living as a translator, at the same time working on his history of the schism of the Russian Church. I was tougher inside, and enjoyed (as I think) a broader vision of the Revolution, as well as having less individualistic sentiment in my make-up. I did not feel disheartened or disoriented. I was disgusted at certain things, psychologically exhausted by the Terror and tormented by the mass of wrongs that I could see growing, which I was powerless to counteract. My conclusions were that the Russian Revolution, left to itself, would probably, in one way or another, collapse (I did not see how: would it be through war or domestic reaction?); that the Russians, who had made superhuman efforts to build a new society, were more or less at the end of their strength; and that relief and salvation must come from the West. From now on it was necessary to work to build a Western working-class movement capable of supporting the Russians and, one day, superseding them. I decided to leave for Central Europe, which seemed to be the focus of events to come. (The condition of my wife, who was now on the verge of tuberculosis as a result of all the privations, was another factor that encouraged me in this direction.) Zinoviev and the comrades on the Executive offered me a post in Berlin, working in illegality. If danger was within us, salvation must lie within us no less.

5

EUROPE AT THE DARK CROSSROADS

1922—1926

The train crossed a dismal no-man's-land furrowed with abandoned trenches, bristling with barbed wire. Soldiers in grey greatcoats, wearing the red star on their cloth helmets, watched us sadly as we went by. They were gaunt and grey as the earth. Farewell, comrades!

From Narva onwards, Narva the first town in Estonia, with its ancient gabled houses in the old German style, one suddenly breathed an air that was both less heavy and less bracing. We were coming from a huge entrenched camp governed by the harsh laws of congealed idealism, and entering instead a small, neat, comfortable bourgeois province whose modest shops we viewed as opulent and whose elaborate uniforms appeared loathsome and grotesque. With its puny million of inhabitants, without an economic hinterland, Estonia made a serious pretence at being a modern State, complete with Parliament, generals, and foreign diplomacy. Three parts Russified, it was now unlearning the language of Tolstoy, dismissing the Russian teachers from the University of Dorpat (now Tartu), and conjuring up a national intelligentsia lacking any idiom in common with the rest of the world. How long would it last, and at what price?

At Tallinn (lately Reval), I stopped, overwhelmed with emotion, in front of some houses that were being built. I had seen so much destruction that the simple work of bricklayers moved me deeply. From its hill the old castle dominated the empty streets, which were paved with the little pointed cobbles of medieval days. A

horse-drawn omnibus went along a street lined with shops and cafés
that sold pastries. At the sight of any one of these shops, our children
of Russia would have shouted for joy. In the Volga territories the
children of Russia were turning into living skeletons, hundreds of
thousands of them. Better than through any theory, I now understood the meaning of the politics of 'self-determination of nationalities', raised as it was to perfection by the blockade of the Revolution.

Myself, my wife Liuba, and my son Vladimir, who was not yet
a year old, were travelling illegally; it was, however, an easy form of
illegality. From Petrograd as far as Stettin and several other Western
cities, there were no obstacles in our path. There were a dozen of us,
delegates and agents of the International, discreetly (or sometimes
openly) accompanied by a diplomatic courier named Slivkin, a
strapping, jovial young man who was entrusted with every imaginable variety of smuggling, and had bought over all the police,
customs, and frontier officials along our itinerary. At the last
moment we had discovered that the O.M.S. office (*Otdiel Mezh-
dunarodnoi Sviazy*, or International Relations Section of the Comintern Executive) had, in entering the details on our Belgian passports,
forgotten to mention our child. . . .

'That's nothing serious,' Slivkin told me. 'During the frontier
examinations I'll make a show of playing with him.' At Stettin
he put himself to more trouble in getting an 'invalid' through:
a tall, thin young man with dark, piercing eyes and an ashen face,
sought by every policeman in the Reich as one of the organizers
(Bela Kun was another) of the March 1921 insurrection. This was
Guralski, whose real name was Heifitz, once a militant in the
Jewish Bund, and now one of the hardest-working agents of the
International.

Without any difficulty, I bought from the Berlin *Polizeipräsidium*,
at the price of ten dollars and a few cigars, a genuine residence
permit which, moreover, transformed me from a Belgian into a Pole.
Soon I had to change my nationality again, this time into a Lithuan-
ian, since the cafés in Berlin were plastered with notices saying:
'No Poles served here.' It was the time when Poland had just
annexed several mining districts in Upper Silesia, although a
plebiscite had yielded a result which in fact favoured the Reich.
Germany was visibly gripped by a cold fury.

Inside post-Versailles Germany, governed as it was by the

Social-Democratic President Ebert, and by the most democratic of republican constitutions, one breathed in the atmosphere of a collapsing world. Everything was just in its place: people were unassuming, kindly, industrious, bankrupt, wretched, debauched and resentful. Right in the middle of town, beyond the dark Spree and the Friedrichstrasse, a huge railway station was being built. Bemedalled cripples from the Great War sold matches outside night-clubs in which girls, who had a price just like everything else, danced naked among the flower-decked tables of the diners. Capitalism was running riot, apparently under the inspiration of Hugo Stinnes,[1] and accumulating immense fortunes in the midst of insolvency. Everything was for sale: the daughters of the bourgeoisie in the bars, the daughters of the people in the streets, officials, import and export licences, State papers, businesses in whose prospects nobody believed. The fat dollar and the puny, puffed-up coin of the victors ruled the roost, buying up everything, even human souls if they could. The Allied military missions, burdened with the impossible task of controlling disarmament, walked around in their smart uniforms, surrounded by a polite but no less obvious hatred.

Permanent conspiracies of various sorts went on in limitless ramifications: the conspiracy of Rhineland separatists, financed from abroad, the conspiracy of reactionary military leagues, and the conspiracy of revolutionaries: our own. In philosophic language, Oswald Spengler proclaimed the Decline of the West: come, look at the corpse of Egypt, ponder on the end of Rome. The revolutionary poets were publishing 'Dämmerung der Menschen' (*The Twilight of Mankind*). The portraits of Oskar Kokoschka palpitated in all their lines, colours, and volumes with a cosmic neurosis; the metallic touch of George Grosz traced the silhouettes of piggy bourgeois and robot jailers, with ghastly prisoners and workers living like grubs beneath them. Barlach made statues of peasants stupefied in fear.

I myself wrote:

> *Life is like a sickness:*
> *Red-hot iron the only cure*
> *But instead they are using poisons.*

[1] Hugo Stinnes (1870–1924): a German industrialist who put his enormous fortune at the service of Nationalist interests; a power behind the Press, most of which was controlled by him, and in the general economy.

The little pointed red-brick churches slumbered on the edges of squares which were carved up into allotments. The Reichswehr's choicest old sweats, in heavy helmets, guarded a War Office whose windows were adorned with flowers. Raphael's Madonna, from within her brilliantly-lit room in the Dresden gallery, gazed deeply, darkly and goldenly at all comers. Organization had been so perfected that even in the utter solitude of the Saxony or Harz forests, I found waste-paper baskets and signboards saying '*Schönes Blick*'—Recommended or (as it were) Starred Landscape. At night the towns were magnificently lit up. After the comparison of our Russian penury, affluence had a lasting shock-effect.

Germany was bled white. Nobody there had any real confidence in the future, and practically nobody had any idea of the public good. The capitalists lived in terror of the revolution. The impoverished petty-bourgeoisie saw the old manners and hopes of yesterday vanishing beneath their eyes. Only the Social-Democrats believed in the future of capitalism, in the stabilization of German democracy and even in the intelligence and benevolence of the victors of Versailles! They had the enlightened, optimistic attitudes of the liberal bourgeoisie of 1848. The youth, which was nationalistic and Socialist-inclined, would have nothing to do with them. My impression was that young people hoped for a revolution, and for an alliance with Russia to wage a revolutionary war. Energy, when it was divorced from reason, took refuge in the military leagues; where it was coloured by dogmatic reasoning, it gathered around the Communist Party. Charles Rappoport, pulling a wry smile on his bearded, cynical face, said to me, 'There will be no German revolution for the same reason that there will be no counter-revolution in Russia: people are too tired and too hungry.'

Seen from here, the Russian Revolution appeared as a superb exploit. It preserved almost all its halo of newly-arisen justice and organization, as well as of unprecedented democracy. This was the case both with us and with the general public, and even with many reactionaries. The Social-Democrats were the only people who saw nothing but the cost of the Revolution, its despotic character, the famine and the long wars. Our Soviet poverty, our improvised egalitarianism (with its very modest privileges for the rulers), our blazing creative will and revolutionists' dedication contrasted with the brutal self-seeking of speculation, the arrogant, imbecile luxury of the rich, and the shameful destitution of the masses; and so we could easily forgive the Revolution her unbending harshness, her errors and Spartan ways. In this decomposing bourgeois world we recovered our confidence.

I was on the editorial staff of *Inprekorr*, the Press agency of the Comintern Executive, which published copious material, intended for the Labour Press of the whole world, in three languages, German, English, and French. At my office at the *Rote Fahne*, I was successively Siegfried and Gottlieb; in town I was Dr. Albert, on my papers Viktor Klein and, in my journeys to Russia, Alexei Berlovsky, a former Russian prisoner-of-war in Germany. Victor Serge datelined his articles (which were reprinted as far away as China) from Kiev, a city to which, as it happened, I had never been. I appeared only very seldom at the Soviet Legation in the Unter den Linden where, all the same, I managed to meet Krestinsky and Yakubovich. If I chanced to pass Radek on the Kurfürstendamm, we would exchange a knowing glance, but never greet one another, in case one of us was being followed.

At Grunewald I used to visit a friendly house, occupied by a celebrated French Communist, living (naturally) under a false name; in the next-door garden we could see a stout gentleman taking a stroll among his rose-bushes: Captain Eckhart, one of the leaders of the 'Black' (i.e. secret) Reichswehr and the military conspiracy. At Zehlendorff, in a rose-pink, solid-looking villa shaded by tall pines (this belonged to Eduard Fuchs, who was an active militant), we outlaws and emissaries of the International would meet from time to time, to talk Socialism or hear a little music. The guests there included Radek, the Vuyovich brothers, Otto Pohl (the Austrian Ambassador), L.-O. Frossard, and various Russians. Fuchs, a social historian, was a collector of works by Daumier and Slevogt, Chinese and Japanese *objets d'art*, and obscure facts about the dark corners of the German Revolution. A man on the fringe of the Communist movement, he was still rendering it services which were by no means devoid of risk.

Several times I just missed being arrested in the most idiotic way. When I was on the point of entering the doorway to the *Rote Fahne* office, my wife held me back by the arm: 'Let's walk on quickly, come on!' The vestibule was full of green *Schutzpolizei* uniforms. All the same it was a good idea to post them so openly.

I took a small, separate office away in town as a commercial broker —what brand of commerce, I never discovered.

The editorial staff of *Inprekorr*, the intellectual and political mentor of the world Communist movement, was of an outstanding mediocrity. In charge was Gyula Alpári, once a high official in the Hungarian Soviet régime, a bloated, artful and well-informed individual, whose sole conception of his role was already that of a functionary discreetly heading, even through illegality, for an undisturbed career. He never committed himself on any issue, but rode along passively and gently in a spirit of revolutionary conformism awaiting its due reward. He would explain to me, grinning fatly: 'When a pretty girl says No, it means Yes; when a diplomat says Yes, it means No; when I say Yes or No, it means neither Yes nor No. . . .'

The German section was run by two deputies of the Prussian *Landtag*, Bartz, the cartoonists' image of the petty official behind his little window, and Franz Dahlem, a young man with hard features, a prominent nose and expressionless eyes: Dahlem, the toiler without personality, the militant without doubts, the fact-gatherer without thoughts, who never asked himself a question of the slightest vital interest but only carried out, all punctiliously, every instruction and directive he received. This was the Communist N.C.O. type, neither a blockhead nor a thinker: obedient only. Bartz has died, a faithful working-class Deputy; Alpári continued his career as Comintern agent right up to the fall of Paris; Franz Dahlem, after Thaelmann's arrest, became the leader of the German Communist Party, was interned in France, and then handed over to the Gestapo by the Vichy Government, in all likelihood to his death.[1] He had conscientiously performed all the infamous routines of totalitarian Communism; he will die (if he has not already died) like a good N.C.O., courageously. Already around 1922, the International was unintentionally modelling factotum officials, who were prepared to give passive obedience.

The march on Rome and the rise of Mussolini were understood by no one in the International except a few isolated militants, who included myself since I had followed the progress of Fascism from

[1] Dahlem survived, becoming a Politburo member and head of the cadres section of the E. German S.E.D.; in 1953, dismissed from all posts for 'political blindness towards imperialist agents'; in 1956-7 reinstated in some posts (Central Committee, Ministry for Higher Education in the G.D.R.); now (1977) writing his memoirs.

fairly close quarters. The opinion of the leadership was that this was a piece of reactionary buffoonery which would soon die away and open the path to revolution. I opposed this view, saying that this new variety of counter-revolution had taken the Russian Revolution as its schoolmaster in matters of repression and mass-manipulation through propaganda; further, it had succeeded in recruiting a host of disillusioned, power-hungry ex-revolutionaries; consequently, its rule would last for years.

The International and the Soviet Government were proceeding along two parallel dimensions, and with two distinct objectives: first, to form disciplined parties over the whole of Europe with a view to events to come; secondly, to achieve toleration from the capitalist world and thence credits for the reconstruction of Russia. If such credits had been forthcoming, the Soviet system would probably have evolved in a liberal direction. I know that, at the time of the Genoa Conference, in May 1922, Lenin and Kamenev were considering the revival of some degree of Press freedom; there was talk of allowing a non-Party daily to be published in Moscow. A certain religious toleration was also envisaged, although the poverty of the State necessitated the seizure of precious metals from the churches, a measure which led to innumerable clashes and subsequent executions. Genoa was a setback for Russia, despite the flexibility displayed by Chicherin and Rakovsky. Chicherin made up for his losses at Rapallo, where he signed a treaty of friendship with Germany, thus ranging the Soviet Union decisively on the side of the losers of Versailles.

The Conference of the Three Internationals assembled the fraternal enemies for the first time around the same table (in one of the study-rooms in the Reichstag): leaders of the Socialist International, leaders of the Two-and-a-Half International (as we mockingly called the little groups conglomerated midway between the reformists and the Bolsheviks), leaders of the Third International. I attended the conference in my capacity as a journalist. These men presented a striking physical contrast. The Socialists, Abramovich, Vandervelde, and Friedrich Adler had the fine profiles of Western intellectuals and the behaviour of competent lawyers; their whole comportment expressed moderation. Facing them was Clara Zetkin's solid, powerful old face, the mobile, sardonic features of Radek, and Bukharin's impervious geniality. The Socialists insisted—and with good reason—that political persecution in Russia must be ended. Bukharin told me, 'That's only an excuse. Those people are determined never to fight for Socialism'; and he added, as though by way of a directive, 'Our Press must attack them mercilessly.'

The trial of the Central Committee of the Russian Social-Revolutionary Party actually ruined any chance of co-operation. The S.-R.s had taken part in the Civil War, against us. In 1918, Semionov, one of their terrorists, had organized the assassination in Petrograd of the Bolshevik orator Volodarsky; Dora Kaplan had shot Lenin. Semionov embraced Bolshevism and made a remarkably full confession. . . . The background to the attempts against Lenin was closely investigated—the authors of the first attempt, in Petrograd, had meanwhile joined the Communist Party—and the trial ended with a suspended death-sentence on the twelve principal defendants, who included Gotz, Timofeyev, and Gerstein.

From Berlin, I observed the proceedings with great distress. Now that the Civil War was over, were we going to shed the blood of a defeated party which, in the old days, had furnished the Revolution with so many of its heroes? The Politbureau hesitated. I heard it said: 'We are moving towards an inevitable collision with the peasantry. This peasant party has certain prospects; consequently it must be beheaded.'

I conspired with several friends to try and prevent this calamity. Clara Zetkin, Jacques Sadoul and Souvarine exerted pressure towards the same end; Maxim Gorky sent Lenin a letter breaking off all relations. . . . No blood was spilt. Thirteen years later, I was to see the aged Gerstein die in almost complete destitution, deported to Orenburg. He was an unyielding, conscience-racked idealist who until his last breath remained loyal to his democratic beliefs. Gotz was deported for a second time in 1936 to a town on the Volga.[1]

Shortly afterwards, at the end of 1922, I paid a short visit to Moscow. Russia was returning to life; Petrograd was bandaging its wounds and emerging from dilapidation. Night-time, with the pitiful state of illumination, exuded a terrible depression, but people

---

[1] Abraham R. Gotz (1882–1937), a former Social-Revolutionary terrorist, and later a strong supporter of Kerensky, was released in 1927. He then worked for many years for the State Bank. It is believed that Stalin had him shot in 1937.

were no longer hungry and a brisk pace of living was in evidence everywhere. The Terror had ceased, without being formally abolished, and everyone tried hard to forget the nightmare of arrests and executions. A new literature was bursting out in the 'Serapion Brothers' circle and among the writers, yesterday unknown, who overnight were now counted among the great: Boris Pilniak, Vsevolod Ivanov, Konstantin Fedin.[1] Their works were intense and impetuous, saturated with virile humanism and a critical spirit. They were rebuked because they were not at all Communistic, indeed very far from being so; but they were published, they were loved. The great tradition of Russian literature, interrupted during the stormy years, was being born again in the second year of peace! It was miraculous.

Small traders were springing up everywhere, crowds swarmed over the markets, the taverns exhaled their music, barefoot youngsters ran in the streets at dawn, following the cabs to offer flowers to lovers. There were plenty of beggars, but they were not dying of hunger. In official circles they were beginning to talk of the Reconstruction Plan advocated by Trotsky. It was a nation in convalescence, a nation on the march.

At the Kremlin I found the familiar atmosphere still there. An enlarged session of the Comintern Executive was studying certain problems whose nature escapes my memory. At it I met Amadeo Bordiga, gloomier, sturdier, and more quarrelsome than ever before, this time picking a quarrel over revolutionary morality. Zinoviev listened to him with a smile.

---

[1] Boris Pilniak (1894–?): novelist, not a Communist Party member; author of *The Story of An Unextinguished Moon* (1926), dealing with the touchy theme of Frunze's death after an operation (ordered by Stalin); *Red Wood* (1929); *The Volga Flows Into The Caspian Sea* (1930), a novel on the Five-Year Plan. Disappeared in 1937. Vsevolod Ivanov (1895–1963): led a varied life as sailor, actor, circus juggler, typesetter, comedian, and wrestler; joined the Red Army in 1917; early stories on the Civil War (*Partisans, Armoured Train No. 1469*); *Adventures Of A Fakir* (1934–5); memoirs of Maxim Gorky (1953); novels on the Second World War. Konstantin Fedin (1892–1963): early works inspired by his experiences as a soldier and prisoner-of-war in 1914–18; Red Army journalist and volunteer (1918); pessimistic at first regarding the future of the intelligentsia, but later adapted himself. Later novels *Early Joys, No Ordinary Summer*; now head of the Soviet Writers' Union, and generally held to be a liberalizing influence. Serge retained a very high opinion of Fedin's record and integrity as a writer (see the excerpt from Serge's *Diaries* in the *New International*, July–August 1950).

Corruption, servility, intrigue, backstage tale-bearing, and the official mentality began to assume an increasing role in the functioning of the International. The worst of it was that anybody who wanted to preserve any influence or political office had to kowtow persistently to the Russians and their emissaries. Besides, they had control of the cash, and the other parties presented the appearance of poor relations. Led by politicians accustomed to bourgeois living, these displayed no capacity for propaganda or action. The International would employ two or three methods to breathe some life into them: it would put 'grey eminences' in charge of them, who were mostly Russian (and therefore strangers to the Western mind), as well as being devotees of Zinoviev; it sent them sizeable funds; or it would remove the old time-honoured politicians and replace them with young militants who were sometimes no more than young careerists. The Parties went from one crisis to another.

At the crossroads of Berlin, I encountered many delegates and emissaries. They included a young engineer from Saint-Denis named Jacques Doriot, who was in high esteem as a 'real force'.[1] Frossard assured me of his intention to serve the Russian Revolution without falling back into the ways of the old Parliamentary Socialism of the Third Republic. Pierre Sémard, secretary of the railwaymen's union, a tall, poised man with a face typical of the Paris worker, spoke of the proletarianizing of the Party. Louis Sellier went into ecstasies over financial reform in Soviet Russia, a subject of which I immediately saw that he knew nothing.

Frossard broke with the International a few months later.[2] Sémard was to remain loyal to the Party till his death, despite many humiliations, despite even the atrocious allegation that he had been a police agent, a charge with which he was hypocritically smeared when he was to be removed from the leadership. (The Nazis shot him in Paris on 15 April 1942.)

---

[1] Jacques Doriot (1898–1945): subsequently built up a strong following in the working-class Paris suburb of St. Denis; he opposed the 'Social-Fascist' line of the Comintern, and broke with the French Communist Party in 1934, advocating a 'Popular Front' with Socialists and bourgeois-liberals. After being unseated in St. Denis, founded the *Parti Populaire Français*, which speedily became a blatant fascist organization. During the Occupation a virulent French Nazi; fought on the Russian front; killed by an Allied plane while travelling in a car.

[2] Frossard rejoined the Socialist Party in 1924, and became a 'moderate'; he left the Socialist Party in 1935 to become Minister of Labour in a succession of bourgeois Cabinets.

Marcel Cachin would relate how he had exhorted Lenin not to march on Warsaw; oh, if only people had listened to him! Cachin was likeable and open-hearted. He had the greying hair and moustachioed face of an old sailor or miner, a passionate voice, and a relentlessly perfect French diction, appropriate for the Parliamentary orator that he was. His thinking was purely that of a platform speaker; he worshipped the Party and lived exclusively on his popularity. To keep his reputation going he would strive always to follow the strongest current of opinion, which he was quick to smell out. A rather intelligent man, who could see practically everything that was going on, he—for a long time I am sure—experienced considerable anguish; but he never rebelled. Where would he have been without his Party, his Parliament, etc?

The crisis over the reparations imposed on Germany by the Versailles Treaty grew worse from day to day. When Vorovsky, the old Marxist humanist and then Soviet Ambassador to Italy, died in Lausanne, riddled with bullets by a young White Russian *émigré*, the atmosphere in Germany was so acute that an order from Moscow came insisting on a great Communist and pro-Soviet demonstration while the corpse was in transit across our territory. The funeral van arrived at the Silesia station on a foggy evening; the gloomy building was surrounded by a dense crowd, complete with red banners. Radek spoke from a lorry laden with flowers and bristling with flags. Torches flamed all around him. His strident voice was carried away in the electric night-air, but his short, austere silhouette could be clearly distinguished. Krestinsky,[1] the Ambassador, followed the procession on foot, protected only by a group of German Y.C.L.ers.

Krestinsky was a man of outstanding intelligence, discretion and courage. His whole life was dedicated to the Party of the Revolution but he was there as a sort of exile, having been dismissed from the General Secretaryship because of his democratic inclinations. He was still young, and astoundingly myopic, so that his shrewd eyes, hidden behind lenses a quarter of an inch thick, seemed to have a timid expression. With his tall, bare skull and his wisp of dark beard,

---

[1] Nikolai N. Krestinsky (1883–1938): a Bolshevik since 1907, repeatedly arrested; People's Commissar for Finance after 1917, later Deputy Commissar for Foreign Affairs; Secretary of the Central Committee 1919–21; defendant in the 1938 Bukharin–Rykov trial; repudiated his confession on the first day and repudiated the repudiation on the next; sentenced to be shot.

he made one think of a scholar; actually he was a great practical technician of Socialism. He was against taking unnecessary risks, but was not afraid of them; indeed he was quite ready, if it came to it, to defend his Embassy at pistol-point, along with his secretaries and office staff. On that evening he refused to take precautions for his own safety, saying that it was proper that Soviet Russia's Ambassador to Berlin should expose himself to a little danger. The torchlight demonstration around Vorovsky's coffin marked the opening of the period of revolutionary mobilization.

The Cuno Government announced that Germany was incapable of paying any more reparations. In this way the *Schwerindustrie* which backed the Government held over the head of Europe the threat of the Reich's bankruptcy and even of a revolution. Poincaré had the Ruhr occupied by French troops, who shot a nationalist agitator named Schlageter. French agents were at work creating a separatist movement in the Rhineland. Events, which I followed hourly, were hurrying onward at a dizzying pace. There was catastrophic inflation, speculation in currency; the rate of exchange of the dollar changed as often as twice a day and, in between telephone-calls heralding the latest rise, the holders of the precious greenbacks issued by the Federal banks of America stripped the shops of all their goods. . . . The central thoroughfares of the big towns could always be seen packed with people running along holding parcels. The Germans, of all people, actually rioted outside bakeries and grocers' shops; there was no rationing to inhibit them. Mobs loitered in the streets. How many trillions did it cost to stamp a letter? At the pay-desk of a Wertheim store I saw an old lady, with a black lace neckband, taking out of her handbag some hundred-mark notes dating from the previous year, the age of Walter Rathenau.

'But they are not worth anything now, *gnädige Frau* (honoured lady).'

'What do you mean? I don't understand. . . .' People guffawed at her. Walter Rathenau lay in his grave, his body hacked all over: this notable Jew had dreamed of a new, intelligently organized German capitalism; and he had held discussions on the subject with Radek.

Not far from the Alexanderplatz and the *Polizeipräsidium*, a little shop was being looted, in the most orderly manner. Nobody is to take more than three tins of food, see! Proletarian discipline. In

another place I saw a shoe-business being looted. Two volunteers kept watch outside while people rapidly tried shoe after shoe for size; some, who had not found shoes to fit, came out scrupulously empty-handed. . . .

The working-class women of Wedding, Neukolln, and Moabit had the grey complexions that I had first seen on convicts in the central jails, and subsequently among the inhabitants of the famished towns of the Russian Revolution. Few lights at the windows, dim groups in the streets. Each day brought its windfall of strikes, and every night the sinister silence echoed with revolver-shots. The voice of the agitator would deliver a commentary in the street, surrounded by faces. The safe Social-Democrat, angry in a safe sort of way, the eager Communists, the patriotic member of the clandestine Leagues were all practically agreed: Versailles is a noose around the German nation's neck; woe unto France, woe unto Poland, woe unto capitalism! The Communists had an attractive scheme: industrial Germany and agricultural Russia could unite to save the world. Radek pushed through his 'Schlageter tactic' of conciliation with the Nationalists. It's playing with fire—all right, let's play with fire! Where shall we begin? Our agitators told us, with a word that snapped out of their mouths: *Loschlagen!*—Strike out! The decision was taken: we strike. After careful and thorough preparations, we have only to choose the moment. Trotsky's talks to the Moscow Military School are published in several languages; their subject—'*Can one lay down the date of a revolution in advance?*' Red Saxony and Thuringia, ruled by working-class governments (Communist and Social-Democrat) recruit two Red divisions. Arms arrive from Czechoslovakia; more are sold by the Reichswehr, and the dollars to pay for them come from Russia. (The consequence is that the Reichswehr deliver a wagonload of carbines one nightfall and, once they have their hands on the brand-new dollars, inform the *Schutzpolizei*, who come at dawn to seize the truck. . . .) The young militants have their orders to establish secret links with the troops; the railway workers, to shunt away and camouflage the ammunitions-wagons; the comrades in charge of transport, to look sharp, for God's sake! At night, outside the barred gates of the barracks, girls whose plaits are drawn into a topknot flirt with helmeted young men. 'You'll bring out some grenades, won't you, dear?' *Liebeslied* and sweet romance. . . .

Will the masses follow us? The Party makes up its mind only
after the first big strikes in the Rhineland; it has held back the
movement so as not to dissipate its forces. Are our forces gathering
or weakening? Hunger has a habit of unnerving men. When the
International has decided everything, what will be going on in the
heads of the average Social-Democrat (who distrusts Communists)
and the man in the street? From Moscow, where the Executive is in
session, Boris Souvarine writes to me, 'We are trying to put ourselves
into Lenin's shoes. . . .'

The Executive fixes the date of the uprising as 25 October, the
anniversary of the seizure of power in Petrograd in 1917. At this
moment the difference in dates between the Julian and Gregorian
calendars is of small importance! I reply to Souvarine, and write to
other contacts in Moscow, to the effect that unless the Party's
initiative joins with the spontaneous movement of the masses, it is
doomed beforehand. Every day I learn of stocks of arms being seized.
The tense expectation in the working-class districts seems to be
slackening strangely. The unemployed are passing, by swift stages,
from an insurgent enthusiasm into weary resignation.

Voya Vuyovich arrives from Moscow: indented forehead, and
grey eyes lighting up his young face. I knew of his history as a
militant which had begun during the retreat from Serbia. Voya
became a Socialist through the fact that among this beaten rabble
there were men who could still think calmly. Then came imprisonment in France, little committees, the International, illegal
journeys, secret messages, and factional intrigue inside the old
Socialist parties. Voya was one of the hidden architects of the split
in the Italian Socialist Party at its Leghorn Congress.

He tells me: 'Our propaganda among occupation-troops in the
Ruhr has brought useful results. A police-spy has been disposed
of in Cologne. . . .' Voya believes that, on the day, we shall win.
'Everything is going to be much better than in Russia. . . .' I hope
you are right, Voya.

Other comrades are forming 'mopping-up' squads with a view
to the aftermath of the rising: these are to liquidate the leading staff
of the counter-revolution. Our top activists are full of zest, but they
are the only ones to be so. A few days before the uprising a militant
from the military section of the *Kommunistische Partei Deutschlands*
gazed into my eyes when I put the question to him, and replied:

'We shall make a good showing when we get defeated, but we shall be defeated all the same.' We all feel like this: but meanwhile the Central Committee of the K.P.D. is allotting the portfolios of a commissars' Cabinet to its members, and Koenen, with his ginger goatee and his schoolmaster's specs, explains to us on behalf of the Central Committee's Information Department that everything is going along wonderfully. Even on the day after our main stocks of arms in Berlin have been seized, he is still proving it. Chance is my principal informer, an excellent one too. I learn that a Party official has been arrested coming out of Willi Münzenberg's house;[1] his briefcase actually contained our arms-accounts, intended for the eyes of the Comintern Executive. Thus the Party has been more or less disarmed in the capital. I also learn that the Government has decided in principle to dissolve it. I warn the members of the Central Committee of these facts, indirectly since it is now impossible for me to see them personally. They send a reply to the effect that this is indeed a current rumour in the streets, but that they know what's what; no one will dare to interfere! 'Of course, we may lose, in which case. . . .' They have already lost, but they still have no inkling that this is so.

Everything is set for the seizure of power on 25 October 1923! Red Saxony and Thuringia are to lead. In accordance with Comintern directives, Brandler, Heckert and Böttcher have entered the Dresden Cabinet under the Social-Democrat Zeigner. The Communists see this Government as the forerunner of insurrection; the Social-Democrats probably only as one more crisis-Cabinet: everything will calm down, just like all the other times. On the 21st, a conference of Factory Committees meets at Chemnitz; this foreshadows the Congress of Workers' Councils which will proclaim the dictatorship of the proletariat. The Workers' Hundreds stand guard outside it: young lads, proud to carry the five-pointed star on their sports shirts, or old Spartakists who have lived through November 1918, the rising of January 1919, the murder, in public, in broad daylight, of Karl and Rosa, the dictatorship of the man of blood, Gustav

[1] Willi Münzenberg (1889–1940): German Communist leader; Secretary of the International Socialist Youth League 1914–21, and then of the Young Communist International; later an outstanding behind-the-scenes organizer of many 'front' movements; broke with the Party in 1937 after the Moscow Trials; found hanged in France in 1940 after escaping from an internment-camp. His death is variously ascribed to the Gestapo and the N.K.V.D.

Noske, the worthy Social-Democrat. These men are ready to do anything that they may be asked. I live with them, they ask me timid questions about Russia, the tall youngsters are studying the technique of street-fighting.

While the Chemnitz conference is on, and Eberlein is seeing to secret preparations in Berlin, the Russian military experts review the strategic situation. They include Yuri Piatakov, who has experience of civil war in the Ukraine, and (I think) Lozovsky. This supply of arms would scarcely be enough even for fighting the campaigns around Kiev! There is nothing for it but to call the rising off. The lads return from Chemnitz, with long faces. Couriers leave with counter-orders for every *Bezirk* (or region) in the country. Will we have the chance to recover our breath and make up our armaments? It would be mad to think so. There are few of us who realize the full extent of the defeat in the first moments that follow.

The counter-order has not reached Hamburg; there 300 Communists start the revolution. The town is frozen in silence and tense expectation; they go off, filled with a terrible enthusiasm, methodically organized. The police outposts fall one after the other, and sharpshooters take up their positions in the top windows over the main thoroughfares. Hamburg is taken, taken by the 300! The whole of Germany has not moved an inch, and neither for that matter has Hamburg itself. The housewives go out shopping, while the police venture out again, having regained their confidence, and start firing against invisible rebels who melt away as they approach. The workers, at home, await the outcome with impatience.

'Another *putsch*,' say the Social-Democrats, 'will you never learn anything after all?' We answer back, 'And you—what have you learnt?' The Left of the Party denounces the leadership, who are Rightists: Thalheimer the dialectician and Brandler the hump-backed bricklayer with malice in his eyes. The Left wonders if the Comintern Executive is at last going to recognize that 'we are the real ones', the only revolutionaries, the only possible leadership for a German revolution. Ruth Fischer, Arkadi Maslow, Heinz Neumann, and Arthur Rosenberg believe that their hour has come. I have met Rosenberg on a number of occasions at the *Rote Fahne*. This brilliant intellectual gives me a slight jolt by asking 'Do you really think that the Russians want a German revolution?' He doubts if they do. Heinz Neumann, a pale, mocking young man, plays at conspiracy with the gusto of a romantic actor, but there is no acting in his courage. He carries false whiskers in his pocket; he has just escaped from a police station in the Rhineland; a house he is in is surrounded, and he gets away at the last minute; he purloins letters addressed to the comrades who are lodging him, members of the opposing tendency in the Party; he conducts, simultaneously, three or four different spheres of activity: one for the Party, one for the Left's Party-within-the-Party, and yet others more dangerous in nature— not forgetting the ladies. . . . Twenty-five years old, he is a young rogue who argues like a cynic. He has an infant prodigy's capacity for absorbing knowledge, a sense of history, merciless views on his elders, and a love for a theoretical working class besides which the actual working class is only highly imperfect human material.

'There are no more real Bolsheviks in Germany. They are all putrid with moderation, wisdom, detachable collars and respect for the *Polizeipräsident*—Do not Break the Glass in the Street Lamps, and all that. The proletariat is respectability itself. We shall have to pass through Fascism before they get cured of all that clap.' Heinz came several times, at dead of night, to air these opinions to me: he, with all the police of Germany after him, coming to see me, a man under observation, living just opposite the Lichterfelde barracks.[1]

The Social-Democratic President, Ebert, deals with the tail-end of the disturbances by granting full powers to General von Seeckt, whose ascetic face suddenly looms out from the newspapers. General Müller enters Dresden with a regiment and dismisses the Zeigner Government; there is no resistance. Every morning von Seeckt goes for a morning ride in the Tiergarten, followed by an *aide-de-camp*. On his route Heinz Neumann stations two workers, good marksmen and armed with revolvers. Twice these workers lose their nerve, and von Seeckt passes on. . . .

On 9 November Adolf Hitler, the puny agitator from a tiny party that is stirring up trouble in Bavaria, opens his absurd *coup* in Munich. The result: one revolver-shot in the ceiling above the beer-mugs, fourteen dead in the street, and the Führer-to-be out on the rocks with an empty belly and a very comfortable prison

[1] Neumann later organized the Canton Communist uprising in 1927. After the rise to power of Nazism, he took refuge in the Soviet Union and perished in the purges of 1937; his widow was handed over to the Gestapo after the Nazi-Soviet Pact.

waiting for him. See now, the Left and the Right are both absolutely useless!

The Weimar Republic only survives the crisis of October to November 1923 through the weight of the masses' inertia. Its opponents, whether revolutionary or counter-revolutionary, have neither guts nor following. The bulk of the population is uninvolved, since it has no confidence in either of them. It will take years of deception before the unemployed will be seen either selling themselves for a crust to the Nazi Party or, like others, hopelessly following a confused ideal. Nothing could be done without the Social-Democratic masses; and these were divided into officials with a stake in the foundering social system and canny workers ridden by fear of the revolution: as for revolution, the Russian one, the only one that had succeeded, had suffered too much famine, waged too much terror, and strangled too much freedom in its early years. Trotsky is to explain the German defeat in terms of 'the crisis of revolutionary leadership', but that crisis is itself an expression of two other crises: that of popular consciousness, and that of an already bureaucratized International.

There had been some talk of summoning Trotsky to Germany in the decisive hours; a suggestion which annoyed Zinoviev intensely: why not he himself, for that matter? The Politbureau had decided in principle to go as far as military intervention, if necessary, in support of the German rising; and divisions of troops were making ready. But now the E.C.C.I., solicitous above all for its own prestige, condemns the 'opportunism' and inefficiency of the two leaders of the K.P.D., Brandler and Thalheimer, who have been so incompetent in managing the German Revolution. But they did not dare move a finger without referring the matter to the Executive! But Brandler only learnt in the train that he had been made a Minister in Saxony! What's that you're saying? So you're trying to discredit the Executive, are you? Which comes first: the Communist International's reputation? Or your version of the truth, and the moral interests of individuals?

Scapegoats had to be found. Out of defeat came the lying, the suppression, the demoralizing discipline that ruins consciences. Nobody talked about the basic fault. The whole Party lived on the involuntary bluff of functionaries whose first concern was not to contradict their superiors. Misinformation was generated at the base through the personal interest of the poor wretch who, simply to keep his job, assured the *Bezirk* or Central Committee organizer that, yes, he had his fifty men available and that the fifty Mausers had been bought—when in fact he had ten men and was searching in vain to find Mausers for sale. Misinformation ascended stage by stage, through the whole hierarchy of secretaries, so that, at the end of it all, the delegate from the Central Committee of the K.P.D., could tell the President of the International, 'We are prepared', when nothing was prepared and everybody in the Party knew it was so, except those who drew up the confidential reports.

On the very morning of the proclamation of von Seeckt's dictatorship, I took the express for Prague, with my wife and four-year-old son. We had lived through critical days, working practically without money, without an identity to fall back on, and packed off in indecent haste at the last minute by the Soviet Embassy, which had no intention of compromising itself by assisting illegal workers. In the carriage some travellers asked my son, whose only fluent language was German, what he was going to do when he grew up, and he answered in a flash: '*Krieg gegen die Franzosen!*' ('War against the French!')

Prague was an oasis of urbane prosperity. Under its sober President Masaryk, it was enjoying affluence and liberty, the fruits of victory. Vienna was recovering painfully from its inflationary crisis: Austria, in the knowledge that it could not live behind its meagre frontiers, was playing for time, building workers' flats and enjoying sweet music in every café down to the smallest. I arrived with a diplomatic passport, which restored my identity with, however, some embarrassment to me, since I was not officially listed.

Andreu Nin, the secretary of the Red International of Labour Unions, who was passing through Vienna with Lozovsky, told me that Lenin was dying. Lenin still seemed to be completely conscious, but had no power to express himself or do any work. He would manage to stutter out a few words with difficulty; the heading of *Pravda* was spelt out to him letter by letter. Sometimes his eyes were heavy with a voiceless tribulation. Once, when he had felt better, he had wished to see the Kremlin again, and his work-table and telephones; he was taken to them.

'You can see him, leaning on Nadezhda Konstantinovna [Krupskaya] and Nikolai Ivanovich [Bukharin], dragging his feet weakly across his study, gazing, terrified in case he will no longer understand it, at the map on the wall, taking pencils between his fingers to make a rough signature, all like a dreamer, like a despairing old man in his second childhood. Bukharin often visits him in his country house out in the Gorky district; Bukharin makes merry in his company, and then hides behind a bush looking at him with tear-dimmed eyes. . . . It's definitely the end, my friend.'

'And afterwards?'

'Afterwards, there's going to be a riot. The unity of the Party nowadays depends upon that shadow of a man, no more than that.'

I remembered what Lenin had said to Dr. Goldenberg, an old Bolshevik who lived in Berlin and was summoned urgently by Lenin for a consultation at the beginning of his illness: 'We have demolished quite a lot! For that, certainly, we have been competent enough!'

I was travelling on a January day in 1924. The train bumped out of tunnels into vast landscapes on a mountain glittering with snow, where sombre armies of firs made a sudden descent. In this compartment full of fat, stodgy men, someone opened a newspaper and I saw: *Death of Lenin*. Then these men talked about the death, showing that they felt someone unique and very great had passed. I looked at their faces, folk from another world, Austrian petty-bourgeois closed to all new ideas, lamenting the death of a revolutionary; and Lenin was there, too, before my eyes, his hands open in the familiar gesture of demonstration, hunching a little towards the audience, marshalling the historical evidence, with his great firm forehead and the smile of a man who was sure of the truth, sure of himself. Together with a few others, this man had endowed an immense movement of faltering masses with a political consciousness that was supremely clear and resolute. Even when favourable social conditions are granted, such a human achievement is rare, unique, irreplaceable at the moment of its happening. Without it, the minds of those who marched would have been several degrees dimmer, the chances of chaos, and of defeat amid chaos, immeasurably greater; for a degree of consciousness, once lost, can never be measured.

Events continued to overwhelm us. Even where they took place at a distance I find it hard to separate them from my personal memories. All we lived for was activity integrated into history; we were interchangeable; we could immediately see the repercussions of affairs in Russia upon affairs in Germany and the Balkans; we felt linked with our comrades who, in pursuit of the same ends as we, perished or else scored some success at the other end of Europe. None of us had, in the bourgeois sense of the word, any personal existence: we changed our names, our posting and our work at the Party's need; we had just enough to live on without real material discomfort, and we were not interested in making money, or following a career, or producing a literary heritage, or leaving a name behind us; we were interested solely in the difficult business of reaching Socialism.

At 5.15 a.m. on 1 December 1924, 227 Estonian Communists, following the orders of the E.C.C.I., attacked the public buildings of Tallinn with the objective of seizing power. By 9 a.m., they were being slaughtered in all corners of the small capital. By noon, nothing was left of their ardour but splashes of blood on the little round cobbles. Yan Tomp was shot.

How could Zinoviev have initiated this imbecile adventure? The man terrified us. He refused to acknowledge the German defeat. In his eyes the rising had been only delayed and the K.P.D. was still marching to power. The riots in Cracow were enough for him to announce revolution in Poland. I felt that he was obsessed by the error in his otherwise sensible judgement which had led him in 1917 to oppose the incipient Bolshevik revolution; in consequence, he had now swung into an authoritarian and exaggerated revolutionary optimism. 'Zinoviev', we used to say, 'is Lenin's biggest mistake.'

In September of 1924 we learnt that a rebellion had just been crushed in Soviet Georgia. The comrades who came from Russia spoke of it, in their confidential discussions, with extreme bitterness. 'Collapse of our agrarian policy. . . . The whole Georgian Party, with Mdivani at their head, is in opposition to the Central Committee, and the whole country is in opposition to the Party. . . .'

Later we heard of the massacre, supervised by Sergo Ordzhonikidze, a former inmate of Schlüsselburg, an honest and scrupulous man tormented by recurrent crises of conscience. I learnt of the background to the tragedy; a people in ferment, their national pride outraged, provocation organized by the Cheka to unmask rebellious tendencies and then liquidate them; the imprisoned members of the Menshevik Central Committee of Georgia, receiving information of the preparation for the revolt, beg to be released for a few days so that they can avert irreparable disaster, even offering to take poison before they set out; they are kept inside, powerless, and later shot. . . . The political problem of the Caucasus was this: could Red Russia, as a great Power, agree that two little countries like Georgia and Azerbaijan, prone to hostile influences and bound to become a hunting-ground for foreign powers, should keep their petroleum, manganese and strategic roads all to themselves?

In Vienna we breathe the turbulent air of the Balkans. Of events there we catch only fragmentary glimpses, but these take in several vistas: propaganda, activity, whether openly acknowledged or disavowed, and secret intrigue. Bulgaria is still pregnant with revolution, despite all its previous miscarriages. In a public meeting at the Kremlin, I had heard Kolarov, an impressive deputy, and the thin Kabakchiev,[1] bearded up to his very eyes, speaking proudly of their Party, the only Socialist Party in Europe that was, like the Bolsheviks, intransigently loyal to principle. They called themselves *Tesnyaki*, The Narrows, by contrast with the broad, flabby opportunists of whatever country. They remarked that they would have already seized power if the Executive had not been dubious about the international complications; it was necessary to wait and allow Stambulisky's Peasant Party to exhaust itself and lose its credit with the rural masses, who would then turn to us. . . . While they were waiting, Professor Tsankov, supported by a military conspiracy, carried out his *coup*, in June 1923. Stambulisky, the huge frizzy-haired giant, was surprised at his country house, and straddled like a beast by brutes who murdered him with all the cruelty of primitive imagination. The powerful Communist Party, under Kolarov, Kabakchiev, and Dimitrov observed a neutrality which they justified in terms of the most strait-laced doctrinal intransigence: 'It is not for a working-class party to support the rural petty-bourgeoisie against the reactionary big bourgeoisie. . . .' When the Party was

[1] Hristo Kabakchiev (1878–1940): Comintern emissary in the early twenties; arrested and imprisoned in Bulgaria in 1923; released in 1926, joining Dimitrov and Kolarov in Russia; a member of the Soviet Communist Party in his last years.

persecuted immediately afterwards, its leaders acknowledged their mistake in Moscow and promised to set it right. It was too late. In September, the Communists took to arms, with poor support from an enfeebled and helpless peasantry. They fought, and were scattered; the noise of these relatively minor fusillades was lost in the great avalanche-roar of the advancing German Revolution. . . .

I was in Vienna when, at the beginning of April 1925, Tsar Boris, whom we dubbed 'the Butcher of the Bulgars', narrowly missed assassination; on 15 April General Kosta Georgiev fell to the bullets of a terrorist. On the 17th, the Government was assembled together for his funeral at the Cathedral of the Seven Saints in Sofia, when an explosive device shattered one of the domes. Twenty-five dead were unearthed from the rubble, including three deputies, thirteen generals, eight colonels, and eight high officials. By a singular chance the Government and the Royal Family were unscathed. The explosion had been organized by officers from the military section of the Communist Party, who were acting perhaps on their own behalf—for the Party was ravaged by dissension—or else in accordance with secret instructions; it surprised the Communists themselves, who were at once assaulted, fired on, tortured, and murdered by the troops and police. Shablin, a handsome, smiling man whom I had known in Russia, was (it seems) burnt alive in a furnace. The two men responsible for the explosion, Yankov and Minkov, were killed resisting arrest. In May, in front of 50,000 inhabitants of Sofia, three Communists were hanged, one of whom, Marko Fridman, had defended the ideas and record of the Party every inch of the way before his judges.[1] A French Communist, Eugène Léger, tried and condemned with these men, was subsequently released in obscure circumstances and took refuge in Moscow, where he disappeared. I was to discover later that he had spent a long period in the secret Isolator at Yaroslavl, whence he was transferred, now insane, to an asylum.

I became interested in the movement for Balkan Federation. The conception was noble: no other remedy was appropriate to the division of the small kindred peoples of the peninsula into feeble states, destined to be destroyed sooner or later through their mutual

---

[1] This is not strictly accurate. Before the end of the trial Fridman broke down and gave evidence on the internal organization of the Communist Party and its military section.

laceration. The Doctor, a big white-haired Bulgarian, scholarly and Parisified, would arrange appointments with me in discreet little local cafés. A taxi, and then the tram; we would head out to the vineyards, between Floridsdorf and Mödling. There we would meet a young stranger in an outsize overcoat, whom I immediately classified as a bodyguard; I thought I could see the enormous Browning revolver, the favourite weapon of Macedonians (who do not trust small bullets), bulging through his coat pocket. The overcoat-man, all smiles, hurried me along urgently: the tram again, and then we came to a village full of charming taverns, and after that to a villa, adorned with flowers like its neighbours, in which lived the last surviving leader of the Communist-influenced *La Fédération Balkanique*,[1] a former Member of the Ottoman Parliament. What, has there been an Ottoman Parliament? Oh yes, convened by Abdul Hamid, and on the day of its opening, bombs explode. . . . V——[2] rarely goes out now. Murder lies in wait for him at every street-corner, and at night trusted men stand on watch in the garden of his villa. In this very city his predecessor, Todor Panitza, was recently killed while watching a performance in a theatre. A short while before that, Panitza's predecessor, Peter Chaulev, had discovered that he was being trailed in these streets and took the train to Milan. In Milan he was murdered. A short while before that, the old leader of I.M.R.O. (*Internal Macedonian Revolutionary Organization*),[3] Todor Aleksandrov, had been killed at the end of a conference in the mountains, in which he had advocated co-operation with the Communists. I had drafted the three obituaries for the Press.

Around the great conception of Balkan Federation there swarmed hordes of secret agents, impresarios of irredentism, pedlars of the influential word, night-walking politicians engaged in six intrigues at a time; and all these smart gentlemen, with their over-gaudy

[1] *La Fédération Balkanique:* a multi-lingual review published in Vienna from 1924, and after 1931 in Frankfurt, with Communist backing but a wider appeal. It advocated a Balkan Federation including a united and independent Macedonia.

[2] V—— is Dimitar Vlahov, a leading Macedonian Communist and Comintern delegate. After 1935 he took refuge in the Soviet Union; in 1943 emerged as a partisan leader with Tito, with special responsibility for Yugoslav Macedonia, and died in 1951 as Vice-President of Yugoslavia.

[3] I.M.R.O. was a Macedonian nationalist and terrorist organization founded in 1893, and financed by a levy on all Macedonians; it was based on local activist bodies called *comitajis* which elected delegates to a national convention.

neckties, sought to harness the unbridled energy of the *Comitajis* and sell it to and fro to any buyer. There was the Italian wing, the Bulgarian wing, the Yugoslav wing, two Greek tendencies, one monarchist and one republican, ideologies, personal cliques, and vendettas. We knew the cafés in which the revolvers of any given group lay in wait, watched from the café opposite by those of another. *La Fédération Balkanique* was a focus for certain revolutionary romantics who were the survivors of other tragedies. Among them I met the Young Serbs of recent memory, friends and disciples of Vladimir Gaćinović, the Bakuninist and nationalist, who died of tuberculosis at the age of thirty after founding the group which was, on 28 June 1914, to carry out the assassination at Sarajevo. They cherished the memory of Gavrilo Princip and of the teacher Ilić. They declared that their leader, Colonel Dragutin Dimitrijević[1]—alias 'Apis', in underground circles—had, before initiating the action, been assured of support from Russia; this had been formally promised by Artamonov, the Russian Imperial military attaché in Belgrade, who had been informed of the project. I published these allegations in *Clarté* (in Paris), and heard them confirmed by a former colleague of Dimitrijević, Colonel Božin Simić, and also, more reticently, by a former Serbian Ambassador, M. Bogićević. As a consequence of this revelation, some Yugoslav friends advised me not to go too near the Yugoslav border in the course of my trips to the Wörthersee, and on no account to enter Yugoslavia; there were, they told me, certain highly confidential instructions of which I was the subject. These survivors of the Serb conspiracies against the Habsburg monarchy were shortly to join the Communist Party. In 1938 I found their names in a Communist newspaper which published the news of their expulsion. They disappeared in Russia.

Despite all these setbacks and the general atmosphere, the Russians still kept their plain integrity and abundant optimism. Men whose usefulness had been exhausted habitually ended by living in Soviet missions abroad, there to observe the decay of the bourgeois world. They were given these sinecures to keep them quiet. They included seasoned veterans of the persecution in the old

[1]Dimitrijević was the chief of Serbian Intelligence and a leading figure in the secret society called 'The Black Hand'; executed after a highly suspect trial in June 1917. Danilo Ilić was executed for his part in the assassination in February 1915; Princip, who actually shot the Archduke, was spared the death-penalty on account of his age and died in jail of tuberculosis in April 1918.

days, former Marxist exiles, and the ex-managers of those first Soviet institutions which had succeeded against everyone's expectation. Some of them were now only chatterers, nursing strained hearts and content to smoke good cigars and be driven out to the Cobenzl Restaurant. An obsequious riff-raff fussed about them, and observing their eccentricities, remarked complacently to themselves: 'That's what they are, these great revolutionaries, when you see them close up.' Of some of these men I will say nothing. But I wish to set down at this point a few character-sketches of worthy men, to whom my memory returns with affection. They typify a vanished generation.

I again met Adolf Abramovich Joffe, a little aged since I last saw him in Petrograd in the desperate days of resistance. He now reminded one of a wise physician, almost affluent in his appearance and almost comical in his gravity, who had been summoned to the bedside of a dying patient. He was now back from China and Japan, having won Sun Yat-sen for the cause of Soviet friendship. A sick man, and in disgrace because of the boldness of his views, he was accredited by the Soviet Union to the Austrian Republic, in other words to the Chancellor-Cardinal Seipel.[1] He was opposed to all adventures. He told me that a Yugoslav officers' league had made him an offer to instal, forcibly, a left-wing government in Belgrade. Stjepan Radić's Croat Peasant Party would give it support. . . . (We often talked of Stjepan Radić, who was worth far more than any Balkan politician; he was to be murdered not long afterwards in front of the whole Yugoslav Parliament.) Joffe, with his bearded Assyrian face, powerful lips, and eyes that disconcerted the newcomer, so severe was their squint, gave a vivid pout of disdain:

'They imagine that revolutions are made like that. No, thank you!' They were all for sale, *coups d'état*, dictatorships, republican leanings, pro-Soviet sympathies, shady dealings, what you like. A man like Joffe knew, better than anyone, the colossal frontier that separates revolutionary action from dubious adventurism. Others preferred not to know: these sponsored the establishment in Albania of a pro-Soviet Left Government under Monsignor Fan Noli.

[1] Mgr. Ignaz Seipel (1876–1932), Minister of Social Administration in the last Habsburg Cabinet, led the Christian-Social Party from 1922 to 1924 and was Chancellor from 1926 to 1929. While in office, encouraged the right-wing paramilitary *Heimwehr* and intrigued against the democratic constitution.

Ahmet Zogu's *putsch* followed it, and Albania passed into the Italian sphere of influence.[1]

This dark frontier-land was often skirted, as a matter of duty, by Dr. Goldstein, the Embassy Secretary. A specialist in Balkan affairs, Goldstein was tall, thin, and artful; a man of great modesty, he was quite straightforwardly a Socialist of the old breed, who carried out the worst possible directives in such a way as to do the least possible damage. Killer-squads from Sofia lay in wait for him all around the Schwartzenbergplatz. Fortunately their assignment was complicated by the fact that they had been told to liquidate him without causing any scandal. He showed me some photographs which had been taken, without my knowledge, of the contents of my drawer: 'I advise you to sack your maidservant. Some of the back-room chaps from the Whites have been paying visits to your papers; however, we have a man planted among them. . . .'

Old Kozlovsky, whose sympathetic face befitted his past as a St. Petersburg lawyer, had been our first People's Commissar of Justice. His function then was to combat excesses. He related to me how the Cheka had drawn up a document defining who was a suspect: '*Social origins:* aristocratic or bourgeois, *Education:* University. . . .' Kozlovsky took the sheet and went to knock on Lenin's door: 'Tell me, Vladimir Ilyich, surely this is a little matter for us two, isn't it?' 'The appalling imbeciles!' said Lenin. A provincial Cheka proposed in 1918 to bring back torture to make foreign spies talk. Kamenev and Kozlovsky were enraged at the idea, which received short shrift.

Yuri Kotziubinsky was a man with whom I could speak frankly of everything. His nimble life had survived only by some chance or miracle. He had been waiting in a Kiev cellar for his turn to go against the wall, when the Reds captured the town, so quickly that the Whites had no time to dispatch the last prisoners. He escaped from encircled townships, joining Piatakov and the last fighters for the Soviets who also functioned as the Government of the Ukraine. The country was subdued village by village; what was captured in the morning was often lost by nightfall. In those parts the names of the heroes of 1918 were Evgenia Bosch, Yuri Kotziubinsky, and Yuri Piatakov. He was a tall, handsome man with a

---

[1] The *coup* was in June 1924. Zogu soon afterwards assumed the royal title of King Zog.

thin line of beard round his jowl, an aquiline profile, and a head in the harmonious proportions of the young humanists of long ago, except that it was much more solidly stocked inside. Kótziubinsky was too popular among the working class of Kharkov, and so was exiled to the world. of diplomacy. He sympathized with the most radical Oppositional group, that of the 'Democratic Centralists': Sapronov, Vladimir Smirnov in the Ukraine, and Drobnis (the one shot in 1937). We would clamber up the steep slopes of the Leopoldsberg and there gaze out on the blue band of the Danube and discuss the problems of the Party. I see him now, laughing into the wind, his silk blouse, with a cord for its belt, billowing away. (From Vienna he went on to be Consul-General at Warsaw; he was shot without trial in 1937.)

Like Yuri Kotziubinsky, N—— usually wore only a Russian blouse under his jacket; but N—— only possessed one old grey suit, and had no idea that it was possible to wear anything else. Young, or rather ageless, without any official job in the Legation, without money (which he despised), known history or personal life, very Jewish, and childlike in his gaze, N—— was a courageous conspirator. His corner of the Embassy was confined to strictly secret duties; it was full of phials, chemical reactives and inks, photographic apparatus, and codes. I wondered if he had forgotten his real name as a result of changing his nationality and identity so many times (but then, what is one's 'real' name?). We talked passionately of our sick Party: sick, but what else on earth is there?

(Years went by. I had just come out of a Soviet prison when N—— called on me in Leningrad. 'Where have you come from, you old ghost?' 'From Shanghai.' Shanghai in 1928 was no sinecure. N—— had reorganized the trade unions there after the 1927 massacre. There he had met men more stoical, more cunning, more nameless than himself. 'The anarchists, too,' he remarked to me, 'they're wonderful—but what an ideology! Fit for twelve-year-old kids!' He had just learned, on his arrival back in Moscow, of the execution of Yakov Blumkin; he had sought out the comrades in the firing squad to discover how our mutual friend had passed his last moments. He came to me with the news.)

Angelica Balabanova, the first Secretary of the Comintern Executive, whose moral objections had often annoyed Lenin and Zinoviev, had just been expelled from the Third International. She lived now

sometimes in Vienna, sometimes in its outskirts, carting her possessions, those of the eternal poor student, from one furnished room to
another: the spirit-stove for tea, the small pan for omelettes, and
three cups for her guests; together with the huge picture of Felippo
Turati, the manly, glowing portrait of Matteotti,[1] files of *Avanti!*,
the correspondence of the Italian Maximalist Party, and notebooks
full of poems. Small, dark, and beginning to age, Angelica still led
her eager militant's life which, with its romantic fire, was about
three-quarters of a century too late. She should have had Mazzin-
ians and *Carbonari* around her, burning with zeal to fight for the
Universal Republic! After a life spent in the company of politicians
like Lazzari and Serrati, in whom a little of this fire still lingered,
decently displayed in their Parliamentary tactics, Angelica had
rushed to the service of the Russian Revolution (suffering in the
process a severe battering from a reactionary mob in Switzerland),
and lived in close contact with that world government of Marxism
which went by the name of the Executive of the Communist International.

It was no longer the atmosphere of Zimmerwald! Seats in the
different Commissions were adroitly packed, and couriers carrying
diamonds were sent to the fraternal Parties abroad (couriers and
diamonds both disappearing); other emissaries were sent to arrange
the expulsion of men who were still being called 'dear comrade'.
Revolutionary politics, when conducted with foresight and courage,
requires at certain decisive times the qualities of a good surgeon,
for there is no character in this world more humane and honest than
that of the good surgeon, even though he works on living flesh, amid
pain and blood. Angelica rebelled both against the political surgery
which led to the unceremonious removal of the reformist leaders
who were inclined to torpedo any offensive tactic, and against
Zinoviev's sordid little tricks of political bone-setting. She was quick
to detect the first symptoms of that moral sickness which after the
passing of some fifteen years was to bring on the death of Bolshevism.
Georg Lukács, the author of *Geschichte und Klassenbewusstsein*, once

---

[1] Felippo Turati (1857–1932): founder and leader of Italian reformist Socialism;
opposed Italian involvement in the First World War; extremely anti-Communist;
after 1926 an exile in Corsica and then France. Giacomo Matteotti (1885–1924):
Italian Socialist and anti-Fascist; peasant leader and Deputy: opposed any 'United
Front' with the Communists; fearlessly outspoken against Mussolini's violence;
murdered on Fascist instructions to silence him.

remarked to me: 'Marxists know that dirty little tricks can be performed with impunity when great deeds are being achieved; the error of some comrades is to suppose that one can produce great results simply through the performance of dirty little tricks. . . .'

Angelica gave me coffee on her window-sill and sent me her friendly criticisms for the benefit of our official publications. I recalled the days of the famine in Petrograd, when, as a present for the birth of our son, she had sent us an orange and a bar of chocolate, delicacies from another world, imported through the diplomatic bag. In her hands lay great kindness, and in her eyes a fortifying passion. I reflected that several times she had narrowly missed the death of a Rosa Luxemburg.[1]

Antonio Gramsci was living in Vienna, an industrious and Bohemian exile, late to bed and late to rise, working with the illegal Committee of the Italian Communist Party. His head was heavy, his brow high and broad, his lips thin; the whole was carried on a puny, square-shouldered, weak-chested, hump-backed body. There was grace in the movement of his fine, lanky hands. Gramsci fitted awkwardly into the humdrum of day-to-day existence, losing his way at night in familiar streets, taking the wrong train, indifferent to the comfort of his lodgings and the quality of his meals; but, intellectually, he was absolutely alive. Trained intuitively in the dialectic, quick to uncover falsehood and transfix it with the sting of irony, he viewed the world with an exceptional clarity. Once, we consulted together about the quarter-million workers who had been admitted at one stroke into the Russian Communist Party, on the day after Lenin's death. How much were these proletarians worth, if they had had to wait for the death of Vladimir Ilyich before coming to the Party?

After the example of Matteotti, like him a Deputy, like him living among menaces, a frail invalid held in both detestation and respect by Mussolini, Gramsci had remained in Rome to carry on the struggle. He was fond of telling stories about his wretched childhood; how he had failed his entry to the priesthood, for which his family had marked him out; with his short bursts of sardonic laughter he exposed certain leading figures of Fascism with whom he was closely acquainted. When the crisis in Russia began to worsen, Gramsci did

---

[1] After the Second World War, Balabanova helped to found the P.S.D.I., the pre-Western Social-Democratic party led by G. Saragat. She died in 1965.

not want to be broken in the process, so he had himself sent back to Italy by his Party: he, who was identifiable at the first glance because of his deformity and his great forehead. He was imprisoned in June 1928, together with Umberto Terracini and some others, and a fascist jail kept him outside the operation of those factional struggles whose consequence nearly everywhere was the elimination of the militants of his generation. Our years of darkness were his years of stubborn resistance. (Twelve years later, when I emerged from my period of deportation in Russia and arrived in Paris, in 1937, I was following a Popular Front demonstration when someone pushed a Communist pamphlet into my hand: it contained a picture of Antonio Gramsci, who had died on 27 April of that year in an Italian prison hospital, after eight years of captivity.)

The Hungarian emigration was deeply split. To the opposition within his Party, Bela Kun was a remarkably odious figure. He was the incarnation of intellectual inadequacy, uncertainty of will, and authoritarian corruption. Several of his opponents were starving to death in Vienna. Of these, I held Georg Lukács in greatest esteem; indeed, I owe him a great deal. A former university teacher in Budapest, and then commissar to a Red division in the front line, Lukács was a philosopher steeped in the works of Hegel, Marx, and Freud, and possessing a free-ranging and rigorous mind. He was engaged in writing a number of outstanding books which were never to see the light of day. In him I saw a first-class brain which could have endowed Communism with a true intellectual greatness if it had developed as a social movement instead of degenerating into a movement in solidarity with an authoritarian Power. Lukács' thinking led him to a totalitarian vision of Marxism within which he united all aspects of human life; his theory of the Party could be taken as either superb or disastrous, depending on the circumstances. For example, he considered that since history could not be divorced from politics, it should be written by historians in the service of the Central Committee.

One day we were discussing the problems of whether or not revolutionaries who had been condemned to death should commit suicide; this arose from the execution in 1919 at Budapest of Otto Korwin, who had been in charge of the Hungarian Cheka, and whose hanging afforded a choice spectacle for 'society' folk. 'I thought of suicide', said Lukács, 'in the hours when I was expecting to be arrested and hanged with him. I came to the conclusion that I had no right to it: a member of the Central Committee must set the example.' (I was to meet Georg Lukács and his wife later, in 1928 or 1929, in a Moscow street. He was then working at the Marx-Engels Institute; his books were being suppressed, and he lived bravely in the general fear. Although he was fairly well-disposed towards me, he did not care to shake my hand in a public place, since I was expelled and a known Oppositionist. He enjoyed a physical survival, and wrote short, spiritless articles in Comintern journals.)

I was present, in my non-existent capacity as a representative of the Soviet Press, at a Rumanian-Soviet peace conference. The head of the Soviet delegation was Leonid Serebriakov, a former metal-worker and inhabitant of Imperial prisons, a soldier for the Revolution in Siberia and all over Russia, organizer of the Soviet Railway-men's Union, reorganizer of our railways. A prominent figure in the democratic Opposition in the Party, he was, at the age of thirty-four, marked out by virtue of his moral authority, talents, and past as one of the future leaders of the Soviet State. He was sent shortly after-wards to the United States where he made a reputation as a great Socialist administrator in the world of business. Plump, vigorous in manner, fair-haired, with a full, round face and an aggressive little moustache, he kept dealing out good-humoured impudence to an elderly Rumanian diplomat of the very oldest school. The negotia-tions failed completely, thank God. (Leonid Serebriakov was to be shot in 1937.)

We had only very little contact with the Austrian Social-Democrats. The tiny Communist Party, which was divided into two warring factions (Tomann versus Frey), each numbering about 100 militants, plastered the walls of Vienna periodically with posters demanding the arming of the workers and the dictatorship of the proletariat. But meanwhile, Austrian Social-Democracy continued in its great career, apparently without any suspicion that it was living out its last years. (Actually it did suspect this, but was cutting a fine figure of bravery, and even nonchalance, in the face of un-favourable odds.) Austro-Marxism organized and influenced over a million proletarians, it was master of Vienna, where it was evolving a municipal Socialism rich in achievement, it could mobilize, in a few hours, 50,000 *Schutzbundler* on the Ring, uniformed in sports-tunics and (as everyone knew) tolerably well armed, it was led by the most able theoreticians in the working-class world; and yet, two or three times in ten years, through its sobriety, prudence, and bourgeois moderation, it failed its destiny.

If only. . . . If only a Red Austria had joined with the Hungarian Soviets, would not troubled Bohemia, and then Germany, have followed their example? Revolution was maturing in Italy during this same period. But perhaps it was already too late. If only, after 1918. . . . If only the commission on the nationalization of the main industries, established by the Socialist Government, had not been such a farce! If only the Social-Democrats of Austria had had a little of the impassioned energy of the Bolsheviks of Russia! All they ever did was to sip sweet white wine in the operetta-land of the Blue Danube, while the Bolsheviks were tramping in chains along Siberian highways. Its opportunities lost, its hours of daring past, little Austria found herself jammed in the middle of the expanding counter-revolutions of Hungary, Italy, and Germany; at home, Socialist Vienna found itself menaced by the countryside and the Catholic bourgeoisie. Prince Starhemberg was recruiting his peasant bands against it. I attended meetings of Social-Democratic Party activists: they were middle-aged men, few of them at all fit, who drank their beer as they listened to the speakers. The *Schutzbund* would march past the Town Hall with 30,000 bicycles garlanded with flowers! Otto Bauer, who was greeted on all sides by affectionate glances, watched the parade of this working-class force, so self-confident, so deserving of a glorious future. If only it had been a matter of just deserving! (Fourteen years later, in Paris, I was unable to recognize Otto Bauer, so cruelly had defeat shrivelled his solid, regular features, stamped not so long ago with a noble certainty. He was to die suddenly, from a heart-attack, but actually from the defeat of working-class Austria. On his death-bed his face recovered a wonderful expression of serenity.)

In the Mariahilferstrasse at night, I saw quite different groups of men, wearing uniforms and berets, marching in step by small detachments to the outlying hills, there to practise the use of weapons. Officers' associations, ex-servicemen, Starhemberg formations, crosses, swastikas . . . the politicians still denied that there was any fascist danger in Austria. I was probably the first to denounce the danger, in 1925, in Paris through the *Vie Ouvrière*, in Russia in an ineffectual pamphlet. This danger quite clearly arose from the fact that a working-class democracy, powerful in numbers, education and achievement, but hemmed in on three sides, was consequently harried by the alternatives of either hopeless resistance or total impotence. So long as the Weimar Republic survived in Germany, working-class Austria could still hope. Once German Socialism collapsed, she was doomed. If only France and Czechoslovakia had not opposed the German-Austrian *Anschluss* when Germany and Austria were both democracies, the united strength of the two working classes could probably have blocked the way to fascism; certainly they would have realized a number of impressive Socialist reforms. *If only.* . . .

Blood and despair hovered in the giddy air of Vienna. One evening, at the time of the New Year, we were walking in a silken snow-fall, surrounded by paper decorations and the *um-pa-pa*, *um-pa-pa* of Strauss waltzes, when an explosion rang out beneath the arcades of the Opera House: an unemployed man was blowing out his brains with a dynamite cartridge. Another fired on the Cardinal-Chancellor Seipel. Hugo Bettauer, a charming journalist who frequented nude dances, was propagating a sentimental Freudian eroticism in certain weekly journals with very special classified advertisements. A young fanatic drilled six bullets into the body of this 'Jewish corrupter of Austria's youth'.

I studied Marx and Freud and ran international Press campaigns against the terror waged by employers and police in Spain, where all my old comrades were dying, one after the other, under the bullets of the *Sindicato Libre*. I inveighed against the White terror in 'Bulgaria ruled by the knife'. I stood with the Opposition in the Russian Party, which in 1923–4 was led by Preobrazhensky and largely inspired by Trotsky. In Russia a struggle was beginning whose gravity was still gauged accurately by no one. At the time when the date of the German Revolution was being fixed, forty-six old militants warned the Central Committee of two sorts of danger: the weakness of an industry unable to satisfy the needs of the country-side, and the stifling dictatorship of bureaucracy. In the spiritual impoverishment of recent years there had been only two flashes of daylight: two close-written little books by Trotsky, the demands in *The New Course* and the analysis in *Lessons of October*—both works vilified by our official Press. We would meet discreetly in some outer district to read and discuss these pulsating pages. Then, bound by discipline, prisoners to our daily bread, we went on endlessly printing our news-sheets, with the same insipid, nauseating condemnations of everything that we knew to be true. Was it really worth while being revolutionaries if we had to ply this trade?

I refused to carry out a dishonest directive from Bela Kun, dealing with the French Party. A letter which had been sent to me from Moscow was mysteriously intercepted. A comrade who held high office in the International, and was about as sincere as a genuine bad penny, tried to make me see reason. After this vile conversation I put in a categorical request for my return to Russia. The atmosphere of the International's departments was becoming impossible for me to breathe. Men like Monatte, Rosmer, and Souvarine were being hounded out of the French Party merely for having shown some evidence of political courage in demanding to see things Russian in their proper light. The Parties were changing their faces and even their language: a conventional jargon was settling upon our publications—we called it 'Agitprop Pidgin'. Everything now was only a matter of 'one hundred-per-cent. approval of the correct line of the Executive,' of 'Bolshevik monolithism', of 'the speedy Bolshevization of fraternal Parties'. Such were the latest ingenuities of Zinoviev and Bela Kun. Why not 300 per cent. approval? The Central Committees of all the Parties, who send appropriate telegrams at the first wink, have not, as yet, thought of that one. The system appears to have been perfected. A crony of mine jokes: 'At the Fortieth Congress in Moscow a ninety-year old Zinoviev will be seen propped up by nurses and waving his Presidential bell. . . .' 'Schools of Bolshevism' are being established, like the French one at Bobigny under Paul Marion (the same who was to become a Minister of Pétain and Laval in 1941), and Jacques Doriot. The International still presents an imposing façade, and has thousands of working-class supporters who trust in it with all their heart; but I am watching it go rotten within. And I see that it can be saved only in Russia, by a regeneration of the Party. I have to go back.

'Above all', 'Yuri' Lukács told me, as we roamed in the evening beneath the grey spires of the Votive Church, 'don't be silly and get yourself deported for nothing, just for the pleasure of voting defiantly. Believe me, insults are not very important to us. Marxist revolutionaries need patience and courage; they do not need pride. The times are bad, and we are at a dark cross-roads. Let us reserve our strength: history will summon us in its time.'

I answered that if I found the Party atmosphere in Leningrad and Moscow too oppressive, I would ask for an assignment somewhere in Siberia and there, in the midst of the snows, far from the tortuosities of politics, I would write the books now maturing in my head, and wait for better days. In an effort to break definitively with an old nightmare which still haunted me from time to time, I had, on the shores of a Carinthian lake, begun to write *Les Hommes dans la Prison*.

6

DEADLOCK OF THE REVOLUTION
1926—1928

It is raining; the jetties are black. Two rows of dotted lamplight extend far back into the night. Between them, the black waters of the Neva. On both sides, cut into two, the dark city: inhospitable. It has not cast its misery aside. Four days ago, I was looking at the great glow outspread in the night sky over Berlin: Berlin that only recently knew an inflation more incredible even than ours. We never paid more than a million for a lemon: in Berlin postage-stamps were charged in trillions. Why does this prostration still weigh down on our Russian land? As we come out of the Customs, we are met by a run-down cab advancing over the puddles of mud; a ghost-horse and a rattling carriage, straight from some wretched town in Gogol's time. It has always been the same. A return to Russian soil rends the heart. '*Earth of Russia*,' wrote the poet Tyutchev, '*no corner of you is untouched by Christ the slave.*' The Marxist explains it in the same terms: 'The production of commodities was never sufficient, the means of communication were always short. . . .' And because of that the poor (and there have been some Christs among them), slaves to necessity, have had to take to the roads, barefoot, knapsacks on back, trailing from one steppe to the next, endlessly fleeing, endlessly seeking. . . .

The atmosphere I find is calm, gloomy, oppressive. Lutovinov has committed suicide.[1] The metalworkers' organizer used to wander at night in Berlin, with Radek. The cocktails of the Kurfürstendamm scorched his throat: 'When all's said and done, the bourgeoisie certainly invents some muck to get themselves drunk on! What am

[1] Yuri Lutovinov had caused offence through his leading part in the Workers' Opposition. His suicide occurred in May 1924.

I going to do if I go back? I have told the Central Committee over and over again: we must take another look at the wages question. Our engineers are starving. After that, the Health Commission of the Party sent me abroad for a cure. . . .'

Glazman has committed suicide. The background to this tragedy is hardly known; it all took place within the circle of Trotsky, President of the Supreme War Council. It is mentioned only in hushed tones. Glazman is not the only one.[1]

Certain young people, expelled from the Party for demanding 'the New Course', have turned revolvers on themselves. Young women, as every one knows, prefer veronal. What use is it to live if our Party refuses us the right of serving it? This newborn world is calling us, we belong to it and it alone—and look! In its name someone spits in our faces. 'You are disqualified. . . .' Disqualified because we are the Revolution's racked flesh, its outraged reason? It is better to die. . . . The graph of suicides is mounting. The Central Control Commission meets in extraordinary session.

Evgenia Bogdanovna Bosch has committed suicide. Nothing has been published abroad about the death of one of Bolshevism's greatest personalities. The Civil War, the Ukraine (where, together with Piatakov, she headed the First Soviet Government), the troubles in Astrakhan, which she dealt with severely, the peasant counter-revolution of Perm, armies under her command: through it all she slept with a revolver under her pillow. The Party debate of 1923, the juggling with workers' democracy in equivocal Central Committee resolutions, the purge of the universities and the dictatorship of the secretaries all combined to depress her, and her strong, plain fighter's face, with its piercing eyes, grew hollow with sickness. Once Lenin died, her mind was made up. What was there left to do, with the Party deceived and divided, with Ilyich gone, what was there left to wait for, since she could no longer do anything herself? She went to bed and shot herself in the temple with a revolver. The Committees deliberated the question of her funeral rites. The more rigorous comrades argued that suicide, however justified it might be by incurable illness, remained an act of indiscipline. Besides, in this particular case suicide was a proof of Oppositional leanings. There was no national funeral, only a local one; no urn in the Kremlin

[1] Glazman was Trotsky's young secretary, often at his side in the Civil War.

wall, only a place befitting her rank in the plot reserved for Communists in the Novo-Devichy cemetery. Forty lines of obituary in *Pravda*. Preobrazhensky exposed the underhand trickery of it all. When she had been handling the Germans, the Ukrainian Nationalists, the Whites, and the rural *Vendée*, what joker would have inquired into her official rank in the Party hierarchy? These very ideas did not exist then: Preobrazhensky was requested to hold his tongue. The spectre of Lenin's flesh, robbed of all substance and spirit, lies under the Mausoleum while the hierarchy is only too alive, voracious even—it has not finished showing us yet.

Sergei Yesenin, our matchless poet, has committed suicide. The telephone rings: 'Come quickly, Yesenin has killed himself.' I run out in the snow, I enter his room in the Hotel International, and I can hardly recognize him; he no longer looks himself. The night before he had been drinking, of course, and then had said good night to his friends. 'I want to be alone. . . .' In the morning he awoke depressed, and felt the urge to write something. No pencil or fountain-pen was at hand, and there was no ink in the hotel inkwell: only a razor blade, with which he slashed his wrist. And so, with a rusty pen dipped in his own blood, Yesenin wrote his last lines:

> *Au revoir, friend, au revoir. . . .*
> *. . . There is nothing new about dying in this life*
> *But there is surely nothing new about living either.*

He asked the hotel to keep everyone out. They found him hanging with a suitcase-strap round his neck, his forehead bruised by falling, as he died, against a heating-pipe. Lying there washed and combed on his death-bed, his face was less soft than in life, his hair brown rather than golden; he had an expression of cold, distant harshness. I observed at the time: 'One would think him a young soldier dying alone after some bitter defeat.' Thirty years old, at his peak of glory, eight times married. . . . He was our greatest lyrical poet, the poet of the Russian campaigns, of the Moscow taverns, of the Revolution's singing Bohemians. He proclaimed the victory of the steel horses over the red-maned colts in the 'fields without a glimmer'. He spawned lines full of dazzling images, yet simple as the language of the villages. He plumbed his own descent into the abyss: *'Where have you led me, you, my reckless head?'* and *'I have been loathsome, I have been wicked—and all so that I could blaze more brilliantly. . . .'*

He had tried to be in tune with the times, and with our official literature. '*I am a stranger in my own land. . . .*'; '*My poems are no longer needed now, and I myself am unwanted. . . .*'; '*Blossom, O young folk, in your healthy bodies. . . . Your life is alien, your songs are alien. . . .*'; '*I am not a new man, I have one foot in the past, and yet I wish, I the stumbler, I the cripple, to join the cohorts of steel once more. . . .*'

> *We have it: unrelenting harshness*
> *Which is the tale of man's suffering!*
> *The sickle cuts the heavy stalks*
> *As one cuts the throats of swans.*

Vladimir Mayakovsky, the most popular of our poets after Yesenin, addressed a reproachful farewell to him:

> *So you have gone off*
> *As the saying is:*
> *To the next world. . . .*
> *The void. . . .*
> *You circle in it,*
> *Hustling the stars.*

Mayakovsky, an athlete poised from top to toe in a bantering style of violence, hammered out his farewell before audiences for whom this death was turning into a symbol:

> *This planet's not well equipped for happiness;*
> *Happiness will only be won at a future date!*

And Mayakovsky is soon to kill himself too, with a bullet in the heart; but that is another story. Through the night, through the snow we carry the corpse of Sergei Yesenin. This is no age for dreaming and lyricism. Farewell, poet.

Lenka Panteleyev, one of the Kronstadt sailors of 1917, who stove in the gates of the Winter Palace with their rifle-butts, has just ended his life's course in Leningrad. A legend has grown up about him in the underworld (for we have an underworld again). When money came back, Lenka felt that his end must be near. He was not a theoretician, but a straight egalitarian. He turned bandit to rob the first jeweller's shops to be opened by the first neo-capitalists of N.E.P. The other night, the militiamen who told me the story—admirers of Lenka—cornered him in his *malina* or hide-out; betrayed, naturally—it was a tale of women and drink. He came, threw off his leather jerkin, downed a glass of vodka and took up his guitar. What should he sing? '*Roll under the axe, O head of Stenka Razin. . . .*' They felled him in the middle of his song. The dangerous guitar was stopped. The militiamen, on pay of forty roubles a month, wear on their caps the red star which the Pantaleyevs had been the first to sport.

There is I——; I had known him in the days when, skinny as a yogi, he had got our ghosts of factories working, without fuel or raw materials. One evening, in that year of ice, 1919—six years ago now—when we were returning from the front at Ligovo, thirty minutes away from the city, he had told me, 'We must throw all our last remaining forces into the firing-line, even the anaemic little seventeen-year-olds, everything except the brains of us. A few thinking heads at the rear, well guarded by machine-guns, and everything else into the firing-line: that's what I say!'

Nowadays even my friend I—— has stopped thinking. We have an evening reunion at his house, where we play cards. An atmosphere of mild affluence reigns in this flat: fine books, miniatures, heraldic tableware, dark mahogany furniture dating back to the Emperor Paul. This is what remains of the spoils of many an expropriation, such as is to be found in the houses of a number of Party stalwarts. I knew fair-haired Lisa I—— in the days when, emaciated and crazy-eyed, she saw her first child die of starvation. Now they have another child, who is far better fed than the children of our unemployed workers. Lisa is now a plump blonde who wears a necklace of heavy gems from the Urals. There is still a slight hint of madness in her eyes, which makes me long to come out with some sharp questions: '*Quite a smash-up in those days, wasn't it? Do you remember Mazin's body under the fir-trees? And the corpse of that little sculptor Bloch who got shot, we never knew why? And his wife's corpse, so childlike she was? Tell me, do you remember?*' But I say nothing of the sort; it would not be nice, the world has changed. Grisha Yevdokimov comes to make up a card-game with us. He is home from Germany, where the Central Committee had sent him for an alcoholics' cure. We talk about the Pushkov affair: and so life goes on. (We do not talk politics, because I am a disgraced Oppositionist and they know it, and because they are anxious for the future and I know it: within the Politbureau an odd coolness has sprung up between Zinoviev, with whom they are friendly, and Stalin.)

Pushkov I met in the old days, when he was running the *Petrokom-muna*, or Central Co-operative of the Petrograd Commune. The reason why he has just been cast into the darkness (which is what expulsion from the Party amounts to) was as follows. The Control Commission's resolution speaks of 'irregular conduct in management (to be referred to the courts) and demoralization'. Pushkov was a married man. At his place, too, people played cards on Sunday evening, with glasses of tea standing by. He loved his wife with a passion whose intensity ill fitted his character as a materialist administrator. When death suddenly took her from him, he forgot that matter is perishable, and that the cult of the dead is sympto-matic of those ancestral ideologies which have been formally con-demned by Party teaching. He had her remains embalmed, and a vault made for her in a cemetery where she could sleep under a canopy of glass. If Lenin could repose in a mausoleum, the better to survive in the memory of mankind, why should not she be likewise preserved for one man's remembrance? Pushkov is honest, but a glass coffin is expensive: he meddled with the funds of the collective. No one will mention him again. I do not know why, but what I find saddest of all in the whole affair is the thought of a dead woman consigned once again to oblivion.

The sordid taint of money is visible on everything again. The grocers have sumptuous displays, packed with Crimean fruits and Georgian wines, but a postman earns about fifty roubles a month. There are 150,000 without jobs in Leningrad alone: their dole varies between twenty and twenty-seven roubles a month. Agricultural day-workers and female servants get fifteen, with their board added, it is true. Party officials receive from 180 to 225 roubles a month, the same as skilled workers. Hordes of beggars and abandoned children; hordes of prostitutes. We have three large gaming-houses in town, where baccarat, roulette and chemin-de-fer are played, sinister dives with crime always hovering around the corner. The hotels laid on for foreigners and Party officials have bars which are com-plete with tables covered in soiled white linen, dusty palm-trees and alert waiters who know secrets beyond the Revolution's ken. What would you like—a dose of 'snow'? At the Europa bar thirty girls show off their paint and cheap rings to men in fur-lined coats and caps who are drinking glasses brimming with alcohol: of these a third are thieves, a third embezzlers, and another third workers and comrades deep in a black mood which, around 3 a.m., breaks out into fights and drawn knives. And then, the other night, I heard someone shouting, with a strange pride: '*I've* been a member of the Party since 1917!' The year when the whole world shook. Here, on snowy nights before dawn, sledges are halted, drawn by proud thoroughbreds, their drivers bearded just like those who served the playboys of Tsarist days. And the manager of a nationalized factory, the wholesaler in textiles from the Lenin Factory, the assassin hunted by informers who are drinking with him—all drive off smartly with some daughter of the Volga or Riazan squeezed up close on the narrow seat, some daughter of famine and chaos with nothing to sell but her youth, and too much thirst for life to join the list of suicides that it is my task as an editor to check. Leningrad lives at the cost of ten to fifteen suicides a day, mainly among the under-thirties.

You could take the lift to the roof of the Hotel Europa, and there find another bar, like any in Paris or Berlin, full of lights, dancing and jazz, and even more depressing than the one on the ground floor. Two of us writers were there in the deserted hall, just starting a drab night out, when Mayakovsky walked in with his usual athletic tread. He came and leant on the bar near us.

'How goes it?'

'All right. Hell!'

'Fed up?'

'No. But one day I'll blow my brains out. Everybody's a bastard!' It was several years before his suicide. Mayakovsky was earning a great deal of money publishing official poetry, which could sometimes be very powerful.

Our aim is still to be a party of poor men, and little by little money becomes master, money corrupts everything—even as it makes life blossom everywhere. In less than five years, freedom of trade has worked miracles. There is no more famine, and an intoxicating zest for life rises about us, sweeping us away, giving us the unfortunate sensation of slipping downhill very fast. Our country is a vast convalescent body, but on this body, whose flesh is ours, we see the pustules multiplying.

When I was Chairman of a co-operative tenement, I had a long struggle to get a girl student given a maid's room in our thoroughly bourgeoisified piece of property; the accounts, presented to me by an engineer, were absolutely crooked, and I had to sign them just the same. One of our fellow lodgers was quite openly enriching himself by re-selling, at high prices, textiles which had been sold him by a nationalized factory at the special cheap rate for the poorly paid. How was it possible? Because the demand for manufactured goods outran supply to the tune of 400,000,000 roubles' worth. The workers went to the taverns to escape their wretched family lives; the housewives in the area of the Red Putilov Works pleaded with the Party Committees to find a way of deducting some part of their drunken husbands' wages to hand over to them. On pay-day some workers could be seen sprawled blind drunk on the pavements, and others greeted all and sundry with cat-calls. They regarded me with particular venom as a bespectacled intellectual. A Committee for Child Relief ran the Vladimirsky Club, a disreputable gambling-den. There I saw a woman hit in the face and thrown down the steps with her clothes half torn off. The manager came over to talk to me and told me quite coolly, 'What are you so shocked about? She's nothing but a whore! Just put yourself in my shoes!' He is a Communist, this manager: we belong to the same Party.

Business livens up society, after a fashion, but it is the most corrupt kind of business imaginable. Retail trade, i.e. the distribution of manufactured articles, has passed into the hands of private enterprise, which has triumphed over the co-operative and State trading systems. Where does this capital, non-existent five years ago, all come from? From robbery, fraudulent speculation, and superbly skilful racketeering. Twisters start up a fake co-operative; they bribe officials to give them credits, raw materials, and orders. Yesterday they had nothing; the Socialist State has given them everything, on burdensome terms it is true, for contracts, agreements and orders are all fixed by corruption. Once launched, they carry on, determined to become the universal middlemen between socialized industry and the consumer. They double the price of everything. Soviet trade, as a consequence of our industrial weakness, has become the hunting-ground for a flock of vultures in whom the shape of tomorrow's toughest and smartest capitalists can be clearly discerned. In this respect, N.E.P. is an unquestionable setback. The prosecutors, from Krylenko downwards, spend their days in useless trials for speculation. One shabby little character named Plyatsky, carroty and talkative, is at the hub of all corruption and speculation in Leningrad. This Balzacian man of affairs has floated companies by the dozen, bribed officials in every single department —and he is not shot, because basically he is indispensable: he keeps everything going. N.E.P. has become one big confidence-trick. The same holds good, although in a different form, in the countryside. A single year's sheep-raising in the south has produced Soviet millionaires of a most curious brand: former Red partisans, whose daughters live in the finest hotels in the Crimea, whose sons play for high stakes in the casinos.

In an entirely different sphere, the gigantic scale of certain royalties encourages the gradual growth of an official literature. The dramatists Shchegolev (the historian) and Alexei Tolstoy are reaping hundreds of thousands of roubles for their slick plays about Rasputin and the Empress, and many of our young writers dream only of imitating them. It is only a matter of writing in a style which fits popular taste and the directives of the Central Committee's Cultural Section. Not that this is so very easy. It is becoming obvious that, despite the sterling resistance of most of the young Soviet writers, we have on our hands a literature that is conformist and corrupt. Things are coming back to life: but everywhere we can see symptoms of a process that eludes us, threatens us, and portends our doom.

It was Konstantinov who gave the solution to the equation. We knew each other, though we had never met. I loathed him, but was beginning to understand him. Somebody told me, 'He is a literary man: he collects original manuscripts. He has some of Tolstoy, Andreyev, Chekhov, and Rozanov. A materialist, but he has begun to join the company of mystics. A bit cracked, but intelligent. Used to be in the Cheka—says he's very fond of you.'

In a tenement on the Right Bank I found a few people in a room lit by a chandelier. An old man spoke to us of Rozanov, in whom there had been something of Nietzsche, Tolstoy, and Freud, all subsumed in a carnal Christianity which was perpetually at war with itself. A saintly obsessive, who had delved very deep into the moral problem and the sex problem. He thought of himself as a moral reptile; not that he wanted to be, but he told himself that everyone is like that at heart anyway; and so, ever so slightly, he really became one. Author of *Fallen Leaves*: meditations on life, death, hypocrisy, fleshly impurity, and the Saviour, a book written on sheets of lavatory paper in the w.c. He had died at the same time as Lenin, and the memories he left among the Russian intelligentsia ran deep. They spoke of him as though he had just gone out of the room.

The company included some young women, and a thin, tall man with a little white moustache. I recognized him at once: Ott, head of the Cheka's administrative section in 1919 and 1920. An Estonian or Lett, gifted with a bloodless imperturbability, he attended to all the form-filling, with the executions going on all round him. Konstantinov had thinning hair, a bony nose, swarthy, lips and spectacles; I did not recognize him, although he treated me as an old acquaintance. It was only later on that he drew me aside and said, 'You know me well, all the same: I was the examining magistrate in the Bayrach case. . . .'

Indeed, how could I have forgotten him? This was the Cheka man against whom, in 1920, a French Communist and I had waged a long struggle for the lives of some indubitably innocent men, whom he wanted shot at all costs. I will not recount this trivial case. There was the incident of the blood-stained shirt that was brought to me out of jail; the incident of the girl with the face of an *odalisque* before whom this sadistic magistrate had dangled fantastic traps, and promises with degrading conditions attached to them. There were indeed many incidents, and finally we did save the accused men, by going to the leading circles of the Cheka, Xenofontov, I believe. At the Petrograd Cheka the comrades had talked of the examining magistrate in ambiguous terms: a hard man, incorruptible (he only pretended to be willing to sell his clemency), a sadist perhaps, 'but you must understand—it's all psychology!' I avoided meeting him, believing him to be a dangerous character, a professional maniac. And, seven years later, here he was offering me tea, treating me as a friend.

'Your protégés went off to Constantinople where, no doubt, they have become big racketeers. You were quite wrong to take so much trouble to stop me liquidating them. I knew of course that, from a formal point of view, they were innocent, but we had plenty on file against them. That's unimportant now. In other cases, I was never prevented from doing my revolutionary duty, even by much more powerful people than you. It was I who. . . .'

He had been one of those Chekists who, in January 1920, just as

Lenin and Dzerzhinsky were issuing the decree to abolish the death-
penalty, had arranged an execution at night, involving the massacre
of several hundred suspects at the very last minute, when presses
were already rolling out the new decree.

'So it was you. And what now?'

Now, he was on the fringe of the Party, not positively expelled,
but pensioned off and tolerated. From time to time he would take
the train to Moscow and go to the Central Committee, where he
would be received by a senior secretary. Konstantinov would bring
out his file of secrets, bulging with fresh titbits and supplemented by
that irrefutable source of accusation, his memory. He would utter
proofs, accusations, and the names of high personages, but still did
not dare to tell everything. They would kill him.

He proposed to tell me nearly everything. Whence came this
confidence in me? 'You are an Oppositionist? You are missing the
real question altogether. You don't suspect anything. . . .' At first
he talked in hints, and we discussed what was going on; what Lenin
had foreseen when he said, 'You think you are driving the machine,
and yet it's driving you, and suddenly other hands than yours are
on the wheel.'

Unemployment statistics, wage-scales; the home market ruled
by private enterprise, itself born out of the plunder of the State;
rural misery, and rise of a peasant bourgeoisie; Comintern in-
competence and Rapallo policies; privation in the towns and
arrogant *nouveaux riches*—do these results strike you as being quite
natural? 'And have we done all that we have done, only to come to
this?'

Konstantinov lays his cards on the table, unveils his secret to me.
The secret is that everything has been betrayed. From the years
when Lenin was alive, treason has wormed its way into the Central
Committee. He knows the names, he has the proofs. He cannot tell
me everything, it's too dangerous: they know that he knows. If
anyone guessed that I have heard it from him I would be a doomed
man. It is all tremendous and appalling. The exposure of this plot
demands infinite clairvoyance, a genius for inquisition, and absolute
discretion. At the peril of his life, he is submitting his analysis of the
gigantic crime, studied over years, to the Central Committee. He
whispers the names of foreigners, of the most powerful capitalists,
and of yet others which have an occult significance for him. He

specifies a city across the Atlantic. I follow his chain of reasoning
with the secret uneasiness that one feels in the presence of some
lunatic logician. And I observe that he has the inspired face of a
madman. But in all that he says, he is driven by one basic idea
which is not the idea of a madman: 'We did not create the Revolution to come to this.'

We leave each other bound by a mutual confidence. It is a white
night, and the trams have stopped running. I walk away with Ott.
Crossing a bridge which lies between dull sky and fog-coloured
water, I notice that my companion has not changed in six years.
He still wears his long cavalry-coat without badges of rank, he has
the same stolid bearing, the same half-smile under his pale little
moustache, as if he were still on his way out of Cheka headquarters
on a winter night in 1920. He is entirely in agreement with Konstantinov. His argument is crystal-clear, isn't it? We hold the threads
of the plot, this plot of blackest treachery and infinite ramifications,
the world-wide plot against the first Socialist republic . . . everything can still be saved, if only . . . there are still a few men in the
Central Committee. But who?

The pale city of two in the morning opened its great, depopulated
vistas to us. It seemed preoccupied: a cold stone model, full of
memories. We had passed by the blue cupola of the Mosque. On the
little hill towards our right the five heroes of the masonic Decem-
brist conspiracy had been hanged in 1825. On our left, in the small
mansion that had once belonged to a favourite of Nicholas II, the
Bolshevik conspiracy of 1917 had been organized. The gilt spire of
the Peter-Paul Fortress poked up above its casemates and the river.
There in his chains Nechayev had dreamed his prodigious plot to
overthrow the Empire. There too the conspirators of *Narodnaya
Volya* had died: left to die of starvation, in the years 1881 to 1883.
Many of their younger comrades are still alive: the link they forged
continues down to ourselves. We were approaching the tombstones
in the Field of Mars, walled around by red granite ramparts: our
own tombstones. Just opposite, in the Engineers' Castle, Paul
I was done to death by his own officers. 'Just one plot after another,
isn't it?' said Ott, with his smile. 'All that was just child's play.
Today. . . .'

I felt an urge to reply (but it would have been useless with a
paranoiac like this): 'Today things are not nearly so easy as that.

It's all quite different. And, my poor Ott, these plots that you are inventing are quite redundant. . . .'

If I have sketched these portraits and recorded these conversations of the year 1926, it is because they reveal a certain atmosphere even then, the obscure early stages of a psychosis. Much later the whole of Soviet Russia was to experience years of tragedy when it would live ever more intensely in the grip of this psychosis, which must be a psychological phenomenon unique in history. (Konstantinov disappeared in the early thirties, after being deported to Central Siberia.)

The calm of the workers' city of Leningrad was suddenly broken by the dramatic incident of Chubarov Alley, which shed a sinister light on the conditions under which our youth lived. About fifteen young workers from the San-Galli works had raped an unfortunate girl, the same age as they, on a piece of waste ground near the October railway station. This took place in the Ligovka quarter, a district where the underworld and the working class met, full of scabby tenements. The Party's Control Commission, now overloaded with nasty little morals-cases, had a sort of epidemic of collective rapes to investigate. Doubtless sexuality, so long repressed, first by revolutionary asceticism and then by poverty and famine, was beginning to recover its drive in a society that had been abruptly cut off from any spiritual nourishment. Promiscuity fed upon the misery of the environment. Books like those by Alexandra Kollontai[1] propagated an oversimplified theory of free love: an infantile variety of materialism reduced 'sexual need' to its strictly animal connotation. 'You make love just as you drink a glass of water, to relieve yourself.' The most sophisticated section of youth, the university students, was discussing Enchmen's theory (contested by Bukharin) on the disappearance of morals in the future Communist society.[2]

The fifteen defendants from Chubarov Alley were given a show-trial in a workers' club-room, with the portrait of Lenin overlooking

[1] Alexandra Kollontai (1872–1952): Menshevik for a while, then a prominent Bolshevik. Commissar of Social Welfare in the first Soviet Government; 'Left Communist' and then leader of the Workers' Opposition; diplomatic activity in Mexico, Norway, and Sweden; sympathized with the Trotskyist Opposition but subsequently conformed.

[2] Emmanuel S. Enchmen, biologist and 'mechanistic' materialist. He did not admit of the existence of 'other minds'.

all. Rafail, the editor of the Leningrad *Pravda*, presided; he was a
tame, crafty-looking, bald official. At no moment did he give the
slighest indication of understanding the tangled complexity of
human baseness and poverty-induced corruption that it was his task
to unravel in the name of working-class justice. A hall full of men
and women workers followed the cross-examination in an atmosphere of suspenseful boredom. The accused fifteen had the typical
faces of Ligovka gutter-kids, fusing the peasant and proletarian
types with primitive brutality as their salient feature. They offered
confessions and denounced one another with no inhibitions about
giving details. If ever the case diverged from the strictly factual they
could not follow it, and found it all a great fuss to be made over
things that often just pass by without any bother. What was more
natural than sex on waste sites? And what if she didn't mind
mating with four, five, or six? She would have got just as pregnant
or diseased if it had only been one. And if she did mind, perhaps it's
because she had 'prejudices'.

Certain parts of the cross-examination are still clear in my
memory. The lack of any insight on the part of the accused was
so primitive in its quality that the magistrate Rafail, good com-
mitteeman that he was, was continually put out by it. He had
just been so foolish as to talk of 'new culture' and 'our wonderful
Soviet morals'. A short, fair-haired lad with a flat nose answered
him:

'Never heard of 'em.'

Rafail went on, 'Of course, you'd prefer foreign bourgeois morals,
wouldn't you?'

It was ridiculous, it was horrible. The boy replied, 'I don't
know nothing about them. Me, I've never been abroad.'

'You could have got to know about them through reading foreign
newspapers.'

'I never even see Soviet newspapers. The Ligovka streets, that's
the only culture I know.'

Five of the accused were condemned to death. In order to be able
to carry out the sentence, the authorities had to twist the law and
accuse them of 'banditry'. On the evening of the verdict, the sky
above the city glowed purple. I walked towards the glow: the whole
of the San-Galli works was in flames. The five condemned youths
were executed on the following day. There was a rumour that the

workers who had started the fire had been executed secretly, but this was impossible to confirm.

I was taken by a sudden yearning to know this social inferno of ours, whose great flames cried out into the night. I burrowed into our Soviet doss-houses. I was there when they rounded up the girls they kept sending, by administrative decree, to the concentration-camps of the Far North. I can honestly say that Dostoevsky did not see everything; in any case, I discovered that since Dostoevsky's day nothing, in certain dark corners of our world, has changed for the better. O my fellow-tramps of Paris, how difficult is social transformation!

It was at this time that Vassily Nikiforovich Chadayev waylaid me in the Leningrad Press Institute on the Fontanka Embankment, where the Countess Panina used to reside.

'*Taras has told me about you. . . .*' Taras was a password name that had been given me in Piatakov's circle in Moscow so that I could contact the clandestine Opposition in Leningrad. The 'Trotskyists' as a group had withdrawn from political activity, and since 1923 had been playing a waiting game. This was the Centre which guided the Left Opposition in the area, and I was invited to join it. We used to meet in a room at the Astoria, usually that of N. I. Karpov, a professor of agricultural science who had been an army commissar. Those who went there consisted of two or three students of working-class origin; two old Bolshevik workers who had been in every revolution in Petrograd for the last twenty years; X——, an un-assuming man, formerly the organizer of a Party print-shop, who had been dropped from various sinecures because of his excessive integrity and who, ten years after the seizure of power, was living as poorly as he always had, pale and scraggy under his faded cloth cap; Feodorov, a huge red-haired fellow, splendidly strapping, with an open face fit for a barbarian warrior, a factory-worker who was soon to leave our group, ultimately to meet his death as a member of the Zinoviev tendency. We also included two Marxist theoreticians of genuine worth, Yakovin and Dingelstedt. Grigori Yakovlevich Yakovin, aged thirty, had returned from Germany, on which country he had just written an excellent book. A sporting enthusiast with a constantly alert intelligence, good looks, and a spontaneous charm, he was to spend some years in ingenious daring and dangerous illegality, and then to do the rounds of the jails for an undetermined period, there to disappear in 1937.

Feodor Dingelstedt had been, at the age of twenty, one of the Bolshevik agitators (together with Ensign Roshal, Ilyin Genevsky, and Raskolnikov) who had been behind the mutiny of the Baltic fleet in 1917. He was in charge of the Institute of Forestry and was having a book published on 'The Agrarian Question in India'. Among us he represented an extreme-Left tendency similar to Sapronov's group, who considered that the degeneration of the régime was now complete. Dingelstedt's face, with its harsh, inspired ugliness, was a picture of invincible obstinacy. 'They will never break *him*.' I used to reflect. I was not mistaken: he was to follow the same path as Yakovin without ever giving in.

'Babushka', or 'Grandmother', usually took the chair at our meetings. Plump, her hair white over her kindly face, Alexandra Lvovna Bronstein was the last word in commonsense and honesty. She had some thirty-five years of militancy behind her, including exile in Siberia; she had been Trotsky's wife in his first years of struggle, and had borne him two daughters, Nina and Zina (who were both to perish . . .). The only work allowed her was elementary instruction in sociology to children of under fifteen, and that was not to last long. I have known few Marxists as free in their basic outlook as Alexandra Lvovna.

Nikolai Pavlovich Baskakov, a small, powerful man with a tall, indented forehead and blue eyes, thought it was now questionable whether the system could be reformed. He went into the jails, where I do not know what became of him. Together with Chadayev and myself, who specialized in international questions, this was the roll-call of the Centre. I insist on one historical point: there was never any other Centre of the Left Opposition in Leningrad.

Chadayev became my friend. He was to be the first of our number who was killed. Long before the Party leadership, he raised the question of the collectivization of agriculture, in a remarkable set of theses. He was the only one of us to put the question of a second party—in private—and the only one to foresee the great trials of deception. A fighter from 1917, an editor on the evening paper *Krassnaya Gazeta*, he was led through his knowledge of the condition of the working class to a realistic appraisal of political problems. He watched the disorders at the Labour Exchange, which was in the end wrecked by the unemployed.

'In that riot', he said, 'I saw a fantastic woman who reminded me of the best days of 1917. She gave purpose, and almost order, to the tumult. Her appearance was insignificant, but I could see that she was cut out to be a leader. And it is working-class women like her that have to come out against us!' Together we watched the disgusting trial of the Labour Exchange officials, who would not send a woman to a factory job unless she were reasonably good-looking and, what was more, obliging. He left behind him several precious booklets filled with observations which, like so many others, probably went to be pulped.

The Party was in a state of slumber. Meetings were hardly noticed by the apathetic public. Since the purge of the universities, the youth had turned in upon itself. All the same, we were, for the time being fairly optimistic, for Trotsky was publishing a series of articles proving that we were on the way 'to Socialism, not capitalism', and supporting the preservation of a marginal private sector (which would take the force of all crises) around the nationalized factories. I discussed these ideas in the Paris journal *Vie Ouvrière*. Victor Eltsin brought me a directive from the Old Man (Trotsky): 'For the moment we must not act at all: no showing ourselves in public but keep our contacts, preserve our cadres of 1923, and wait for Zinoviev to exhaust himself. . . .' Writing good books and publishing Leon Davidovich's *Collected Works* was to be our means of keeping up morale. Victor Eltsin had the cool temperament of a tactician. He also told me that in Moscow the Left Opposition could muster more than 500 comrades. Sermuks was a fair-haired, gentlemanly type, refined and circumspect, Poznansky a tall Jew with untidy hair. These were the three secretaries of Trotsky, all of them aged about thirty to thirty-five; towards the Old Man they would keep faith unshakeably, until Heaven knows what terrible death.[1]

The storm broke quite out of the blue. Even we were not awaiting its coming. Certain remarks of Zinoviev, whom I had seen weary and dull-eyed, should have warned me. . . . Passing through Moscow in the spring of 1925, I learnt that Zinoviev and Kamenev, who were

---

[1] Poznansky and Sermuks tried to join Trotsky in exile at Alma Ata. They were arrested, and disappeared. At the end of the voyage in which Trotsky was deported to Constantinople, a G.P.U. official accompanying him promised that Poznansky and Sermuks would be released and allowed to join him abroad. Nothing more was heard of this promise. (Serge, *Vie et Mort de Trotsky*.)

to all appearances still all-powerful as the two foremost figures in the Politbureau since Lenin's death, were about to be overthrown at the forthcoming Fourteenth Party Congress, and that Stalin was offering the Department of Industry to Trotsky. . . . The 1923 Opposition asked itself who its allies should be. Mrachkovsky, the hero of the Urals battles, declared, 'We will not ally ourselves with any one. Zinoviev would end by deserting us and Stalin would trick us.' The militants of the old Workers' Opposition proved to be non-committal, since they believed us to be too weak and, as they said, distrusted Trotsky's authoritarian temper. My own opinion was that it was impossible for the bureaucratic régime stemming from Zinoviev to get any harsher; nothing could be worse than it. Any change must offer some opportunity for purification. I was very much mistaken, as is now obvious.

Grossman-Roschin, a leader of the syndicalist group *Golos Truda* (*Voice of Labour*), who was also the only member of the group still at liberty, came to tell me how disturbed he was: 'Stalin is grumbling about the clowns and stooges in the Comintern, and is getting ready to cut off their rations once he has sacked Zinoviev. Aren't you afraid of some damage happening to the Communist International through this?' I answered, 'Nothing could be better for the International than to have all its rations cut off. The commercial characters will go elsewhere, the artificial Parties will die away, and the working-class movement will be able to recover its health.'

As a matter of fact, the Fourteenth Congress, of December 1925, was a well-rehearsed play, acted just as its producer had planned over several years. All the regional secretaries, who were appointed by the General Secretary, had sent Congress delegates who were loyal to his service. The easy victory of the Stalin-Rykov-Bukharin coalition was an office-victory over Zinoviev's group, which only controlled offices in Leningrad. The Leningrad delegation, led by Zinoviev, Yevdokimov, and Bakayev and supported by Kamenev —all doomed to the firing-squad in 1936—found itself isolated when it came to the vote. Zinoviev and Kamenev were paying for years of responsibility devoid of any glory or success: two defeated revolutions, in Germany and Bulgaria, the bloody and imbecilic episode of Estonia; at home the revival of class-distinctions, about 2,000,000 unemployed, scarcity of goods, conflict simmering between the peasantry and the dictatorship, the extinction of all democracy; in the Party, purges, repression (still mild, but shocking because it was new), the multiplication of slanders against the organizer of victory, Trotsky. Certainly Stalin had a share in the responsibility for all these doings, but he wriggled out of it by turning on his colleagues in the triumvirate. Zinoviev and Kamenev were quite literally falling under the weight of their own errors, and yet we could see that at this particular hour they were more or less right. They opposed the makeshift doctrine of 'Socialism in a single country', in the name of the whole tradition of International Socialism. Kamenev used the expression 'State capitalism' in speaking of the wretched condition of the workers, and advocated that the wage-earners should share in their factories' profits. Zinoviev's crime was that he demanded the right to take the platform at Congress to present his own report. The whole Central Committee Press chose to see in this an attack on the unity of the Party. Bukharin was sick of the reign of mediocrity; he hoped to become the 'brain' behind Stalin. Rykov, President of the Council of People's Commissars; Tomsky, the head of the trade unions; Voroshilov, the head of the army; and Kalinin, the President of the Central Executive, were all carefully watching the state of peasant discontent and uttering condemnations of international adventure. The mass of Party officials wanted nothing more than to live a quiet life.

Zinoviev, whose demagogy was quite sincere, believed every word he said about the warm support of Leningrad's working-class masses for his own clique. 'Our fortress is impregnable', I heard him say. He took the opinions which his subordinates cooked up in the Leningrad *Pravda* as being representative of real public opinion. He came back to make his appeal to the Party and the masses at a time when the Party was no more than a phantom in the imagination of bureaucrats and the masses were apathetic and dormant. The resistance of Leningrad, which I had seen for myself, was crushed in a fortnight, even though on certain nights workers loyal to Zinoviev came to mount guard over the newspaper's print-shop in anticipation of a forcible *putsch*. The proletarian district of Vyborg, which had been famous ever since the days of March 1917, was the first to give in. The same men were no longer there, neither was the same spirit. In every local committee there were shrewd folk who knew that a declaration in favour of the Central Committee was the first step in a career. The better members were disarmed by their respect, or rather fetishism, towards the Central Committee. The Central Committee sent Gusev and Stetsky along to us to instal new committees. Stetsky, a man of 35, was a disciple of Bukharin: his pose was that of the 'Soviet American'—neatly dressed, clean-shaven, genial, round head, and round glasses, very friendly to the intellectuals, joining them in investigating 'the problems'. (Later he was to betray Bukharin, temporarily replacing him as a theoretician in Stalin's circle, and then to develop a blatant theory of the totalitarian State, before disappearing into jail around 1938.)

I heard Gusev speaking to big Party meetings. Large, slightly bald and well-built, he got at his audience through the degrading hypnotism which is associated with systematic violence. In order to argue in this particularly foul manner one must, first, be sure of having force at one's elbow, and, secondly, make up one's mind to stop at nothing. It is, at bottom, a fear-making technique. Not a single word of his won conviction, but the losers had got themselves into hot water, there was nothing for it but to vote for the Central Committee. . . . We of the Opposition walked out before the vote was taken, silence all round us. The very low level of education of some of the listeners, and the material dependence of all of them on the approval of Party committees, guaranteed the success of the operation. Under Gusev's hammer-blows the formal majority that Zinoviev had enjoyed in Leningrad since 1918 crumbled away in a week.

Our own 'Leading Centre of the Left Opposition' had abstained in this battle. We were taken aback by the news that Trotsky had concluded an agreement with the 'Leningrad Opposition'. How could we sit at the same table with the bureaucrats who had hunted and slandered us—who had murdered the principles and ideas of the Party?

The old leaders of the Leningrad Party, nearly all of whom I had known since 1919, Yevdokimov, Bakayev, Lashevich, Zorin, Yonov, Makhimson, and Gertik, seemed to have undergone a change of heart overnight; I could not help thinking that they must have felt enormously relieved to escape from the stifling fog of lies and shake us by the hand. They spoke admiringly of Trotsky, the same man that they had covered with odious abuse a couple of days ago. They described, in considerable detail, the first talks he had held with Zinoviev and Kamenev. Their relationship was 'better than ever—just like in 1918'. This was the time when Zinoviev and Kamenev

presented Trotsky with letters testifying how, in conference with
Stalin, Bukharin, and Rykov, they had decided to fabricate a
doctrine of 'Trotskyism' against which they could unloose smear
campaigns. They made even more serious revelations with which I
will deal later. They signed a declaration recognizing that on the
question of the Party's internal régime the 1923 Opposition (Preobrazhensky, Trotsky, Rakovsky, and Antonov-Ovseyenko) had
been right as against themselves.

Twenty or so sympathizers were gathered around our Leningrad
Centre. The Zinoviev tendency declared that it could count on a
clandestine membership of between five and six hundred. We had
our doubts about this figure, but decided to open a recruiting
campaign aimed at creating an organization of similar size, in
preparation for the time when the forces of both tendencies would be
brought face to face. The Zinoviev group, knowing our weakness,
demanded the immediate fusion of the two organizations. We
hesitated to hand over the list of our leading members to them.
What would they be up to tomorrow? A number of us suggested that
we conceal certain names from our newly-found allies—a proposi-
tion we rejected as being disloyal. Our agitators set to work. We held
semi-clandestine meetings from district to district. Chadayev, the
organizer of the central area, would come to see me at night, eyes
blazing out of his wrinkled face, and announce the day's results:
'I tell you that we shall have 400 comrades organized on the day of
the merger!' We were actually to surpass this total, but out of
suspicion we kept putting off the merger.

Nechayev and Chadayev went to Moscow to inform Trotsky of
our fears. I followed them for the purpose of briefing Leon Davidovich and presenting our objections to him. On that day Leon
Davidovich was shivering with fever; his lips were violet-coloured,
but his shoulders were still set firmly and the cast of his face displayed intelligence and will. He justified the amalgamation on the
grounds of the necessity to unite the political forces of both the two
working-class capitals, Leningrad and Moscow. 'It is a battle which
will be difficult to win,' he said calmly, 'but we have excellent
chances, and the salvation of the Revolution depends on it.' Someone brought coded telegrams in to him. In the large waiting-room
at the Concessions Commission two bearded peasants in sheepskins
and clogs of plaited bark were parleying with Sermuks for an

interview with Trotsky, to whom they were anxious to submit an interminable legal dispute they had been having with the local authorities of a distant country district. 'Now that Lenin is dead', they kept repeating stubbornly, 'there is only Comrade Trotsky to give us justice.' .

'He will certainly see you,' Sermuks would answer patiently, all dapper and smiling, 'but he can do nothing now; he is no longer in the Government.' The *mujiks* shook their heads, visibly annoyed that someone was trying to make them believe that 'Trotsky can do nothing now'.

'Pretend to be blowing your nose when you go out,' one of the secretaries told me. 'The G.P.U. has put men with cameras in the house opposite. Apart from that, some of the "comrades". . . .'

Preobrazhensky and Smilga were sent to us by the Moscow Centre to unify the leadership of the two Leningrad oppositions. Preobrazhensky had the broad features and short auburn beard that befitted a man of the people. He had driven himself so hard that during the meetings it seemed that he might at any moment drop off to sleep; but his brain was still fresh, and crammed with statistics on the agrarian problem.

Smilga, an economist and former army leader who in 1917 had been Lenin's confidential agent in the Baltic fleet, was a fair-haired intellectual in his forties with spectacles, a chin-beard, and thinning front hair, ordinary to look at and distinctly the armchair sort. He spoke for a whole evening in a little room to about fifty workers who could not move at all, so closely were they squeezed together. A Latvian giant with gingerish hair and an impassive face scrutinized all who came in. Smilga, sitting on a stool in the middle of the room, spoke, in an expert's tone and without one agitational phrase, of production, unemployment, grain and budgetary figures, and of the Plan that we were hotly advocating. Not since the first days of the Revolution had the Party's leadership been seen in an atmosphere of poverty and simplicity like this, face to face with the militants of the rank and file.

Together with Chadayev, I was a member of the Party cell at the *Krassnaya Gazeta*, the big evening newspaper. (I had, of course, been removed from all committees and 'responsible' positions after my return from Central Europe.) There were about 400 of us: printers, typographers, linotype operators, clerks, editorial staff, and political activists attached to the paper. Three Old Bolsheviks, lost in this multitude, occupied managerial posts. Ten or so comrades had been in the Civil War. The other 387 (or thereabouts) were from the 'Lenin enrolment': workers who had joined the Party only at the death of Lenin, after the consolidation of power and at the height of N.E.P. We Oppositionists numbered five, one of whom was shaky; we were all of the Civil War generation. It was a miniature of the situation in the Party as a whole; many things are explained thereby.

The battle of ideas was joined on three issues, on which the maximum possible silence was maintained: agricultural system, Party democracy, Chinese Revolution. Chiang Kai-shek, with Blücher (Galen) and my comrade Olgin (lately one of the victors at Bokhara) as his counsellors, was beginning his triumphal march from Canton to Shanghai and winning startling victories on the way; the Chinese Revolution was in its ascendancy. From the very beginning the discussion in the whole Party was falsified, on orders from the bureaucracy. The cell committee, in obedience to the district committee, called an aggregate meeting every fortnight. Attendance was compulsory and all names were checked off at the door. A hack orator took two hours to prove the possibility of constructing Socialism in a single country and denounce the Opposition's 'lack of faith'. All he did was to spin out the statements published by the Central Committee's Agitation Department. The next to speak were those termed the 'activists', always the same ones, long-winded old workers who were favourites of the committee or eager young careerists who were actually offering themselves as eligible candidates for a minor position. I can still hear a young soldier expounding painfully from the platform how Marx and Engels doubtless did not conceive of one of the 'little Western countries', like France, Britain, or Germany, being able to build Socialism out of its own resources; but the U.S.S.R. constituted a sixth of the world. . . .

The Bureau, which consisted of workers loyal to the management, was always keen to have a long list of speakers, both to limit the time available for Oppositionists to speak and to give statistical proof of the participation of the masses in the life of the Party. Of the Oppositionists, three were lying low; Chadayev and myself were the only ones to go to the platform, and we were allowed five minutes. It was essential not to lose a second of the time, and accordingly we had invented a special style. We spoke in detached sentences which were all either declarations, statements of fact, or questions. Each one of them had to register, even if the shouting of the 'activists' drowned what came before. As soon as we opened our mouths to speak, interruptions and shouts, mingled with insults, would burst out at once: '*Traitors! Mensheviks! Tools of the bour-geoisie!*' One had to stay calm, remark to the chairman that half a minute had been lost by interruptions and start the mangled sentence over again. Somebody, a member of the Bureau, would be taking down hurried notes for the benefit of the city committee and the Central Committee. The body of the hall watched this duel in absolute silence. Twenty of the onlookers filled the place with their shouts; we only had them to face, and were troubled by the silence of the others.

The Chinese Revolution galvanized us all. I have the impression of a positive wave of enthusiasm heaving up the whole Soviet world —or at least the thinking part of it. The country felt, however confusedly, that a Red China could be the salvation of the U.S.S.R. Then came the Shanghai fiasco. I was expecting it; I had stated beforehand that it would happen. In Moscow I took part in the International Commission set up by the Oppositional Centre, together with Zinoviev's spokesman Kharitonov, Fritz Wolf (who soon capitulated, which did not stop him being shot in 1937), Andrés Nin, the Bulgarian Lebedev (or Stepanov, a clandestine Oppositionist who betrayed us and later worked as a Comintern agent during the revolution in Spain) and two or three other militants whose names I have forgotten. I was well briefed, by comrades who had come back from China and by material from Radek (then Rector of the Chinese University in Moscow), Zinoviev and Trotsky. Incredibly enough, the only non-Communist French newspaper that came into the U.S.S.R., *Le Temps*, a Conservative organ but reputable (money having no smell, as they say), provided me with valuable points of confirmation.

When he arrived before Shanghai, Chiang Kai-shek had found the town in the hands of the trade unions, whose rebellion had been superlatively organized with the assistance of the Russian agents. Day by day we followed the preparation of the military *coup*, whose only possible outcome was the massacre of the Shanghai proletariat. Zinoviev, Trotsky, and Radek demanded an immediate change of line from the Central Committee. It would have been enough to send the Shanghai Committee a telegram: 'Defend yourselves if you have to!' and the Chinese Revolution would not have been beheaded. One divisional commander put his troops at the disposal of the Communist Party to resist the disarmament of the workers. But the Politbureau insisted on the subordination of the Communist Party to the Kuomintang. The Chinese Party, led by an honest man, Ch'en Tu-Hsiu, had disavowed the peasant uprisings in Hopei and left the insurgent farmers of Chan-Sha to be slaughtered in their thousands.

On the very day before the Shanghai incident Stalin came to the Bolshoi Theatre to explain his policy to the assembled activists of Moscow. The whole Party noted one of his winged remarks: 'We are told that Chiang Kai-shek is making ready to turn against us again. I know that he is playing a cunning game with us, but it is he that will be crushed. We shall squeeze him like a lemon and then be rid of him.'

This speech was in the press at *Pravda* when we heard the terrible news. Troops were wiping out the working-class quarters of Shanghai with sabre and machine-gun. (Malraux was later to describe this tragedy in *Man's Estate*.)

Despair was in us all when we met. The arguments within the Central Committee were repeated with equal violence in every Party cell where there were Oppositionists. When I began to speak in my own branch, just after Chadayev, I felt that a paroxysm of hatred was building up and that we would be lynched on the way out. I ended my five minutes by flinging out a sentence that brought an icy silence: 'The prestige of the General Secretary is infinitely more precious to him than the blood of the Chinese proletariat!' The hysterical section of the audience exploded: 'Enemies of the Party!'

A few days later our first arrest took place: they arrested Nechayev, a new member of our Centre, a thoughtful worker who had once been an army commissar, with a rough, weary face and gold spectacles, about forty years of age. We spoke of the arrest at a meeting. The Bureau did not dare to accept any responsibility for it. We had prepared two angry interventions: Chadayev made his from the platform, but I spoke from the floor, the better to defy the fanatics in the front rows. I shouted 'You have arrested Nechayev. To-morrow you will have to arrest us in thousands. Know then that in the service of the working class we will accept prison, deportation, the Solovky Isles. Nothing will silence us. The counter-revolution is rising behind you, stranglers of the Party!' The activists kept up bursts of rhythmic chanting '*Slanderers! Traitors!*' These arguments were conducted in a hall where we suddenly felt, members of the same Party as we were, that the enemy was in front of us and prison was a step away; it had a shattering effect upon me.

On one other occasion we scored a point—but what a dismal point it was! I asked the audience to stand in homage to the memory of Adolf Abramovich Joffe; I had just kept watch by him as he lay on his death-bed in Moscow, dead for the Revolution's sake. The cell Secretary, who was always briefed by a confidential circular, gazed at us in fury, but yielded. We rendered homage, since the circular did not expressly forbid that. . . .

'And now, tell us why he died, and how!'

'The district committee has given me no information on those points,' answered the Secretary, adding that nobody had the right to speak on those points before the Central Committee did so. In the memoranda that passed from committee to committee, a death like this could disappear without trace. On this sacrifice the newspapers were silent; it was being squeezed into nothing under half a ton of paper.

We began to tire of this sterile battling in a low-level organization. Once, as Chadayev and I were walking along there in the rainy street, we looked at each other, each with the same thought in his eyes: 'What if we kept quiet this evening?' I forget now what was being discussed. After the activists had finished haranguing us, the Chairman announced, in a puzzled voice, that the list of speakers had no more names. Then, for the first time, the apathetic audience stirred. There was a flurrying all around us: 'Hey, what about you chaps?' Chadayev rose smiling and I saw him, looking very tall, and putting up his hand to ask to speak.

And this time, when it came to the vote on the final motion, when we were always the only ones to vote against—against 250 others—a third hand was raised at the same time as ours. A young printer was exclaiming: 'They're right! I am with them!'

He joined us in the street. We learnt that about forty workers, all bound by mutual confidence, were prepared to support us, but would only do so discreetly, for fear of losing their jobs. An equal number of sympathizers were around them. We went home in the darkness, tense but happy. The ice was beginning to break. From other sources we discovered that the same situation held in the Party as a whole.

'I think', Chadayev said to me, 'that they'll crush us to pulp before the big thaw ever happens.'

Now that Zinoviev had been dismissed from the Chairmanship of the Leningrad Soviet, he had not been in the city for months. He came along there with Trotsky for a session of the Central Soviet Executive, which of course was a purely formal gathering. Grey drizzle was falling over the stands decked in red calico, and on the demonstration marching past near the Tauride Palace. The leaders of the Opposition were standing on the platform well away from the official group. The crowd had eyes only for them. After delivering hurrahs to order before Komarov, the new Chairman of the Soviet, the procession found itself level with these legendary men who no longer meant anything in the State. At this point the demonstrators made a silent gesture by lingering on the spot, and thousands of hands were outstretched, waving handkerchiefs or caps. It was a dumb acclamation, futile but still overwhelming.

Zinoviev and Trotsky received the greeting in a spirit of happy determination, imagining that they were witnessing a show of force. 'The masses are with us!' they kept saying that night. Yet what possibilities were there in masses who were so submissive that they contained their emotions like this? As a matter of fact everybody in that crowd knew that the slightest gesture endangered his own and his family's livelihood.

Together with the two leaders we conducted a campaign of agitation, a legal one that is: the Party rules did not forbid members of the Central Committee to talk to militants. Fifty people packed a small room, sitting around a pale, plump Zinoviev, him of the curls and the low voice. At the other end of the table sat Trotsky, now obviously ageing, almost hoary but well-set, his features boldly chiselled, ever ready with a shrewd answer. A woman worker, sitting cross-legged on the floor, asked: 'What if we are expelled?' Trotsky explained that 'nothing can really cut us off from our Party'. It was a simple, reassuring sight: the men of the proletarian dictatorship, who had yesterday been the greatest in the land, coming back like this to the districts of the poor, there to seek support from man to man.

I was with Trotsky as he left one of these meetings in some ramshackle apartment scarred by poverty. In the street Leon Davidovich put up his overcoat collar and lowered the peak of his cap so as not to be recognized. He looked like an old intellectual in the underground of long ago, true as ever after twenty years of grind and a few dazzling victories. We approached a cabman and I bargained for the fare, for we had little money. The cabman, a bearded peasant straight out of old Russia, leaned down and said, 'For you, the fare is nothing. Get inside, comrade. You are Trotsky, surely?' The cap was not enough of a disguise for the man of the Revolution. The Old Man had a slight smile of amusement: 'Don't tell any one that this happened. Everybody knows that cabmen belong to the petty-bourgeoisie, whose favour can only discredit us. . . .'

Using assumed names, I spoke in outlying districts. One of my groups, consisting of half a dozen working men and women, held its meetings in the shade of low fir-trees in an abandoned cemetery. I would stand on the graves and discuss the confidential reports of the Central Committee, the news from China, and Mao Tse-tung's articles. (The future military leader of Soviet China was very close to us in his ideas; but he stayed within the Party line to keep his supplies of weapons and munitions.)

I had no confidence that we would win: I was even sure in my own heart that we would be defeated. I remember saying this to Trotsky, in his big office at the Concessions Commission. In the old capital we could count on only a few hundred militants, and the mass of the workers was indifferent to our case. Leon Davidovich spread his hands wide: 'There is always some risk to be run. Sometimes you finish like Liebknecht and sometimes like Lenin.' As far as I was concerned everything was summed up in one conviction: even if there were only one chance in a hundred for the regeneracy of the Revolution and its workers' democracy, that chance had to be taken at all costs. I was unable to confess these sentiments openly to any one. To the comrades who, under the firs in the cemetery, or on a waste plot near a hospital, or in poverty-stricken houses, demanded some promise of victory from me, I would answer that the struggle would be prolonged and harsh. So long as I confined this way of talking to personal conversations with a few people, it worked, it made their faces harden; but if it was used against a more numerous audience, it cast a chill. 'You behave too much like an intellectual,' I was told by one of my friends in our Centre. Other agitators were lavish with promises of victory and I think that they themselves lived on such hopes.

We decided to use surprise tactics to occupy a hall in the Palace of Labour, where we would hold a big meeting with Zinoviev. (Kamenev had done this at Moscow, speaking by the glow of a few candles since the Central Committee had had the electricity cut off.) At the last minute Zinoviev cried off, afraid of being called to account, and Radek refused to speak by himself. So the hundred-odd of us went off to demonstrate at an engineers' conference at the Mariinsky Theatre. One of us was badly beaten.

Our Centre held a meeting at my lodgings with Radek, around the tea-table. Karl Bernardovich munched his pipe between his thick lips; his eyes were very tired. As usual he gave an impression of extreme intelligence, which was, at first encounter, disagreeable because of a certain flippancy; but beneath the sarcastic retailer of anecdotes, the man of principle shone through. Somebody had recalled the Workers' Opposition, which in 1920–1 had analysed the bureaucratization of the Party and the condition of the working class in terms which we scarcely dared repeat aloud seven years later. At the idea that this bygone Opposition had been right against Lenin, Radek was nettled. 'A dangerous idea. If you take it up, you will be finished as far as we are concerned. In 1920 there was no Thermidor in sight, Lenin was alive, and the revolution was simmering in Europe. . . .'

I questioned him about Dzerzhinsky, who had just died, on the couch where he had collapsed with a heart-attack on the way out of a stormy session of the Central Committee. Nobody doubted Dzerzhinsky's absolute incorruptibility. The petty deceit that had become current among our leadership must have made him ill. . . .

Radek remarked, 'Felix died just in time. He was a dogmatist. He would not have shrunk from reddening his hands in our blood.' At midnight the telephone rang: 'Scatter, look sharp! You're all going to get locked up, the orders have been given by Messing!'[1]

---

[1] S. A. Messing: a leading Soviet official of the Cheka and later of the G.P.U., himself to be arrested after the fall of Yagoda. He died in 1946.

Everyone dispersed unhurriedly. Radek lit his pipe again. 'Plenty of things are going to start happening again. The main job is not to do anything silly.'

The Central Committee authorized the 'activists' to break up 'illegal meetings' by force. Squads of husky fellows, ready to beat up anyone on behalf of the Central Committee, were formed in the various districts of the city, and provided with lorries. Concerned for its dignity, the Opposition recoiled from the prospect of fist-fighting; meetings were stopped or else held in absolute secrecy.

For some years now the country had been living on political formulae many of which were obsolete and some downright deceitful. The Opposition decided to give itself a programme, thereby proclaiming that the ruling party now had either no programme, or else one which no longer had anything to do with the Revolution. Zinoviev undertook to work out the chapters on agriculture and the International in collaboration with Kamenev; the chapter on industrialization was assigned to Trotsky; Smilga and Piatakov, helped by some young comrades, also worked on the draft, which was submitted, as each section came out, to our meetings and, wherever possible, to groups of workers. For the last time (but we had no suspicion that this was so) the Party returned to its tradition of collective thinking, with its concern to consult the man in the workshop. Typewriters clattered throughout entire nights in apartments where the Kremlin was still unable to intrude. The daughter of Vorovsky, the Ambassador who had been assassinated in Switzerland, wore herself out in this work (she was soon to die of the combined effects of tuberculosis, work, and privation). Some of the comrades got three or four typewriters together in a little room in Moscow. Agents of the G.P.U. besieged these premises quite openly. One of the Red Army leaders, Okhotnikov, came complete with the tabs on his collar and ordered this surveillance to be called off; we were able to save some of our stocks. The next day the newspapers announced the discovery of a 'clandestine printing-press'! A further crime: a former White officer was implicated in the plot—and this was partly true, except that the ex-officer was now a member of the G.P.U. For the first time a squalid police-intrigue was interfering with the life of the Party.

This odious legend was automatically publicized by the Communist Press abroad. Vaillant-Couturier put his name to the official statement. A few days later I met him in Moscow at an international writers' conference. I pushed away the hand he offered me. 'You know perfectly well that you have given your signature to a slander!' His large chubby face grew pale and he stammered, 'Come along this evening and I'll explain to you. I received the official reports. How could I check if they were true?' That night I knocked on his door, in vain. I will never forget his face, helpless with shame. For the first time I witnessed the self-debasement of a man who wanted to be a sincere revolutionary—who was, moreover, talented, eloquent, sensitive and (physically at least) courageous. They got him in a corner: 'You must write that, Vaillant; the Executive demands it!' Refusal meant breaking with the all-powerful Comintern that could make and break reputations, meant joining a minority without a press or resources. . . . He would more willingly have risked his neck on the barricades, than his Parliamentary career in this particular way. Besides, shame makes its impact only the first time.

All legal means of expression were now closed to us. From 1926 onward, when the last tiny sheets put out by anarchists, syndicalists and Maximalists had disappeared, the Central Committee had enjoyed an absolute monopoly of printed matter. Fishelev, an old companion of Trotsky in Canada and now the manager of a print-shop in Leningrad, published our *Platform* clandestinely; it was signed by seventeen members of the Central Committee (Trotsky, Zinoviev, Kamenev, Smilga, Yevdokimov, Rakovsky, Piatakov, Bakayev, etc.). Fishelev was convicted of misappropriating paper and plant, and sent to a concentration-camp in the Solovietsky Islands. Meanwhile we collected signatures to the *Platform*. 'If we get 30,000 of them', said Zinoviev, 'they won't be able to stop us speaking at the Fifteenth Congress. . . .' We managed, with considerable difficulty, to gather five or six thousand. Since the situation was taking a rapid turn for the worse, only a few hundred, the names of the men of the Bolshevik Old Guard, were sent to the Central Committee. Events were speeding to a conclusion which would make all this petitioning appear in its true light: as mere child's play.

The 100 pages of the *Platform* attacked the anti-Socialist forces that were growing under the N.E.P. system, embodied in the *Kulak* or rich peasant, the trader and the bureaucrat. Increase in indirect taxation, bearing heavily on the masses; real wages held static at an excessively low level, barely that of 1913; 2,000,000 unemployed; trade unions fast becoming executive organs of the employer-State (we demanded the preservation of the right to strike); 30–40 per cent. of the peasantry poor and without horses or implements, and a rich 6 per cent. cornering 53 per cent. of the corn reserves; we advocated tax-exemption for poor peasants, the development of collective cultivation (*kolkhozes*) and a progressive tax-system. We also advocated a powerful drive for technological renewal and the creation of new industries, and mercilessly criticized what was the first, pitifully weak version of the Five-Year Plan. On the other hand, we demanded the abolition of the State alcohol trade, which brought in a considerable revenue. We quoted Lenin's saying: 'We will sell everything, except ikons and vodka.'

On the political level, it was essential to restore life to the Soviets, to apply the principle of self-determination of nationalities 'in sincerity', and above all to revitalize the Party and the trade unions. The 'Party of the proletariat' was only one-third working class (no more than that) in its composition: 430,000 workers compared with 465,000 officials; 303,000 peasants (over half of whom were rural officials), and 15,000 agricultural day-labourers. We disclosed that two tendencies existed within the Central Committee. One of these, the moderate one, envisaged the formation of a rich peasant petty-bourgeoisie; this Right tendency was quite capable of precipitating an involuntary slide towards capitalism. It comprised Rykov (Chairman of the Council of Trade Unions), Kalinin (President of the Executive of the U.S.S.R.), Chubar (Chairman of the Ukrainian Council of People's Commissars), Petrovsky (Chairman of the Ukrainian Soviet Executive), and Melnichansky and Dogadov, of the Council of Trade Unions. (With the exception of Kalinin, and Voroshilov, all these men were to perish in 1937–8.)

'Centrist' was our designation of the Stalin tendency (Molotov, Kaganovich, Mikoyan, Kirov, Uglanov), because its only apparent motive was the preservation of power, to which end it would resort by turns to the policies of the Right and of the Opposition. Bukharin was unstable and drifted between the two. (In fact he belonged to the Right.) The Central Committee replied to this 'foul slander' by stating that 'never, even while Lenin was alive, had it been so perfectly unanimous' (I quote verbatim). In conclusion, the Opposition openly demanded a Congress for the reform of the

Party, and the implementation of the excellent resolutions on internal democracy that had been adopted in 1921 and 1923. The *Platform*, of course, fiercely criticized the policies of the Comintern, which in China were resulting in an uninterrupted series of bloody disasters.

By a significant coincidence of dates, the Soviet Thermidor was realized in November 1927, the anniversary of the seizure of power. In ten years the exhausted Revolution had turned full circle against itself. On 7 November 1917 Trotsky, Chairman of the Petrograd Soviet, organized the victorious insurrection. On the second day of November 1927 *Pravda* published the report of his latest speech, delivered in October to the Central Committee beneath a hail of shouting. While he was speaking from the rostrum, protected on all sides by a human rampart, he was constantly overwhelmed by gross insults, duly recorded by the shorthand-writers, from Skrypnik, Chubar, Unschlicht, Goloschekin, Lomov, and several others who, well-fleshed as they might be, had no suspicion that they were really no more than the restless ghosts of future suicides and firing-squad victims: 'Menshevik! Traitor! Scoundrel! Liberal! Liar! Scum! Despicable phrasemonger! Renegade! Villain!' Yaroslavsky threw a heavy book at his head. Yevdokimov rolled up his sleeves like the old worker he was, ready to take on a fight. Trotsky's voice, intolerable, sarcastic, beat on: 'Your books are unreadable nowadays, but they are still useful for knocking people down. . . .'

Pravda reported: '*The speaker:* Behind the bureaucrats stand the renascent bourgeoisie . . . (*Commotion. Cries of* Enough!) *Voroshilov:* Enough! Shame! (*Whistling. Uproar. The speaker can no longer be heard. The Chairman rattles his bell. Whistles. Shouts:* Get off the platform! *Comrade Trotsky continues to read, but not a single word can be distinguished. The members of the Central Committee begin to leave.*)'

Zinoviev left the rostrum overwhelmed by boos after saying: 'Either you will reconcile yourselves to letting us speak to the Party or you will have to imprison us all . . . (*laughter*).' Did these revilers believe what they were shouting? They were mostly sincere men, narrow-minded and zealous. These uncultured upstarts of the Revolution's victory justified their sharp practices and privileges by reference to their service to Socialism. Outraged by the Opposition, they saw it as treason against them; which in a sense it was, since the Opposition itself belonged to the ruling bureaucracy.

We decided to take part in the November demonstrations under our own slogans. In Leningrad, adroit marshals allowed the Oppositionists to march past the official dais under the windows of the Winter Palace, before cramming them away between the caryatid statues of the Hermitage Museum and the Archives building. I ran foul of several barriers, and was unable to join the procession. I stopped for a moment to survey the multitude of poor folk carrying their red flags. From time to time an organizer turned back to his group and raised a hurrah which found a half-hearted chorus in echo. I went a few paces nearer the procession and shouted likewise—alone, with a woman and child a few steps behind me. I had flung out the names of Trotsky and Zinoviev; they were received by an astonished silence. From the procession an organizer, roused from his sluggishness, answered in a spiteful tone: '—to the dust-bin!' No one echoed him, but all at once I had the very distinct impression that I was about to be cut to ribbons. Burly characters sprang up from nowhere and eyed me up and down, a little hesitant because after all I might be some high functionary. A student walked across the clear space that had arisen all around me and came to whisper in my ear, 'Let's be off, it might take a turn for the worse. I'll go with you so that you won't be hit from behind.' I knew that all that was needed was a proclamation, in the public square of a civilized town, that a man could be struck with impunity, and instantaneously all the suppressed violence would converge on his head. I tried to rejoin my comrades by means of a detour.

On the bridge at Khalturin Street (once the Millionaya) mounted militiamen were holding back groups of onlookers. A disturbance, stationary and curiously unmalicious, was flaring up at the feet of the grey granite statues that supported the Hermitage portico. Several hundred Oppositionists were there engaged in fraternal battle against the militia. The horses' breasts were constantly pushing back the crowd, but the same human wave returned to meet them, led by a tall, beardless, open-faced soldier, Bakayev, the former head of our Cheka. I also saw Lashevich, big and thick-set, who had commanded armies, throwing himself, together with several workers, on a militiaman, dragging him from the saddle, knocking him down, and then helping him to his feet while addressing him in his commander's voice: 'How is it that you are not ashamed to charge at the workers of Leningrad?' Around him billowed his soldier's cloak, bare of insignia. His rough face, like that of some drinker painted by Franz Hals, was crimson red. The brawl went on for a long time. Around the tumultuous group, of which I was part, a stupefied silence reigned.

That evening we held a meeting attended by Bakayev and Lashe-vich, whose uniforms were torn. Excited voices exclaimed, 'Oh, you've been fighting!' 'Who against?' others asked heatedly, 'Against our own people?' At home my son, seven years old, hearing all the talk of fights, charges and arrests, was most disturbed: 'What's happening, Daddy? Have the capitalists and fascists come here?' For he already knew that Communists never got charged in the street except by capitalists or fascist police. How could I explain to him? The newspapers accused us of fomenting an insurrection.

On 16 November the expulsion of Trotsky and Zinoviev from the Central Committee was published: this ensured that they would be unable to speak at the forthcoming Congress. Zinoviev, in his small apartment in the Kremlin, feigned a supreme tranquillity. At his side, covered by glass, lay a death-mask: Lenin's head lying aban-doned on a cushion. Why, I asked, had not copies of so poignant a mask been generally distributed? Because its expression held too much in the way of grief and mortality; considerations of propa-ganda compelled a preference for bronzes with uplifted hands. Zinoviev told me that he was about to be evicted, since only Central Committee members had the right to live in the Kremlin. He left the place, taking with him the death-mask of old Ilyich.

Trotsky had slipped past the watchers on his tail, and moved house discreetly; for a whole day the G.P.U. and the Politbureau, seized by a comical fright, had asked each other what plots he was up to. He was at Beloborodov's, in the House of the Soviets on Cheremetievsky Street. I found Radek, too, in the Kremlin but being ordered out of it, in the process of sorting and destroying his papers, which were scattered in the middle of a deluge of old books heaped in confusion over the carpets. 'I'm selling all this for buttons,' he told me, 'and then I'm clearing out. We've been absolute idiots! We haven't a halfpenny, when we could have kept back some pretty spoils of war for ourselves! Today we are being killed off through lack of money. We with our celebrated revolu-tionary honesty, we've just been over-scrupulous sods of intellec-tuals.' Then, without a pause, as though it were about the most commonplace matter: 'Joffe killed himself tonight. He left a political testament addressed to Leon Davidovich, which the G.P.U. of course stole in a flash. But I got there in time, and I've fixed a nice scandal for them abroad if they don't give it back.' (Officialdom maintained that all the papers of any top-rank militant belonged, once he was dead, to the Central Committee.) Radek deplored the fact that we had broken, on Trotsky's advice, with the Group of Fifteen (Sapronov and Vladimir Smirnov), which believed that the dictatorship of the proletariat had been replaced by a bureaucratic police régime. 'They exaggerate a bit; they're not as wrong as all that, maybe, don't you agree?' 'Quite,' I said. Kamenev and Sokolnikov dropped in. This was the last time that I met Kamenev, and I was surprised to see that his beard had become all white: a handsome old man with unclouded eyes. 'Would you like some books?' Radek asked me. 'Take away whatever you like. It's all being cleared out.' As a souvenir of that day, I took away a volume of Goethe bound in red leather: *The West-Eastern Divan.*

Joffe lay outstretched on a large table in the office where he had worked in Leontievsky Street. A portrait of Lenin, larger than life-size and with an enormous forehead, dominated the room, hanging just above the bureau at which the old revolutionary had written the last pages—wonderful pages—expressing his convictions. He slept, his hands placed together, his forehead bare, his greying beard neatly combed. His eyelids were tinged with blue, his lips dark. In the small black-edged hole in his temple, someone had stuffed a plug of cotton wool. Forty-seven years—prisons, the revolt of the fleet in 1905, Siberia, escapes, exile, Congresses, Brest-Litovsk, the German Revolution, the Chinese Revolution, embassies, Tokyo, Vienna. . . . Near by, in a little room full of children's toys, Maria Mikhailovna Joffe, her face dry and burning, talked to some of the comrades in a low voice. Since the correspondent of the *Berliner Tageblatt*, Paul Scheffer, had revealed the existence of Joffe's political testament, the Central Committee consented to release a copy to its intended recipient, Trotsky.

Joffe had, now that his mind was made up, written at great length. First he affirmed his right to commit suicide: 'All my life I have been of the opinion that the political man has the duty to depart at the right time . . . having most assuredly the right to abandon life at that moment when he is aware that he can no longer be useful to the cause which he has served. . . . Thirty years ago, I adopted the philosophy that human life has no meaning except in so far as it exists in the service of something infinite—which for us is humanity; since anything else is limited, to work for the sake of anything else is devoid of meaning. . . .' The man who wrote these lines, prepared to seal them with his own blood, here touched on heights of faith where neither reason nor unreason counts any longer; there has been no better expression of the revolutionary's communion with all mankind in all ages.

'My death is a gesture of protest against those who have reduced the Party to such a condition that it is totally incapable of reacting against this disgrace' (the expulsion of Trotsky and Zinoviev from the Central Committee). 'Perhaps these two events, the great one and the little' (Joffe's own suicide) 'in occurring together, will re-awaken the Party and halt it on the path that leads to Thermidor. . . . I should be happy to think so, for then I would know that my death was not in vain. But, though I have the conviction that the hour of awakening will sound one day for the Party, I cánnot believe that it has already sounded. In the meantime, I have no doubt that today my death is more useful than the prolongation of my life.'

Joffe addressed certain friendly criticisms to Trotsky, exhorted him to intransigence against orthodox Leninism, authorized him to make changes in the text of the letter before publishing it, and entrusted him with the care of his widow and child. 'I embrace you firmly. Farewell. Moscow, 16 November 1927. Yours, A. A. Joffe.'

The letter signed, the envelope closed and placed in full view on the writing-table. Brief meditation: wife, child, city; the huge eternal universe, and myself about to go. The men of the French Revolution used to say: Death is an everlasting sleep. . . . Now to do quickly and well what has been irrevocably decided: press the automatic comfortably against the temple, there will be a shock and no pain at all. Shock: then nothing.

The path of agitation was closed to Joffe because of his sickness. For the last time at his funeral we breathed in the salty air of times long past. The Central Committee had arranged two o'clock as the time for the departure of the procession which would accompany the body from the Commissariat for Foreign Affairs to the Novo-Devichy Cemetery; working people would not be able to come as early as that. The comrades delayed the removal of the body for as long as they could. At about four o'clock a crowd, singing and slowly tramping through the snow, and bearing a few red flags, went down towards the Bolshoi Theatre. It already numbered several thousand people. We went along Kropotkin Street, the old Ostozhenka. Long ago, on this very road, I had seen Kropotkin off to the self-same cemetery, accompanied by quite different victims of persecution; now our own persecution was beginning, and I could not but see a secret justice in this. At the approaches to the cemetery, incidents began. Sapronov, his aged, emaciated face surrounded by a mane of bristling white (at the age of forty), passed along the ranks: 'Keep calm, comrades, we mustn't let ourselves be provoked. . . . We'll break through the barrier.' A man who had organized the Moscow rising of 1917 was now organizing this painful struggle at the cemetery. We marked time for a moment in front of the high embattled gateway; the Central Committee had issued an order that only twenty or so persons should be allowed to enter.

'Very well,' replied Trotsky and Sapronov, 'the coffin will go no further and the speeches will be delivered on the pavement.' For a moment it looked as though violence would break out. The representatives of the Central Committee intervened, and we all went in. For one last instant the coffin floated above men's heads in the cold silence, then it was lowered into the pit. Some functionary, whose name I forget, presented official condolences from the Central Committee. Murmurs were heard: 'That's enough! Why doesn't he clear off?' It was so ponderous. Rakovsky towered over the crowd, stout and smooth-shaven; his words snapped out, carrying a great distance; '*This flag—we will follow it—like you—right to the end—on your tomb—we swear it!*'

The country at large did not hear Joffe's pistol-shot, and his last message remained secret. The country knew nothing of our *Platform*, an illegal document. We had copies of these texts circulated, and the G.P.U. came at night to search our quarters for them. The reading of either of them became an offence punished by imprisonment—in contravention of all legal procedure, be it noted. Official Russia was organizing the tenth anniversary of the October Revolution: congresses, banquets, etc. Foreign delegates, hand-picked by the Communist Party, the Friends of the U.S.S.R. and the secret service, poured into Moscow. Among them were two young Frenchmen, ex-surrealists, singularly upright in character and unflinchingly acute in intelligence, Pierre Naville and Gérard Rosenthal.[1] They had come with me to keep watch over Joffe's body. I took them to see Zinoviev and Trotsky. The interview with Zinoviev took place in the little apartment of Sachs-Gladnev, an old Marxist scholar who was a timid, fastidious man, myopic and bearded up to his eyes. Storks in white silk were visible in flight upon a Chinese tapestry. On his bookshelves, the twenty-five volumes of Lenin. The two French comrades questioned Zinoviev on the prospects for the Opposition in the International. Zinoviev said, more or less, 'We are starting the Zimmerwald movement all over again. Think of Europe at war and that handful of internationalists gathered in a Swiss village; we are already stronger than they were. We have cadres practically everywhere. In our time, history moves faster. . . .'

As we went out, Naville, Rosenthal, and myself exchanged glances, all somewhat horrified by this crude approach. Did Zinoviev believe what he told us? I think so, more or less. But he had besides a second and a third set of possibilities kept in reserve, and these he did not disclose. Poor Sachs-Gladnev, our host for that day, disappeared in 1937, classified as a 'terrorist'.

There was not a single Oppositionist among the 1,600 delegates of the Fifteenth Party Congress; Stalin, Rykov, Bukharin, and Ordzhonikidze waxed large on the theme of uninterrupted success in all fields. Bukharin denounced the crime of Trotskyism, which was preparing the establishment of a second party; behind this second party all those who hated the régime would rally; and so the split would lead to the undermining of the dictatorship of the proletariat, and the Opposition would be no more than the spearhead of that hidden 'third force', reaction. The Opposition greatly feared this mode of reasoning, whose accuracy it admitted, and sent the Congress yet another message expressing its loyalty in spite of all. The idea that the 'third force' was already organized in the heart of the ruling bureaucracy had occurred only to an unknown young comrade named Ossovsky, who was disowned by everybody.

[1] Pierre Naville (1903–): edited the review *La Révolution Surréaliste* (1924–5); then a Trotskyist; a prolific author in politics, psychology, and Marxist sociology. Gérard Rosenthal (1903–): lawyer and writer. Active first in the surrealist movement, and then in French Trotskyism, the Maquis, and in Sartre's *Rassemblement Démocratique et Révolutionnaire*; author of *Avocat de Trotsky* (1975).

The Central Committee knew what was going on inside the Opposition. The Leningrad tendency, Zinoviev, Kamenev, Yevdokimov, and Bakayev, favoured capitulation. 'They want to hound us from the Party; we have to stay in it at all costs. Expulsion means political death, deportation, the impossibility of intervening when the coming crisis of the régime begins. . . . Nothing can be done outside the Party. Humiliations are of small account to us.' Kamenev and Zinoviev, themselves builders of the system, realized the power of the bureaucratic machine outside which nothing could live; but they failed to see the nature of the transformation that had been accomplished within this machine, which was henceforth destined to crush all vital initiative not only outside but also within the ruling Party.

The Oppositional Centre sat in ceaseless debate throughout the Congress. Our Leningrad allies finally proposed: 'Let us throw ourselves on their mercy and drink the cup of humiliation.' The following exchange of replies took place between Zinoviev and Trotsky, on slips of paper passed from hand to hand. Zinoviev: 'Leon Davidovich, the hour has come when we should have the courage to capitulate. . . .' Trotsky: 'If that kind of courage were enough, the revolution would have been won all over the world by now. . . .'

The Fifteenth Congress decreed the expulsion of the Opposition, which it termed a Menshevik or a Social-Democratic deviation. Kamenev, who had just asked from the rostrum, in crushed tones, 'Is it to be demanded that we forswear our convictions overnight?' now spoke again to say, 'We submit unreservedly to the decisions of the Congress, painful as they may be for us.' They had got rid of Trotsky: what a relief! Bukharin, inexhaustibly sprightly and mocking, used an impressive phrase: 'The iron curtain of History was falling, and you got out of its way in the nick of time. . . .'

Iron curtain indeed, and even guillotine, but so much was not yet obvious. Rykov announced that the Party would be pitiless in the use of repressive measures against those who were expelled. Thus, in a single word, Soviet legality was liquidated and freedom of opinion received its death-blow. We saw the capitulation of Zinoviev and Kamenev as political suicide, doubly so because of their wretched recantation. Rakovsky, Radek, and Muralov for the last time affirmed the unshakeable loyalty of the expellees to their Party. And in this ecstasy of loyalty the split achieved its consummation.

Expulsion from the Party, as we had repeated often enough, amounted to our 'political death'. How could living people, full of faith, ideas and devotion, be turned into political corpses? There are no two ways of doing it. The general mood was still not set for harsh forms of repression. The Central Committee entered into negotiations with the most prominent of those expelled, and the local committees did the same with the less prominent. Since they declared themselves to be loyal despite everything, they were offered posts in Bashkiria, Kazakhstan, the Far East, or the Arctic. Trotsky was supposed to go off in this way, 'of his own free will', to Alma-Ata, on the frontier of Chinese Turkestan. He would have nothing to do with the hypocrisy of friendly deportation, and was given an administrative sentence by the G.P.U. under Article 58 of the Penal Code, which dealt with counter-revolutionary plotting. In order to make the business known at least to some extent in Moscow and the country as a whole, he decided to put up a resistance.

He was lodging with Beloborodov, the Bolshevik from the Urals who in 1918 had had the task of deciding the lot of the Romanov dynasty and had even lately been People's Commissar of the Interior; this was in the House of the Soviets in Granovsky (formerly Cheremetievsky) Street. It was there that I went to take leave of him, a few days before he was forcibly taken off and deported. Comrades kept watch night and day in the street and in the building itself, themselves watched by G.P.U. agents. Motor-cyclists took note of the comings and goings of any cars. I went up by a service staircase; on one floor, a doorway with guards outside: 'Here it is.' In the kitchen my comrade Yakovin was supervising the defence arrangements and at the same time drafting a document. The Old Man received me in a little room facing the yard, in which there was only a camp-bed and a table loaded with maps of all the countries of the world. He had on an indoor jacket that had seen much wear. Vigilant, majestic, his hair standing nearly white on his head, his complexion sickly, he exhaled a fierce, caged energy. In the next room the messages he had just dictated were being copied out; the dining-room was used to receive the comrades who kept arriving from all corners of the country, with whom he held hasty conversations between calls to the telephone. At any moment it was possible that we would all be arrested. After arrest, what then? We did not know, but we hurried to make the best of these last hours, for they assuredly were the last.

My own conversation with Trotsky turned chiefly on the Opposition abroad, whose activity had at all costs to be expanded and articulated. The Old Man had just received from Paris the first numbers of *Contre le Courant*, published by my friends Magdeleine and Maurice Paz, with my co-operation. He was pleased with the tone and tendency of this publication, and advised me to leave, illegally if necessary, for France, in order to work on the spot. For a moment we examined the possibilities. 'We have begun a fight to the finish', he said, 'which may last for years and require many sacrifices. I am leaving for Central Asia: you try and leave for Europe. Good luck!' We embraced one another. The lengthening shadows helped me to throw off the spies in the street. On the next day, if it was not the one after, the crowd blocked the Old Man's departure by occupying a station. The G.P.U. made a surprise call to take him away. To make sure that there could be no lies put out about the manner of his departure, the Old Man let the political police break down the door; he refused to walk, and let himself be carried out to the car which left for a small, deserted station. I reflected that he had reached the peak of his exalted destiny. If, as we all feared, he were mysteriously assassinated, he would still be the symbol of the murdered Revolution. Alive, he would continue his struggle and his work as long as a pen remained between his fingers, a single breath in his lungs, be it in the depth of dungeons. . . .

He had gone, vanished. *Izvestia*, in minute print, announced his deportation for 'insurrectionary plotting', a fantastic accusation. Eighteen months previously, a *coup* against the Politbureau of Zinoviev, Kamenev, and Stalin would have been possible, and in our Oppositional circles we had weighed this possibility. The army and even the G.P.U. would have plumped for Trotsky if he had wished; he was always being told this. I do not know if there were any formal deliberations on this subject among the leaders of the Left Opposition, but I do know that the question was discussed (end of 1925, beginning of 1926) and it was then that Trotsky deliberately refused power, out of respect for an unwritten law that forbade any recourse to military mutiny within a Socialist régime; for it was all too likely that power won in this way, even with the noblest intentions, would eventually finish in a military and police dictatorship, which was anti-Socialist by definition. Trotsky wrote later (in 1935):

'No doubt a military *coup* against the Zinoviev-Kamenev-Stalin faction would have presented no difficulty and even caused no bloodshed; but its consequence would have been a speedier triumph for the very bureaucracy and Bonapartism against which the Left Opposition took its stand.'

Rarely has it been made more sharply obvious that the end, far from justifying the means, commands its own means, and that for the establishment of a Socialist democracy the old means of armed violence are inappropriate.

Rakovsky was sent off to Astrakhan, Preobrazhensky to the Urals, Smilga to Minussinsk in Central Siberia, Radek to North Siberia, Muralov to the Tara forests, Serebriakov, Ivan Smirnov, Sapronov, Vladimir Smirnov, Sosnovsky, and Voya Vuyovich elsewhere; where we did not know, since everything was done in secret. I had just seen Christian Rakovsky, back from the Embassy in Paris, lodging at the *Sophiiskaya Naberezhnia*, the hotel reserved for diplomats. In the corridors there one might run into Krestinsky with his forehead of fine ivory, grave and wary even in the way he walked; and Karakhan,[1] splendidly elegant however carelessly he dressed, on account of the extraordinary nobility of his features and bearing.

Rakovsky had come back from Paris penniless; without illusions and in good humour, at the age of fifty-four, he contemplated the long struggle yet to be endured. His massive, regular face expressed a composure which almost smiled. His wife was more nervous— on his account. He said that Europe was entering a period of unresolved instability, on which it was necessary to wait. To someone who invited him to capitulate to the Central Committee, he replied gently: 'I am getting old. Why should I blot my biography?'

Now and then I saw Ivan Nikitich Smirnov, People's Commissar for Posts and Telegraphs, in his little office on the Varvarka. A little over fifty, he was tall, upright, and gaunt, with timorous but resolute eyes, an introverted manner, and a good deal of youthfulness

---

[1] Lev N. Karakhan (1889–1937): former Menshevik, then a Bolshevik and participant in the October Revolution; negotiator for the Soviet side at the Brest-Litovsk Treaty (1918); Ambassador to China (1923). Shot at the end of 1937 without public trial.

reflected in the grey-green gaze behind his pince-nez. When I asked him one day whether all correspondence addressed abroad was opened (postal censorship did not exist officially), he answered briskly, 'All of it is. Don't trust anything to it. There's a positive factory run by the G.P.U. in my place dealing just with that and I haven't the right to go in there.' When his Ministerial portfolio was withdrawn he was quite content. 'It does us all good to go back to the ranks for a time.' Not having a farthing, he went to sign on at the Labour Exchange register of unemployed, in his old occupation of precision engineer. He hoped naïvely that he would soon be taken on in an factory. Some snooty little official saw this tall, greying, bright-eyed innocent bending in front of his window, and writing on the form he had to fill in, under the heading *Last Employment*: 'People's Commissar for Posts and Telegraphs'. The Labour Exchange contacted the Central Committee, and the G.P.U. deported Ivan Nikitich to the Caucasian Riviera; repulsive as it was, repression was beginning mildly.

At the battle of Sviazhk in 1918, along with Trotsky and Rosengoltz, typists and engineers from the Army's special train, cooks and telegraph-operators, Ivan Smirnov had swiftly halted the routing of the Reds and the victorious offensive of the Whites under Kappel and Savinkov. On that day the newly-born Republic was saved by this handful of men. Later, in 1920–1, it was Smirnov that Lenin commissioned to restore order in the chaos of Siberia and to bring Russian Asia under Soviet control. For the young generation, he was the incarnation of the idealism of the Party, devoid of gestures or fine phrases.

Deportations were very quick to follow, and in hundreds. The revolutionaries of October 1917 had been not at all demoralized,.it seemed, by their ten years of power, the last years of which had passed smoothly for the most well-known, in legations, ministries, administrative councils and posts of command. What had seemed the bourgeoisification of smartly-dressed folk was revealed as so superficial that it was with positive gaiety that they went off to rough it in the desert wastes of Central Asia and Siberia, all for the salvation of the Revolution. I felt inexpressibly reassured at the sight of their various departures. A certain number of Communists had attached themselves to the Opposition out of design, believing that in it they saw the next government; experience showed that they were very few. We lost them forever and for good riddance at the first dark turning, after a few months. In their different ways, all the Oppositionists of 1927, whether they chose endless humiliation through loyalty to the Party, or endless resistance through loyalty to Socialism, followed the same terrible road right to its end.

What a striking contrast it was between these men and the foreigners, whether noted writers, Communist delegates or distinguished liberal guests, who were in Moscow at that time to celebrate the tenth anniversary of the Revolution. And they actually offered us lessons in wisdom! Jacques Sadoul gave me a friendly lecture. We had been friends, and had in common some pleasant and stirring memories of Russia and Germany. I loved his lively, mocking intelligence, his epicurean nonchalance, his political adroitness. The French Communist Party would not let him undertake any activity, although he could have made a first-rate Parliamentary leader. His mind and temperament were those of a moderate Socialist, but his need for good living bound him to the service of the Soviet State. Old Kalinin had just decorated him with the Order of the Red Flag, and he told me how Vaillant-Couturier, wishing to play down the importance of this honour, had proposed the simultaneous decoration of certain old Communards, some of whom, for all any one really knew, might be old hoaxers.

'The leaders of the Opposition', he said, 'will be shut up in comfortable villas on the Crimea and allowed to write tomes which nobody will read. But you others, Serge—you're going to catch it!' We were having dinner at the table for foreign visitors; young Indian girls draped in dark-coloured silks, who were sitting near us, caused our conversation to wander a moment. Jacques insisted, 'You're going to get yourselves persecuted still, and life is so beautiful! Look at those figures, how charming they are, think how. . . .' And so, affectionately, we parted. Jacques, bemedalled and equipped with sinecures, returned to Paris; I made ready to start all over again: prisons, hard living, etc.[1]

Sadoul at least did not pretend to be a saint. At that time Barbusse was writing his mystical books, *Jesus* and *The Judases of Jesus*; now he was in Moscow, the guest of other Judases. I admired his *Under Fire*, and the lyricism of some pages in *Jesus* impressed me as

[1] After Serge's return to France in 1936, Sadoul vigorously defended the Moscow Trials and tried to discredit Serge's testimony.

ringing true. I found Barbusse, with whom I had had some correspondence, at the Hotel Metropole, guarded by a male interpreter-secretary (G.P.U.) and accompanied by a very pretty female doll-secretary. I had just come from the overcrowded rooms of the outer city, from which comrades disappeared every night; I saw their wives with eyes too reddened, too racked with anxiety for me to incline to any indulgence towards the great official consciences from abroad now visiting our country; moreover, I knew who had been chased out of the hotel so that the great writer could stay there.

Barbusse had a large, thin, pliant body, topped by a small, wax-like and concave head, with the thin lips of a man who has known suffering. Right from the first I saw him as a quite different kind of person; concerned above all not to be involved, not to see anything that could involve him against his will, concerned above all to disguise opinions he could no longer express openly, sliding past any direct questioning, scurrying off along all conceivable tangents, his eyes vague, his slender hands circumscribing curves in the air around obscure words like 'immensity', 'profundities', 'exaltation' —and all with the real aim of making himself the accomplice of the winning side! Since it was not yet known whether the struggle had been definitively settled, he had just dedicated a book, at great length, to Trotsky, whom he did not dare to visit for fear of compromising himself. When I told him about the persecution, he pretended to have a headache, or not to hear, or to be rising to stupendous heights: 'Tragic destiny of revolutions, immensities, profundities, yes . . . yes. . . . Ah, my friend!' My jaws shuddered as I realized that I was face to face with hypocrisy itself. Some days later I learnt that International Class-war Prisoners' Aid,[1] then run by Helena Stassova, was devoting a considerable sum to the foundation of a 'cultural' weekly in France, under the control of Barbusse. This was *Monde*. And Barbusse enrolled me in the list of co-sponsors.

In the course of our struggles I had deployed my activity in two directions: in the Centre at Leningrad, and in Moscow and abroad (mainly in France) through my writings. I belonged to the editorial board of *Clarté* in Paris. In this review I published my articles—under

---

[1] International Class-war Prisoners' Aid: officially a relief and defence organization, founded around 1923, 'to accord assistance to all victims of the revolutionary struggle'.

my own name—on the Platform of the Opposition and the Chinese Revolution. For some months these articles forecast events with an accuracy that overwhelmed even myself. The last one had been signed by a comrade on my behalf, but its contents are still transparent. During the Party Congress, on 11 and 12 December 1927, the lightning success of the Canton Commune had supervened in a manner peculiarly suited to refute the Opposition, which considered that the Chinese Revolution had been defeated for a long time to come. The Press was in raptures. *Pravda* published decrees, strikingly similar to those of the Russian Revolution, which had been promulgated by the Communist dictators of the Chinese city—behind whom, on the very spot, stood the envoys of the General Secretary of the C.P.S.U., Lominadze and my late comrade Heinz Neumann; these were under pressure to supply the Fifteenth Congress with triumphal telegrams. Twenty-four hours later, the torch of Canton was doused in a sea of blood; the coolies who had thought they were fighting for the cause of social justice died in thousands for the cause of an official dispatch; and the staff of the Soviet consulate, both men and women, perished by impalement. I met Preobrazhensky, who asked,

'Have you written about Canton?'

'Yes, and sent it off.'

'But you must be mad! That could cost you several years in jail. Stop it from being published. . . .'

I changed the name under which it was signed. I was expecting to be deported anyway.

At last I was summoned before the Control Commission of the Leningrad Central District, and so appeared before the Party tribunal. A dejected old worker, Karol, was the Chairman; there were a woman worker, a young man with spectacles, and two or three others, sitting around a red tablecloth (the Party committee was housed in the old baroque palace that had belonged to the Grand Duke Sergei). Karol did not seem particularly keen to expel me, and offered me several ways out of the mess. But he had to ask the treacherous and decisive question: 'What is your attitude to the decision of the Congress pronouncing the expulsion of the Opposition?'

I answered, 'In accordance with discipline, I comply with all decisions of the Party, but I regard this decision as a grave error whose consequences will be fatal if it is not speedily mended. . . .'

The woman worker in a red head-scarf stood up, and said in a stupefied voice, 'Comrade, did you really say an *error*? Do you think then that the Party Congress can be mistaken, and commit errors?'

I cited the example of German Social-Democracy voting for the war on 2 August 1914, with only Karl Liebknecht and Otto Rühle voting against. This blasphemous comparison horrified the Commission. I was expelled forthwith. Vassili Nikiforovich Chadayev was called in. He likewise was expelled after a few minutes. We went out. 'Here we are, political corpses. . . .' 'That's because there's nobody but us left alive.'

A few days passed. My bell rang at about midnight. I opened the door, and understood at once (which was not difficult): a young soldier, and a young Jew in a leather outfit. They conducted a search, and made a bee-line for some translations of Lenin. 'You're seizing those too?' I asked ironically. 'Don't joke,' replied one of the pair, 'we are Leninists too, you know.' Perfect: we were all Leninists together.

Dawn hovered over Leningrad, in a blue like the depths of the sea, when I left the house between those two comrades, who apologized for not having a car at their disposal. 'We have so much to do every night. . . .' 'I understand,' I said. My son of seven wept when I embraced him before I left, but explained to me: 'Daddy, I'm not crying because I'm afraid, it's because I'm angry.' I was taken to the old House of Arrest.

The fire-blackened brick shell of the old Palace of Justice vividly recalled the great days of liberation. But inside the squat masonry, little had changed over half a century. A warder explained to me that he had served there for twenty years: 'I took Trotsky out for his walks after the 1905 Revolution. . . .' There was still an arrogant air about him; he was ready to get back to the same job. In a corridor, during one of those waiting periods which precede incarceration, I sat next to a fine-looking young lad who recognized me and whispered in my ear: 'Arnold, the Oppositionist from the Vyborg district, and B—— and C—— have been arrested.' Good enough. What else could we have expected? Through the half-gloom, I clambered up iron stairways linking the different floors of the prison. At long intervals from each other, lamps were burning in corners on the tables of the block supervisors. A door was opened for me in the dark, thick stonework, on the fifth or sixth floor. The dingy cell was already occupied by two men; a former officer, a municipal engineer accused of having sold ice from the Neva for his own profit instead of supplying it to the Soviet; and a creature of filth, babbling madness and futile suffering, a kind of lunatic tramp who had been arrested for vagrancy near the Catholic cemetery—he had been selling little metal crosses there. Since he was of Polish origin, he was charged with espionage. This creature with a shrunken old face never washed, and never spoke, except that he was perpetually mumbling prayers. Several times a day he knelt down to pray, banging his forehead against the side of the bed. At night a rather frightening babble would wake me, and I would see him on his knees, hands pressed together. Later a little book-keeper came in, accused of having served in Admiral Kolchak's White army. The examining magistrate declared that he recognized him as a White officer. It was all inhumanly grotesque.

I discovered that the prison was packed with victims, all targets for the hatred of functionaries who were obsessives, maniacs, and torturers by profession. In the never-ending twilight I read Dostoevsky once again; it had been kindly passed on to me by some harmless sectarian convicts who ran the library. The servant-lads gleefully brought us soup ('bum-wash' they called it) twice a day, uneatable at first but awaited impatiently from the fourth day on. One of these lads, a strapping, fair-haired boy with a pale smile, did not appear one morning, and the others had sullen faces. We knew that the absentee had been shot during the night. He had not expected it so late; the sentence had been on him for months and he had assumed he was pardoned. They came to fetch him a little before dawn. 'Say good-bye to your mates, and let's have no trouble, eh!' He was a boy from the frontier-zone, charged with crossing illegally to Poland and back again. His death did not even serve as an example since it was kept secret.

A shirtmaker from the Sadovaya, accused of tax evasion, was next door to us; he skipped over the parapet in the corridor, jumped into space and found his eternal rest. Someone else near us tried to hang himself, and another to open his veins. . . . We heard only faint echoes of these tragedies. Our days went by peacefully, without any particular anxiety or peevishness, since there were two of us, out of the three in the cell, to keep some sense of balance; we

discussed Socialism. In my screeds to the Procurator I invoked the
Constitution and Soviet law: a pretty joke.

My arrest had caused some commotion in Paris, and so was considered awkward in high circles. I had made up my mind not to
agree to any recantation; they were content with an undertaking
from me not to engage in any 'anti-Soviet activity'. It was a revolting distortion of language, for we had nothing whatever to do with
anything anti-Soviet.

I shall never forget the wonderful sweetness of the young greenery
along the Fontanka embankments, in the white night when I
returned home after seven or eight weeks' absence. The porter of the
house had explained my arrest very plausibly. 'The same under the
old régime,' he said. 'The intellectuals were always arrested like
this, just before the first of May. . . .' In Paris, Vaillant-Couturier
reported in *L'Humanité* that I had been treated with the greatest
possible consideration while in prison. Barbusse sent me embarrassed
letters apologizing for the fact that, on learning of my arrest, he had
deleted my name from the list of sponsors of *Monde*.

Chadayev, in whom Paris showed no interest, remained in jail
for six months; then a personal friend who was a member of the
Government got him out. Since he did not recant, his presence in
Leningrad was deemed undesirable. The *Krassnaya Gazeta* sent him
on an assignment to investigate the *kolkhozes* of the Kuban. His life
was to end just when he believed that it was starting anew, in the
enthusiasm of a fresh departure. We spent several hours rowing on
the lake at Dietskoe Selo, among the scenery of the Imperial Park.
Vassili Nikiforovich sang me the praises of prison, that benevolent
retreat where a man takes stock of himself. He had his doubts about
the regeneration of the Party, which many people believed to be
now going on.

In the Kuban he pounced, with his writing-pads, his inquisitive
eyes and his precise questions, upon all kinds of highly dubious
rackets. Racket in building the harbour at Tuapse, racket in the
layout of the beaches, racket in the repairing of roads, racket in the
collectivization of agriculture!

'Banditry' on the dark roads intervened to dispose of these in-
discreet interrogators. On 26 August 1928, on a summer evening
filled with the cicadas' song, the local authorities vigorously pressed
Chadayev to go off in a carriage with a number of other passengers

to the neighbouring market-town. It was a night journey across the steppe and the fields of maize. A militiaman accompanied the caravan; he was the first to make himself scarce when rough voices came from out of the night: '*Stoy!* Halt!' Chadayev's carriage was the only one held back by the roadside. The coachman heard my poor Vassili arguing with the bandits: 'What's the matter with you? We're all human beings. What is it?' All I ever saw of him again were some dreadful photographs: the dumdum bullets, fired from sawn-off rifles, had harrowed his face and chest monstrously. We wanted to give him a funeral in the town that he loved. Was he not a fighter of the Year Seventeen? The Leningrad Committee opposed this: was he not expelled? His murderers remained unknown, naturally. A stone with an inscription, erected on the spot where he died, was broken into fragments.

7

THE YEARS OF RESISTANCE
1928–1933

These constituted five years of resistance waged by a solitary man—surrounded by his family, that is to say by weak creatures—against the relentless, overwhelming pressure of a totalitarian system. For his daily bread, his ration-card, his lodging, his fuel in the harsh Russian winter, the individual is dependent on the Party-State, against which he is totally defenceless. And he who, in the name of freedom of opinion, stands out against the Party-State, bears the brand of 'suspect' wherever he goes. The small amount of liberty that he still has left, and even his own courage (which seems quite mad), stand for him as a source of astonishment, mingled with anxiety.

The leaders of the now vanquished Opposition hoped to set up a clandestine organization strong enough to achieve rehabilitation in the Party at some future date with freedom of speech and propaganda. I did not share this illusion. I said that illegal methods would fail for two reasons: the unlimited power of the secret police would crush everything—and our own ideological and sentimental loyalty to the Party made us vulnerable both to political manœuvrings and, even more, to police provocation. I declared that, rather than allow ourselves to be bundled away into illegality, we should defend, absolutely openly, our right to exist, think, and write; we should form, also quite openly, an opposition which was strictly loyal (as being without any organization) but also strictly intransigent. It was a purely academic discussion, since both alternatives were equally impossible.

At the beginning of 1928, Alexandra Bronstein and myself were the only known Oppositionists in Leningrad still at liberty; in Moscow, Andreu Nin was free, but he had 'resigned' from the

Secretaryship of the Red International of Labour Unions, and was kept under close watch in the Lux Hotel. His status as a foreigner saved him from imprisonment. Of the Russians, Boris Mikhailovich Eltsin, a Bolshevik since 1903 and founder-member of the Party, former Chairman of the Soviet in Ekaterinberg (Sverdlovsk) in 1917, was also free because the G.P.U. needed his presence in the capital for a while. In an effort to maintain the connexions and inner life of the tiny circles of militants, old Eltsin, a sick man, confided in a young, vigorous—and invulnerable—fellow-activist, one Mikhail Tverskoy, who was an agent of the G.P.U. Tverskoy drew up idiotic leaflets, shortly to be classed as 'anti-Soviet' documents—the very purpose for which they were written. After having had the last Oppositional sympathizers in the Moscow factories arrested, he came to us in Leningrad in order, he said, to 'help us re-organize'. Alexandra Bronstein and myself refused to receive him. Without our being able to stop him he speedily set up a shadow-organization consisting of fifty or so workers, only to have it rally noisily to the 'general line' within two months, while those who resisted were thrown into jail. This police manœuvre was repeated in all the working-class centres. It was made easier by the moral confusion of the Communists. Oppositionists and officials outbid each other in loyalty to the Party, the Oppositionists being by far the most sincere.

Nobody was willing to see evil in the proportions it had reached. As for the idea that the bureaucratic counter-revolution had attained power, and that a new despotic State had emerged from our own hands to crush us, and reduce the country to absolute silence—nobody, nobody in our ranks was willing to admit it. From the depths of his exile in Alma-Ata Trotsky affirmed that this system was still ours, still proletarian, still Socialist, even though sick; the Party that was excommunicating, imprisoning, and beginning to murder us, remained our Party, and we still owed everything to it: we must live only for it, since only through it could we serve the Revolution. We were defeated by Party patriotism: it both provoked us to rebel and turned us against ourselves.

Three months after our expulsion, the grain crisis that we had forecast broke out, endangering supplies to the towns and the army. The peasants, having paid off their taxes, now refused to deliver their grain to the State because they were not being paid enough for it. The Central Committee decreed requisitions, applying, quite improperly, Article 107 of the Penal Code on concealment of stocks. Detachments of young Communists scoured the countryside, stripping the fields of their grain, flax, tobacco, or cotton, depending on the district. Just as in the years of the Civil War, Communists were found at the roadsides with their skulls split open. The stacks of confiscated grain were set on fire. There was no fodder at all; the countryfolk besieged the bakeries in the towns so that they could feed their livestock with black bread bought at the regulation price.

The requisitioning was no more than an expedient. The real policy had been outlined by Molotov at the Fifteenth Party Congress: the development of collective agricultural cultivation (*kolkhozes*) or of State grain-factories (*sovkhozes*). A slow development was envisaged, spread over many years, since collective agriculture could only replace piecemeal cultivation stage by stage as the State supplied the farms with the equipment that was indispensable to mechanized cultivation. But, as it was, war had been declared on the peasantry through the requisitioning. If the State confiscates the grain, what is the use of sowing? In the following spring, statistics will show that the area under wheat has shrunk: a peasants' strike. There is only one way of forcing them: compulsory co-operatives, administered by the Communists. Will persuasion succeed? The independent farmer who has resisted the agitation, or rather coercion, turns out to be freer and better fed than his fellows. The Government draws the conclusion that collectivization must be total and abrupt. However, the folk of the soil are putting up a bitter defence. How can their resistance be broken? By expropriation and mass deportation of the rich peasants or *kulaks* and of any that may be classified as *kulaks*. This is what is called 'the liquidation of the *kulaks* as a class'.

Will it ever be known how terrible was the disorganization of agriculture that resulted? Rather than hand over their livestock to the *kolkhoz*, the peasants slaughter the beasts, sell the meat and make boots out of the leather. Through the destruction of its livestock the country passes from poverty to famine. Bread-cards in the cities, black market, a slump in the rouble and in real wages. Internal passports have to be issued, to keep the skilled manpower in the factories against its will. Since total collectivization is heading towards disaster, its completion is declared when it has reached 68 per cent., and even then too late, in March 1930, when famine and terror are at their height.

The women came to deliver the cattle confiscated by the *kolkhoz*, but made a rampart of their own bodies around the beasts: 'Go on, bandits, shoot!' And why should these rebels not be shot at? In a Kuban market-town whose entire population was deported, the women undressed in their houses, thinking that no one would dare make them go out naked; they were driven out as they were to the cattle-trucks, beaten with rifle-butts. Sheboldayev of the Central Committee was in charge of the mass deportation in this region, never suspecting that, for his very enthusiasm, he would be shot in 1937. Terror reigned in the smallest hamlets. There were more than 300 centres of peasant insurrection going on simultaneously in Soviet Eurasia.

Trainloads of deported peasants left for the icy North, the forests, the steppes, the deserts. These were whole populations, denuded of everything; the old folk starved to death in mid-journey, new-born babies were buried on the banks of the roadside, and each wilderness had its crop of little crosses of boughs or white wood. Other populations, dragging all their mean possessions on wagons, rushed towards the frontiers of Poland, Rumania, and China and crossed them—by no means intact, to be sure—in spite of the machine-guns. And in a long message to the Government, couched in a noble style, the population of Abkhazia pleaded for permission to emigrate to Turkey.

A Russian scholar, Prokopovich, made the following calculation from official Soviet statistics—at a time, be it noted, when the statisticians were being imprisoned and shot. Up to 1929 the number of peasants households grew uninterruptedly:

> 1928: 24,500,000 households
> 1929: 25,800,000 households

When collectivization ended in 1936, there were no more than 20,600,000 households. In seven years over 5,000,000 families disappeared.

The transport system was worn down, and all plans for industrialization were turned inside-out to cope with the new demands. It was, to quote Boris Souvarine's expression, 'the anarchy of the plan'. Agricultural technicians and experts were brave in denouncing the blunders and excesses; they were arrested in thousands and made to appear in huge sabotage-trials so that responsibility might be unloaded on somebody. The rouble was in the process of disappearing; hoarders of silver coin were shot (1930). Crisis in the coal industry, Shakhty sabotage-trial, fifty-three technicians in court, executions. Naturally there is a meat shortage: execution of Professor Karatygin and his forty-seven co-defendants for sabotage of the meat supply—an execution without trial. On the day of the massacre of these forty-eight men, Moscow received Rabindranath Tagore; there were speeches about abundance and the new humanism, and a splendid official reception. In November 1930 there was the trial of the 'Industrial Party': Ramzin, the engineer and *agent provocateur*, who was pardoned, confessed to being its leader and to plotting military intervention against the Soviet Union in London, Paris, and Warsaw. It was raving madness, and five were shot.

At the same period a 'Peasant Party' including Professors Makarov and Kondratiev, who were opposed to total collectivization, was liquidated off-stage. There was the lunatic trial of the old Socialists (of Menshevik inclinations) in the Planning Commission: Groman, Ginsberg, the historian Sukhanov, Rubin, and Sher. There was the secret trial of the officials of the Finance Commissariat, Yurovsky and others. There was the secret trial of bacteriologists, several of whom died in prison. There was the execution of the thirty-five leading figures in the Commissariat of Agriculture; among them, several noted Old Communists (Konar, Wolfe, the People's Vice-Commissar, and Kovarsky). There was the secret trial of physicists and the deportation of Academician Lazarev. There was the secret trial of the historians Tarle, Platonov, and Kareyev. . . .

The accusation of sabotage which was directed at thousands, or rather tens of thousands of technicians, was in general a monstrous slander, justified solely by the need to find culprits for an economic situation that was now insupportable. Close examination of a whole number of cases proves this irrefutably, apart from the fact that the patriotism of the technicians was constantly appealed to in the course of wringing confessions out of them. The whole business of industrialization proceeded in the midst of such chaos, and under an authoritarian system of such rigidity, that it was possible to find 'sabotage' in any place, at any moment. I may add that in my experience the whole mentality of the technician is quite antagonistic to sabotage, dominated as it is by love of technique and a job well done. Even in these hellish conditions Soviet technical experts were full of enthusiasm for their tasks and, all things considered, worked wonders. The 'Industrial Party', just like the 'Peasant Party' of the leading agronomists—was no more than a police invention sanctioned by the Politbureau. All that there was in fact was a fairly widespread 'technocratic mentality'. Technicians saw themselves as indispensable and as distinctly superior to the men in the Government.

Many of them were punished for having actually foreseen the disastrous consequences of certain Government decisions. The old Socialist Groman was arrested after having had a sharp quarrel at the Planning Commission with Miliutin. Groman, at the end of his tether, shouted that the country was being led to the abyss.[1]

Although foreign espionage did exist, the technicians' plotting with the governments of London, Paris and Warsaw, and with the Socialist International, was ascribable purely and simply to con-spiracy-psychosis and political deception. In the so-called 'Men-shevik Centre' trial, the accused (who of course confessed) allowed themselves to be caught in a flagrant lie by inventing, all to order, a journey to the Soviet Union by the old Menshevik leader Abram-ovich. Later, the historian Sukhanov, when incarcerated in the Isolator of Verkhne-Uralsk, had documents passed around among the political prisoners relating how the text of confessions had been laid down for him and his fellow-defendants by the G.P.U. in-structors, how an appeal to their patriotism had been combined with threats of death, and what kind of pledges their inquisitors had given them. (Sukhanov undertook lengthy hunger-strikes to obtain the liberty he had been promised; he disappeared in 1934.) During the 'Menshevik Centre' trial, I met people every day who were connected with the accused, and I was in a position to trace, line by line, the progression of the lie in their evidence.

The Politbureau knew the truth perfectly well. The trials served one purpose only: to manipulate public opinion at home and abroad. The sentences were prescribed by the Politbureau itself. The G.P.U. organized Labour Departments for the condemned

---

[1] Valentin G. Groman (1873–?): former Menshevik; a statistician and econo-mist, he was one of the chief inspirers of a planned economy and occupied a number of important planning posts with Gosplan under the Soviet régime.

technicians, which continued working for industrialization. Some of the technicians were promptly rehabilitated. Once I had dinner with an outstanding expert in energetics who, in the space of twenty months, had been condemned to death, pardoned, sent to a concentration-camp (a Labour Department), rehabilitated, and decorated. The physicist Lazarev was similarly rehabilitated. The historian and Academician Tarle, the only non-Marxist Soviet historian of repute, spent long months in prison and was deported to Alma-Ata; today (1942) he is the most official of all historians in the Soviet Union. The engineer Ramzin, an accomplice (if it is to be believed) of Poincaré and Winston Churchill in the 'preparation of war against the U.S.S.R.' and condemned to the supreme penalty, was pardoned, continued his scientific work in mild captivity and was rehabilitated at the beginning of 1936, with his principal co-defendants, for distinguished services to industrialization.

On the other hand the old Socialists of the pretended 'Menshevik Centre' disappeared.

I was on very close terms with several of the scientific staff at the Marx-Engels Institute, headed by David Borisovich Riazanov, who had created there a scientific establishment of noteworthy quality. Riazanov, one of the founders of the Russian working-class movement, was, in his sixtieth year, at the peak of a career whose success might appear exceptional in times so cruel. He had devoted a great part of his life to a severely scrupulous inquiry into the biography and works of Marx—and the Revolution heaped honour on him: in the Party his independence of outlook was respected. Alone, he had never ceased to cry out against the death-penalty, even during the Terror, never ceased to demand the strict limitation of the rights of the Cheka and its successor, the G.P.U. Heretics of all kinds, Menshevik Socialists or Oppositionists of Right or Left, found peace and work in his Institute, provided only that they had a love of knowledge. He was still the man who had told a Conference to its face: 'I am not one of those Old Bolsheviks who for twenty years were described by Lenin as old fools. . . .'

I had met him a number of times; stout, strong-featured, beard and moustache thick and white, attentive eyes, Olympian forehead, stormy temperament, ironic utterance. . . . Of course his heretical colleagues were often arrested, and he defended them, with all due discretion. He had access to all quarters and the leaders were a little afraid of his frank way of talking. His reputation had just been officially recognized in a celebration of his sixtieth birthday and his life's work when the arrest of the Menshevik sympathizer Sher, a neurotic intellectual who promptly made all the confessions that any one pleased to dictate to him, put Riazanov beside himself with rage. Having learnt that a trial of old Socialists was being set in hand, with monstrously ridiculous confessions foisted on them, Riazanov flared up and told member after member of the Politbureau that it was a dishonour to the régime, that all this organized frenzy simply did not stand up and that Sher was half mad anyway.

During the trial of the so-called 'Menshevik Centre', the defendant Rubin, one of Riazanov's protégés, suddenly brought his name into the case, accusing him of having hidden in the Institute documents of the Socialist International concerned with war against the Soviet Union! Everything that was told to the audience was engineered in advance, so this sensational revelation was inserted to order. Summoned on that very night before the Politbureau, Riazanov had a violent exchange with Stalin. 'Where are the documents?' shouted the General Secretary. Riazanov replied vehemently, 'You won't find them anywhere unless you've put them there yourself!' He was arrested, jailed and deported to a group of little towns on the Volga, doomed to penury and physical collapse; librarians received the order to purge his writings and his editions of Marx from their stocks. To anybody who knew the policy of the Socialist International and the character of its leaders, Fritz Adler, Vandervelde, Abramovich, Otto Bauer, and Bracke,[1] the fabricated charge was utterly and grotesquely implausible. If it had to be admitted as true, Riazanov deserved to die as a traitor; but they merely exiled him. As I write this book I learn that he died a couple of years ago (in 1940?) alone and captive, nobody knows where.

Was there then no basis of truth at all in the trial of the 'Menshevik Centre'? Nikolai Nikolayevich Sukhanov (Himmer), a Menshevik won over to the Party, a member of the Petrograd Soviet from its inception in 1917, who had written ten volumes of valuable notes on the beginnings of the Revolution and worked in the

---

[1] Otto Bauer (1881–1938): Austrian Socialist, friend and colleague of Fritz Adler; Foreign Minister 1918–19; exiled after the destruction of the Austrian Left in 1934. Alexandre Bracke (Desrousseaux) (1861–1956): French Socialist and Deputy; editor of *Le Populaire* in 1936; a considerable classical scholar.

Planning Commissions with his fellow-defendants Groman, Ginsberg, and Rubin, did have a kind of *salon*, in which talk between
intimates was very free and the situation in the country as of 1930
was judged to be utterly catastrophic, as it undeniably was. In this
circle, escape from·the crisis was envisaged in terms of a new Soviet
Government, combining the best brains of the Party's Right (Rykov,
Tomsky, and Bukharin, perhaps), certain veterans of the Russian
revolutionary movement and the legendary army chief Blücher. It
must be emphasized that for practically three years between 1930 and
1934, the new totalitarian régime maintained itself by sheer terror,
against all rational expectations and with every appearance, all the
time, of imminent collapse.

From 1928–9 onwards, the Politbureau turned to its own use the
great fundamental ideas of the now expelled Opposition (excepting,
of course, that of working-class democracy!) and implemented them
with ruthless violence. We had proposed a tax on the rich peasants—
they were actually liquidated! We had proposed limitations and
reforms of N.E.P.—it was actually abolished! We had proposed
industrialization—it was done, on a colossal scale which we, 'super-
industrializers' as we were dubbed, had never dared to dream of,
which moreover inflicted immense suffering on the country. At the
height of the world economic crisis foodstuffs were exported at the
lowest possible price to build up gold reserves, and the whole of
Russia starved.

Beginning in those years, a good many Oppositionists rallied to
the 'general line' and renounced their errors since, as they put it,
'After all, it is our programme that is being applied'; also because
the Republic was in danger, and finally because it was better to
capitulate and build factories than to defend lofty principles in the
enforced indolence of captivity. Piatakov had been a pessimist for
years. He kept saying that the European and Russian working class
was going through a long period of depression, and that nothing
could be expected from it for a long time; more, that he had only
engaged in battle for the Opposition from a sense of principle and
out of his personal attachment to Trotsky. He capitulated, to be put
in charge of banking and industrialization. Ivan Nikitich Smirnov
told one of my friends something like this: 'I can't stand inactivity.
I want to build! In its own barbaric and sometimes stupid way, the
Central Committee is building for the future. Our ideological

differences are of small importance before the construction of great new industries.' He capitulated. So did Smilga. The movement of surrender to the Central Committee in 1928–9 carried off the greater part of the 5,000 Oppositionists under arrest (there had been five to eight thousand arrested).

Six months after the expulsion of the Party's left wing—us, that is—the Politbureau and the Central Committee was torn by savage quarrels: the right-wing Opposition, Rykov, Tomsky, and Bukharin, ranged itself against Stalin, against his policy of forced collectivization, against the dangers of premature industrialization (with no material basis and with famine as its price), against the ways of totalitarianism. The head of the G.P.U., Henry Grigorievich Yagoda, was another sympathizer of the Right. From personal motives whose nature is still obscure Kalinin and Voroshilov, despite their right-wing beliefs, gave a majority to Stalin and Molotov.

The Right Opposition was more of a state of mind than an organization; at certain junctures it included the great majority of officials, and enjoyed the sympathy of the whole nation. However, inspired as it was by men of moderate temperament, who on several occasions were insufficiently decisive, it suffered itself to be constantly outmanœuvred, slandered and finally annihilated. At the end of 1928, Trotsky wrote to us from his exile at Alma-Ata to the effect that, since the Right represented the danger of a slide towards capitalism, we had to support the 'Centre'—Stalin—against it. Stalin sounded the leaders of the Left Opposition even while they were in prison: 'Will you support me against them if I have you rehabilitated in the Party?' We discussed the question with some uncertainty. In the Isolator, that is the prison, at Suzdal, Boris Mikhailovich Eltsin demanded that a conference of expelled Oppositionists be summoned as a precondition, and raised the issue of Trotsky's return. The negotiations got no further than this.

In 1929, the hard core of our Opposition is reduced to the following: Trotsky; Muralov, in exile on the Irtysh, in the Tara forests; Rakovsky, now a petty planning official in Barnaul, Central Siberia; Fedor Dingelstedt in a market-town in Central Siberia; Maria Mikhailovna Joffe in Central Asia; a fine team of youngsters in prison, including Eleazar Solntsev, Vassili Pankratov, Grigory Yakovin. In Moscow Andreu Nin is at liberty, in Leningrad Alexandra Bronstein and myself. Leon Sosnovsky is in jail. Inside the prisons a few hundred comrades keep up hunger-strikes and struggles that are sometimes bloody; in deportation a few hundred others wait for prison to come their way. Our intellectual activity is prodigious, our political action nil. Altogether there must be less than a thousand of us. Between us and the 'capitulators' there is no contact, only a sharp and growing hostility.

As for the two irreconcileables, Timofey Vladimirovich Sapronov and Vladimir Mikhailovich Smirnov, the first has been deported to the Crimea, ill as he is, and the second to an Isolator where he is slowly dying.

Panaït Istrati[1] and myself paid a visit to Mikhail Ivanovich Kalinin, the President of the Central Soviet Executive. We were going to see him about certain criminal measures that were in hand against my relatives. Kalinin worked in a small, brightly-lit office, very soberly furnished, in an unpretentious house next to the Kremlin. His skin was weathered, his eyes lively, his goatee lank and groomed—an old slyboots of a peasant intellectual. We talked with a fair amount of freedom. I asked him the reason for these arrests of Oppositionists, which were contrary to the Constitution. He gazed calmly straight into our faces, putting on his most sympathetic air, and said, 'That's quite untrue . . . there are so many tales being put about! We have arrested only those involved in anti-Soviet conspiracy, no more than a few dozen people. . . .' Were we to call the Head of State a liar? But could he have said anything else to us? Outside in the street Panaït remarked, 'Pity, because he has a fine face on him, that old slyboots. . . .'

In these days there died in a Moscow jail, after a hunger-strike lasting either fifty-four or thirty days according to different reports, Georgi Valentinovich Butov, one of Trotsky's former secretaries; they had tried to extort confessions from him which might be used to implicate the Old Man. Let us pass this by in silence, please! Above all, let us not be embittered by the misfortunes of individuals! Only politics counts. In the October and November of 1929, I made

---

[1] Panaït Istrati (1884–1935): Rumanian novelist; led a vagabond existence for much of life life and won a reputation as 'a Balkan Gorky'. Conducted revolutionary work with Christian Rakovsky; disillusioned with Soviet Russia after a sixteen-months' stay in 1927–8; returned to Rumania and, destitute, offered all his rights as an author to King Carol's Government in return for a pension. It is not clear whether the bargain was accepted; in any case, Istrati died of tuberculosis in great privation.

some effort to shed light on another tragedy, this time in Leningrad, but with no success. On 21 October Albert Heinrichsohn had been arrested, one of our ordinary working-class comrades from the Red Triangle factory, a militant of 1905 and a Civil War Communist. Ten days later his wife was called to the House of Arrest, where all she found of him was a mutilated corpse, its mouth torn. The superintendent explained to the widow that the prisoner had committed suicide, and handed her a 100 rouble note. . . . The Party committees promised an inquiry, which they hushed up. We made our own inquiry, which took me to a tenement of old St. Petersburg: six floors of overpopulated apartments. The dead man's small son told us how he had been taken off there, to rooms which he described in detail, to attend a meeting of 'Daddy's friends'; these 'comrades' had interrogated him at length about the activities and statements of his father. G.P.U.? Or hysteria? We solved nothing.

A few months passed and there was the mysterious case of Blumkin. I had known and loved Yakov Grigorievich Blumkin since 1919. Tall, bony, his powerful face encircled by a thick black beard, his eyes dark and resolute, Blumkin then lived next to Chicherin in a freezing room at the Metropole. Recovering from an illness, he was making ready to conduct certain confidential assignments in the East. In the year before, even while the Foreign Ministry officials were assuring the Germans that he had been shot, the Central Committee was placing him in command of perilous operations in the Ukraine.

On 6 June 1918 Blumkin—then nineteen years old—had, on the orders of the Left Social-Revolutionary Party, killed the German Ambassador in Moscow, Count Mirbach. He and his comrade Andreyev had been sent along by the Cheka to look into the case of a German officer; the Ambassador received them in a small drawing-room. 'I was talking to him, looking into his eyes, and saying to myself: I must kill this man. . . . My briefcase contained a revolver among all the documents. "Wait," I said, "here are the papers," and I fired point-blank. Mirbach, wounded, fled across the big drawing-room, and his secretary flopped down behind the armchairs. In the drawing-room Mirbach fell, and then I threw my grenade hard on the marble floor. . . .'

It was the day of the Left Social-Revolutionary rising against the Bolsheviks and the Brest-Litovsk peace; the insurgents hoped to resume the revolutionary war, fighting side by side with the Allies. They lost. Blumkin also told me, 'We knew that Germany, as disintegrated as she was, could not start a new war against Russia. We wanted to give her a stinging reverse. We were banking on the effect of this action in Germany itself.' Again: 'We were negotiating with German revolutionaries who asked us to help them organize an attempt on the Kaiser's life. The attempt fell through because we insisted that the principal actor should be a German. They didn't find anyone.'

A little later, in the Ukraine, towards the time his comrade Bonskoy would be assassinating Field-Marshal Eichhorn, Blumkin rallied to the Bolshevik Party. His late party was now outlawed. His late comrades fired several bullets into him and came to throw a grenade into the hospital ward where he was; he threw it back out of the window. In 1920-1 he was sent to Persia to start a revolution, together with Kuchik Khan, in Gilan on the Caspian coast.[1] And I met him again in Moscow, in the uniform of the Staff Academy, more poised and virile than ever, his face solid and smooth-shaven, the haughty profile of an Israelite warrior. He declaimed lines from Firdousi[2] and published articles on Foch in *Pravda*. 'My "Persian tale"? There were a few hundred of us ragged Russians down there. One day we had a telegram from the Central Committee: *Cut your losses, revolution in Iran now off.* . . . But for that we would have got to Teheran.' I saw him later on his return from Ulan Bator, where he had just organized the army of the People's Republic of Mongolia. The Red Army's Secret Service entrusted him with missions in India and Egypt. He stayed in a small apartment in the Arbat quarter, bare except for a rug and a splendid stool, a gift from some Mongol prince; and crooked sabres hung over his bottles of excellent wine.

Blumkin belonged to the Opposition, without having any occasion to make his sympathies very public. Trilisser, the head of the G.P.U.'s secret service abroad, Yagoda, and Menzhinsky were well acquainted with his views. All the same, they sent him to

---

[1] Gilan is the northernmost province of Persia. In May 1920 an independent Soviet Republic was established there under Kuchik Khan, with Soviet recognition and military assistance. A march on Teheran was initiated, but repudiated by the Soviet Government which withdrew its troops. In October 1921 Persian troops entered Gilan and hanged Kuchik as a rebel.

[2] Firdousi: Persian national epic poet (tenth century A.D.).

Constantinople to spy on Trotsky—perhaps also to arrange some plot against the Old Man. Did Blumkin turn the tables by becoming Trotsky's bodyguard? At all events he met the Old Man in Constantinople and undertook to bring us a message from him, which was actually quite harmless. In Moscow he became suddenly aware of being watched at every turn: this surveillance was so minute that he knew he was lost. There is good ground for supposing that a woman G.P.U. agent called Rosenzweig, who had become a confidante of his, betrayed him. When he was on the point of being arrested, knowing that the code of the Secret Service left him without a chance, he went to see Radek. Radek advised him to go at once to the Chairman of the Central Control Commission, Ordzhonikidze, a harsh but scrupulous character who was now the only man who could save his life. Radek arranged the meeting—too late. Blumkin was arrested in the street. He betrayed nobody. After being condemned to death by the G.P.U.'s secret Collegium, I know that he requested and obtained a fortnight's reprieve to write his memoirs; they made a first-rate book. . . . When they came to take him to the execution-cellar, he asked if the newspapers would publish the news of his decease; they promised him this—a promise which, of course, was never kept. The news of Blumkin's execution was published only in Germany. Leon Sedov spoke to me later of Blumkin's secretary, an enthusiastic young French Communist of bourgeois origin who was shot at Odessa. Sedov's recollection of this young man was full of warmth; but my overburdened memory has let his name slip.

I can see us now, the few survivors that we were, in the gardens of the Marx-Engels Institute, gathered around a charming girl-comrade, assembling the different hints and scraps we had on the last days and death of Blumkin. Should we now, we asked one another, publish the letters of Zinoviev and Kamenev which told how in 1924 the General Secretary had suggested that they get rid of Trotsky 'by a Florentine technique'? Would we not cast discredit on the régime by publishing this abroad? I was of the opinion that, whatever else, the information about 'Florentine techniques' should be sent to our comrades in the West. I do not know if this was done.

Duplicity began its rule over the Party: a natural consequence of the stifling of free opinion by tyranny. The 'capitulator' comrades

kept their ideas, of course, and met together; as they were absolutely forbidden to participate in political life, they amounted to
no more than a circle viewed with suspicion by the Politbureau. I
came across Smilga, who gave me an admirable account of the way
these men were thinking. (This was in 1929.) He was sore at the
pin-pricks that Trotsky had dealt him in *My Life*, and shocked by
the apotheosis of Stalin; but he said:

'The Opposition is all astray with its sterile bitterness. One's
duty is to work with and in the Party. Think of what is at stake in
these struggles: the agony of a nation of 160,000,000 souls. See how
the Socialist revolution is already advancing over its predecessor,
the bourgeois revolution: with Danton, Hébert, Robespierre, and
Barras, all discussion ended on the guillotine. I am back from
Minussinsk. What do our petty deportations amount to? Oughtn't
we all to be walking around by now with our heads tucked underneath our arms?' Again: 'If only we can bring off this victory'
(collectivization) 'over the antiquated peasantry, without exhausting
the working-class, it will be quite splendid. . . .' He had his doubts
about it, to tell the truth. (He disappeared into jail in 1932, where he
died, doubtless after torture, in 1937.) The programme that we
hard-core Oppositionists have drawn up will not change now till
1937: the reform of the Soviet State by a return to working-class
democracy. The few of us that there are in the hard core are the
only ones to be saved from double-dealing by our intransigence;
but we too are just 'political corpses'.

Within the Party, the Right resists expulsion, and the Zinoviev
tendency, reinstated but humbled, keeps its forces intact. One of
the last actions of our Moscow 'Centre' had been the publication,
in 1928, of pamphlets which told of the confidential discussions
between Bukharin and Kamenev. Bukharin, who was still a member
of the Politbureau and the Party's official theoretician, said, 'What
can one do before an adversary of this type: a Genghis Khan, a
debased product of the Central Committee? If the country perishes,
we all perish [i.e. the Party]. If the country manages to recover,
he twists around in time and we still perish.' Bukharin also told
Kamenev, 'Nobody must know of this conversation. Don't phone me,
the line is tapped. I'm being shadowed and you are being watched.'
Our 'Centre' (B. M. Eltsin) may very well have much to answer for
in publishing these documents. From that moment onward, the

Right of Bukharin, Rykov, and Tomsky is *de facto* ousted from power.

In these critical years plot will succeed plot, in a Party where anyone who allows himself to think in terms of the national interest has to have two faces, one for official use and one for other purposes. I shall merely enumerate. At the end of 1930 the President of the Council of People's Commissars of the R.S.F.S.R., Sergei Ivanovich Syrtsov, disappears with a whole group of leaders accused of opposition (and his successor, Danil Yegorovich Sulimov, will later suffer the same fate). Together with Syrtsov go Lominadze, Shatskin, and Yan Sten, alias the 'Young Stalinist Left'. (Lominadze will kill himself around 1935; Yan Sten, classed as a 'terrorist', will be shot around 1937.)

At the end of 1932 the 'Riutin group' is imprisoned. Riutin, once the Secretary of the Moscow Committee, who had organized gangs of thugs against us, is close to several intellectuals of the Bukharin tendency, such as Slepkov, Maretsky, Astrov, and Eichenwald (all 'Red professors') and also with the old Bolshevik worker Kayurov. They have drawn up a programme of reform for nation and Party, had it distributed in some Moscow factories, and communicated its contents to Zinoviev, Kamenev, and several of us. It is a merciless indictment of the policies of the General Secretary, and concludes by calling for a fresh departure, with the implication that all expelled members, including Trotsky, should be reinstated. The situation of the régime is painted in such bold terms that the following speculation comes at the end: 'One might wonder whether these are not the fruits of an immense and quite conscious provocation. . . .' The General Secretary is compared to the police-spy Azev of olden times. Riutin, condemned to death by the secret Collegium, is pardoned for a short while. . . . For having read this document without informing on its authors, Zinoviev, himself betrayed by Yan Sten, is once more expelled from the Party: when Yaroslavsky tells him the verdict, he clutches at his throat, chokes and whispers 'I'll never live through it!' before falling into a faint.

At the end of 1932 two Old Bolsheviks in the Commissariat of Agriculture, freshly back from the Caucasus, denounce the results of collectivization in a circle of intimates, are arrested and disappear: this is the case of Eismont and Tolmachev. 1933 sees the beginning of the 'nationalist deviation' cases in the federated republics: imprisonment of Shumsky and Maximov in the Ukraine, the suicide of Skrypnik, who was one of Stalin's most determined partisans, purges in the governments of Central Asia. An engineer, back from deportation in distant Siberia, tells me, 'My prison train had three kinds of carriage: one kind lice-ridden and freezing, out of which corpses were cleared—this was for common criminals and abandoned children (*besprizornyi*); another kind, fairly tolerable, for technicians and "hoarders of currency"—the old Liberal Nikolai Vissarionovich Nekrassov, a former minister of Kerensky, died in one of them; and a privileged carriage for the People's Commissars of Central Asia. . . .'

Our communications with Trotsky were almost completely cut off. Communication among ourselves was so difficult that for months we thought Rakovsky was dead; he was in fact only sick. I had managed, in 1929 I think, to send Trotsky a voluminous correspondence passed out from the Verkhne-Uralsk prison, written in microscopic characters on thin strips of paper; it was the last he ever received from his persecuted comrades. The *Bulletin of the Opposition* that Trotsky published reached us only occasionally and in fragments, and ceased to reach us altogether at around this time. I was astonished at the thoroughness with which it was possible, in a country so large, to seal off hermetically the frontiers of the intellect, at all events in so far as these could be subject to police control. We knew of the line of Trotsky's thought only through officials imprisoned after returning from abroad, who discussed it all in the prison-yards, now the last resorts of free Socialist inquiry in the U.S.S.R. We were upset at the discovery that on several serious issues Trotsky, under the unfortunate influence of his Party patriotism, was grossly mistaken. At the time of Blumkin's execution, a normal G.P.U. crime, he still defended this Inquisition on principle. Later, he accepted as true the tales of sabotage and 'conspiracy' by technicians and Mensheviks, being unable to imagine the state of inhumanity, cynicism, and mania that our police-apparatus had sunk to. We had no means of informing him, though the views expressed on these monstrous impostures by the Socialist Press of the period were very sensible.

Together with Trotsky, we were against reckless industrialization, against forcible collectivization, against the inflated Plans, against the sacrifices and the infinitely dangerous strain inflicted on the country by bureaucratic totalitarianism. At the same time we recognized, through all the disasters, the successes achieved by this same industrialization. This we ascribed to the enormous moral capital of the Socialist revolution. The storehouse of intelligent, resolute popular energy which it had built up was now revealed as inexhaustible. The superiority of planning, clumsy and tyrannical as it was, in comparison with its absence, was also visibly manifest to us. But we could not, like so many foreign tourists and bourgeois journalists with a naïve propensity to the worship of force, fail to note that the cost of industrialization was a hundred times multiplied by tyranny. We remained convinced that the achievements of a system of Socialist democracy would have been better, infinitely better and greater, with less cost, no famine, no terror, and no suppression of thought.

A few days after my release from prison in 1928, I was laid out by an unendurable abdominal pain; for twenty-four hours I was face to face with death. I was saved by chance, in the shape of a doctor friend who came in at once, and another friend, a Menshevik, who would not leave my side in the Mariinsky Hospital till I was out of danger. It was an intestinal occlusion. I can still see the dim night illumination of that hospital ward in which quite suddenly, seized by a great fit of shivers, I emerged from semi-delirium to recover a rich and tranquil inner lucidity.

'I think that I am going to die,' I told the nurse, 'fetch the house-doctor.' And I reflected that I had laboured, striven and schooled myself titanically, without producing anything valuable or lasting. I told myself, 'If I chance to survive, I must be quick and finish the books I have begun: I must write, write. . . .' I thought of what I would write, and mentally sketched the plan of a series of documentary novels about these unforgettable times. A Russian nurse's pretty, broad-cheeked face was leaning over me, a doctor was giving an injection; I felt utterly detached from myself, and it occurred to me that my son was, at eight years, already old enough not to forget me. Then I saw the doctor making weird passes with his hand above my face. I managed to sit up, and saw that he was flicking away some great, bloated lice. 'Do you think that I shall live?' I asked him. 'I

think so,' he replied seriously. 'Thank you for that.' On the following morning he told me that I was safe. I had taken my decision:
that is how I became a writer.

I had renounced writing when I entered the Russian Revolution.
Literature seemed quite a secondary matter—so far as I personally
was concerned—in an age like this. My duty was dictated by history
itself. Besides, whenever I did any writing, there was such a striking
discrepancy between my sensibility and my opinions that I could
actually write nothing of any value. Now that nearly ten years had
rolled by, I felt sufficiently in tune with myself to write. I reflected
that our own reactionary phase might be lengthy; the West, too,
might be stabilized for years to come; and since I was refused the
right to join the work of industrialization, except at the price of my
freedom of opinion, I could (while remaining uncompromising as an
Oppositionist forced into inactivity) provide a serviceable testimony
on these times. Because of my love of history I had accumulated a
pile of notes and documents about the Revolution. I set myself to
writing *L'An Un de la Révolution Russe* and to gathering material
for *L'An Deux*. I finished *Les Hommes dans la Prison*.

Historical work did not satisfy me entirely; apart from the fact
that it demands both resources and undisturbed leisure of an order
that I shall probably never enjoy, it does not allow enough scope for
showing men as they really live, dismantling their inner workings
and penetrating deep into their souls. A certain degree of light can
only be cast on history, I am convinced, by literary creation which is
free and disinterested, which is to say devoid of any market pre-
occupations. I had, and still have, an immense respect for literary
activity—and an equally great contempt for 'Literature'. Many
authors write for pleasure (especially the rich ones) and may do it
well; many others practise a conscious profession for the sake of
earning a living and winning a name. Those who have a message
within them express it in the process, and their contribution has
human value. The others are simply suppliers to the book trade. My
conception of writing was and is that it needs a mightier justification:
as a means of expressing to men what most of them live inwardly
without being able to express, as a means of communion, a testimony
to the vast flow of life through us, whose essential aspects we must try
to fix for the benefit of those who will come after us. In this respect,
I belonged to the tradition of Russian writing.

I knew that I would never have time to polish my works properly. They would be worthwhile without that. Others, less engaged in combat, would perfect a style; but what I had to tell, *they* could not tell. To each his own task. I had to struggle bitterly for my family's daily bread, in a society where all doors were closed to me, and where people were often afraid to shake my hand in the street. I asked myself every day, without any special emotion, but engrossed by the problem of rent, my wife's health, my son's education, whether I would not be arrested in the night. For my books I adopted an appropriate form: I had to construct them in detached fragments which could each be separately completed and sent abroad post-haste; which could, if absolutely necessary, be published as they were, incomplete; and it would have been difficult for me to compose in any other form.

Individual existences were of no interest to me—particularly my own—except by virtue of the great ensemble of life whose particles, more or less endowed with consciousness, are all that we ever are. And so the form of the classical novel seemed to me impoverished and outmoded, centring as it does upon a few beings artificially detached from the world. The commonplace French novel, with its drama of love and self-interest focussed, at best, upon a single family, was an example I was determined to avoid at all costs. My first novel had no central character; its subject was not myself, nor this or that person, but simply men and prison. I next wrote *Naissance de Notre Force*, sketching the surge of revolutionary idealism across the devastated Europe of 1917–18. After that *Ville Conquise*, a stern documentary on Petrograd in 1919. If anyone influenced me it was John Dos Passos, though I was not attracted by his literary impressionism. I had the strong conviction of charting a new road for the novel. Among Russian writers Boris Pilniak was venturing on a similar path.

Between 1928 and 1933 I thus completed one historical book and three novels, which were published in France and Spain. From Paris I received encouragement from Jacques Mesnil, Magdeleine Paz, the brilliant poet Marcel Martinet, Georges Duhamel, Léon Werth, and the review *Europe*.[1] I needed it to some small degree, since I was

---

[1] Jacques Mesnil (1872–1940): Socialist writer and journalist; supporter of Romain Rolland's anti-militarism during the First World War; later a companion of Serge in the early days of the Comintern in Russia. Magdeleine Paz: novelist and essayist; friend and supporter of Serge in both his periods of confinement in

working almost entirely alone, persecuted, and 'more than half beaten', as I wrote to my distant friends. In Paris itself, my books met hostility from two quarters. Bourgeois criticism viewed them as revolutionary works which were best passed over in silence (besides the author was the devil of a long way off, wasn't he?); left-wing critics, dominated, influenced or paid by the Soviet Union, boycotted me even more thoroughly. Despite it all, my books lived out their lives tenaciously; but they earned me very little.

In Russia my situation was critical. My old friend Ilya Yonov, the head of the literary publishing-house of the State Press, a former convict and once a Zinovievite Oppositionist, stopped the printing of my first novel when it was already translated, proof-read and made up in pages. I went to see him. 'Is it true what they tell me?' 'It's true. You can produce a masterpiece every year, but so long as you are not back in the line of the Party, not a line of yours will see the light!'

I turned my back on him and walked out.

At the time when my second novel was published in Paris, I raised the issue with Comrade Leopold Averbach, the General Secretary of the Association of Proletarian Authors. Our acquaintance was of long standing. He was a young Soviet careerist possessed of an extraordinary talent for the bureaucratic callings. Less than thirty, he had the hairless head of the young senior official, the verbal fluency of a Congress demagogue, and the dominating, false-sincere eyes of the manipulator of meetings.

'I will see to it, Victor Lvovich! I know about your attitude, but as for boycotting you let's just see! We've not got as bad as that!' While this was going on, the Leningrad Writers' Publishing Co-operative, which was about to sign a contract with me, ran foul of the categorical veto of the Regional Party Committee's Cultural Section. The hazards of politics did, it is true, give me my revenge on Averbach and his uniformed *literati*. I published in Paris a small book entitled *Literature and Revolution*, which inveighed against the conformism of so-called 'proletarian literature'.

the Soviet Union. Marcel Martinet (1887–1944): revolutionary poet; friend of Trotsky from the First World War until the latter's murder; resigned as literary editor of *L'Humanité* after the rise of Stalinism; campaigner on behalf of Serge. Georges Duhamel (1884–1966): the noted author of the sequence of 'Pasquier Chronicles'. Léon Werth (1879–1955): anti-colonialist French novelist; friend of Serge during the late thirties.

Scarcely had this volume left the press when Leopold Averbach learnt from the Soviet newspapers that the Association of Proletarian Authors had been dissolved by the Central Committee and that he was no longer the General Secretary of anything at all! He was still the nephew of Yagoda, the head of Security, and a good bureaucrat to boot. He delivered a number of speeches condemning his own 'cultural politics' of yesterday. People asked each other, smiling, 'Have you read Averbach's diatribe against Averbach?' And the Central Committee gave him the task of managing a Communist organization in Magnitogorsk. There Leopold Averbach initiated a sabotage-trial, acted himself as prosecutor against the technicians concerned, had them condemned to death according to the rite—and disappeared from my view. (He was, in 1937, after the fall of Yagoda, denounced in the Soviet Press for a traitor, saboteur, terrorist, and Trotskyist, and thence shot.) Although my little book on *Literature and Revolution* had anticipated the Central Committee's decision, it was banned in the U.S.S.R.

At this point I should have dealt at length with the Soviet writers whose life I shared; with their resistance, timid and stubborn at once, to the smothering of their creative freedom; with their humiliations and their suicides. I should have outlined portraits of remarkable men. I have no space to do so; and of these men, some are still alive. In speaking of them I might put them in danger. What I must tell here briefly is the tragedy of a literature of mighty spiritual sources, strangled by the totalitarian system—and also the diverse reactions evoked by this tragedy in men supremely gifted for creative work, whether poets or novelists.

Poets and novelists are not political beings because they are not essentially rational. Political intelligence, based though it is in the revolutionary's case upon a deep idealism, demands a scientific and pragmatic armour, and subordinates itself to the pursuit of strictly defined social ends. The artist, on the contrary, is always delving for his raw material in the subconscious, in the pre-conscious, in intuition, in a lyrical inner life which is rather hard to define; he does not know with any certainty either where he is going or what he is creating. If the novelist's characters are truly alive, they function by themselves, to a point at which they eventually take their author by surprise; and sometimes he is quite perplexed if he is called upon to classify them in terms of morality or social utility. Dostoevsky,

Gorky, and Balzac brought to life, all lovingly, criminals whom the Political Man would shoot most unlovingly. The new totalitarian states, constraining their writers by directives of strict ideology and absolute conformism, succeeded only in killing the creative faculty within them. Between 1921 and 1928 Soviet literature had its glorious season of full flower. From 1928 onwards it declines and dies out. Printing, no doubt of it, goes on; but – what gets printed?

Max Eastman found the right expression for it: 'Writers in uniform'. The conscription and uniforming of Russia's writers took several years to complete; creative freedom disappeared side by side with freedom of opinion, with which it is inseparably bound. In 1928 or 1929 the Leningrad writers were on the point of protesting openly against the censorship, the Press campaigns of slander and threatening, and the administrative pressure. Nothing was done, apart from interviews with high officials (who offered reassurances) and routine acts of petty cowardice. When the Press denounced Zamyatin and Pilniak as public enemies, the first for a biting satire on totalitarianism, the other for a fine realist novel, my author friends voted everything that was expected of them against their two comrades; this done, they were free to go and ask their pardon privately. When, at the time of the technicians' trial, the Party organized demonstrations in favour of the execution of the culprits, and universal votes for the death-penalty, the writers voted and demonstrated like everybody else; this although they numbered men who knew what was going on and were troubled by it, such as Konstantin Fedin, Boris Pilniak, Alexei Tolstoy, Vsevolod Ivanov, and Boris Pasternak.

During the Ramzin trial the Leningrad Writers' Union summoned me to an important meeting. Knowing that it was to concern itself with demanding executions, I did not go to it. A member of the Bureau came to see me:

'Doubtless you were ill, Victor Lvovich?'

'Not at all. I am on principle opposed to the death-penalty in our country at this present time. I think that the revolver has been abused in such excess that the only way of restoring any value to human life in the U.S.S.R. would be to proclaim the abolition of the death-penalty in accordance with the 1917 Programme. I request you to take note of this statement.'

'Certainly, certainly. In that case, will you kindly take note of our resolution, unanimously carried, on the trial of the Industrial Party, and give us your approval with your reservation about the death-penalty?'

'No. I think that trials are the affair of the courts, not of the unions.'

And yet . . . nothing happened to me. Two schoolmistresses who adopted the same attitude (I did not know them) were forthwith expelled from their union, hounded from their jobs, arrested as counter-revolutionaries and deported. The worst of it all was that after having gone to so much trouble to obtain an outcry for bloodshed, the Central Committee reprieved the condemned men.

Every time this sort of voting took place, the writers felt a little more domesticated. Our social tea-gatherings were divided into two parts. From eight to ten at night conversation was conventional and directly inspired by the newspaper editorials: official admiration, official enthusiasm, etc. Between ten and midnight, after a few glasses of vodka had been drunk, a kind of hysteria came out, and conversations—now diametrically at odds—were sometimes punctuated by fits of anger or weeping. Face to face with his neighbour, each one dropped the official style, and displayed instead an alert critical intelligence, a tragic gloom, a Soviet patriotism proceeding from living souls completely exposed.

Andrei Sobol, a notable novelist and a good revolutionary (once a convict), had killed himself at the same time as Sergei Yesenin, in 1926. There were several suicides of young folk; I remember that of Victor Dmitriev and his wife. On 14 April 1930, Vladimir Mayakovsky fired a bullet into his heart. I wrote of this (in Paris, anonymously): 'He was a wonderful "fellow-traveller"; he wasted his best talents in a weary quest for God knows what ideological line, demanded of him by petty pedants who made a living out of it. Having become the most-requested rhymester of hack journalism, he allowed his personality to be sacrificed to this daily drudgery. He felt that he was going to the dogs. He never stopped justifying himself and pleading that it was a surrender to superior force. . . .' Mayakovsky had just joined Leopold Averbach's Association of Proletarian Authors. In his last poem, 'At the Top of my Voice!' he wrote of '*the petrified crap of the present. . . .*'

I know that he had spent the previous evening drinking, in bitter self-justification, before his friends who kept telling him harshly, 'You're finished; all you ever do is piss out copy for the hacks.' I had only held one conversation of any significance with him. He was annoyed at a long article I had devoted to him in *Clarté* at a time when he was unknown in the West. 'Why do you say that my Futurism is no more than Past-ism?'

'Because your hyperboles and shouts, and even your boldest images, are all saturated with the past in its most wearisome aspects. And you write

> *In men's souls*
> *Vapour and electricity.* . . .

Do you really think that's good enough? Surely this is materialism of a peculiarly antiquated variety?'

He knew how to declaim before crowds; but not how to argue. 'Yes, I'm a materialist! Futurism *is* materialist!'

We parted cordially, but he became so official that I never met him again and most of the friends of his youth dropped him.

I no longer saw anything of Gorky, who had come back to the U.S.S.R. terribly changed. My near relatives, who had known him since he was a youth, had stopped seeing him since the day he refused to intervene on behalf of the five condemned to death in the Shakhty trial. He wrote vile articles, merciless and full of sophistry, justifying the worst trials on grounds of Soviet humanism! What was going on inside him? We knew that he still grumbled, that he was uneasy, that his harshness had an obverse of protest and grief. We told each other: 'One of these days he'll explode!' And indeed he did, a short while before his death, finally breaking with Stalin. But all his collaborators on the *Novaya Zhizn* (*New Life*) of 1917 were disappearing into jail and he said nothing. Literature was dying and he said nothing.

I happened to catch a glimpse of him in the street. Leaning back alone, in the rear seat of a big Lincoln car, he seemed remote from the street, remote from the life of Moscow, reduced to an algebraic cipher of himself. He had not aged, but rather thinned and dried out, his head bony and cropped inside a Turkish skull-cap, his nose and cheekbones jutting, his eye-sockets hollow like a skeleton's. Here was an ascetic, emaciated figure, with nothing alive in it except the will to exist and think. Could it, I wondered, be some kind of inner drying, stiffening, and shrinking peculiar to old age, which had begun in him at the age of sixty? I was so struck with this idea that, years later in Paris, at the very time when Romain Rolland, then sixty-five, was following exactly the same spiritual path as old Gorky, I was inexpressibly reassured by the humanity and clear-sightedness of André Gide, and I thought gratefully of John Dewey's honest perspicacity.

After this encounter I tried to see Alexei Maximovich, but was barred at the door by his secretary (G.P.U.), a robust character with pince-nez, generally despised and singularly well-named since he was called Kriuchkov, i.e. Hook.[1]

Boris Andreyevich Pilniak was writing *The Volga Flows Into the Caspian Sea*. On his work-table I saw manuscripts under revision. It had been suggested to him that, to avoid banishment from Soviet literature, he should remodel *Forest of the Isles*, that 'counter-revolutionary' tale of his, into a novel agreeable to the Central Committee. This body's Cultural Section had assigned him a co-author who, page by page, would ask him to suppress this and add that. The helpmate's name was Yezhov, and a high career awaited him, followed by a violent death: this was the successor to Yagoda as head of the G.P.U., shot like Yagoda in 1938 or 1939.

Pilniak would twist his great mouth: 'He has given me a list of fifty passages to change outright!' 'Ah!' he would exclaim, 'if only I could write freely! What would I not do!' At other times I found him in the throes of depression. 'They'll end up by throwing me in jail. . . . Don't you think so?' I gave him new heart by explaining that his fame in Europe and America safeguarded him; I was right, for a while. 'There isn't a single thinking adult in this country', he said, 'who has not thought that he might be shot. . . .' And he related to me details of killings which he had picked up drinking with tipsy executioners. He wrote a wretched article for *Pravda* on some technicians' trial, received a passport for travel abroad on Stalin's personal recommendation, visited Paris, New York, and Tokyo, and came back to us dressed in English tweed, with a little car to himself, dazzled by America. 'You people are finished!' he told me, 'Revolutionary romanticism is out! We are entering an era of Soviet Americanism: technique and practical soundness!' He was childishly pleased with his fame and material comforts.

[1] Kriuchkov was shot in 1938, after the Moscow Trial of that year, in which he 'confessed' to having caused the death of Gorky under Yagoda's instructions.

A little before my arrest, we took a long car trip together, to enjoy vistas of sunshine and unsullied snow. Suddenly he unbent and turned to face me, his eyes saddened: 'I do believe, Victor Lvovich, that one day I too will send a bullet into my head. Perhaps it would have been better if I had done that. I cannot emigrate like Zamyatin: I could not live apart from Russia. And I have the feeling that as I come and go, there is a gun in my back, with a pack of blackguards on the trigger. . . .'

When I was arrested he had the courage to go and protest to the G.P.U. (He disappeared without trial in 1937, quite mysteriously: one of the two or three real creators of Soviet literature, a great writer translated into ten languages, disappeared without anyone in the Old World or the New—except myself, and my voice was stifled—inquiring after his fortune or his end!) One critic has said that the works he had written with Yezhov 'shout the lie and whisper the truth'.

The star of Count Alexei Nikolayevich Tolstoy was climbing gently to its zenith. I had met him in Berlin in 1922, an authentic counter-revolutionary *émigré*, negotiating his return to Russia and his future royalties. Highly esteemed by the educated classes under Tsarism, a discreet liberal and honest patriot, he had fled with the White forces from the Revolution. He was a decent stylist and now and then a good psychologist, skilful enough to adapt to the public taste, to turn out a successful play or a novel of contemporary interest. In character, manner, and morals he was really a high Russian lord of olden days, loving beautiful things, good living, polite literature, cautiously liberal opinions, the odour of power— and, what is more, the Russian people: 'our eternal little *mujik*'.

He invited me out to his villa at Dietskoe Selo, where his furniture came from the Imperial palaces, to hear the first chapter of his *Peter the Great*. At this time he was not particularly well regarded, and was deeply distressed by the sight of the devastated countryside; he conceived of his great historical novel as a defence of the peasant folk against tyranny as well as an explanation of the present tyranny in terms of one of the past. A little later, the analogy he drew between Peter the Great and the General Secretary turned out to be strangely satisfying to the latter. Alexei Tolstoy, too, now began to protest aloud, when he was in his cups, that it was almost impossible to write in such an oppressive atmosphere. He told the General

Secretary himself as much, in the course of a writers' reception, and the General Secretary drove him home in his car, reassured him, lavished him with pledges of friendship. . . . On the following day, the Press stopped attacking the novelist; Alexei Tolstoy was revising his manuscripts. Today he is the official 'great writer' of Soviet Russia. But has he ever inquired after the fate of Boris Pilniak— or of so many others who were his friends? The quality of his writings has sunk quite incredibly, and falsifications of history can be found in them on a scale that is simply monstrous. (I am thinking of a novel of his about the Civil War.)

Three men far removed from this rising official celebrity used to meet in an old cottage in Dietskoe, and through them I made contact with a different set of values. These were representatives of the Russian intelligentsia of the great period from 1905 to 1917. The ancient, shabby interior of the place seemed pervaded through and through with silence. Andrei Bely and Feodor Sologub would be playing chess. Sologub, the author of the novel *The Petty Demon*, was in his last (the sixty-fourth) year of his life: a small man of an astounding pallor, his oval face well-proportioned, his forehead high, bright-eyed, timid and introverted. Since the death of his wife he had been delving into mathematics for some proof of an abstract form of immortality. His work had been concentrated variously on the mystical world, the sensual world, and the Revolution. His utterances displayed a childish ingenuity, and it was said of him that all he lived on now was 'his big secret'.

In the visionary eyes and passionate voice of Andrei Bely an inextinguishable flame still burned. He was fighting for his imprisoned wife and writing his autobiography, *At the Frontier of Two Epochs*; he lived even now in a state of intellectual fever. Ivanov-Razumnik, now failing, his face cadaverous and his suit threadbare, would from time to time emit some mordant observation; he was allowed to deal only with subjects of literary scholarship, writing his study of Schedrin—until he disappeared.

Censorship, in many forms, mutilated or murdered books. Before sending a manuscript to the publisher, an author would assemble his friends, read his work to them and discuss together whether such-and-such pages would 'pass'. The head of the publishing enterprise would then consult the *Glavlit* or 'Literature Office', which censored manuscripts and proofs. Once the book was published, official critics would issue their opinion, on which depended the sales of the book to libraries, whether it would be tolerated, or whether it would be withdrawn from circulation. I saw the entire edition of the first volume of an *Encyclopaedic Dictionary*, which had cost the intellectuals of Leningrad years of toil, sent to be pulped. Success was manufactured wholly by the Party offices. The chosen book, recommended to all the libraries in the land, was printed in tens of thousands of copies; the Foreign Languages Publishing House translated it into several languages, and the author, loaded with money and praise, became a 'great writer' in the space of a season, which of course deceived nobody. Such was the case with Maria Shaginyan and her novel *Hydrocentral*. In the same period, censorship and 'criticism' achieved the silencing of a masterly Communist writer who had risen from the people, Artem Vesioly. But then—the title he had given his outstanding novel was *Russia Washed in Blood*!

What I cannot reproduce is the atmosphere of overpowering, sickening absurdity that surrounded some of the meetings of writers who were compelled to fanatical obedience. One day in a small, dark meeting-room in Herzen House, we heard a report from Averbach on the spirit of the proletariat, the collective farm, and Bolshevism in literature. Lunacharsky, frozen in a stance of weary boredom, kept passing me ironical little notes—but he spoke nothing but a few quasi-official remarks, in terms more intelligent than the official speaker had used. Between the two of us Ernst Toller was seated, lately released from a Bavarian prison. Bit by bit the whole deadening speech was translated for him, and in his great dark eyes, in his face of strength and gentleness, a kind of confusion could be seen. Surely in his years of imprisonment as an insurgent poet, he had pictured the literature of the Soviets as altogether different from this. I remember a meeting of our Leningrad writers' union in which some young men of letters, who were none the less practically unlettered, suggested the formation of 'mopping-up' squads, to go to the second-hand bookshops and remove from them historical works which the Leader had just attacked. An uneasy silence fell across the room.

I certainly had no place in this literature of sacred cows; and my very relationships with its writers were not at all easy. My non-conformist attitude was a reproach to them, and my presence compromised them. The friendships I had left were brave ones; I have no right to speak of them here. How and on what could I live? For some time after my expulsion from the Party I was allowed to carry on with my translations of Lenin for the Lenin Institute, though my name was kept out of the published volumes and I was checked, line by line, by experts charged with the task of uncovering possible sabotage in the disposition of semicolons. I knew that Nadezhda Konstantinovna Krupskaya was working in similar conditions on her memoirs of Lenin; a committee was reviewing her every line. Gorky was altering his own memoirs on the demand of the Central Committee. Kreps, the head of International Social Publishing, a little red-eyed Tatar, greeted me rubbing his hands: 'I've just started up a bookshop in the Philippines!' He put on a friendly voice to let me know that, because of my correspondence abroad, I was in grave danger of being indicted for treason (a capital charge). This said, he invited me to reflect, hinting at a glorious future for me if I returned to the Party: 'One day you will run the Lenin Institute of Paris!' (Poor Kreps disappeared himself in 1937.)

Then came the years of rationing, famine, and black-marketeering. Authors with the right ideas received fantastic secret rations from the G.P.U. co-operatives, including even butter, cheese and chocolate! 'Do have a little taste', a friend asked me, 'of this highly confidential Gruyère. . . .' Doubtful writers, that is any who were lyrical, mystical, or unpolitical, got mediocre official rations. I got nothing except for an occasional bit of fish; and some of the comrades came to tell me that they had had to battle hard in committee to stop my name from being deleted from the list.

I lived with my wife and son in a small apartment in the centre of Leningrad, 19 Zhelyabova Street, in a 'communal flat' of a dozen rooms, occupied by, on average, a good thirty people. In several cases a whole family lived in one room. A young G.P.U. officer, plus his wife, child, and grandmother, lived in a small room overlooking the courtyard; I knew that he had been put there, in the room vacated by a jailed technician, so as to have 'someone' near me. In addition, a Bessarabian student was spying on me, watching my comings and goings and listening to my conversations on the telephone (which was situated in the corridor). A little G.P.U. secret agent lived in a hidey-hole next to the bathroom; he assured me of his friendship, without concealing the fact that he was always

being interrogated about me; he was the amiable type of informer.
Thus, even at home, I was under constant watch from three agents.
A sham Oppositionist, who was visibly annoyed at the role he had to
assume, visited me once or twice a week for confidential political
discussions—and I knew that our conversation was filed away
verbatim the next day in my dossier. A young relative on my wife's
side came one night to knock on my door. He was a delicate youth,
recently married, who lived poorly: 'Listen, I've just left the G.P.U.
They want me to make detailed reports on the people who visit you
—I'll lose my job if I refuse. What can I do, God, what can I do?'

'Don't fret,' I replied. 'We'll draw up your reports together. . . .'

Another time, also at night, an oldish intellectual, bespectacled,
asthmatic and terrified by his own audacity, came in and sat for a
long time recovering his breath in an armchair. Then, gathering all
his courage together:

'Victor Lvovich, you do not know me, but I know you, and have a
high opinion of you. . . . I am a censor in the Secret Service. Be
discreet, discreet: they're always paying attention to you.'

'I have nothing to hide. I think what I think. I am what I am.'

He repeated, 'I know, I know, but it's very dangerous. . . .'

In my frequent sojourning in Moscow, I felt more and more
that I was a hunted man. Stay at a hotel? Impossible, the hotels are
reserved for officials. My relatives, who usually put me up, found
my visits too compromising and begged me to go elsewhere. Most
often I spent the night in houses that had just been emptied out by
the G.P.U.; there, people had no fear of compromising themselves
any further by being my hosts. Acquaintances avoided me in the
street. Bukharin, whom I ran into just outside the Lux Hotel,
slipped by with a furtive 'How's things?'—eyes right, eyes left,
then off sharp. Pierre Pascal's small room, in a converted hotel
on Leontievsky Street, was another spot that was devilishly spied on,
but one breathed a free air there. The Italian Rossi (Angelo Tasca),
who was still on the Comintern Executive, came there to stretch out
on the couch. He had the broad, indented brow of a dreamer—and
he still hoped to bring the International back to health! He was
planning to join with Ercoli (Togliatti), in winning over a majority
of the Central Committee of the Italian Party, and then offer support
to Bukharin. (Ercoli betrayed him and Rossi was expelled.) He
told me, 'I can assure you, Serge, that every time there are three of

you together, one of you is an *agent provocateur*.' 'There are only
two of us,' I answered, alluding to Andrés Nin, with whom, never
out of temper, his long hair tossing in the wind, I used to stroll
through Moscow, shadowed at each step.

Luck was on my side. One night I was going back through
twenty degrees of frost to the house of some comrades to sleep in
the bed of a friend who had been arrested. A frightened little
girl half-opened the door to me: 'Get away quickly. They are turning
the flat inside out. . . .' I did not know where to go, but I went.
Another time I was asked to a private party, but missed the telephone-
call inviting me; that evening all the guests were arrested. Perhaps
my presence there had been anticipated? Still another time, I
escaped from Maria Mikhailovna Joffe's house while the police were
surrounding it. One of them, naturally, clung behind my heels;
without turning round I hurriedly skirted the white façade of the
Comintern building, turned the corner and made an acrobatic leap
to grab a tram going along at full speed. How long could it be kept
up? (The young widow of our great comrade Joffe disappeared for
ever, deported to Central Asia with her son—who died there—and
then imprisoned several times; her life ended in captivity in 1936,
no one knows exactly where or how. I had known her as a fair-
haired young girl, proud and coquettish; when I met her again she
was a woman, charming in the way of Russian peasant women,
earnest and yet playful; her moral stamina formed a salutary influence in the Oppositionist deportee-colonies of Turkestan. She
struggled for eight years without weakening.)

Later on, they uncovered a whole series of conspiracies. How could
anyone conspire in these conditions—when it was scarcely possible
to breathe, when we lived in houses of glass, our least gestures and
remarks spied upon?

Our crime as Oppositionists lay simply in existing, in not disowning ourselves, in keeping our friendships and talking freely in
each other's company. In the two capitals, the total extent of those
relationships of mine which were based on free thinking was no more
than twenty individuals, all differing in their ideas and characters.
Spare, tough, dressed as the true proletarian that he in fact was, the
Italian syndicalist Francisco Ghezzi, of the *Unione Sindicale*, emerged
from imprisonment at Suzdal to tell us ardently of the victories of
industrialization. His hollow face was lit up by his feverish eyes.

And he came back from the factory with a troubled brow. 'I have seen workers falling asleep under their machines. Do you know that real wages have sunk to one-twentieth during my two years in the Isolator?' (Ghezzi disappeared in 1937.)

Gaston Bouley, as full of whimsy as a seasoned Paris street-urchin, now working in the Commissariat of Foreign Affairs, was making plans to return to France, but did not dare ask for a passport: 'They'd lock me up straight away!' (He was deported to Kamchatka in 1937.) That much-mellowed anarchist Herman Sandomirsky, also on the staff of the Foreign Affairs Commissariat, was publishing his powerful studies of Italian Fascism, and acting as our middleman with the G.P.U.; he was putting up a quiet fight for the Kropotkin Museum. (He disappeared in 1937, deported to Yenisseisk and probably shot.) Zinaida Lvovna Bronstein, Trotsky's youngest daughter, was ill: she managed to go abroad, where she too soon committed suicide. Her character was, point for point, like that of her father, with a lively intelligence and a fine spiritual toughness. Her husband, Volkov, was in prison, never to be released. Andreu Nin sent parcels to the victimized comrades, gathered material on Marx, and translated Pilniak into Catalan. In order to get permission to leave for Spain, then in the midst of revolution, he sent the Central Committee a positive ultimatum, framed in dauntless language. He was allowed to leave—and I shall speak later of his dreadful end. Occasionally we would indulge in a few fantasies. I remember saying: 'If a madman were to shoot some satrap or other, there is a grave risk that we would all be shot before the week was out.' I did not know how truly I spoke.

The persecution went on for years inescapably, tormenting men and driving them crazy. Every week the system devoured a new class of victim. In this atmosphere my wife lost her reason. I found her one evening lying in bed with a medical dictionary in her hand, calm but ravaged. 'I have just read the article on *Madness*. I know that I am going mad. Wouldn't I be better off dead?' Her first crisis had come during a visit to Boris Pilniak's; they were discussing the technicians' trial, and she pushed back the cup of tea offered her, with revulsion—'It's poison, don't drink it!' I took her to psychiatrists, who were generally excellent men, and she settled down in the clinics. However, the clinics were full of G.P.U. people who won over the patients' confidence while curing their nervous difficulties.

She came home again a little better, for a while, and then the old story began again: bread-cards refused, denunciations, arrests, death-sentences demanded over all the loudspeakers placed at the street corners. . . .

She had suffered much from the disgusting persecution which was visited upon my in-laws—simply because they were my in-laws, and libertarians to boot. And always, at the root of it, was the 'struggle for life' in destitution. My father-in-law, Russakov, had fought in the 1905 revolution at Rostov, acted as Secretary to the Russian Seamen's Union in Marseilles, and was expelled from France in 1918 for organizing a strike on ships loaded with munitions for the Whites. Now he was a cloth-capped worker, living with his family in a princely couple of rooms in the same communal apartment as ourselves; from the moment that he became defenceless there were plans afoot to take them off him. People from the Party and the G.P.U. came to insult him in his own home and hit my wife in the face; they denounced him as a counter-revolutionary, ex-capitalist, anti-Semitic, and terrorist! He was hounded that same day from his job and his union, and indicted. To a signal from the agitators, whole factories demanded the passing of the death-penalty upon him—and they were on the way to obtaining it. This took place at a time when I was in Moscow, and the informers who kept watch on me at home thought I was under arrest, since they had lost sight of me. Actually I was staying with Panaït Istrati in a little villa lost in the depths of the Bykovo woods. Having learnt the news from the papers, Istrati, Dr. N——, and I took the train and, once in Leningrad, ran to the editorial office of the local *Pravda*. 'What is this senseless crime you are committing?' we asked angrily of the editor, Rafail, a hardened, spiritless official with a shaven head. 'We can prove a hundred times over that all this stuff is lies and that at the most there has been a half-hearted scuffle in a corridor, in which a young woman has been attacked and an old worker insulted!'

'I personally respect working-class democracy,' replied this perfect functionary, 'and I have here ten resolutions from factories demanding the death-penalty! However, out of consideration for you, I will suspend this campaign pending the investigation!'

The Party leaders, by contrast, proved to be understanding and moderate. Naturally the inquiry fizzled out. A public trial ended in the acquittal of my wife and her parents, to applause from the spectators. On the same day, the Communist cells ran meetings to demand the quashing of 'this scandalous judgement' and the District Attorney, yielding, as he told me, to 'the voice of the masses', obliged. A second trial took place, before a suitable magistrate. When Russakov was relating his life-history, complete with documentation, and was telling of his trips to New York (twenty years ago, as a dish-washer) and Buenos Aires (in the bilge with the other emigrants), this magistrate replied sarcastically, 'You pretend to be a proletarian, but I see you have made trips abroad!'

However, since all that was behind the case was a provocation on the part of a G.P.U. woman informer, the second trial resulted only in a verdict of censure, passed, it is true, upon the victims of the crime. This sordid affair lasted a whole year, during every month of which the Russakovs were refused bread-cards, on the grounds that they were 'ex-capitalists'; Russakov himself could find no work. The Workers' and Peasants' Inspectorate held its own trial and had him reinstated in the union, without managing to find him a job. . . . The investigator for the Inspectorate was a tall, thin young man with untidy hair and grey eyes, who displayed a singular honesty. His name was Nikołayev—and subsequently I wondered if this was the same Nikolayev, a former G.P.U. and Inspectorate officer, who shot Kirov in 1934.

Istrati went back to France, heartbroken by these experiences. It is with deep emotion that I recall his memory. He was still young, with the leanness of the Balkan highlander, rather ugly with his large, salient nose, but despite his tuberculosis so alive, so enthusiastic for living! Whether as a sponge-fisherman, a sailor, a smuggler, a tramp or a bricklayer's mate, he had passed through every port on the Mediterranean; then he began to write, and cut his throat to end it all. Romain Rolland rescued him; literary fame and the sweet money of royalties came to him out of the blue, with the publication of his Haiduk tales. He wrote without any idea of grammar or style, as a born poet madly in love with simple things like adventure, friendship, rebellion, flesh and blood. He was incapable of theoretical reasoning, and so could not fall into the trap of convenient sophistry. People told him, in my hearing: 'Panaït, one can't make an omelette without breaking eggs. Our revolution . . .' et cetera. He exclaimed, 'All right, I can see the broken eggs. Where's this omelette of yours?'

We came out of the model penal colony of Bolshevo, where hardened criminals worked in freedom under their own supervision. Istrati's only comment was, 'A pity that you can't have all this comfort and such a wonderful system of work unless you've murdered at least three people!' Of the editors of reviews who paid him 100 roubles per article he would ask sharply, 'Is it true that a postman here earns fifty roubles a month?' At every turn he would burst into fits of violent indignation. It took Istrati's inborn mulishness to enable him to resist the corrupt approaches that were made to him, and leave the Soviet Union saying, 'I shall write a book, full of enthusiasm and pain, in which I shall tell the whole truth.' The Communist Press immediately accused him of being an agent of the Rumanian *Siguranţa*. . . . He died, poor, forsaken, and utterly confused, in Rumania. It is partly owing to him that I am still alive.

Shortly afterwards I found great consolation in doing a little work alongside another great, indeed exemplary, character: Vera Nikolayevna Figner. I was translating her memoirs, and she overwhelmed me with corrections framed in her fastidious tones. She was, at 77 years of age, a tiny old woman, wrapped in a shawl against the cold, her features still regular and preserving the impression of a classical beauty, a perfect intellectual clarity and a flawless nobility of soul. Doubtless she looked upon herself proudly as the living symbol of the revolutionary generations of the past, generations of purity and sacrifice. As a member of the Central Committee of the *Narodnaya Volya* (People's Will Party) from 1879 to 1883, Vera Figner was responsible, together with her comrades, for the decision to take to terrorism as a last resort; she took part in organizing ten or so attempts against Tsar Alexander II, arranged the last and successful attack of 1 March 1881, and kept the Party's activity going for nearly two years after the arrest and hanging of the other leaders. After this she spent twenty years in the prison-fortress of Schlüsselburg, and six years in Siberia. From all these struggles she emerged frail, hard and upright, as exacting towards herself as she was to others. In 1931, her great age and quite exceptional moral standing saved her from imprisonment, although she did not conceal her outbursts of rebellion. She died at liberty, though under surveillance, not long ago (1942).

From week to week from 1928 onwards, the ring closes in relentlessly. The value of human life continuously declines, the lie in the heart of all social relationships becomes ever fouler, and oppression ever heavier; this will last up to the economic relaxation of 1935 and the subsequent explosions of terror. I asked for a passport for abroad, and wrote the General Secretary a resolute and forthright letter to this effect. I know that it reached him, but I never had a reply. All I got out of it was military demotion, though on friendly terms. I was the Deputy Commander of the Front Intelligence Service, corresponding to a rank of colonel or general. I expressed my astonishment at keeping this post at a time when the whole Opposition was being imprisoned, and the Commandant of Staff Selection told me with a smile. 'We know perfectly well that in the event of war the Opposition will do its duty. Here we are practical men first and foremost.' I was amazed by this display of sense. So that I might be free to obtain a passport the military authorities reduced me to the ranks and discharged me, on the grounds that I had passed the age limit for military service.

At the end of 1932, the economic and political situation suddenly grew even worse. An actual famine was raging through three-quarters of the countryside; news was whispered of an epidemic of plague in the Stavropol region in the northern Caucasus. On 8 November Stalin's young wife, Nadedzha Alliluyeva, committed suicide in the Kremlin, with a revolver-shot in the breast. A student, she had seen the portraits of her husband in the streets, covering whole buildings; she had lived not only at the summit of power, surrounded by the official lie and the tragedies of conscience, but also in the simple reality of Moscow. Kamenev's daughter-in-law, a young woman doctor who had given first aid to Alliluyeva, was held in custody for some days, and a legend ascribing the death to appendicitis was spread abroad.

Mysterious arrests began among the former Oppositionists who had rallied round the 'general line'. At long intervals, and with minute precautions, I would go and visit Alexandra Bronstein in Leningrad, on the other side of the Neva, in the great, red-brick workers' city of the Vyborg district. Her face calm beneath her white hair, she gave me first-hand news of the Old Man, then in exile at Prinkipo, on the Golden Horn. She corresponded with him openly, and was to pay for this bravery with her life (disappearing in 1936). She told me of the suicide of Zinaida Lvovna Bronstein in Berlin, and showed me a letter from Trotsky, which said that he was surrounded by so many dangers that he never went out, and took the fresh air only very discreetly in his garden. A few days later, the villa he occupied caught fire, perhaps by accident. . . .

I learnt of the arrests of Smilga, Ter-Vaganian, Ivan Smirnov and Mrachkovsky. Mrachkovsky, an unrepentant Oppositionist who had submitted to the Central Committee, was building a strategic railway-line to the north of Lake Baikal, and Stalin had a short while ago received him in a friendly fashion. The leader had complained of having only idiots around him: 'A pyramid of idiots! We need men like you. . . .' I saw Evgeny Alexeyevich Preobraz-hensky, and we opened our hearts for a moment in a dark little yard beneath leafless trees. 'I do not know where we are going,' he said. 'They are stopping me from breathing, I expect anything to happen. . . .' Symptoms of moral treason were being uncovered in his economic works on the world crisis. Hands in his pockets, melancholy and hunched against the cold night air, he was, as I inexplicably sensed, a doomed man.[1]

My own surveillance had grown so close that arrest was percept-ibly in the offing. It seemed to me that, in my communal apartment, the old mother and the wife of the G.P.U. officer and even this young officer himself, so punctilious and pleasant, were looking at me in a peculiar way. The old lady sought me out timidly and said, 'How terrible his job is! Every time my son goes out at night, I pray for him. . . .' She gave me a meaning look and added: 'And I also pray for *the others*. . . .'

I judged that I had a 70 per cent. probability of disappearing in the very near future. As a unique opportunity came my way to get a message to some friends in Paris, I drew up a letter, or testa-ment, addressed to Magdeleine and Maurice Paz, Jacques Mesnil and Marcel Martinet, asking them to publish the essentials of it if I disappeared. In this way the last years I had spent in resistance would not have been completely wasted.

I am sure that, in this document, I was the first person to define the Soviet State as a totalitarian State. 'For many, many years', I wrote, 'the Revolution has been in a phase of reaction. . . . One must not conceal the fact that Socialism carries seeds of reaction within itself. Cast on the soil of Russia these seeds have brought forth

[1] Preobrazhensky subsequently disappeared, it seems around 1937. He was never given a public trial or reported as having made a 'confession'.

a thriving blossom. . . . This régime is in contradiction with every-thing that was stated, proclaimed, intended and thought during the Revolution itself.'

I wrote:

'On three essential points, which take precedence before all tactical considerations, I remain and shall remain, though it may cost me dear, an open and dedicated intransigent, who will have to be coerced to keep quiet:

'I.—*Defence of man. Respect for man.* Man must be given his rights, his security, his value. Without these, there is no Socialism. Without these, all is false, bankrupt and spoiled. I mean: man whoever he is, be he the meanest of men—"class-enemy", son or grandson of a bourgeois, I do not care. It must never be forgotten that a human being is a human being. Every day, everywhere, before my very eyes this is being forgotten, and it is the most revolting and anti-Socialist thing that could happen.

'And on this point, without wishing to erase a single line of what I have written on the necessity of terror in revolutions threatened by death, I must state that I hold as an abomination unspeakable, reactionary, sickening, and corrupting, the continued use of the death-penalty as a secret and administrative measure (in time of peace! in a State more powerful than any other!).

'My viewpoint is that of Dzerzhinsky at the beginning of 1920 when, as the end of the Civil War appeared, he moved—and Lenin willingly ratified—the abolition of capital punishment for political offences. It is also that of those Communists who for several years have advocated a reduction in the inquisitorial powers of the Extraordinary Commissions (Cheka and G.P.U.). So low has the value of human life fallen, and so tragic is the result, that all capital punishment in the present régime must be condemned.

'Equally abominable, and unjustifiable, is the suppression, by exile, deportation, and imprisonment more or less for life, of all dissent in the working-class movement.

'II.—*Defence of the truth.* Man and the masses have a right to the truth. I will not consent either to the systematic falsification of history or to the suppression of all serious news from the Press (which is confined to a purely agitational role). I hold truth to be a precondition of intellectual and moral health. To speak of truth is to speak of honesty. Both are the right of men.

'III.—*Defence of thought*. No real intellectual inquiry is permitted in any sphere. Everything is reduced to a casuistry nourished on quotations. . . . Fear of heresy, based on self-interest, leads to dogmatism and bigotry of a peculiarly paralysing kind. I hold that Socialism cannot develop in the intellectual sense except by the rivalry, scrutiny and struggle of ideas; that we should fear not error, which is mended in time by life itself, but rather stagnation and reaction; that respect for man implies his right to know everything and his freedom to think. It is not against freedom of thought and against man that Socialism can triumph, but on the contrary, through freedom of thought, and by improving man's condition.' Dated: 'Moscow, February 1st, 1933.' I had no time to read it over. The friends who could see this message to its destination were on their way—and they fully expected to be arrested at the last minute.

On the day that this letter reached Paris my forebodings were proved true. Nobody knew what had become of me, and I did not know myself what would become of me next.

8

THE YEARS OF CAPTIVITY
1933–1936

My poor invalid has that look of absolute agony in her face. . . .
I go out in the cold morning to find her some sedatives and telephone
the psychiatric clinic. I also want to see the newspapers posted up
by the Kazan Cathedral, because somebody has just told me that
Thaelmann has been arrested in Berlin.[1] I am aware of being
followed, which is quite natural. Except that this time, 'they'
are trailing so close behind me that I begin to be worried. As I
come out of the chemist's they stop me. This on the pavement of
October 25th Prospect, with everybody bustling past all round me.

'Criminal Investigation. Kindly follow us, citizen, for purposes of
identification.'

Speaking low, they take out their red cards and station themselves on either side of me. I shrug my shoulders.

'I have quite certainly nothing to do with criminal investigations.
Here is my card from the Soviet Writers' Union. Here are some drugs
for a sick woman who cannot wait. Here is the house where I live; let
us go and see the caretaker; he will make my identity clear to you.'

No, it is absolutely necessary for me to come with them for ten
minutes, the misunderstanding will obviously be cleared up immediately. . . . All right. They have a consultation: which car? They
look carefully at the cars parked near by, pick the most comfortable
one, and open its door for me. 'Kindly take a seat, citizen.'

They have a curt exchange with the dumbfounded driver. 'To
the G.P.U., fast, come on!'

[1] Ernst Thaelmann (1866–1944): leader of the German Communist Party after
its Stalinization; 1924–33, leader of the Communist Party's Reichstag fraction;
arrested in 1933 and murdered at the end of the war in a concentration-camp.

'But I can't! The Director of the Trust will be coming out, I have to . . .' 'No discussions. You'll be given a chit. Move off!' And off we moved, straight to the new G.P.U. building, the handsomest in the new Soviet Leningrad, fifteen storeys high with façades of clean granite, at the angle made by the Neva and the former Liteynaya Prospect. A side-door, a spy-hole. 'Here's the criminal.' (The criminal is myself.) 'Kindly enter, citizen.' I only just find myself in a huge waiting-room when a friendly young soldier comes up to me and shakes my hand: 'Good day, Victor Lvovich! Did everything go off properly?'

Yes, more or less. . . .

'So,' I said, 'there is no doubt of my identity?'

He gave a knowing smile.

The building is spacious, stern and magnificent. A bronze Lenin welcomes me as it does everybody else. Five minutes later I am in the vast office of the investigating magistrate responsible for Party cases, Karpovich. He is a large, ginger-haired man, coldly cordial, sly and guarded.

'We are going to have some long talks together, Victor Lvovich. . . .'

'I have no doubt of that. But we shall have none at all unless first you grant some requests I have. I must ask you to arrange to have my wife transferred, no later than today, to the Red Army's psychiatric clinic; after that I want to talk over the telephone to my son—he is twelve years old—as soon as he comes home from school.'

'Certainly.'

Before my eyes Comrade Karpovich telephones the instructions to the clinic. He takes kindness so far as to offer to telephone my home while my sick wife is being collected. Then:

'Victor Lvovich, what is your opinion on the general line of the Party?'

'What? You don't know? Is it just to ask me this that you have caused all this trouble?'

Karpovich answers: 'Must I remind you that we two here are Party comrades?'

'In that case let me ask you the first questions. Is it true that Thaelmann has been arrested in Berlin?'

Karpovich thinks that the report must be treated with caution but that in Berlin 'things are going badly'. My second question bothers him:

'Has Christian Rakovsky died in deportation?'

The ginger-haired figure hesitates, looks into my eyes, says 'I can't tell you anything,' and indicates *No* by a motion of his head.

The interview which we are beginning is to last from midday to past midnight, interrupted by the meal I am given and by rests during which, when I feel the need to relax, I go for a walk along the big corridor outside. We are on the fourth or fifth floor, and through the huge window-panes I stare at the bustle of the town, I see twilight and then night falling over the teeming view, and I wonder when I shall again see this city that I love above all—if indeed I ever see it again? We talk of everything, point by point: agrarian question, industrialization, Comintern, inner-Party régime, etc. I have objections to the general line on all points; they are Marxist objections. I see them bring in all the papers that have been seized at my home, several trunkfuls. We shall not be short of subject-matter for theoretical discussion! We have tea. Midnight. 'Victor Lvovich, it is with great regret that I must have you transferred to the House of Arrest; however, I am giving orders that you are to be well treated there.'

'Thank you.' It is quite near by. A young plain-clothes policeman, clean-shaven and open-faced, goes with me and, since I ask it, we lean for a while on the embankment overlooking the dark waters of the Neva. The air from the open sea is bracing. I always find this river so charged with turbulent power that I am stirred by it as though by some Russian song.

The old House of Arrest has not changed since 1928—nor, doubtless, over the last fifty years. Are prisons then so durable as to prevail over revolutions and the fall of empires? Formalities of entry, a registration-office, and a series of partitions through which a man passes like a grain on its way into some intricate milling mechanism. In passing I meet a tall, elegant old man with a noble head of white hair; he tells me that he is from the Academy of Sciences, and that they have just taken his spectacles off him, which is the worst nuisance of all. . . . Iron staircases, ascended in dusk, then a door opens for me in the thick stonework, opens and then shuts. A poky cell, lit feebly by one pitiful bulb, just like an underground passage. Somebody rises from one of the two bunks, hails me and then introduces himself. He is a sorry kind of figure and I find it hard at first to follow him:

'Petrovsky, Writers' Union, Poets' Section. . . .'

'I'm a prose-writer myself,' I say.

I am shivering with nervous exhaustion under my heavy leather coat. The poet is shivering too beneath his old sheepskin-lined cloak, from cold and weakness. He is young, thin and wan, with a sparse, discoloured beard. We strike up an acquaintance. He talks and talks, and I sense that my presence is an event for him, which is true enough: he has been living alone for months in this underground solitude, wondering if he was going to be shot. A kindred restlessness keeps us awake for a long time, and brings us close together, strangely moved, each checking the same outflow of feeling, not knowing what to do for one another. I can do only one thing for him: listen to him and reassure him. I prove to him that they cannot shoot him, that the examining magistrate who threatens him is a ruffian using a professional stratagem; arrests are submitted to the secret Collegium which, however slightly, still does ponder possible repercussions. I am calm and reasonable, and I think I see the poet straighten a little, his confidence restored.

He is a child of highways and famine. Self-trained, he became a schoolteacher, and began to write simple poems—which I found full of charm—because he loves to gaze on the rustle of cornfields, the clouds racing above the country scenes, the brushwood and the roads shining by moonlight. 'A peasant poet, do you follow?' Along with two or three friends, he published a hand-written journal at Dietskoe Selo; a subversive tendency was unearthed in it. Why, they asked him, is there not a single reference to collectivization in your poems? Because you are hostile to collectivization? The worst of it was that he belonged to a literary circle—in no way clandestine—run by the philosopher Ivanov-Razumnik, a former Left Social-Revolutionary. Thus I learn that my friend Ivanov-Razumnik, that great, idea-hungry idealist, is also in jail. 'Say some of your poems to me again, comrade poet, I find them very beautiful. . . .' He recites them in an undertone, eyes ablaze, shoulders huddled for warmth under his fur, neck emaciated. We go to bed at dawn, never to forget this past night.

On the following day I was transferred to Moscow, discreetly, in a passenger compartment, accompanied by two G.P.U. men, one in plain clothes and the other in inconspicuous uniform, both of them comradely and polite. The transfer proved that the case was serious. But what case? There was not and could not be anything against my name except the crime of my opinions, which had been common knowledge for years and could easily have been dealt with on the spot. It is true of course that, where facts are absent, there is a free hand for fiction. An *agent provocateur*'s visit came back to my memory. I reflected too that my message to my friends in Paris could have been intercepted. That would be very serious, but on what passage in it could they lean to justify a heavy charge? Persons corresponding abroad were often charged with espionage (a capital offence). I had written: 'I sometimes begin to wonder whether we are not bound to be murdered one way or another in the end, for there are plenty of ways of going about the job . . .'

Was not that discrediting the régime in a most criminal manner? But then, the letter was only to be published if I disappeared. I thought I had hit on it: I had also written: 'And the lies that one breathes in like the air! The whole Press was proclaiming a few days ago that the fulfilment of the Five-Year Plan was resulting in a 68 per cent. increase in wages. . . . However, the value of the rouble has sunk to about a thirtieth while this increase in nominal wages was being achieved. . . .' In the eyes of the secret Collegium, that could justify a charge of 'economic espionage'. In short, I reached Moscow pretty disturbed, but quite determined to resist unyieldingly.

I was at once driven to the Lubianka, that big building in Dzerzhinsky Square built in the commercial style of the last century. Within the hour I found myself in a minute cell, perhaps in the cellars, windowless but powerfully lit, in the company of a stout-bodied worker with a forceful chin who told me that he had been a G.P.U. car-driver, now arrested for having heard a counter-revolutionary leaflet read out among some friends without denouncing everybody immediately. This suffocating box where we were, two yards long by two across, was driving him to distraction. He finally told me that it was here that prisoners condemned to death waited before being taken off for execution. . . . By about three in the morning there were ten or so of us in this cell, now stuffy and over-hot with our breath. Some of us were on the two iron bedsteads, others were standing on the chilly tiling, others again tucked themselves into the door recess. I had a headache and my heart was paining me. We all behaved very deferentially towards each other, with the affability of undertaker's men. I remember how much we were cheered by an old Jew who recalled having been arrested a year ago to the very day. Now, at last, he was being charged with having allegedly deducted a commission on the sale of a typewriter by one office to another. 'There is no evidence', he said naïvely, 'and besides it is not true; but there is a difference between the two sets of accounts. How do you think *I* can explain that away?' Our little corner of Hell shook in a burst of laughter, with no ill-will.

A few hours later, when it was morning, I was taken into a spacious ground-floor barrack-room which looked like a camp of shipwrecked mariners. About fifteen men had been living more or less at home there for weeks or maybe months, waiting for goodness knows what. Several of them had mattresses, the others made their beds on the cement floor. The atmosphere was heavy with anxiety, and breathed a forced good humour. A young soldier standing near the window talked aloud to himself incessantly; one sentence that he kept obstinately repeating could be heard quite clearly: 'Ah well! Let them shoot me!' followed by a tremendous oath. I found myself a place and asked: 'Citizens, can any of you lend me a haversack or suitcase, anything for me to rest my head on?' A big fellow in Siberian dress, his face flecked with the traces of smallpox, offered me a briefcase covered with a towel, and as he lay down next to me introduced himself—'N——, lecturer in agronomy at Irkutsk. . . .' Another agronomist, this one from Moscow, dressed very smartly and with an expression of extreme distress on his face, joined us as we were talking together. He had been arrested the night before and could not get over the shock; all the leading figures in the People's Commissariat for Agriculture had just been whisked off by the G.P.U., and, a fact that most deeply affected this 'non-Party technician', his Communist superiors were now somewhere in this self-same prison, yes, even Deputy People's Commissar Wolfe, and Konar and Kovarsky! He felt as though he was in the middle of an earthquake.

That day, I was taken up by lift to the floors that constituted the inner prison. A short medical inspection, then my fifth search: absolutely nothing was left on me of those trivial objects that people tend to carry about with them, but this final search was so careful that it disclosed the pencil hoarded away in my lining, and the half razor-blade that I had taken the precaution to conceal in my lapel. And so at last I entered the prison of prisons, which was obviously reserved for prominent persons and those charged with the gravest offences. It was a prison of noiseless, cell-divided secrecy, built barely into a block that had once been occupied by insurance company offices. Each floor formed a prison on its own, sealed off from the others, with its individual entrance and reception-kiosk; coloured electric light-signals operated on all landings and corridors to mark the various comings and goings, so that prisoners could never meet one another. A mysterious hotel-corridor, whose red carpet silenced the slight sound of footsteps; and then a cell, bare, with an inlaid floor, a passable bed, a table and a chair, all spick and span. A big, barred window with a screen masking it from the outside. On the freshly painted walls, not a single scribble or scratch. Here I was in the void, enveloped in a quite astonishing silence. Except that, far away, with a jangle of bells and ironmongery, the trams were passing by in Miasnitskaya Street, which at all hours of the day was full of people. . . . Soldiers of the Special Corps, with the smart style and polish of purely mechanical functioning, shut the door gently behind me. I asked their N.C.O. for books and paper. 'You will present that request to the Examining Magistrate, citizen.'

Here, in absolute secrecy, with no communication with any person whatsoever, with no reading-matter whatsoever, with no paper, not even one sheet, with no occupation of any kind, with no open-air exercise in the yard, I spent about eighty days. It was a severe test for the nerves, in which I acquitted myself pretty well. I was weary with my years of nervous tension, and felt an immense physical need for rest. I slept as much as I could, at least twelve hours a day. The rest of the time, I set myself to work assiduously. I gave myself courses in history, political economy—and even in natural science! I mentally wrote a play, short stories, poems. I bent a great effort of will to avoid going over my 'case' except in a purely utilitarian manner and for a limited time; this as a precaution against becoming obsessed with it. My inner life was most intense and rich, in fact not too bothersome at all. In addition, I did a little gymnastics several times a day, and this did me a great deal of good. My diet—black bread, with wheaten or millet batter, and fish-soup—was tolerable but inadequate, and I had hunger-pains every evening. On 1 May (festival of the world's workers!) I was given an extraordinary meal: mincemeat cutlets, potatoes, and stewed fruit! I got thirteen cigarettes and thirteen matches a day. Out of breadcrumbs I made myself a set of dice and a kind of calendar.

The monotony of this existence was broken up by the investigation. I had half a dozen interrogations, spaced out at intervals. Magistrate Bogin (sharp features, spectacles, uniform) opened the series. Probably an alumnus of the G.P.U. training-school (advanced course, naturally), he had a ready flow of talk, doubtless to try out his little psychological tricks, and I let him go on, being well aware that in a situation like this it is best to speak as little as possible yourself and listen carefully to everything you are told. I was awoken around midnight—'Investigation, citizen!'—and taken via lifts, cellars, and corridors to a floor lined with offices which, I discovered, was just next door to my cell-section. All the rooms along these endless corridors were set aside for the use of inquisitors. The one to which I was taken was numbered 380 or 390. I only met one person on the way: a sort of bishop, most imposing, came out of one of the offices, leaning on a cane. I said to him aloud, just for the pleasure of dismaying our warders, 'Take care of yourself, *batiushka* (Father)!' And he answered me gravely with a motion of his hand. That must have started some pretty reports for them to study.

I went into my first examining session in an aggressive mood. 'So! You are resuming the tradition of interrogations at night! Just as in the worst days of Tsarism. Congratulations!'

Bogin was not put out: 'Ah! how bitterly you speak! If I call you in at night, it is because we work day and night, we people! We have no private life, we people!'

We were smiling now, in excellent wit. Bogin stated that he knew all. 'All. Your comrades are so demoralized—I have their depositions here, you wouldn't believe your eyes. We should like to know whether you are an enemy or, despite your disagreements, a real Communist. You can refuse to answer my questions, just as you please: the investigation will be closed this very day and we shall view you with the esteem befitting an open political adversary.'

A trap! You'd like me to make your job easy by giving you *carte-blanche* to go and cook up all kinds of findings against me with your secret reports—findings which would earn me years in the Isolator at the very least. 'No. I am anxious to reply to the examination. Carry on with it.'

'Well then, let us talk together like the Communists we both are. I am at the post that has been assigned me by the Party. You wish to serve the Party, yes, I quite understand you. Do you admit the authority of the Central Committee?'

A trap! If I admit the Central Committee's authority, I have joined in the game, they can make me say what they like in the name of devotion to the Party. 'Excuse me. I have been expelled. I have not asked to be re-admitted. I am not bound by Party discipline any longer. . . .'

Bogin: 'You are deplorably formalistic!'

Myself: 'I demand to know what I am accused of, so that I can refute the charges. I am sure that no blame in Soviet law can be attached to me.'

Bogin: 'Formalism! So you'd like me to lay my cards out on the table?'

Myself: 'Are we in a card-playing mood?'

Eventually he told me that documents from Trotsky had been found at my home. 'That is not true,' I said. And that I often went to see Alexandra Bronstein; we discussed the number of visits I had paid her.

'You talked Opposition matters with her, admit it!'

'No. We talked about our state of health and about literature!'

'You have been in touch with Andrés Nin, who is a counter-revolutionary, haven't you?'

'Yes, by post, on postcards. Nin is a model revolutionary: you know that he is in jail at Algeciras?'

Bogin offered me cigarettes, and explained that my outlook was visibly that of a hardened counter-revolutionary, which was extremely dangerous for me. I interrupted him:

'Must I conclude that I am being threatened with the death-penalty?' He protested, 'Not at all! But, all the same, you are well on the way to destroying yourself. Your only hope for safety lies in a change of attitude and a complete confession. Think it over.'

I was returned to my cell at about 4 a.m.

After a number of night interviews of this kind, neither of us had got anywhere. All I learnt was that they were trying to link me with some person called Solovian, who was quite unknown to me. This information both puzzled and worried me: it was a door opening on to some conspiracy or other.

Every time I went to an examining session, the electric signals operated all along my route, so efficiently that I did not even see any warder other than my own. One night I noticed that several of the warders were gazing at me in a peculiarly attentive way as I went out. When I returned, at dawn, I found them crowded around the reception-office; they seemed to be looking rather benevolently upon me, and the one who searched me was so friendly as to venture a little joke. I discovered later that on that very night the thirty-five agricultural experts had been executed, along with Konar, Wolfe, and Kovarsky, all of them prominent officials, and including several influential Communists. They had gone off just as I had, down these very corridors, summoned just as I had been 'for the examining session' and the warders knew no more than that they had been shot somewhere down there in the cellars. Doubtless they assumed that I was earmarked for the same end—and so looked upon me with the humane attentiveness that I had noticed. When I came back, the warders were both surprised and pleased to see somebody return from that last 'examining session'. As I went to and from interrogations, I happened to pass in front of the gaping mouth of a cement-lined corridor on the ground floor, which was lit with brutal brilliance. Was that the door to the final descent?

Abruptly, the investigation was cut short. I had a strong sense of danger. I was summoned in the middle of the day and received by some high-ranking person, gaunt, grey, and wrinkled, with a cold little face perched on a bird-like neck, and thin, straight lips. I recognized the examining magistrate for serious Oppositional cases, Rutkovsky, the personal aide to the Head of the Department, Molchanov, and a member of the secret Collegium. (Molchanov was shot in the period of the Yagoda trial.) Rutkovsky was crisp and vicious:

'I can see that you are an unwavering enemy. You are bent on destroying yourself. Years of jail are in store for you. You are the ringleader of the Trotskyite conspiracy. We know everything. I want to try and save you in spite of yourself. This is the last time that we try.'

I was chilled to the bone. I felt I had to gain a few moments and interrupted him. 'I'm very thirsty. Could you get me a glass of water?' There was none there; Rutkovsky had to stand up and call someone. I had time to think, and his effect was ruined. He resumed:

'So I'm making one last attempt to save you. I don't expect very much from you—I know you too well. I am going to acquaint you with the complete confessions that have been made by your sister-in-law and secretary, Anita Russakova. All you have to do is say, "I admit that it is true", and sign it. I won't ask you any more questions, the investigation will be closed, your whole position will be improved, and I shall make every effort to get the Collegium to be lenient to you.'

So Anita Russakova had been arrested! She used to take down quite insignificant translations at my dictation. She was an unpolitical girl whose only interest was in music, innocent in all things as a new-born baby. 'I am listening,' I said.

Rutkovsky began to read and I was terrified. It was sheer raving. Anita related that I had made her send messages and take parcels to addresses which were completely strange to me, to people I did not know at all, notably to a certain Solovian who lived in a 'Red Army settlement'. This heap of impostures, coupled with the address of a 'military settlement' came as an immediate revelation to me. Therefore, they intended to shoot me. Therefore, Anita had been tortured into lying like this. Therefore, she was doomed just as I was. I burst out:

'Stop! Not one more line. You are reading a detestable falsehood, every line is false. What have you done to this child to make her lie like this?'

I was in a rage and I felt that I had to be, that I no longer had anything to gain by discretion. I might as well get myself shot and have done with it.

My inquisitor pretended to be angry, or else really was:

'Do you know that you are insulting me? And that that is another serious offence?'

'Let me calm down and I will answer you more soberly. Out of respect for myself, out of respect for you and for the rank that you hold, I refuse to hear another line of this deposition, which is a pack of lies; I demand to be confronted with Anita Russakova.'

'You're destroying yourself.'

As a matter of fact, I was demolishing the whole case, thereby saving myself and Anita as well. One moment of cowardice meant the triumph of falsehood, and then they could shoot us. I knew that the G.P.U. inquisitors worked under the scrutiny of different committees, especially the Central Committee's Control Commission, and that, before they could bring about the verdicts they wanted, they had to prepare their briefs according to the rules.

Every day I wrote to Rutkovsky demanding a confrontation with Anita so that I might unmask what I called her 'lies'. 'Let her describe the places where she pretends to have gone!' I was aware of being in a dilemma. Clearly I had caught my inquisitors in a flagrant fabrication. I was putting the G.P.U. on trial. After that, could I be allowed to live, whether released or sent to an Isolator where I would meet other comrades and tell them about it, from which I could write to the Government authorities? Rutkovsky stood to lose at the very least his career if he failed to break me (I am convinced that he perished with his superiors Molchanov and Yagoda in 1938). I decided to prepare myself for the worst.

My second examination by Rutkovsky. This time he was a little deflated, and ventured a smile. A brief admonishment for form's sake:

'You would be far better advised, I can assure you, to change your attitude and stop treating us as enemies. I tell you this in your own interest . . .', etc.

I heard him out politely, shaking my head.

'All right then, I can see we can do nothing with you. I am going to close the examination. Too bad for you.'

'As you will.'

Up till now not a word had been written down during the interrogations. Perhaps a shorthand writer was at work, concealed from my view. The inquisitor took out some large sheets of headed paper and began to copy the questions and my replies. There were six insignificant questions and six uninteresting replies. Do you know such-and-such persons? Did you and they take an interest in what happened to the deportees? Yes, of course. We used to meet quite openly, and sent letters and parcels to deported people equally openly. Have you had any subversive conversations with them? Of course not. That will be all. Sign here.

'And my confrontation with Anita Russakova? I want to prove to you that she is innocent. When she lied about me she lied about herself too. She hasn't an Oppositional idea in her head. She is just a child.'

My inquisitor's grey eyes gazed at me with a kind of meaningful smile.

'Will it satisfy you if I give you my word that we attach no importance at all to Russakova's evidence, and that this whole business will have no serious consequences for your sister-in-law?'

'Yes.'

'Good! That's that, then. The investigation is closed.'

I asked for news of my wife and son.

'They are doing well.'

I then asked for books. 'What, haven't they given you any yet? It is a piece of unforgivable negligence!'

'No,' I said quietly, 'it's not negligence. . . .'

'You will have some in a few minutes.'

'And might I have an hour's exercise walking, as in all the prisons of the civilized world?'

Rutkovsky pretended to go into fits of amazement. 'What? Do you mean you haven't had that?'

In the evening a warder brought me a pile of books: a *History of the Moslem World*, an *Economic History of the Directory*, Nogin's *Siberian Memoirs*—riches indeed! The Political Red Cross sent me onions, a little butter, a roll of white bread, and a bit of soap. I knew now that my disappearance had been made known in Paris and that, since they could not wring any signature from me which would have justified a legal condemnation, they wanted to avoid any disagreeable fuss on my account. If I had been only a Russian militant, instead of a French author as well, matters would have taken quite a different turn.

If I have lingered so long in describing my examination this is because it was a great help later on, along with what I know from other sources, in enabling me to understand how the great Trials were fabricated.

Alone and at night, I was taken across Moscow in a prison-van; I found myself in a bare, brightly-lit cell in the old Butyrki jail, a city within the city. I stayed there only for two or three days, provided with books and left untroubled. I reflected that there were plenty more prisons waiting for me to see from the inside. On the second or third day they took me downstairs and locked me in a cell with green-tiled walls, like a bathroom, next to a spacious corridor. A lad from the Moscow streets was there with me for a short while, and told me how his father and brother had certainly been shot, but he himself had been spared—yes, a very complicated case. . . . I could hear people going to and fro in the corridor. A G.P.U. officer bustled in with a little paper slip in his hand. 'Read it and sign!' I read it: '*Counter-revolutionary conspiracy. Condemned by the*

Special Collegium to three years' deportation at Orenburg. . . .' I signed, angry and glad all at once: angry because I could do nothing, glad because deportation was, after all, an open-air life, with the free sky above one's head.

Deportees were forming up in the lobby, in a kind of funeral procession. Among them I saw a girl, and a young intellectual with heavy features who shook everyone's hand, introducing himself as 'Solovian' and repeating rapidly: 'I am not in any Oppositional group: supporter of the General Line. . . .' 'Best of luck with the General Line,' I told him. I was taken by open car, together with the girl and several uniformed men, in the direction of a station. Farewell, Moscow! The city, lit by the spring sun, dazzled my eyes. The girl was a Moscow worker, the wife of an imprisoned Oppositionist and a Left Oppositionist herself; she was being deported to the Volga. She gave me news of some of the women comrades locked up in the female prison, and shared her riches with me: a cube of compressed tea and twenty roubles. She whispered, 'Oh, so it's you, Sergo—Sergo for whom we were so afraid! We thought that you would stay in jail for years!' We parted with a hearty embrace in a little station in the Tartar Republic.

Several G.P.U. soldiers guarded the compartment; an extremely stylish, extremely stupid officer, adorned with a pair of superb pincenez whose lenses were cut at right angles in the opticians' latest fashion, sat in various poses on the seat opposite, enticing me into political conversation; I always let the subject drop, and talked about the moon. The train shot through the plains of Russia. One night, in a forest filled with nightingales in song, on the banks of the Volga, I experienced a momentary thrill of wonder. I traversed Samara (Kuibyshev) in the small hours, walking through the sleeping streets in the rose-coloured light with a soldier carrying a lowered rifle behind me, ready to open fire if I looked like running. At the local G.P.U. headquarters, under the shower—a blessing indeed—I came across a dark, bearded, emaciated figure who was frisking about nimbly under the jets of hot water.

'You there, with the intellectual's head—who are you?' he asked me in jovial tones. He went on: 'I'm a Right Communist myself, Secretary of the —— District, Stalingrad region, served in the Civil War, Ivan Yegorovich Bobrov.' I introduced myself in turn. Bobrov had, as punishment for a cruelly accurate report on the course of collectivization in his area, practially died of hunger in some hellish prison-cellar where ten of the thirty inmates were at death's door; now he was, like myself, on the way to Orenburg. Our friendship, which was to endure, began in a comfortable cellar furnished with straw.

On the next day a dozen soldiers from the G.P.U. special cavalry, clicking their spurs against the paving-stones, took us to the station and stood guard round us in the middle of the public traffic. I was amused to see my reflection on a glass door. I had an unkempt beard, black-grey and bristling, and I had leather and fur clothing on, though it was the height of summer; Bobrov was the perfect model of a tramp—jacket in holes at the elbows, trousers in tatters and gone at the knees, and lean as a scarecrow. Our eyes were merry and proud. The folk around viewed us with sympathy, and a peasant woman asked our escort to allow her to offer us some wheatcakes. They were delicious.

Orenburg, on the Ural river, is a metropolis of the steppes, solitary under a glorious sky, on the line from Kuibyshev to Tashkent. Although it is geographically situated on the border between Europe and Asia, it belongs to Asia. Up to 1925 it had been the capital of the Autonomous Republic of the Kazakhs (or Khirghiz), a nomadic people of Central Asia, Turkish in origin and orthodox Moslems, who were still divided into three great hordes. Since then Kazakhstan has become one of the eleven federal republics of the U.S.S.R., with its capital at Alma-Ata. Under the Tsars, Orenburg, the central market for the copious livestock of the steppes, had been a wealthy city, crowned with fifteen or so Orthodox churches and several large mosques. There in the Civil War, the working class had undergone battles of legendary ferocity, marked by frightful massacres of the poor, against a Cossack ataman, General Dutov. During the N.E.P., the town had recovered its substantial prosperity, thanks to the steppe from which it drew its life. When we arrived in June 1933, a hideous famine was raging there, in an environment of destruction and decay.

There was hardly any vegetation, apart from a shady wood on the other bank of the Ural, strewn with silvery leaves. It was a lowly town, whose streets were lined with charming little houses built in peasant style. Tall, raw-boned camels trundled along gloomily under their burdens. There were two central thoroughfares of a

European type, the Sovietskaya and the Kooperativnaya, and a number of pretentious buildings in that Imperial style, with massive white pillars, which the governors-general of old times planted everywhere. All the churches, except for one in the near-by Cossack township of Vorstadt (or Orenpossad), had lately been destroyed. The rubble of the dynamited cathedral formed an islet of quaint little rocks in the middle of one of the squares. There was a little old white church on the hill over the river, which had associations with Pugachev's rebellion of 1774; not even this had been spared. All the priests and the bishops had been deported to the north; religion functioned illegally. The synagogue was either closed or demolished; in the absence of a kosher butcher, the Jews were now refusing to eat meat. On the other hand, the mosques had not been damaged, for fear of provoking the Moslem masses, with whom the authorities had quite enough trouble already. The finest mosque had been converted into a Khirghiz high school. One or two Christian churches, their domes split open and their crosses obliterated, were used as goods warehouses by the co-operatives, but there were no goods in them. The vast bazaar of the caravans, which not long ago had been glutted with merchandise, was now deserted, and the caravanserai was empty. Beside these ruins a new city was beginning to grow, with barracks and military schools. Cavalry, tank units, and the Air Force filled the town with well-clad, well-fed young men. Numerous airfields extended far into the adjoining steppe, the Flying School was housed in brand-new buildings of red brick, and if you passed young women in the street with plump cheeks and gaudy silk dresses you knew that they were the wives of airmen. The State retail-trade was at death's door: neither cloth nor paper, shoes nor food was to be found in the shops. In all the three years I spent there, no shoes were sent to Orenburg, except to the co-operatives reserved for the Party and the G.P.U. There were several technical schools for the training of agronomists, vets and teachers; a garment-factory; a railway-repair workshop; a number of prisons, all packed out; and a small concentration-camp. I often saw a great herd of men passing under my windows, ragged and mostly barefoot, surrounded by watchdogs and soldiers with lowered rifles. These were the labour brigades of the penitentiary department; we dubbed them, sarcastically, 'the enthusiasts' brigades', since some of them were actually called by that name and took part in 'Socialist labour emulation'. An immense, flea-ridden market ran out from the town into the steppe, bounded by the Moslem cemetery (now occupied by abandoned children and bandits), the dismal garment-factory, the cavalry school, a maternity hospital and the endless sands.

The G.P.U. issued us with bread-cards, which were valid from the beginning of the current month (a stroke of luck). 'It is forbidden to leave the town, except to go out for fresh air in the woods; from now on you may find any work and lodging that you can; only no employment can be taken up without our authorization.'

We thought that the light from the sky was rich and pellucid as nowhere else; and so it was. The town itself gave the impression of being sun-scorched, exciting, picturesque, and overwhelmed with heat, poverty, and sand. We went on to the barber's and acquired heads of civilized hair again; a dark-skinned urchin stole my three last roubles off me; we hocked my leather-and-fur overcoat at the municipal pawnshop for eighty roubles, and with that our experience of hunger began. The room in the Peasant's Hostelry cost two roubles a night, and the sheets were so filthy that after inspecting them by the light of a match I decided to sleep in my clothes. The inn had an enormous four-sided courtyard, littered with carts, horses, camels, and nomads who slept there, whole families of them, on mats close to their beasts. It was, in the delightful coolness of early morning, a touching spectacle. At that hour the Khirghiz families would have risen, which is to say that they would be squatting in silence or busy at their morning toilet: biblical ancients, mothers with Mongol eyes suckling their babies, children of all ages cleaning themselves of fleas in deep concentration, often cracking the lice between their teeth. It often looked as if they ate them, saying, 'You eat me and I eat you.' A row of crouching Asiatics would be relieving themselves in the latrines and I noticed that several of them excreted blood. Rags, rags everywhere. Some slender girls stood out from the mob, because of their perfect beauty, like Israelite or Persian princesses.

I heard shouting from the street, and then a shower of vigorous knocks on the door. 'Quick, Victor Lvovich, open!' Bobrov was coming back from the bakery, with two huge eight-pounder loaves of black bread on his shoulders. He was surrounded by a swarm of hungry children, hopping after the bread·like sparrows, clinging on his clothes, beseeching: 'A little bit, uncle, just a little bit!' They were almost naked. We threw them some morsels, over which a pitched battle promptly began. The next moment, our barefooted maidservant brought boiling water, unasked, for us to make tea. When she was alone with me for a moment, she said to me, her eyes smiling, 'Give me a pound of bread and I'll give you the signal in a minute. . . . And mark my words, citizen, I can assure you that I don't have the syphilis, no, not me. . . .' Bobrov and I decided to go out only by turns, so as to keep an eye on the bread.

Afterwards the two of us would meander through the town and the woods, as hungry as those children. One rouble was the price of meat-soup in the restaurant, where little girls waited on you so as to be able to lick your plate when you had finished and glean your bread-crumbs. We rationed ourselves strictly, gaining time until work should come our way, or else the relief I hoped to receive from Leningrad or Paris. Twice a week we would buy bunches of unripe onions and some mutton-bones from the market, and make a soup, which smelled delicious, over a wood fire in the courtyard. Then we would lie down and let it digest, in a state of positive bliss. Once we fell ill after the feast. Our usual nourishment consisted of dried bread and sweetened tea made in a samovar; we owed this last to the compressed tea I had been given by the girl-comrade I met at the Butyrki prison. At long last we had some news: Bobrov, that his father had died of hunger in the village; I, that my wife was getting better and would be sending me a parcel. . . .

Among the ruins of churches, in abandoned porches, on the edge of the steppe or under the crags by the Ural, we could see Khirghiz families lying heaped together, dying of hunger. One evening I gathered up from the ground of the deserted market-place a child burning with fever; he was moaning, but the folk who stood around did not dare to touch him, for fear of contagion. I diagnosed a simple case of hunger and took him off to the militia-post, holding him by his frail, boiling wrist. I fetched him a glass of water and a morsel of bread from my place; the effect on the lad was that of a small but instantaneous miracle.

'What do you want us to do with him?' asked the soldiers.

'Take him to the Children's Home.'

'But they're running away from there, because they're starving to death!'

When I returned home, I discovered that someone had stolen my stock of bread that was to last several days.

The Khirghiz folk lay on waste lots in the sun; one could not be sure if some of them were alive or dead; and people passed by without looking their way: the poor people, hurrying and shabby, the functionaries, the military, their bourgeois-looking womenfolk, in brief all those we termed 'the satisfied 8 per cent.' The market, bordered by sky and desert and invaded by the sands, teemed with an incongruous multitude. There people traded back and forth to each other, chiefly in the perpetual bric-à-brac of poverty: lamps patched up a hundred times and still giving out smuts, if no light; precious lamp-chimneys of the wrong sizes; ruined stoves, nomads' garments, stolen watches which went for no longer than five minutes (I knew experts who, out of three watches and a stock of odds and ends, would make four . . .), livestock. The Khirghiz had long arguments around a haughty, regally white camel. Troglodytic old women, their skin so brown as to appear black, practised palmistry. A weird Turkmenian in a turban divined the future by throwing goats' vertebrae upon engravings from an erotic book in French published at Amsterdam in Voltaire's time. Here, even on the worst days, one could find bread, butter, and meat, all at outrageous prices and light-years away from any hygienic regulation. Famished thieves of all ages and all varieties from as far away as Turkestan and Pamir strayed in these crowds, snatching a carrot or an onion from your hands and popping it immediately down their throats. My wife witnessed the following piece of thievery: a housewife had just bought a pound of butter costing fifteen roubles (three days' wages for a skilled worker); an Asiatic smartly nipped it from her hands and made off. He was pursued and caught easily enough; but he curled up on the earth like a ball and for all the blows from fists or stones that rained on him from above, ate the butter. They left him lying there, bloody but full.

For the rest, it was a decently managed town. Three cinemas, and a travelling theatre in the summer, of a fair standard; and an ornamental garden, called *Topoli* (The Lime-trees). About 160,000 inhabitants, a tenth of them unloaded there by the G.P.U. A healthy climate: five months of extremely harsh winter with up to forty-two degrees of frost; five months of extremely hot summer, with hot spells of up to forty degrees. All the year round, violent winds from the steppes, the savage *buran* which in winter whirled the snow around and heaped it into white dunes in the squares, and in summer worked up squalls of warm sand. Among the poor inhabitants at least 70 per cent. suffered from marsh-fever; naturally there was no quinine. I have seen the same ague shaking the grandmother of eighty and the suckling baby; and they did not die of it.

When I first arrived, there were about fifteen political deportees: Social-Revolutionaries, Zionists, anarchists, ex-Oppositional capitulators. Orenburg was considered a privileged spot for deportation. The G.P.U. only used it for leading figures, and for convicts who already had behind them years of imprisonment or exile in other parts. There were in fact a number of grades of deportation. I knew men who had lived inside the Arctic Circle in settlements of five houses; others again at Turgai in the Kazakhstan desert, where the primitive Kazakhs dwelt in hovels of mud, practically without water for five months of the year. In this town of ours L. Gerstein, of the Social-Revolutionary Party's Central Committee, was living out his last years undisturbed; and the G.P.U. was collecting influential 'Trotskyists', those known to be intransigent, for purposes whose very obscurity made us anxious. Soon there was a whole little fraternal group of us, in excellent spirits. An old Georgian Menshevik, Ramishvili, arrived, now in the fourteenth year of his captivity; then another Menshevik, Georgi Dimitrievich Kuchin, a late member of his party's Central Committee; and some ex-Oppositionists of the Right, who, having become supporters of the General Line, had been high in authority only the day before—with these last we never exchanged a word.

Life under deportation was characterized by its instability. The G.P.U. made up exiles' colonies in a fairly homogeneous composition, so as to allow a limited intellectual activity to arise, foment divisions and betrayals and then, under some easily arranged pretext, pack the irreconcilables off to prison or transfer them to regions more squalid and obscure. The deportee, dependent in regard to letters from relatives, work and medical attention, lived literally on the mercy of a few officials. He was obliged to report to the G.P.U. daily, or every three, five or seven days as the case might be. No sooner would he get his life organized a little than it would all be undone by unemployment, prison, or transfer. It was an endless cat-and-mouse game. The deportee who repented and apologized politely to the Central Committee would (though not always) be better treated and find a comfortable job as an economist or librarian; but the others would boycott him. For example, a woman who had been a Trotskyist and was the wife of a capitulator still in jail was given the task of purging the public library, i.e. of withdrawing the works of Trotsky, Riazanov, Preobrazhensky, and a host of others, in accordance with lists that were issued from time to time; the books were not burned after the Nazi pattern, but sent for pulping to provide material for fresh paper.

It was clearly indicated to me that I would receive no work except by seeking the favour of the G.P.U. Once I went to discuss a possible job in the Ural Gold Trust, and had the following fragment of conversation with the local head of the secret police:

'Have you any intention of seeking readmission to the Party?'

'None at all.'

'Or of appealing against your sentence to the Special Collegium of the Interior?'

'None at all.'

Any employment was now out of the question. I was determined to fight back. I had a historical work, three novels, and various other publications on sale in Paris. In Orenburg there was a *Torgsin* shop where, even at the height of famine one could buy, at prices sometimes below the world level, foodstuffs and manufactured goods on which the whole town gazed greedily. The only acceptable payment for them was in gold, silver, or foreign currency. I saw Khirghiz and *mujiks* coming to the counter with ancient necklaces fashioned from Persian coinage or embossed silver icon-frames; these *objets d'art* and rare coins were bought by the weight of metal in them and paid for in flour, cloth or hide. Former bourgeois now in exile brought along their false teeth. On 300 francs a month, the equivalent of about fifteen dollars, I was able both to live myself and to provide a livelihood for some comrade or other who might just be out of prison.

My wife arrived from Leningrad with some books; the G.P.U. gave me back my manuscripts and uncompleted works, as well as my typewriter. I decided to work on, just as though I had some kind of future; which, after all, was still possible. It was an even chance whether I would survive or vanish into the jails. At all costs I would, in opposition to despotism, keep this irrevocable minimum of my rights and my dignity: the right to think freely. I began to write two books at once, one of them an autobiographical work on the struggles of my youth in Paris, and to gather notes on the history of the years 1918–20. I was in the terrain of Chapayev's partisans,[1] and I met some of the survivors of that era. While their glory was being hymned throughout the world in Soviet films, they were just scraping a living, alcoholic and demoralized—but wonderful personalities all the same. I studied that particular phase in the Civil War and the folk-world around me, which, though primitive, had much of human value.

In particular, I was a close observer of a case of banditry, which amounted to no more than the spontaneous violence of a few youngsters who, in a drunken condition, had thought it gallant to have a fight to the death. I saw the most formidable of these youths being tried in a workers' club. He had several deaths on his conscience and had no clear idea of what he was being charged with. His name was Sudakov, and they shot him. Around his name I noted the phenomenon of legend-making. I left the court an hour before the verdict, it being a stifling August night. On the following day several bystanders told me, in great excitement and with all the details, that Sudakov had escaped. He had saluted the audience by bowing, in the old Russian fashion, to the four points of the compass, and then jumped through a window and disappeared in the park outside. People had seen it and the whole town was talking of the affair; only, none of it was true. When they sobered down, people declared that Sudakov had been pardoned; then the G.P.U. sent his clothes to his family.

The dry, scorching summers and the glaring, relentless winters made every hour one of struggle. The first priority was to obtain wood. The stupid regulations of the Soviet, and the G.P.U.'s habit of requisitioning on some pretext or other any peasant homes that were at all comfortable, forced people to abandon the big, well-built houses and build new ones, barely habitable by a single family and so forming no temptation for the military. A big house would be left to rot; permission would then be obtained to demolish it (in view of its condition), and the timber in it was sold for firewood —a brilliant transaction! I followed the smart example of the experts and kept myself warm by this technique. The area covered by

[1] Vassili I. Chapayev (1887–1919): an outstanding Red commander in the Civil War. Fought against the Czechoslovak Legion and Kolchak's troops.

housing diminished regularly, while the town's excess population
increased. Through the snow-storms my son and I would drag
toboggans loaded with the usual sack of potatoes or drum of
paraffin bought on the black market. On some mornings the snow's
onslaught on the house would bury it almost completely, and we had
to fight it with our shovels to get the doors and windows free. Then
too we had to chop and saw the wood, and hide it in case it was
stolen. I made wooden barricades which we piled in front of the
blocked front door. We had to go and find our bread in the far end
of town, sometimes only to push our noses up to a tiny notice:
The bread-ration for the 10th is cancelled. At the rationing-office a poster
announced: 'Grandparents have no right to food-cards.' All the
same, people managed to keep those 'useless mouths' alive.

Besides this, we used to go on long ski trips over the frozen Ural
and in the woods. The iridescent snow would, every so often,
show the tracks of wild beasts, which we proceeded to trail. At the age
of thirteen my son had become a first-rate skier, though he had no
skis, properly speaking, only old planks fastened to his feet. He was at
school, where they had one textbook between three pupils and three
exercise books per pupil per session; here the little terrors used to
fight one another with knives and go marauding in the market. The
little *Frantzuz* (Frenchman) acquitted himself well, without a knife,
and was respected by all. As a deportee's son, he was a source of
anxiety to the Communist senior staff, who actually upbraided him
for not breaking off relations with his father. For a short while he
was expelled from school for declaring in the social-science lesson
that in France the trade unions functioned freely. The headmaster of
the school carpeted me for the 'anti-Soviet activities' which I was
encouraging in my son. 'But', I told him, 'it is a fact that trade-
union freedom and even political freedom exist in France; there is
nothing anti-Soviet about that.'

'I find it hard to believe you', replied the headmaster, 'and in any
case it is our duty to impress upon our children that true liberty
exists here and not in the capitalist dictatorship of the so-called
democratic countries.'

At Orenburg the G.P.U. had gathered (doubtless for the purpose of
working up a 'case' at some time) half a dozen deportees from the
Left Opposition, together with a few young sympathizers; we were a
family circle. They were men and women of a truly wonderful

stamp. In my novel *S'il est Minuit dans le Siècle* I have taken some
pains to recapture the spiritual atmosphere of deportation. Journeying over the years from prison to prison, from exile to exile, tormented
by privation, these comrades kept their revolutionary faith, their
good spirits, their sparkling political intelligence. Fanya Upstein, less
than thirty years old, was an Odessa intellectual, a devoted student;
Lydia Svalova was a worker from Perm, still young, who had been
deported to the White Sea coast for raising her voice about wages in
a meeting; in the north she had been put to work as a waggoner.
Lisa Senatskaya, a kindly and steadfast person, was the wife of
Vassili Pankratov, an Oppositionist in jail for the last five years,
and had herself been deported for refusing to divorce him, 'a fact
which proves her solidarity with her husband'. They were expecting
to be reunited here.

The men had all fought in the Civil War. Boris Mikhailovich
Eltsin, a Bolshevik since 1903, and a member of the Opposition's
'Leading Centre', was a little man with heart trouble and rheumatism; his powerful head was topped with black hair which stood out
in rebellious tufts: black chin-beard and moustache, swarthy skin,
deep wrinkles, lively eyes, and a thoughtful, spontaneously sarcastic
way of talking. Over fifty-five, he came to us from Suzdal prison,
where he had bargained with Stalin. He had been deported at first to
Feodossia in the Crimea, along with a son who was dying of tuberculosis; but the climate there had been considered too easy for a man
so obdurate. Hegel's *Collected Works* were his constant companion. I
used to see him having his dinner, a few potatoes and half a herring;
he would then make tea, like the old student he was, and at last
smile, bright-eyed, and say: 'Tonight I read a page of Hegel over
again: it's a tremendous stimulant for the mind!' He remarked too:
'Our unity is the work of the G.P.U.; in fact we have as many tendencies as there are militants. I don't find this at all objectionable.'
His son, Victor Borisovich, was deported to Archangel after being
five years in prison.

Vassili Feodorovich Pankratov was sent to us after release from
a five years' stay in an Isolator (Suzdal, I think). Aged forty, well-
set shoulders and head, in vigorous trim, his features athletic and
clean-cut as his nature. Once a sailor in the fighting fleet, he
had helped to lead the revolutionary movement at Kronstadt in
1917; after that he was in the Civil War, and headed the G.P.U.

at Vladikavkaz (Northern Caucasus); imprisoned in 1928 for three years; when these three years had expired, the G.P.U. asked him if his ideas had changed, and upon his replying in the negative, added another two years to his term. It was only after the prison-inmates threatened to have a hunger-strike to the death that the secret Collegium stopped doling out increased sentences of this kind, and Pankratov recovered his liberty—by being deported. His wife Lisa had waited for him; in our midst they found happiness together— for a little while.

Chanaan Markovich Pevzner, an economist from the Finance Commissariat, had been seriously maimed in the Manchurian campaign. He had done only four years in the Isolator owing to the pitiable condition of his left arm, which had seven bullets in it and dangled like a rag. The G.P.U. arranged employment for him in the regional treasury, to enable him to deal with an incipient attack of scurvy by eating his fill, or as near as might be. Pevzner was young, lively, a strong swimmer and a pessimist. 'We are in for years of it,' he kept saying; 'I do not believe that the Terror will die down: the economic situation demands it.' He had the sharp, bold features of a fighter from old Israel.

Vassili Mikhailovich Chernykh, lately a high G.P.U. official in the Ural area, had, in bygone days, captured Rostov with a little army of miners, sailors and students. He had come to us from the prison at Verkhne-Uralsk. Tall, the very model of a timberman in the Nordic forests with his powerful arms, toughened face, blond mane, and mocking eyes, he was a warm-hearted warrior with a serious head on his shoulders. He argued that, through the absence of an intelligent and decisive leadership, the Petrograd Soviet had missed the chance of a revolution in February–March 1917 at the time of the autocracy's collapse; and that power should have been seized at that time, thus saving a year of semi-bourgeois Kerenskyism. Chernykh was (like myself) one of the tribe of revisionists, who maintained that all ideas, as well as all recent history, should be reviewed from top to bottom. On this issue the Opposition was divided roughly into two halves: there were the revisionists and there were the doctrinaires, themselves subdivided into the orthodox, the extreme Left, and the followers of the theory that the U.S.S.R. was establishing State capitalism.

Ivan Byk came to us from the concentration-camp on the

Solovietsky Islands. A young man, he had fought in the Ukraine, campaigned for the Workers' Opposition, and undergone confinement at Verkhne-Uralsk: there, he had been one of the organizers of a widespread hunger-strike against the 'doubling' of sentences by administrative decision. The strikers did drink water, which enabled them to hold out for longer; on the eighteenth day the strike committee was carrying on as usual. The formidable Andreyeva, who was in charge of political prisons, came to negotiate with the committee. She began by threatening them with forced labour. Byk answered her, 'If you're afraid of labour, I'm not: I'm a worker.'

In the concentration-camp Byk was informed that, in a short telegram published in the newspapers, Christian Rakovsky had announced his support for the Central Committee 'to stand against the war-danger side by side with the Party'. A conciliator by nature, Byk thought this quite reasonable, and accepted Rakovsky's formulation of 'a united front'. He was flown to the Butyrki prison in Moscow. 'You are in favour of a united front between the Opposition and the Central Committee?' 'Yes.' 'Rakovsky goes further than that. . . . Read this article of his. If you sign it, we release you.' Having read the article, Byk simply asked to be sent back to the concentration-camp. After he had finished his sentence, the G.P.U. passed him to us.

Alexei Semionovich Santalov, a proletarian from the Putilov Works, had been in all the revolutions of Petrograd for twenty years and more. An educated, thoughtful person, but sluggish in outward appearance, he used to defend trade-union rights and factory legislation in whatever workshop he found himself: a serious offence. 'A spineless lot of youngsters, this working class of today!' he would say, 'They've never seen an electric light bulb in their lives—it'll take them ten years or more before they get round to demanding decent lavatories!' The G.P.U. deferred to him, but he eventually landed in trouble. During a revolutionary festival Santalov got a little drunk and wandered into a workers' club, where he stopped short before the Leader's portrait. 'You've got to admit it,' he cried noisily, 'a fine face he has, this grave-digger of the Revolution!' He was arrested and we never saw him again.

I have described these men because I am grateful to them for having existed, and because they incarnated an epoch. Most probably all of them have perished.

Ch——, a history professor at Moscow, had been arrested because it was imagined that certain allusions could be heard in his lectures on the French Revolution (Thermidor!). He was so seriously ill that we asked the G.P.U. to send him to a clinic in Moscow. Our demand was granted. He came back to us far less shaky and brought us news: Trotsky, of whom we had heard absolutely nothing for a long time, was founding the Fourth International. With what forces? What parties? we speculated. Ch——, on behalf of some mysterious 'comrades' whom he had, so he said, managed to contact while in hospital, suggested to me that Eltsin and I should establish an illegal committee of the Opposition: 'We need a brain!' We were sitting on the steps of my house, facing the steppe. I asked him questions about the comrades in Moscow, trying to discover their identity; I looked deep into his eyes, and thought to myself: 'You, my friend, are an *agent provocateur!*' I explained to him that even when shut away in prisons we still embodied a basic principle of life and liberty, and that we had no need to organize ourselves into clandestine committees. His attempt failed, then; but he was pardoned some time later. I had been right. If I had listened to him I should be lying dead at this very hour, with a little hole in the back of my neck.

The winter of 1934-5 was frightful, despite the lessening of the famine towards the New Year, the abolition of bread-rationing and the revaluation of the rouble at the equivalent of a kilo of black bread. For a long while my wife, a victim to crises of insanity, had been away from me for treatment in Leningrad. I was left alone with my son, and the G.P.U. suddenly cut off my supplies. A consignment of money posted from Paris via the *Torgsin* was intercepted and 'lost'. I asked the G.P.U. for work, and the Secret Service ironically offered me a night-watchman's job, adding by the way that it was not certain that I could be given a permit to carry arms and this would be contrary to regulations. I now understood that a directive was out to choke me to death—or else that the protest campaign in France on my behalf was annoying Moscow and so they were trying to break me. Try, try again! Our morale was excellent. We had passionately followed the battles in the Asturias in October 1934; in the talks that I gave in the woods by the River Ural, I proclaimed the Spanish Revolution to my comrades; and I was not wrong. A great popular victory in the West could save us by blowing a gust of fresh air across the U.S.S.R. This news coincided with rumours of a political amnesty; the G.P.U. officials told us that Trotsky was begging to come back, offering to submit to the Central Committee. I learned later that Lozovsky was likewise announcing my own impending submission to my comrades in Paris; this, he said, would mean the end of 'the Victor Serge affair'. Rakovsky had just surrendered, but this did not worry us. We told each other, 'He is getting old, and they've played a classical trick on him, showing him confidential documents about the approach of war. . . .' Meanwhile, most of the comrades were being thrown out of work by the G.P.U.

My son and I rationed ourselves to the limit, so that all we fed on now was a little black bread and 'egg-soup' which I made to last two days with some sorrel and just one egg. Fortunately we did have wood. Soon I began to suffer from boils. Pevzner, famished and homeless besides, came to sleep at our house, bed-ridden by attacks of a strange ague. Later we discovered that he had scarlet fever. An enormous anthrax tumour under my left breast laid me flat on my back, and I saw the abscess devouring me. The G.P.U. refused to send me a physician, and the doctor from the Vorstadt dispensary, a young, overworked little woman, tended us as best she could, with no medicines at her disposal. Rumour grew in the neighbourhood that Pevzner was dying (and indeed he was delirious), and that I was dead. The G.P.U. woke up, since they had to answer for us to the Central Collegium. One morning, the most eminent surgeon in town, a tireless and remarkably talented neurotic, burst into the house, wagged his head, told me, 'Don't worry, I'll save you', and had me conveyed immediately to the hospital. Pevzner was already there, in the huts reserved for contagious patients. This was a little after Kirov's assassination.

I left for the hospital lying in straw on a low sledge, on a day dazzling with sunshine and snow. A bearded, wrinkled peasant would turn round to me every now and then to inquire if I was being jolted too much. My son walked along beside the sledge. I could not move an inch; all I could see was a luminous blue of surpassing purity. Vassili Pankratov had just disappeared; he was arrested obscurely, leaving his young wife pregnant. The comrades thought that my condition would prevent my being arrested, but that I would be imprisoned immediately upon discharge from hospital. Such was the fate of Pevzner, whom we never saw again. Once he was convalescent, policemen waited for him at the exit to the huts and took him away to the cellars of the G.P.U.

Pevzner and Pankratov, in common with many other notable deportees who had recently been let out of Isolators and arrested at this time, were to be enrolled into a 'prison conspiracy', invented in the panic over the Kirov affair. We heard no more of them, except that after several months Pankratov arrived at the prison of Verkhne-Uralsk, which held Kamenev and Zinoviev. His message to us said only one thing: 'The investigation has been frightful. Nothing we have so far experienced can be compared with what is going on. Be ready for anything!' And ready we were.

I no longer know how many weeks I spent in the 'gangrenous' department at Orenburg's surgical hospital, during the bitterest part of winter. The hospital was run as efficiently as the general destitution permitted; what it treated primarily was poverty. It was filled with cases of sickness or accident-casualties whose true sickness or accident lay in chronic undernourishment aggravated by alcoholism. The worker who lived on sour-cabbage soup, without fat content, would acquire an abscess as a result of a simple bruise, the abscess would be followed by septic inflammation and this, since the hospital fed its inmates very poorly, would last indefinitely. Children were covered in cold sores; whole wards were full of peasants with frozen limbs; bellies empty, clothes worn and threadbare, they offered small resistance to the cold.

Disinfectants, anaesthetics, analgesics, gauze, bandages, even iodine, came in inadequate quantities, so that dressings which should have been changed daily were only attended to every three days. In the bandaging-room I heard arguments and bargaining going on among the nurses: 'Give me back the three yards of gauze I lent you the day before yesterday, I've a patient here who can't wait any longer!' 'But you must know, the delivery they promised hasn't come. . . .' The same bandages were washed and used over and over again. I saw gangrenous flesh being torn from the frozen limbs with pincers; indescribable scars resulted. To treat me the doctors had to ask for vaccines and drugs from the G.P.U.'s privileged infirmary, the only one which went short of nothing. True, I was in the hospital for the poor—along with Chapayev's old partisans. Official, technical, and military personnel had special clinics reserved for their use. The medical and ancillary staff, which was generally very underpaid, was extraordinarily conscientious.

In the long winter evenings, the convalescing patients used to gather round a big stove in the passageway, and sing, underhandedly, a tragic ballad of love and brigandage; its refrain was:

> *And money, money all the time:*
> *With no money, you can't live. . .*

I got better, largely I believe because the G.P.U. allowed the next dispatch of money to reach me, and so I was able to buy butter, sugar, and rice at the *Torgsin*. I shall never forget the way in which some of the sick people gazed at me when I was brought such food, or their deference when they took their share of it. Nor, for that matter, shall I forget how on the most wretched of our days of misery we all heard a radio broadcast from a regional meeting of *kolkhoz* workers. Passionate voices went on endlessly thanking the Leader for 'the good life we lead'; and twenty or so patients tormented by hunger, half of them *kolkhoz* workers themselves, listened to it all in silence.

Contrary to all our predictions, I did not disappear, but returned home. This was due to the stubborn battle that was raging around my name in France. Militants and intellectuals were demanding that either I be released or my deportation be justified. They were promised that I would have a proper trial—and the trial never took place; they were promised documentation on the case—and no documents were forthcoming. They were promised that I would be freed forthwith; and I was not. At a time when Soviet policy was seeking the support of left-wing circles in France, it was all rather embarrassing.

I am convinced that at the end of 1934, just at the moment when Kirov was murdered, the Politbureau was entering upon a policy of normality and relaxation. The *kolkhoz* system had been modified so far as to permit the farmers to keep their private property even in the *kolkhoz* itself. The Government was anxious to present the Soviet Union in a démocratic role within the League of Nations and was seeking the support of the enlightened bourgeoisie and petty-bourgeoisie in other countries. The revolver-shot fired by Nikolayev ushered in an era of panic and savagery. The immediate response was the execution of 114 people, then the execution of Nikolayev and his friends, fourteen young folk in all; then the arrest and imprisonment of the whole of the former Zinoviev and Kamenev tendency, close on 3,000 persons as far as I could make out; then the mass deportation of tens of thousands of Leningrad citizens, simultaneously with hundreds of arrests among those already deported and the opening of fresh secret trials in the prisons themselves.

Certain mysterious happenings at the top of the Party have come to light: for example, the Yenukidze case. Aveli Yenukidze, whom I have mentioned a number of times in these reminiscences, was a Caucasian Old Bolshevik, a companion of Stalin's youth and, like Stalin, a Georgian; he had also been Secretary of the Central Soviet Executive since the foundation of the Soviet Union. In the discharge of these high offices he proved himself a man of human feeling, and as liberal and large-hearted as was possible in that age. His honesty was evidently an obstacle to the great settling of political accounts whose preparation was in hand. Relieved of his duties and shifted to a subordinate position, Yenukidze gradually disappeared from view (eventually to be shot in 1937, without 'confession' or trial).

On Nikolayev's crime, the world has seen the publication of a number of successive versions, all of them lavish in improbabilities, but not of the original papers, whether the terrorist's own statements or the documents of the investigation. It was almost certainly an individual act committed by an enraged young Communist. The Left or Trotskyist Opposition was, in all likelihood, represented in Leningrad at that time solely by Alexandra Bronstein; I cannot doubt, with my intimate knowledge of its members, ideas, and general condition, that it had nothing whatsoever to do with the assassination. We still viewed ourselves as the partisans of 'Soviet reform', and reform excluded any appeal to violence. I was too well acquainted with the followers of the Zinoviev tendency, as well as those of the Right Opposition, men tragically cautious and loyal, to suspect them for a single moment. The murder was a spontaneous act, but it confronted the Politbureau with a frightful problem: not only their own responsibility for the years of darkness, but also the existence of a reserve team of government in the persecuted Opposition who, for all the abuse directed so incessantly against them, were more popular among the informed sections of the population than the leaders of the State. 'Just think of it', one official said to me, terrified, 'one of the Party leaders has been deliberately shot by a young Party member who didn't even belong to any Oppositional tendency!'

Throughout the whole of the year 1935, the Politbureau was secretly torn between contrary inclinations, towards normalization on the one hand, towards terror on the other. The first-named tendency seemed to be on the winning side. Executions, jailings, and deportations had long ceased to interest the masses. By contrast, the abolition of bread-rationing made everybody happy. This country, for the sake of a little progress in the direction of prosperity, would walk over any number of corpses without noticing. I told myself that Stalin only had to increase real wages a little, allow the collective farmers room to breathe, wind up the concentration-camps, and shout pardon to any political opponents who were either mere invalids or else interested only in supporting him without loss of face—and he could at once soar into imperishable popularity. I was of the opinion that he was about to enter this course with the new Soviet Constitution, on whose drafting Bukharin was at work.

And so, for what was left of our family of deportees, the year glided past with a deceptive tranquillity. A number of Communist exiles arrived, who all continued to declare their loyalty to 'the General Line'; we avoided their company except for a few of them.

I was finishing my books in a state of uncertainty. What would their destiny be, and mine? There was an autobiographical piece on the French anarchist movement just before the First World War (*Les Hommes Perdus*), and a novel, *La Tourmente*, which followed on from my published novels. In it I reconstructed the atmosphere of the year 1920, the zenith of the Revolution. I had also completed a small collection of poems, *Résistance*, and amassed a great pile of notes for a historical work on War Communism. I finished these writings in two and a half years; they were the only works I have ever had the opportunity to revise at leisure. I wrote in French, in a town where no one understood French; unable to converse in this language myself except with my son. Although I am inured to efforts of will-power, I have to recognize that it was often only an actual hardening of my nature that enabled me to persevere. It is not easy to work without respite, wondering if all one's writing may not tomorrow be seized, confiscated, or destroyed. By one of those strokes of irony that are so frequent in Russia, the Soviet Press was, quite appropriately, commemorating an anniversary of the Ukrainian national poet Taras Shevchenko, who in 1847 had been exiled for ten years to the steppes of Orenburg, 'forbidden to draw or to write'. He did, all the same, write some clandestine poetry which he concealed in his boots. In this report I had an overwhelming insight into the persistence in our Russian land, after a century of reform, progress, and revolution, of the same wilful determination to wipe out the rebellious intelligence without mercy. Never mind, I told myself, I must hold on: hold on and work on, even under this slab of lead.

I made several copies of my manuscripts, and made an arrangement through the post with Romain Rolland to send him my books; he was perfectly willing to forward them to some publishers in Paris. Rolland had no love for me, since long ago I had strongly attacked his doctrine of non-violence which had its inspiration in Gandhism; but he was worried by the repression in the U.S.S.R. and wrote to me in very friendly terms. I posted him a first manuscript in four registered envelopes, not forgetting to inform the G.P.U. that I had done so. All four envelopes were lost. I went to complain to the head of the secret police and he exclaimed, 'Just see how deplorably the Post Office works! And then you say we're exaggerating when we uncover sabotage! Why, my own letters to my wife go astray! I promise you that a proper inquiry will be made and that the Post Office will pay you the lawful compensation without delay!'

He even offered, very kindly, to supervise the transmission, still to Romain Rolland, of another set of manuscripts which the G.P.U. would see were visaed by the literary censors. I entrusted them to his care—and of course they never reached their destination.

While this was going on, my correspondence with abroad was cut off. The head of the secret police shook his head gravely: 'Oh dear! What would you have us do to put the Post Office right?' The Post Office regularly paid me hundreds of roubles for the registered letters that I continued to send at the rate of five a month and which 'went astray'. This afforded me the income of a well-paid technician.

Meanwhile, in France, the 'Victor Serge affair' was proving a troublesome business in working-class and intellectual circles. In its annual conferences the United Teachers' Federation was demanding my release, or else some justification for my confinement. At the 1934 conference of this body the Soviet teachers' delegation had promised that I would be tried before a duly constituted court. At the Rheims conference in 1935, the Russian delegation, which was greeted with chants of '*Victor Serge! Victor Serge!*' raised by the whole hall, provoked a storm of booing by declaring that I was mixed up in the Kirov affair! The League for the Rights of Man published the detailed documentation assembled by Magdeleine Paz. *La Révolution Prolétarienne*, *L'Ecole Emancipée*, *Le Combat Marxiste*, *Les Humbles* (under Maurice Wullens) took up the campaign. Georges Duhamel, Léon Werth, Charles Vildrac, Marcel Martinet, Jacques Mesnil, Maurice Parijanine, Boris Souvarine, and the wavering editorial board of *L'Europe*, all in different ways took an interest in the case. In Holland, Henriette Roland-Holst, in Switzerland Fritz Brupbacher, in Belgium Charles Plisnier lent their support to the protests. Brupbacher was told quite baldly by Helena Stassova, the secretary of International Class-war Prisoners' Aid in Moscow: 'Serge will never get out.'[1]

In June 1935 an 'International Congress of Writers for the Defence of Culture' took place in Paris, formally upon the initiative of such left-wingers as Alain, Barbusse, Romain Rolland, Elie Faure, André Gide, André Malraux, and Victor Margueritte.[2] The actual initiative came from certain Communist back rooms which specialized in organizing congresses of this kind; their objective was to arouse a pro-Stalinist movement among the French intelligentsia and buy over a number of famous consciences. My friends decided to attend the congress and demand to be heard. Some of them got themselves ejected by the stewards. Aragon and Ehrenburg manipulated

---

[1] Maurice Wullens: 'libertarian veteran' referred to on page 347. Maurice Parijanine: writer, poet, and collaborator with Serge in the translation work of the Communist International's executive; the subject of Serge's memoir, *Deux Recontres*. Fritz Brupbacher (1874–1945): Swiss physician and Socialist over forty years; expelled from the Socialist Party in 1914 for his revolutionary internationalism and from the Communist Party in 1933 for his anti-Stalinism, which was of a semi-anarchist rather than a Trotskyist variety. Charles Plisnier (1896–1952): Belgian novelist and former Communist militant; expelled from the Communist Party in 1928 as a Trotskyist; subsequently turned exclusively to literary work.

[2] Alain (1868–1951): an outstanding French teacher and author in philosophy; formed no system of his own. Elie Faure (1873–1937): nephew of the Reclus brothers; physician, art historian, biographer, and philosopher, of broad progressive sympathies. Victor Margueritte (1866–1942): ex-officer and subsequently anti-militarist writer; prominent pacifist.

the assembly in accordance with secret directives. Barbusse, Malraux, and Gide presided with some embarrassment. Heinrich Mann and Gustav Regler spoke of the persecuted intellectuals of Germany, Gaetano Salvemini of those in Italy and of freedom of thought in general. Salvemini caused a scene by condemning 'all the oppressions' and mentioning my name.[1] Gide, amazed to find that fierce efforts were being made to hush up the dispute, insisted on the ventilation of the matter, and Malraux, who was chairing the session, finally allowed Magdeleine Paz to speak: she spoke harshly, in fighting terms. Charles Plisnier, the novelist and mystical poet, and a Communist militant not long ago, supported her. Henry Poulaille, the author of *Damnés de la Terre*, a true son of the workers' suburbs who did not mince his words, demonstrated in the hall.

The delegation from the Soviet writers included two men with whom I had been on friendly terms, the poets Boris Pasternak and Nikolai Tikhonov, and also a person in the innermost circle of Party confidence, whom I had met in Moscow, the official journalist Mikhail Koltsov, a man as remarkable for his talent as for his pliant docility; besides these there were the successful playwright Kirshon and the hack agitator-novelist Ehrenburg. Pasternak, who is at once the Mallarmé and Apollinaire of Russian poetry, a truly great writer and a victim of semi-persecution besides, kept in the background. The other four fulfilled instructions and declared without a blink that they knew nothing of the writer Victor Serge—these, my good colleagues of the Soviet Writers' Union! All they knew of was a 'Soviet citizen, a confessed counter-revolutionary, who had been a member of the conspiracy which had ended in the murder of Kirov'. As he declaimed this from the platform, Koltsov did not suspect that in 1939 he himself would disappear, in complete obscurity, into the G.P.U. prisons.[2] Kirshon did not suspect that

---

[1] Heinrich Mann (1871–1950): German novelist and playwright, an exile in France and the United States after the rise of Hitler. Gustav Regler (1898–1963): German novelist and former Communist; political commissar with the International Brigades in Spain; broke with the Party in 1939; a companion of Serge's exile in Mexico. Gaetano Salvemini (1873–1957): Italian historian and independent Deputy (1919–21); in exile after the rise of Mussolini; at Harvard University from 1934 to 1948.

[2] Koltsov was arrested in 1938 after his return from reporting on the Spanish Civil War, and perished in 1942. Kirshon, a friend of Yagoda, and author of *Bread* (1930), a play on the extermination of the *kulaks*, was arrested and shot in 1938. Both men have been officially 'rehabilitated' in recent years.

two years later, he would disappear himself, dubbed a 'terrorist-Trotskyist'—he whose pen had never been anything other than strictly conformist. Ehrenburg forgot his flight from Russia, his banned novels, his accusation against Bolshevism of 'crucifying Russia'. Tikhonov forgot his hymns to Courage, in those splendid epic ballads of his which I had translated into French. Nobody there could foresee the grim tumbrils of the Moscow Trials, but they knew of the 127 executions of innocents; these had been publicly announced the day after Nikolayev's deed and, according to the Soviet Press, were even stoutly approved by humanists such as Jean-Richard Bloch and Romain Rolland. The shameless statement that justified my captivity by a murder committed two years after my arrest sent a shiver down more than one spine. André Gide went to see the Soviet Ambassador, who could give him no enlightenment at all.

Almost at the same time Romain Rolland, who had been invited to Moscow and received by Stalin, spoke to him of the 'Victor Serge affair'. Yagoda, the head of the political police, was consulted, and could find nothing in his files (if he had found the least confession of complicity signed by myself, I should have been lost). Stalin promised that I would be authorized to leave the U.S.S.R., together with my family.

But where could I go? For a moment the battle for visas seemed hopeless. The French Prime Minister Laval refused us the entry-permit into France for which my friends pleaded. Approaches made in London were fruitless. Approaches made in Holland were fruitless. Copenhagen promised. Then Emile Vandervelde, now in the government of Belgium, arranged for us to be granted permission to reside there for three years. If these negotiations had dragged on a few weeks longer, I should never have left the country; I should have been no more than a dead man on bail.

Suddenly I was given three days to get ready to leave for Moscow, and thence for an 'unknown destination' which the G.P.U. Collegium would fix. When the Political Red Cross sent me forms to sign for a Belgian visa, I thought I could understand. Above all, I believed, I had enough standing and support in France to ensure that they would not dare to prolong my confinement. My comrades Bobrov and Eltsin, and others who had just come from Isolators, such as Leonid Girchek and Yakov Belenky, thought that I had fallen victim to unfortunate illusions: 'You'll have a rude awakening when you find yourself in a nice dark prison or some desert in Kazakhstan. . . .'

'It is not to the G.P.U.'s advantage', I replied, 'that I should be in a position to observe its machinery any further. They know quite well that I will never capitulate and that in the end I shall just have to be released, able to write about it all. . . . I would be doomed only if Fascism won in France, and it failed in its *coup* of 6 February 1934.' Old Eltsin, crippled with rheumatism, was living in an icy little room in a house without a w.c.; I asked him, 'Should I start a campaign in the Press abroad to get you out?' and he answered, 'No. My place is here.'

I took the precaution of giving away my household goods only on condition that they be kept at my disposal for a month and sent on to me if, from the heart of some Siberia or other, I asked for them back. All I took with me was papers, useful books, and personal keepsakes. I went off with my son on a freezing day in April. Chernykh, usually so sprightly with his vigorous manner and his wild, Russian plainsman's hair, was gloomy when he said good-bye to me. 'Those of us who are still alive', he told me, 'will be old, forgotten and obsolete on the day that a new liberty is born in Russia. We shall be like that old revolutionary who came back to St. Petersburg after thirty years of exile during the March days in 1917, met nobody he knew in all the chaos and died of neglect in a hotel room. After it was all over, they recognized him . . .!'

My heart was utterly ravaged as I left; I was severing attachments of a unique quality. I should have liked to have those dear faces, that I would never see again, imprinted on my brain, and those land-scapes of white countryside, and even some image of our great Russian misery, lived out by this brave, gritty, patient people. If I could have believed in any reasonable chance that I would not ultimately have been obliterated in a voiceless struggle which was already sterile, I should have been content to remain there—even if it were in some little Mongol fishing village inside the Arctic Circle. But we do not live for ourselves; we live to work and fight.

The white plains fled past endlessly in the windows of the train. Two seedy-looking policemen had taken their seats not far from us. At Kuibyshev the Volga was still frozen. Tartar Republic, busy little stations, young women with coloured kerchiefs over their hair, peasant dwellings surrounded by birch-trees and little wooden paddocks. . . . In the station at Syzran a great clang of ironmongery made the passengers jump, and we saw an implausible goods-train slewing to and fro over yielding, dancing metals. It was only a small, unimportant derailment: the ballast gone, the soil dissolved with the early thaw, and a false move. The railwaymen chuckled bitterly about it: 'That's where Stakhanovism gets you, citizen! They still have to learn that the stock gets tired just like people!' In another spot the train slowed down in the middle of the steppe and I saw workmen with iron bars holding together the broken rails over which we were gingerly moving. Our train had to alter its route—and arrived several hours late—because of a serious accident on the line.

Moscow. The bustle of the streets and memories, memories! The luxurious Metro with its granite paving, its walls in Ural stone, its exits, huge underground avenues—but without benches for travellers, and expensive. We know how to build subterranean palaces, but we forget that a working-class woman coming home from work would love to be able to sit down beneath all these rich-hued stones.

At the Political Red Cross, in overcrowded little offices on the Kuznetsky Bridge, a stone's throw from the tall, square tower of the G.P.U. building, we saw Ekaterina Pavlovna Peshkova and her colleague Vinaver, a former Liberal lawyer. Ekaterina Pavlovna still bore the name of Gorky, whose wife she had been and whose devoted friend she still was. Having won Lenin's confidence she was allowed, during the Red Terror, to found a relief organization for political detainees, of whatever kind; it was tolerated, first by the Cheka, then by the G.P.U., with a mixture of respect, trust, and hostility. Peshkova was able to manage the amazing moral feat of retaining the trust simultaneously of victims and inquisitors! For year after year this sad, thin woman, with lovely grey eyes and a style of dress whose very artlessness was elegant, aided by a tiny band of untiring fellow-workers, lavished intervention, intercession, and relief on behalf of all the victims of the various terrors that followed hotfoot upon one another. Nobody else in the whole world during this century, I am convinced, has known, and at such close quarters, so many disasters, deaths, atrocities, and tragedies, some inevitable, some senseless. Peshkova lived in a private hell, the repository of countless secrets, all of them deadly as the strongest poison. She was never too tired, never disheartened, however dark the times were—and for her, only for her, all the times of the Revolution were dark. Pledged to secrecy, she has remained unknown to the great world outside.

Ekaterina Pavlovna informed me that my wife, my poor invalid, was waiting for me, along with Jeannine, the baby that had been been born to us while I was in hospital at Orenburg a little over a year ago. She informed me also that I would not see Anita Russakova, who had just been arrested and deported for five years to Viatka. I immediately understood why: now I should not be able to talk to Anita and resolve the mystery of her lying confessions. I was told that we had to leave for Warsaw that same evening. I asked Ekaterina Pavlovna to request a twenty-four hours delay from the G.P.U. so that I could have an exit-permit for my manuscripts (which had obligingly been promised me for the following day) from the censorship, and for my baggage from the head customs-office. When she came back, Peshkova told me, 'Go this very evening, don't press for anything. The secret-police officer just told me that you were not out of the country yet, and that he was sending Yagoda a fresh memorandum about you. . . .' I demurred no longer. I was never to be given any of my manuscripts although their exit had been authorized by *Glavlit*, the literary censorship. Of our baggage we took away only a few small articles in our attaché-cases. All the rest of it was ultimately seized, or rather stolen, by the G.P.U.

Francesco Ghezzi, gaunt and unbending, now a worker in a Moscow factory and the only syndicalist still at liberty in Russia, came with us to the train. Off we went, travelling third class, alone in our carriage, with a few roubles and ten dollars between four persons. In the smart and empty station at Negoreloye, ornamental uniforms surrounded us and searched us minutely: we were made to undress, and even the soles of my shoes were scrutinized with attention. The train entered the grey no-man's-land of the frontier. Behind us we were leaving the boundless grey fields of the collective farms; now we were crossing a sort of desert laid out for war. We had the feeling that we were the only travellers in this wilderness. Oh, our great Russia of agonies, how hard it is to tear ourselves away from you!

So ended my seventeen years' experience of victorious revolution.

9

DEFEAT IN THE WEST
1936–1941

Once we were over the Polish border we could see charming little houses, newspaper-kiosks selling the journals of Paris, Berlin, London, and New York, decently-clad railwaymen, relaxed faces. By the illuminations of evening, Warsaw was a picture of tall façades, garnished with tasteful arrays of blue electric light. All the clothes in the Marszalkowska seemed elegant, and the very bustle of the street seemed to have an air of nonchalance and prosperity. The shops, full of everything to dream of, were an even greater contrast, compared with our meagre co-operatives. All these comparisons we found heartrending. We did not get out of the train when we were crossing Nazi Germany. I could only manage, from the prominence of a bridge, to glimpse a square that I had known not long ago, near the Silesia Station in Berlin. Germany showed no sign of change to the passing eye: efficiency and neatness everywhere, architecture designed for privacy or sheer size, elaborate garden-plots. Some Jewish travellers whom I questioned told me that they could keep alive, only in fear. I had the impression that, since each of them was looking to his own fortune in a large country in which terror was nothing if not secret, they knew little of the dark side of the régime, and were afraid to speak even of this little, even with a Russian traveller. Still, they regarded the U.S.S.R. as a privileged land.

In Brussels we found refuge in the small home of a syndicalist militant of Russian origin who had lately been in jail at Suzdal, and then expelled from the Soviet Union. He lived off his un-employment benefit and went to the Town Hall for the meals provided at minimum cost to the unemployed. When he offered to give me a share of his dinner, which consisted of a rich soup, stew, and potatoes, I exclaimed, 'Back home over there, this is the kind of meal that a high Party official would eat!' He had three rooms, and possessed a bicycle and a gramophone. This unemployed Belgian lived as comfortably as a well-paid technician in the U.S.S.R.

The day after our arrival, as soon as I got up, I went to explore this provincial scene. The freshly-painted houses still had the look of old Flemish towns, with modern buildings carefully styled to maintain an individual flavour; the square paving-stones were newly-washed. My son and I would stop in front of the shops, moved beyond words. The little windows overflowed with hams, chocolates, ginger-bread, rice, and such improbable fruits as oranges, mandarins, and bananas! These riches were within reach, within reach of an unemployed man in a working-class area, without benefit of Socialism or a Plan! It was disconcerting. I had known of all this beforehand, but the reality of it shocked me as if I had been ignorant. It was enough to make one weep in humiliation and grief for our Russia of revolutions.

On May Day we saw these provincial streets full of workers out in their Sunday best with their families; young girls with red-ribboned hair, men with red badges in their buttonholes, all of them with well-fed faces, the women fat at thirty and the men fleshy at forty or so. They were off to a Socialist demonstration, and looked just like the bourgeoisie as pictured by the popular imagination in Russia under the influence of the cinema. Peaceable, content with their lot: I gathered that these workers of the West now had no desire whatsoever to fight for Socialism, or for anything else for that matter.

The city centre, with its commercial opulence, its illuminated signs, its Bourse set solid in the middle of town, was the cause of much astonishment to my son, then in his sixteenth year and a Soviet schoolboy; my answers to his questions seemed incredible, and only confused him the more.

'This big building then, with all these shops and waterfalls of fire on the roof—does it belong to one man, who can do just what he likes with it? Does this shop, with enough shoes for the whole of Orenburg, belong to just one owner?'

'Yes, son: his name is written there in lights. The gentleman probably owns a factory, a country house, several cars. . . .'

'All for him?'

'Yes, you might say.'

It all seemed mad to my Soviet adolescent. He went on:

'But what does he live for, this man? What is his aim in life?'

'His aim', I replied, 'is, broadly speaking, to make himself and his children rich. . . .'

'But he's already rich! Why does he want to get any richer? In the first place it's unjust—and then too, living just to get rich is simply idiotic! Are they all like that, these shop-owners?'

'Yes, son, and if they heard you talking, they would think you were a madman—a rather dangerous madman. . . .'

I have not forgotten this conversation; it taught me more than it taught my son.

I went to Ixelles to see the streets of my childhood once more: nothing had changed there, nothing at all. In the Place Communale I discovered Timmerman's bakery again; there were the same superb rice-tarts, powdered with sugar, so dear to my twelve-year-old self, in the very same shop window. The bookseller in whose shop I bought Redskin tales as a child had prospered: I had known him as an anarchist with a defiantly careless neck-tie, and now he was a Communist sympathizer, white-haired, wearing an artistic cravat, and fat, of course. . . . All those blazing ideas, all those struggles, all the bloodshed, wars, revolutions, civil wars, all our imprisoned martyrs—and all the time in the West here nothing was changing, and the tasty rice-tarts in the baker's window told of the drowsy permanency of things.

The slum districts inspired me with quite different reflections; they *had* changed. La Marolle, Rue Haute, Rue Blaes, and all the wretched alleys near by had become healthy, smart, prosperous streets. This paupers' town, once decked out in rags and saturated in filth, now breathed an air of well-being: wonderful pork-butchers' shops, a fine brand-new hospital, the hovels replaced by working-class flats with flowers lining the balconies. It was the work of reformist Socialism, as splendid as in Vienna.

There I saw Vandervelde, whom we had called 'social-traitor': he was coming back from a demonstration, with several Socialist leaders by him, and a great, loving murmur ran along the street, a sort of whispered acclamation: *'Le Patron! Le Patron!'* I went to see him at his house. His seventy years had spread weight upon him; his voice was weak and he had to listen with a hearing-aid, head bent and eyes set in concentration. His small pointed beard was still dark and his eyes still held the same animated, vaguely sad expression behind their lenses. Shaking his head to and fro, he asked me about Russian prisons, about Trotsky, whose 'aggressive manner' he could not understand—and how could I explain it to him? He told me, 'This contented Belgium that you see is a positive oasis in the midst of dangers, terrible dangers.'

Another time, after the execution of the Sixteen in Moscow, I found him dreadfully depressed, still crushed under the incomprehensibility of it all. 'I have read Kamenev's confession: raving madness. . . . How can you explain it to me? I knew Kamenev: I can see him before me now, with his white hair, his noble head—I cannot believe that they have killed him after this outburst of stark lunacy. . . .' How could I begin to explain such crimes to this old man who, on the threshold of the grave, incarnated half a century of Socialist humanism? I was dumbfounded, even more than when my son asked me his questions.

The friends who came from Paris to visit me said, 'Don't write anything about Russia, perhaps you may be too bitter. . . . We are just at the start of a tremendous movement of popular enthusiasm. Oh, if you could see Paris, the meetings, the demonstrations! Limitless hope is being born. We are allied with the Communist Party, which is winning over splendid masses of people; for these Russia is still an unsullied star. . . . Besides, no one would believe you. . . .' Only Boris Souvarine thought otherwise. 'The truth!' he said. 'Absolutely naked, as undiluted, as brutal as possible! We are witnessing an epidemic of highly dangerous stupidity!'

The strikes of May and June 1936 burst suddenly upon France and Belgium, with their new form of struggle, unplanned by anybody: the occupation of the factories. At Antwerp and in the Borinage the movement started spontaneously, as soon as the workers read the newspaper reports of the events in France. My Socialist friends, some of whom were trade-union leaders, were surprised, enraptured, and embarrassed. Léon Blum came to power, announcing social reforms which only the other day nobody had dreamt of—paid holidays, nationalization of war industries. The employing class was actually seized with panic.

The Belgian *Sûreté* called me in and accused me, on the lines of several Press reports, of 'agitating among the Borinage miners'. I had been 'seen at Jumet'! Most fortunately, I had not gone out of Brussels, but spent practically every evening there in the company of influential Socialists. 'The G.P.U. has not forgotten me,' I remarked, 'you can be sure of that.'

For years hence, denunciations were going to rain around me: sometimes public, launched by the Communist Press, which in Belgium demanded my expulsion 'in the name of respect for the right of asylum'; sometimes secret, passed on mysteriously to the police authorities of the West. The welcoming telegram sent me by Trotsky from Oslo got lost—intercepted, no one knew how. A letter from Trotsky's son which mentioned the *agent provocateur* Sobolevicius[1] (Sénine) never reached me. In the house where I lived, the first floor was rented by strangers who kept watch over my comings and goings with no pretence of concealment. When the Spanish Civil War broke out, a police superintendent called on me with a search-warrant, looking even in my baby daughter's cradle for arms intended for the Republicans. 'I know, of course,' he apologized, 'that we can't take it seriously, but you have been denounced.'

Two days after I arrived, a gentleman who seemed over-tanned, overdressed, and over-affectionate, approached me in a café: 'Dear Victor Serge! How good it is to meet you!' I recognized Bastajić, of *La Fédération Balkanique*; he said he was living in Geneva, and pressed me to fix a meeting with him. 'Geneva?' I said to myself, 'You are a secret agent, then', and did not keep the appointment. I learned later that he had been sent by the G.P.U.; he helped to arrange the murder of Ignace Reiss.[2]

All my close relatives in Russia had now been arrested, including two girls and two young men, all of them unpolitical; of these, my brothers-in-law and sisters-in-law, I never heard again. My eldest sister, an intellectual and equally unpolitical, disappeared too. My mother-in-law was torn from her children and deported alone, God knows where.

In 1938 I was living in the outskirts of Paris. Leopold III visited the city, with an entourage of officials which included several Socialists who were friends of mine. Information was laid, and

---

[1] Sobolevicius later emerged in the United States as an anti-Trotskyist agent under the name of Jack Soble, and was arrested under that name for espionage in 1957.

[2] Pavle Bastajić, a former Young Serb militant before his conversion to Communism, made his return to occupied Yugoslavia in 1940 but was arrested the following year, and later murdered in a concentration-camp.

passed from one department to another at the last moment, accusing me of 'preparing the assassination of the King of Belgium'. A senior Paris police official told me, 'You can guess where that comes from, they're plaguing you and laughing at me!' However, a card classifying me as 'suspected of terrorism' was sent around every police force in Europe, and my dossier swelled, terrifying the officials at the Préfecture. I had no end of trouble as a result.

In the meantime, now that I had made my anguished protest against the first Moscow Trial, the Soviet Legation in Brussels withdrew our passports. Antonov, the First Secretary, informed me that we had been 'deprived of Soviet nationality'.

'My daughter Jeannine too, who is not yet eighteen months old?' I asked ironically.

'That is so.'

Antonov refused me any written certificate of this fact. The Belgian Foreign Ministry received only a verbal confirmation from him, and that after much insisting.

The Communist Press now began a fantastic campaign of slander against me; it was led by a man with whom I had old ties of friendship and who personally, I was to learn, was shocked and sickened by the whole business. For a short while I was the most calumniated man in the world, for in accordance with some directive those scandalous sheets were translated into all languages. Agencies offered to send me all the cuttings at one franc twenty centimes a copy. The Communist cell-organization in the Press and the French reviews was admirably complete. The review *Europe*, to which I contributed, was more or less in bond to them. On the *Nouvelle Revue Française* they were on close terms with Malraux. The left-wing intellectuals' weekly, *Vendredi*, was backed by industrialists doing good business in Russia, and so was 'on the line'. I had to give up my well-paid work on Léon Blum's *Le Populaire*, because of pressures influencing the editorial staff. The publishing-house of Rieder, which had put out my novels, no longer showed them in its window-display, and deleted them from its catalogue. I found myself under a boycott that was practically total; it was impossible for me to live by writing. The only platform I had left was in the Liége Socialist daily, *La Wallonie*, and in extreme left-wing publications with a limited circulation.

I decided to resume one of the crafts of my youth, and become a proof-reader. This was no longer an easy matter since I could not find work in any print-shops where there were Communists. Luckily, the trade union was outside their sphere of influence. I worked in the *Croissant* printing-works; I loved its old-fashioned nineteenth-century buildings, the noise of machines, the smell of ink and dust, and the neighbourhood around—pubs, small hotels catering for the love-life of workers and their girls, houses of Old Paris, the little restaurant where Jaurès was murdered. Cyclists would drink a glass or two, waiting for the last edition. As the 'run' ended, faces would relax, and trade-jokes pass back and forth over the 'stone'. I corrected the proofs of reactionary sheets; and left-wing ones, too, to which I was denied access as a writer, such as *Messidor*, the C.G.T. weekly, which was run nominally by Jouhaux but actually by men who went to Moscow for their instructions, if they did not take them from secret and semi-secret agents.

Bernard Grasset published my books: an essay on Russia (*Destiny of a Revolution*) and a novel (*S'il est Minuit dans le Siècle*). Grasset was something of a reactionary, but of a free-ranging disposition, and he had colleagues who, like himself, loved any book, provided it was good. One knew that really great works would never come near this house. But in it a book retained its whole personality; the publishers never asked any writer to alter a single line.

An expression arose in France which tried to characterize the feeling of strength and confidence in the future generated by the Popular Front: 'euphoria', it was called. Trotsky wrote to me from Norway that it was leading straight to disaster, and I disagreed, wrongly, for at that juncture he saw far and true. For a short while I moved among some of Léon Blum's friends: Blum's brilliance, integrity, deep nobility, and warm popularity gave him such extraordinary prestige that people in his circle were afraid that he might be murdered by the Right. 'It would be better', I said, 'if he were also a man of authority—much less of a great Parliamentarian and much more of a leader for militant masses.' They assured me that he was. At this time he was refusing to avail himself of secret funds to manipulate the Press and back his own Party; I observed, from rather close quarters, an instructive piece of negotiation between the head of his Press Office and a large daily newspaper influenced by Mussolini, which only demanded money—which it eventually got —to turn its support to the Popular Front.

I did not share the opinion voiced by several extreme left-wingers who thought that in June 1936 the opportunity for revolution had been lost through a failure of nerve. I regarded the successful strikes as marking the re-emergence of the French working class which, enfeebled by the bloodshed of war, was now managing to recover its strength. It still needed several more years, in my opinion, to reach a fresh maturity, which would come with the passing of twenty or more years after the days of slaughter. For the same reason, I had immense confidence in the working-class movement of Spain; not having been involved in the war, the Spanish populace lived in the sure knowledge of its own brimming energy.

In any case, the 'euphoria' was snapped quite suddenly by two events which had a historical connexion. 18 July 1936 saw the outbreak of the Spanish military uprising, the coming of which was incisively predicted from the tribunal of the Cortes by my comrade Joaquín Maurín. Meanwhile, over the whole of the Soviet Union, arrests were being made—and were publicly reported—of well-known Communist officials. Trotsky sent me a scandalous cutting from *Pravda* proclaiming that 'the monsters, enemies of the people, will be annihilated with a mighty hand'. The Old Man wrote to me: 'I fear that this may be the prelude to a massacre. . . .' For long months, perhaps for years, he had had no first-hand news from Russia, and what I told him shocked him. I began to tremble for all those left behind there. And on 14 August, like a thunderbolt, came the announcement of the Trial of the Sixteen, concluded on the 25th—eleven days later!—by the execution of Zinoviev, Kamenev, Ivan Smirnov, and all their fellow-defendants. I understood, and wrote at once, that this marked the beginning of the extermination of all the old revolutionary generation. It was impossible to murder only some, and allow the others to live, their brothers, impotent witnesses maybe, but witnesses who understood what was going on. 'Why this massacre?' I speculated, in *La Révolution Prolétarienne*, and could find no other explanation except the urge to wipe out all reserve teams of government on the eve of a war now considered as imminent. Stalin, I was convinced, had not specifically planned the trials; but in the Spanish Civil War he saw the beginning of the war in Europe.

I am conscious of being the living proof of the *unplanned* character of the first trial and, at the same time, of the crazy falsity of the charges brought up in all the Trials. I had departed from the U.S.S.R. in mid-April, at a time when practically all the accused were already in prison. I had worked with Zinoviev and Trotsky, I was a close acquaintance of dozens of those who were to disappear and be shot, I had been one of the leaders of the Left Opposition in Leningrad and one of its spokesmen abroad, and I had never capitulated. Would I have been allowed to leave Russia, with my skill as a writer and my firm evidence as a witness whose facts were irrefutable, if the extermination-trials had been in the offing? Then too, not one mad accusation had been made against me in the whole course of the Trials; which proved that lies were being spread only about those with no means of defending themselves. The case of Trotsky is different: his was the most brilliant head, which had to be struck down at all costs.

In Paris we set up a 'Committee for Inquiry into the Moscow Trials and the Defence of Free Opinion in the Revolution', which included the surrealist poet André Breton, the pacifist Félicien Challaye, the poet Marcel Martinet, Socialists like Magdeleine Paz and André Philip, writers like Henry Poulaille and Jean Galtier-Boissière, worker-militants like Pierre Monatte and Alfred Rosmer, Left journalists such as Georges Pioch, Maurice Wullens and Emery, and the historians Georges Michon and Dommanget. I got the Committee's long title accepted through my insistence, ever since the summer of 1936, that we would also have the task of defending, within the Spanish Revolution, those whom Soviet totalitarianism would attempt to liquidate in Madrid and Barcelona by the same methods of lying and murder. We used to meet in café back rooms, first in the Place de la République, then in the Odéon. We had no money at all, and the Popular Front's Press was closed to us. *Le Populaire* reduced its reports on the Trials to a minimum and never published our documents. For years there would be this struggle of no more than a handful of individual consciences against a total suppression of the truth, in the face of crimes which were beheading the Soviet Union and would soon bring about the downfall of the Spanish Republic. Often we felt like voices crying in the wilderness. We were heartened by the formation in the United States of the Commission of John Dewey, Suzanne LaFollette, and Otto Rühle to conduct the same inquiry. (And even now, as I write these lines, I learn of the mysterious murder in New York of one of the great idealists who worked with that Commission, the old Italian anarchist Carlo Tresca. . . .[1])

The most shameless lying conceivable blazed out before our very eyes. But as witnesses we were practically gagged. In *Pravda* I could read the accounts (all of them mangled) of the Trials. I picked out literally hundreds of improbabilities, absurdities, gross distortions of fact, utterly lunatic statements. But it was a deluge of delirium. Scarcely had I analysed one billow of flagrant deceit than another, more violent, would wash away my day's work into futility. The torrent was so overwhelming that one could never find one's bearings. The British Intelligence Service blended with the Gestapo; railway accidents became political crimes; Japan entered the act; the Great Famine of collectivization had been organized by 'Trotskyists' (all of them in jail at the time); crowds of defendants whose trials were pending disappeared for evermore into the shadows; the succession of executions went on into thousands, without trials of any sort. And in every country of the civilized world, learned and 'progressive' jurists were to be found who thought these proceedings to be correct and convincing. It was turning into a tragic lapse of the whole modern conscience. In France the League for the Rights of Man, with a reputation going back to Dreyfus, had a jurist of this variety in its midst. The League's executive was divided into a majority which opposed any investigation, and an outraged minority which eventually resigned. The argument generally put forward amounted to: 'Russia is our ally. . . .' It was imbecilic reasoning—there is more than a hint of suicide about an international alliance which turns into moral and political servility—but it worked powerfully. The Chairman of the League for the Rights of Man, Victor Basch, one of the brave souls of the old battles against the General Staff, gave me an interview lasting several hours; at the end of it, prostrate with melancholy, he promised me that a commission would be called. It never was.

With no resources, with no assistance, I published irrefutable analyses of the three great lying Trials. Events have validated every line of them, even down to certain 'fine points': I announced that Radek, condemned to ten years of imprisonment, would not live for long: he was murdered in prison. The mechanism of extermination was so simple that one could forecast its workings. Months in

[1] In January 1943. Tresca's murderers were never discovered.

advance, I foretold the end of Rykov, Bukharin, Krestinsky, Smilga, Rakovsky, Bubnov; Antonov-Ovseyenko, the revolutionary who had led the attack on the Winter Palace in 1917, the wretch who had just had my friend Andreu Nin and the anarchist-philosopher Camillo Berneri murdered in Barcelona, was recalled from his post in Spain to take up that of People's Commissar of Justice, now lying vacant through the disappearance of Krylenko into the shadows; I foretold that he was doomed—and so he was. Yagoda, head of the G.P.U., organizer of the Zinoviev trial, was appointed People's Commissar of Posts and Telegraphs; I foretold that he was doomed—and so he was. One's foresight was absolutely useless. The dreadful machine carried on its grinding, intellectuals and politicians snubbed us, public opinion on the Left was dumb and blind. From the depth of a meeting-hall, a Communist worker shouted at me: 'Traitor! Fascist! Nothing you can do will stop the Soviet Union from remaining the fatherland of the oppressed!' I spoke wherever I could, in Socialist branches, trade-union meetings, at the League for the Rights of Man, in masonic lodges, at receptions held by the *Esprit* group. I could carry a meeting quite easily; contradiction I encountered never, insults and threats rather often. Officials of the Paris police advised me to change my lodgings and take precautions (I had no money, and so could not).

Everywhere, well-intentioned men, troubled to the depth of their souls, would ask me: 'But give us an explanation of the mystery of the confessions.' And when I gave them the threefold Russian explanation, through the selection of defendants, their devotion to the Party, and the terror, they would shake their heads, and appeal to 'the individual conscience which. . . .' They were unable to understand that revolutions and totalitarian systems create quite a different sort of individual conscience, and that we are in an age in which the human conscience is being turned inside out. Sometimes, angry in my own turn, I would shout at them: 'You then, you give me an explanation of the *conscience* shown by the famous intellectuals and Western party-leaders who swallow it all—the killing, the nonsense, the cult of the Leader, the democratic Constitution whose authors are promptly shot!' Romain Rolland had not long ago undertaken, at my request, to intervene if there was any fear of death-sentences. I wrote to him, 'Today in Moscow a trial is opening. . . . No more blood, no more blood upon this poor butchered Revolution!

You alone have a moral authority in the Soviet Union which means that you may—which means that you must—intervene. . . .' Romain Rolland kept his mouth shut and thirteen executions followed.

Georges Duhamel told me, 'I understand this drama. I have been enlightened by a personal experience whose nature I cannot disclose. But I feel that I can do nothing, nothing. . . .' There he was, living in his tranquil study over the Rue de Liége, surrounded by his tall sons (all eligible for the next war), and closeted with his vision of a dying civilization. 'I am a bourgeois, Serge, this world is dear to me because, whatever you may say, it has achieved so much for man, and now it looks as if it is all going to go under. . . .'

Henri Sellier, the Socialist Minister of Health, noted for his efforts in working-class housing, explained to me that the interests of the Popular Front demanded the humouring of the Communists. Around the review *Esprit* I met left-wing Catholics like Jacques Lefranc and Emmanuel Mounier, genuine Christians of fine, honest intellect. They sensed sharply that they were living at the end of an era; they loathed all lying, especially if it formed an excuse for murder, and they said so outright. In their simple teaching of 'reverence for the human person', I felt immediately at one with them. And what teaching could be more wholesome in an age in which civilization itself is cracking like rocks in a volcanic eruption?

On the eve of his journey to Russia I had addressed an open letter to André Gide. In it I said:

'We are building a common front against Fascism. How can we block its path, with so many concentration-camps behind us? Let me say this to you: one can only serve the working class and the U.S.S.R. by seeing absolutely clearly. And let me ask this of you in the name of those over there who have every kind of courage: have the courage to see clearly.'

We met several times in Brussels and Paris. Though well past sixty, he was still surprisingly young in manner and mind. His hairless face, with its tall, bare spread of brow, was austere, as if its contours had been shaped by an unresting inner effort. The immediate impression he gave was of extreme timidity which was, however, mastered by a scrupulous moral courage. I saw him weighing every word of his notes on the Soviet Union. He was full of hesitations, but only as far as concerned the act of publishing; his spirit knew no hesitation, but pronounced sentence, not without hope even then.

His manuscript, entrusted to the printer with instructions for strict secrecy, had nevertheless been read by Ehrenburg: 'These people have their ways and means....' Militiamen on the Madrid front (and how did they know of it?) sent a telegram to Gide begging him not to publish a book which could prove 'a mortal blow' for them. Gide hated all intrigue, but the militiamen of Madrid were infinitely close to his heart. His words had a tone of almost absolute gloom:

'I thought I would be able to do so much in Moscow, for so many victims.... I saw at once that one could do absolutely nothing. They overwhelmed me with banquets—as if I went there to feast! Twice Bukharin tried to get near me, and was stopped. All the same, I do not want there to be the slightest touch of pessimism in my book.... What a flood of abuse I'm going to face! And there will be militiamen in Spain who will believe that I am actually a traitor!' Underlying all his words was the anguish of wondering 'What use can I be now?'

What I was expecting duly happened. In March 1937 (the date has a certain importance), while paying a visit to a friend's house in Brussels, I met a young woman whose eyes were wide with terror. 'I am afraid', she said, 'to believe what I've just heard. A prominent Communist from Spain has been to see my husband. I heard him say that in Barcelona they're getting ready to liquidate thousands of anarchists and P.O.U.M. militants, and that it's going along very nicely....'

At once I warned the comrades of P.O.U.M. The *Partido Obrero de Unificación Marxista*, a minority party of dauntless revolutionaries, had a division of volunteers at the front and a membership of 40,000 or so; its leaders, Maurín (now lost in Franco territory), Juan Andrade, Andreu Nin, Julián Gorkín, Gironella, Jordi Arquer and Rovira, all had some background in the various Communist Oppositions, and had pronounced their judgement, in terms no less clear for being temperate, upon the Moscow Trials. They had serious disagreements with Trotsky, but viewed him with comradely admiration. They published my articles and my pamphlet *Seize Fusillés*. They had a first-rate understanding of the methods of the Comintern, and maintained an uncompromising defence of working-class democracy. Unless it crushed them the Communist Party would be unable to press its concealed authority upon the Spanish Republic.

Julián Gorkín passed through Brussels, and we both went to see the leaders of the Socialist International, Fritz Adler and Oscar

Pollak.[1] Adler had lately published a moving and intelligent pamphlet on the 'Witchcraft Trial' in Moscow. He was the image of despair. Pollak answered us, 'What do you want us to do? Since the Russians are sending arms to Spain, they control the situation!'

From day to day during April, I observed from Paris the preparation of Barcelona's bloody days of May. I scattered my futile warnings in the left-wing Socialist Press, as far as the United States itself. Forces with superior weapons, which could have captured Saragossa, stayed back in Barcelona, for reasons that were obscure—and Catalonia was not sent the arms that Russia had promised. If Franco had begun his attack on that region in the spring of 1937, he would probably have taken it. The Communist provocation came duly at the appointed time, on 4 May. There was a battle in the streets, and rather than begin a civil war behind the lines, the C.N.T. (*Confederación Nacionale del Trabajo*) submitted. A few days went by, and then the P.O.U.M. was outlawed; its leaders were arrested and taken to a secret destination, not by the regular Republican police but by the police force of the Communist Party. I knew that once Andreu Nin fell into Russian hands he would never come out alive: he knew Moscow too well. Fearless, optimistic, and physically weakened by illness, he did not go into hiding. Our Committee in Paris lost no time in sending Magdeleine Paz, Félicien Challaye, and Georges Pioch on a deputation to the Spanish Embassy. There they had an icy reception. An Embassy Secretary gave them guarantees of justice for all the prisoners, but added with a little gesture of despair, 'As for Nin. . . .'

'What do you mean, as for Nin?'

'Nothing, nothing. I know nothing, I can tell you nothing.'

The great flyer Edouard Serre, the head of Air-France and a sincere Socialist with a record of solid service to the Republic and Russia, went to see Suritz, the Soviet Ambassador in Paris.[2] He begged Suritz to save Nin, whose death would lead to

---

[1] Oskar Pollak (1893–1963): journalist for the Second International and the Austrian Socialist Party (Brussels 1936–8, Paris 1938–40); Executive member, Austrian Socialist Party.

[2] Yakov Suritz (1882–1952): an ex-Menshevik whose sympathies appear to have been genuinely liberal; active in many diplomatic posts abroad; in 1940 recalled, after being declared *persona non grata* by the French Government for an Embassy telegram to Stalin in which Britain and France were denounced as 'war-mongers'; Ambassador to Brazil 1946–9.

repercussions infinitely damaging to the cause of Spain. 'Thank you for coming to see me,' the Ambassador said. 'Draw up a short memorandum on the matter without delay, and I will forward it.' Serre told us of his visit later.

The delegations we had dispatched to Spain managed, after great efforts, to retrace Nin's tracks up to a frontier of darkness where the trail disappeared. Incarcerated in an isolated villa at Alcalá de Henares, just outside Madrid, close to an airfield occupied by Soviet planes, Nin was then kidnapped by uniformed men, and disappeared for ever into the shadows. A Socialist official in the Madrid political police and an examining magistrate opened an investigation, which at once implicated certain leading Communist officials. The police official, Gabriel Morón, had to resign and the magistrate eventually fled. Largo Caballero, the head of the Government, resigned too, and was replaced in office by Negrín. We learnt that old Caballero had refused to outlaw the P.O.U.M., since it was a working-class party, and that the installation of a more docile government had come about through Communist pressure. All we could cry now was: 'The Spanish Republic is doomed!' For indeed it was impossible to defeat Fascism while creating within the Republic a system of concentration-camps and murder directed against the most forceful and reliable anti-Fascists; those methods destroyed the moral standing of democracy.

The Russian Socialist engineer Marc Rhein, the son of the Menshevik leader Abramovich, had gone before Nin into the same obscure graveyard. Kurt Landau, the Austrian Socialist, followed. Erwin Wolf, a student of Czech-German nationality and bourgeois origins, had been Trotsky's secretary in Norway. He came to see me in Brussels and told me that he could not live in peace, studying Marxism, while a revolution was struggling for its life. He was off to Spain. I told him: 'You are going to certain murder.' However, he had all the pugnacious confidence of youth. Tall forehead, fine features, the rigidity of the young theoretician, a mind that was single-track, schematic and keen. He had just married a Norwegian girl, the daughter of the Socialist Knudsen: he was happy and sure of himself. Once in Barcelona, he was of course arrested. The Czechoslovak and Norwegian consulates applied their influence and he was released. A few days later he was kidnapped in the street and disappeared, this time for ever.

Each one of these crimes was enveloped in the thick, suffocating clouds wafted by the Communist Press. The P.O.U.M., the victims of kidnapping, assassination or (as in Mena's case) the firing-squad,[1] the revolutionaries in jail, all were unendingly denounced as 'Trotskyists, spies, agents of Franco-Hitler-Mussolini, enemies of the people' in the undiluted style of the Moscow Trials. The average man, who cannot conceive that lying on this scale is possible, is taken unawares by stupendous, unexpected assertions. Outrageous language intimidates him and goes some way to excuse his deception: reeling under the shock, he is tempted to tell himself that there must, after all, be some justification for this madness, some justification of a higher order passing his own understanding. Success is possible for these techniques, it seems clear, only in epochs of confusion, and only if the brave minorities who embody the critical spirit are effectively gagged or reduced to impotence through reasons of State and their own lack of material resources.

In any case, it was not a matter of persuasion: it was, fundamentally, a matter of murder. One of the intentions behind the campaign of drivel initiated in the Moscow Trials was to make any discussion between official and oppositional Communists quite impossible. Totalitarianism has no more dangerous enemy than the spirit of criticism, which it bends every effort to exterminate. Any reasonable objection is bundled away with shouts, and the objector himself, if he persists, is bundled off on a stretcher to the mortuary. I have met my assailants face to face in public meetings, offering to answer any question they raised. Instead they always strove to drown my voice in storms of insults, delivered at the tops of their voices. My books, rigorously documented, and written with the sole passionate aim of uncovering the truth, have been translated for publication in Poland, Britain, the United States, Argentina, Chile, and Spain. In none of these places has a single line ever been contested, or a single argument adduced in reply: only abuse, denunciation and threats. Both in Paris and in Mexico there were moments when in certain cafés people discussed my forthcoming assassination quite as a matter of course.

Perhaps, for the sake of the reader ignorant of those past dramas, I must press home one example. Andreu Nin had spent his youth

[1] Marcía Mena was a P.O.U.M. member from Lerida, shot on the orders of the Stalinist General Lister after the arrest of the P.O.U.M. Executive.

in Russia, first as a loyal Communist, then as a militant of the Left Opposition. When he returned to Spain he had undergone imprisonment by the reactionary Republic, translated Dostoevsky and Pilniak, attacked the incipient Fascist tendencies and helped to found a revolutionary Marxist party. The Revolution of July 1936 had elevated him to the Ministry of Justice in the Generalitat of Catalonia. In this capacity he had established popular tribunals, ended the terrorism of irresponsible elements and instituted a new marriage-code. He was a scholarly Socialist and a first-rate brain, highly regarded by all who knew him and on close terms of friendship with Companys, the head of the Catalan Government. Without the slightest shame the Communists denounced him as 'an agent of Franco-Hitler-Mussolini', and refused to sign the 'pact against slander' proposed to them by all the other parties; they walked out of a meeting at which the other parties asked them, all calmly, for proofs; in their own Press they appealed continually to the evidence of the Moscow Trials, in which, however, Nin's name had never once been mentioned. All the same, Nin's popularity increased, and deservedly; nothing else remained but to kill him.

We succeeded in opening an international campaign in defence of the persecuted Socialists of Spain. In Britain the Independent Labour Party, including Fenner Brockway, Maxton, McGovern and MacNair, in Holland Sneevliet's Revolutionary Socialist Party gave us their tireless support. In France the revolutionary Left in the Socialist Party was very active; this included Marceau Pivert, Collinet, Edouard Serre, and Paul Schmierer.[1] Only in minority parties and among isolated individuals did conscience still burn. Rossi, an editor on *Le Populaire* and the historian of Fascism, exclaimed to me, 'The conscience of the masses—my friend, it doesn't exist!

[1] Marceau Pivert (1895–1958): prominent revolutionary militant in the Socialist Party and teachers' unions; led the Left of the Socialist Party in the Popular Front era, but founded the P.S.O.P. (see page 347) in 1938 as a breakaway; companion of Serge's exile in Mexico; after the war re-entered the Socialist Party as an Executive Member, but lost his position through his opposition to the Party's complicity in the Algerian war. Michel Collinet (1904–1977): member of the Communist Youth (1925–8) and later of Trotskyist groups; an active member of the Socialist Party from 1935; co-founder of the P.S.O.P.; active in the Resistance movement, especially in journalism; author of a number of important works of sociology and social history from a 'Marxist-revisionist' standpoint. Paul Schmierer (1905–): physician; Socialist militant since 1922; Secretary of the Aid Committee for the Spanish Revolution (1936–9), where he met Serge; as organizer for the *Centre Américain de Secours* in Marseilles (1940–4) assisted in Serge's escape; Resistance leader.

The dirty tricks of a man like Marcel Cachin add up to nothing—he can supply funds to Mussolini in 1915, slander Lenin in 1917, worship Lenin in 1920, lament perpetually in private over Moscow's methods, applaud all the shootings over there at the top of his voice, call Léon Blum a Social-Fascist yesterday and pledge his friendship to him today—and the Red suburbs idolize him! We, with our outmoded idealism, are properly blocked!' All this was in order to explain to me how very difficult it would be to insert, in a Socialist newspaper, a short note on the trial of the P.O.U.M.

Maxton of the I.L.P. and Sneevliet of the Dutch R.S.P. were at the head of our deputations to Spain. We briefed our delegates carefully: 'Trust nobody at their word. If someone points a man out to you in a prison yard and says that it is Nin, insist on speaking to him and touching him! If they tell you that Gorkín's prison is a sanatorium, insist on going there—that same day! If they bring you a whole cartload of "evidence", insist on an expert opinion for a single page of it—and without delay!' They harassed Republican Ministers with their questions and protests, and proceeded to knock on the doors of the Communist Party's secret prisons. Maxton the imperturbable, with his angular face and steady grey eyes, pipe in mouth, heard the Spanish ministers Irujo and Zugazagoitia—honest Republicans who did their utmost to save the victims—reply to him: 'These abominable acts are done against our will. Do you think that we are safe ourselves? And please remember that it is the Russians who are giving us arms!' Twenty times, if once, we expected to hear it announced that the members of the P.O.U.M. Executive had been executed summarily in some Communist jail. Our campaign saved their lives. Their trial, held at the hour when the Republic was already entering its death-agony, was a real moral triumph.

Black was the spring of 1937. Hardly were the Barcelona troubles ended, and the murdered corpses buried or else mysteriously incinerated when, as I had been able easily to predict, the tragedies of Russia once more cast their peculiar stupor over the world. The incessant massacre of an entire revolutionary generation moved scarcely anybody. Reactionaries were, on the contrary, satisfied with the sight of a victorious revolution discrediting itself in the extermination of its best men. An Italian Fascist magazine wrote that Bolshevism itself was coming round to the formation of a Fascist style of

State. The Socialist adversaries of Bolshevism, who were of course outraged, emphasized that it was all the irresistible march of History.

The annihilation of the Soviet General Staff—Marshal Tukhachevsky and his companions in ill-fortune—did make a profound impression. 'Just think of it!' one French journalist said to me, 'Every general in the whole world is shocked! Shooting marshals—it just isn't done!' It was, besides, realized that the decapitation of the Red Army High Command could, in the context of a Europe approaching war, have serious consequences. There was no mystery in the logic of these events: impossible to destroy the nucleus of the revolutionary régime without touching that of the army; the army was well aware of this, and perhaps its old leaders would have liked to turn the blow. On 11 June the leaders of the Red Army were executed in the shadows.

Scarcely had the Tukhachevsky case passed from the front pages when I read the report on the crime of Bagnoles-sur-Orne: two men stabbed to death in their car on a country road in Normandy. I immediately recognized the picture of one of them: a splendid comrade, the Italian anti-Fascist Carlo Rosselli, editor of *Giustizia e Libertà*. As in Matteotti's case, the order to kill had come from Mussolini himself. With him fell his brother, the historian Nello Rosselli, who had been allowed to leave Italy (to take a holiday!) so that he could be got rid of in this way. At that very time Mussolini was viewed by all right-thinking folk in Europe and America as 'the enlightened dictator of Latin civilization'. We felt that we were being knifed from two sides at once.

In Russia, writers were disappearing, notably one of the greatest, Boris Pilniak; the P.E.N. Clubs kept a discreet silence. . . . The 'judges' of Tukhachevsky (who had probably been executed without even a faked trial) disappeared too. Generals and leaders of war-industry were followed to the grave by admirals and aeroplane-designers. My unending task of unravelling these tragedies was a nightmare without respite.

September 1937. . . . I had formed a close acquaintance with Hendricus Sneevliet. In the previous year we had spoken on the same platform at evening meetings in Amsterdam and Rotterdam, for solidarity with the Republicans of Spain. Our audiences had been working-class and wonderfully sensible. I was aware of the high calibre of his party. He now informed me that a leading official in the

G.P.U.'s Secret Service, resident in Holland, had been heart-broken by the Zinoviev trial and crossed over to the Opposition: Ignace Reiss was warning us that we were all in peril, and asking to see us.

Reiss was at present hiding in Switzerland. We arranged to meet him in Rheims on 5 September 1937. We waited for him at the station buffet, then at the post office. He did not appear. Puzzled, we wandered through the town, admiring the cathedral, which was still shattered from the bombardment, drinking champagne in small cafés, and exchanging the confidences of men who have been saddened through a surfeit of bitter experiences. Both of Sneevliet's sons had committed suicide—the second out of despair because virtually nothing could be done to help the anti-Nazi refugees in Amsterdam, or prevent them from being turned back at the frontier. Several young men of his Party had just died in Spain. Of what use was their sacrifice? Long ago, Sneevliet had been deported to the Dutch East Indies, where he had founded a popular party;[1] the friends of his youth had been sentenced to penal servitude for life and the pleas he had since made on their behalf came to nothing. In his own country, the forces of Fascism were openly growing, although they had the bulk of the population opposed to them. Sneevliet sensed the approach of the war in which Holland, its working class, and its developed culture would be inevitably smashed: doubtless only at the beginning, only to rise again later —but when, how? 'Is it necessary for us to pass through bloodbaths and utter darkness? What can one do?'

All this had aged him a little, so that his face wore a persistent frown amid its close lines, but he never lost heart. 'It is strange', he remarked, 'that Reiss hasn't come. He is such a punctual man. . . .' As we took the train back to Paris we read in a newspaper that on the previous day the bullet-riddled body of a foreigner had been picked up on the road from Chamblandes, near Lausanne. In the man's pocket was a railway ticket for Rheims.

Three days later Elsa Reiss, the widow, told us in a broken voice of the trap that had been laid. A woman comrade named Gertrude Schildbach had arrived. She, like them, had wept in anguish at the news of the Moscow executions. She had known Reiss for fifteen years, and came now to ask his advice. They went out

[1] This was the Indies Social-Democratic Union, founded by Sneevliet in 1913, which later became the Indonesian Communist Party.

together; the comrade left chocolates for the wife and child. These were filled with poison. In the convulsed fingers of the murdered man a handful of grey hair was found. . . . The Communist-influenced Press in Switzerland wrote that a Gestapo agent had just been liquidated by his colleagues. Not a single newspaper in Paris would take our disclosures, detailed as they were.

I paid a visit to Gaston Bergery at the office of *La Flèche*. Bergery was running a left-wing movement called *Le Frontisme*, which was directed simultaneously against the monopolies and against Communism. He was an elegant, pugnacious character with open but subtle features, and with talents equally appropriate, it seemed, either for mass-agitation or a Government position. He was also fond of rich living and quite evidently ambitious; we all knew that he could quite easily turn one day either to the Fascist Right or towards revolution.[1] Within the Popular Front he maintained a position of independence. 'We will publish!' he told me. The silence was broken. Our investigation laid the crime open to the light of day. Senior Russian officials, protected by diplomatic immunity, were asked to pack and be out within three days. The inquiry revealed that minute preparations for a kidnapping were being hatched around the person of Leon Sedov, Trotsky's son.

A certain somebody, who was sure that he was about to be killed, telephoned, demanding to see us. Leon Sedov, Sneevliet, and myself met this person in the office of a Paris lawyer, Gérard Rosenthal. He was a little thin man with premature wrinkles and nervous eyes: Walter Krivitsky, whom I had met several times in Russia. Together with Reiss and Brunn (or Ilk) he had headed the Secret Service and was engaged in amassing arms for Spain. Against his wishes he had taken part in preparing the ambush for his friend; he was then ordered to 'liquidate' Reiss's widow before returning to Moscow.

Conversation was painful at first. He told Sneevliet, 'We have a spy in your party, but I do not know his name', and Sneevliet, honest old man as he was, burst out in anger: 'You scoundrel!' He told me that our mutual friend Brunn had just been shot in Russia, like most of those who had been secret agents in the first period of the Revolution. He added that, despite all, he felt very distant from us and would remain loyal to the revolutionary State; the historic

---

[1] Bergery subsequently served the Vichy Government as Ambassador to Moscow, 1940–2, and Ankara, 1942–4.

mission of this State was far more important than its crimes, and besides he himself did not believe that any opposition could succeed.

One evening I had a long talk with him on a dark, deserted boulevard next to the sinister wall of the Santé prison. Krivitsky was afraid of lighted streets. Each time that he put his hand into his overcoat pocket to reach for a cigarette, I followed his movements very attentively and put my own hand in my pocket.

'I am risking assassination at any moment', he said with a feeble, piqued smile, 'and you still don't trust me, do you?'

'That's right.'

'And we would both agree to die for the same cause: isn't that so?'

'Perhaps,' I said, 'all the same it would be as well to define just what this cause is.'

In February 1938 Leon Sedov, Trotsky's eldest son, died suddenly in obscure circumstances. Young, energetic, of a temperament at once gentle and resolute, he had lived a hellish life. From his father he inherited an eager intelligence, an absolute faith in revolution, and the utilitarian, intolerant political mentality of the Bolshevik generation that was now disappearing. More than once we had lingered until dawn in the streets of Montparnasse, labouring together to comb out the mad tangle of the Moscow Trials, pausing from time to time under a street lamp for one or other of us to exclaim aloud: 'We are in a labyrinth of utter madness!' Overworked, penniless, anxious for his father, he passed his whole life in that labyrinth. In November 1936 a section of Trotsky's archives, which had been deposited in secret a few days previously at the Institute of Social History, 7 Rue Michelet, were stolen in the night by criminals who simply cut through a door with the aid of an acetylene torch. I helped Sedov in his pointless investigation; what could be more transparent than a burglary like this?

Later on he apologized for refusing to give me his address when he went away to the Mediterranean coast for a rest: 'I am giving it only to our contact-man—I really have to become frightened of the least indiscretion. . . .' And we discovered that down at Antibes two of Reiss's murderers had lived near to him; another was in lodgings actually next door to his own. He was surrounded at every turn, and suffered fevers of anxiety each night. He underwent an operation for appendicitis in a clinic run by certain dubious Russians, to which he had been taken under an assumed identity. There he died, perhaps as a result of culpable negligence. . . . We carried his coffin of white wood, draped with the red Soviet flag, to the Père Lachaise cemetery; the inquest revealed no definite findings. He was the third of Trotsky's children that I had seen die; and his brother had just disappeared into Eastern Siberia.

At the cemetery, a tall, thin, pale young man came to shake my hand. His face was downcast, his grey eyes piercing and wary, his clothes shabby. I had known this young doctrinaire in Brussels and we did not get on together: Rudolf Klement, secretary of the Fourth International. In his efforts to infuse some life into this feeble organization he worked at a fanatical pitch, committing in due course gross political blunders which I had many a time rebuked. On 13 July of the same year (1938), I received an express message: 'Rudolf kidnapped in Paris. . . . In his room everything was in order, the meal ready on the table. . . .' Forged letters from him—or genuine ones dictated at pistol-point—arrived from the Spanish border. Then, a headless body resembling Klement was fished out of the Seine at Meulan. The Popular Front Press said nothing, of course. Friends of the missing man identified the decapitated corpse by the characteristic shape of the torso and hands. The Communist daily papers *L'Humanité* and *Ce Soir* joined the argument, and a Spanish officer, actually a Russian who was afterwards nowhere to be found, declared that he had seen Klement at Perpignan on the day of his disappearance. The trail having now been confused, the case was closed.

Shortly after this, Krivitsky left for the United States, where he published his book *I Was Stalin's Agent*. In February 1941 he was found dead in a Washington hotel-room, with a bullet-hole in his head.

The Spanish collapse provoked a catastrophic moral breakdown in France; however invisible this might have been to the superficial observer, it was absolutely clear to the initiated eye. The most deep-rooted Socialist affections, which amount to the same as the noble affections of mankind in general, were almost erased within a few months. Thousands of refugees were crossing the Pyrenees, only to be met by a French constabulary that robbed them, bullied them, and interned them in unspeakable concentration-camps. The C.G.T., which was reasonably prosperous, would not dream of lavishing its funds upon assistance for this flood of heroes and victims. Consumed by discord, governments veered towards the Right, as the Premiership swung from Léon Blum to Daladier, then to Daladier with Reynaud at his elbow. Little by little, merciless legislation (which was never rigorously applied, precisely because it was so merciless) was enacted against the refugees. The masses abandoned the losers of the war, and the issues which they dumbly embodied. It would have been quite easy to accept them in ordinary life, settle them in districts with a declining population, arrange for families to take in the children and youngsters—and even to recruit from their numbers one or two crack divisions for the defence of France, herself under threat of attack. None of these ideas occurred to anybody.

I could see how the psychological mechanism of repression worked. Enjoying so much prosperity themselves, men turned away from so much suffering. Living themselves beneath the shadow of so many dangers, men turned away from the spectacle of so many defeats, inflicted after so many struggles. They were annoyed with the Spaniards for having been beaten. Comrades who had welcomed them at first began to disengage from them, with a kind of anger. Later, on the highways at the time of France's fall, I heard excellent folk speaking contemptuously of the Spanish refugees. I could illustrate factually each line that I am writing; but what purpose would it serve? In the proof-readers' union we had refugees from abroad dying of hunger, and their brothers allowed them to have one or two days' work a week—this at the end of endless, persistent pleading, although most of our members lacked nothing. I battled for months to secure a miserable 300 francs grant to an old man of seventy, one of the founders of the C.N.T., José Negre, who was dying on a wretched bed in a concentration-camp. I roused the 'Elders of the C.G.T.', I had an interview with Jouhaux, all in vain. Several old and devoted friends whom I had known as men full of generous enthusiasm now changed out of all recognition, and we more or less broke off relations. What could we talk about?

Munich was a reflection of this state of mind in the realm of high politics. It was a surrender before Nazi force, a betrayal of our ally Czechoslovakia, a betrayal of the Soviet Union. I knew that

French politicians, reactionaries but (I believe) sincere men, had come back from Berlin and were calling working-class militants in for homilies, saying how afraid they were for France—we must have peace, peace at any price, or ruin would follow. It is a fact that the immense majority of the population welcomed the shameful Munich transaction with inexpressible relief. When Daladier returned from his talks with Chamberlain, Hitler, and Mussolini, his face gloomy as usual (all his photos showed him heavy and downcast—the Prime Minister officiating over the funeral of a political system), he was amazed to find himself acclaimed; he was expecting to be hissed.

I must confess that I too felt a sense of relief at Munich. It was clear to me that this particular French nation, in this particular phase of depression, was incapable of fighting. If they had not fought to save the Republic, if they had not even been able to stop non-intervention from turning into a bloody farce, could one ask them, the day after this disappointment, to go to war for the sake of faraway Czechoslovakia? From this time they would require a period of years, a fresh accretion of energy, before they could recover their full moral integrity.

In the working-class movement, depression becomes expressed and even accentuated by division. As all values begin to be questioned, minorities stiffen into intolerance and majorities lose their bearings. The Socialist Party split at its Royan Congress. The revolutionary Left, now harried by Paul Faure's stupid disciplinary measures, resigned and established the Socialist Workers' and Peasants' Party (P.S.O.P.). By this act it lost its audience in a party of over 300,000 members, isolated its few thousand followers, and started a revolutionary movement just at the time when the working class was retiring into its own demoralization. The split at Royan weakened the Socialist Party and created an unworkable alter----·' party.

The trade unions were shedding their activ< them pacifism and anti-Stalinism, both neg; ranged against warmongering and the blin Communists. I had to break off relations with the far Left edited by a libertarian veteran, ust man, because it was invoking the principle of f; excuse to print apologies for Nazism!

It is from this period, too, that my break with Trotsky can be dated. I had held aloof from the Trotskyist movement, within which I could not detect the hopes of the Left Opposition in Russia for a renewal of the ideology, morals and institutions of Socialism. In the countries I knew at first hand, Belgium, Holland, France, and Spain, the tiny parties of the 'Fourth International', ravaged by frequent splits and, in Paris, by deplorable feuding, amounted only to a feeble and sectarian movement out of which, I judged, no fresh thinking could emerge. The life of these groups was maintained by nothing but the prestige of the Old Man and his great, unceasing efforts; and both his prestige and the quality of his efforts deteriorated in the process. The very idea of starting an International at the moment when all international Socialist organizations were dying, when reaction was in full flood, and without support of any kind, seemed quite senseless to me. I wrote to Leon Davidovich and told him as much. I was also in disagreement with him on certain important issues in the history of the Revolution: he refused to admit that in the terrible Kronstadt episode of 1921 the responsibilities of the Bolshevik Central Committee had been simply enormous; that the subsequent repression had been needlessly barbarous; and that the establishment of the Cheka (later the G.P.U.) with its techniques of secret inquisition had been a grievous error on the part of the revolutionary leadership, and one incompatible with any Socialist philosophy.

In what concerned Russia's contemporary problems, I recognized Trotsky's outstanding vision and his capacity for outstanding insights. At the time when he was writing *The Revolution Betrayed*, I had prevailed on him to include in the Opposition's programme a declaration of freedom for all parties accepting the Soviet system. Blended with the flashes of his superb intelligence I could see the systematic schematizing of old-time Bolshevism, whose resurrection, in all countries of the world, he believed to be inevitable. I understood his inflexibility: he was, after all, the last survivor of a generation of giants. However, convinced as I was that great historical traditions are prolonged only by renewal, I believed that Socialism too had to renew itself in the world of today, and that this must take place through the jettisoning of the authoritarian, intolerant tradition of turn-of-the-century Russian Marxism. I recalled, for against Trotsky himself, a sentence of astounding vision which he had written, in 1914 I think: 'Bolshevism may very well be an excellent instrument for the conquest of power, but after that it will reveal its counter-revolutionary aspects.'

The only problem which revolutionary Russia, in all the years from 1917 to 1923, utterly failed to consider was the problem of liberty; the only declaration which it had to make afresh, and which it has never made, is the Declaration of the Rights of Man.

I expounded these ideas in an article published in Paris as *Puissances et limites du marxisme* and in the New York *Partisan Review* as *Marxism of Our Time*. The Old Man, true to his habitual stereo-types, was pleased to see nothing in it except 'an exhibition of petty-bourgeois demoralization. . . .' Deplorably misinformed by his acolytes, he wrote a long polemical essay against me—imputing to me an article of which I was not the author and which was totally at variance with my frequently expressed opinions. The Trotskyist journals refused to publish my corrections. In the hearts of the persecuted I encountered the same attitudes as in their persecutors. Contagion through combat has its own natural logic: thus the Russian Revolution proved, despite itself, to be the continuation of certain ancient traditions stemming from the despotism it had just overthrown; Trotskyism was displaying symptoms of an outlook in harmony with that of the very Stalinism against which it had taken its stand, and by which it was being ground into powder. . . . I was heartbroken by it all, because it is my firm belief that the tenacity and will-power of some men can, despite all odds, break with the traditions that suffocate, and withstand the contagions that bring death. It is painful, it is difficult, but it *must* be possible. I abstained from any counter-polemic.

Our Oppositional movement in Russia had not been Trotskyist, since we had no intention of attaching it to a personality, rebels as we ourselves were against the cult of the Leader. We regarded the Old Man only as one of our greatest comrades, an elder member of the family over whose ideas we argued freely. And now, ten years later, tiny parties like that of Walter Dauge in Belgium, which had no more than a few hundred members in a district of the Borinage, termed him 'our glorious leader', and any person in the circles of the 'Fourth International' who went so far as to object to his propositions was promptly expelled and denounced in the same language that the bureaucracy had employed against us in the Soviet Union. Doubtless all this had little importance; but the very fact that such a vicious circle could be set up was a terrible psychological symptom of the movement's inner disintegration.

I came to the conclusion that our Opposition had simultaneously contained two opposing lines of significance. For the great majority of its members it had meant resistance to totalitarianism in the name of the democratic ideals expressed at the beginning of the Revolution; for a number of our Old Bolshevik leaders it meant, on the contrary, the defence of doctrinal orthodoxy which, while not excluding a certain tendency towards democracy, was authoritarian through and through. These two mingled strains had, between 1923 and 1928, surrounded Trotsky's vigorous personality with a tremendous aura. If, in his exile from the U.S.S.R., he had made himself the ideologist of a renewed Socialism, critical in outlook and fearing diversity less than dogmatism, perhaps he would have attained a new greatness. But he was the prisoner of his own orthodoxy, the more so since his lapses into unorthodoxy were being denounced as treason. He saw his role as that of one carrying into the world at large a movement which was not only Russian but extinct in Russia itself, killed twice over, both by the bullets of its executioners and by changes in human mentality.

And war was speeding on its way. I had known a time when the Spanish Republic could almost certainly have won in the space of a few weeks or months. In the days after the military uprising, when it was still based upon Morocco, the Moroccan Nationalists had offered to fight Franco if the Republic would only come to a generous settlement with them. The negotiations (which were conducted by a number of my friends) failed, probably because the chancelleries of Europe intimated some hostility to a reform as daring as this. Everything that had happened subsequently fitted the assumption that the Soviet Union, far from desiring victory for a Republic in which the Communist Party would not have preserved its hegemony, had instead sought to prolong the anti-Fascist resistance merely for the sake of gaining time. Once demoralization had done its work, Franco entered Barcelona in January 1939 without meeting any resistance. Towards the middle of March, the Nazis entered Prague.

It was during that same month of March that I read the *Pravda* report of Stalin's speech to the Eighteenth Party Congress. The

Leader accused Britain and France of trying to 'sow discord between
the Soviet Union and Germany'. A speech by Voroshilov confirmed
the authenticity of the details of Soviet military power which had
been published in a Nazi military review. Through Reiss and
Krivitsky we were aware that Soviet agents had been in continual
contact with the Nazi rulers. On 5 May Litvinov, the advocate of
'collective security' and of the Politbureau's 'peace policy' within
the League of Nations, resigned abruptly. These clues, among
others, were a clear indication that Soviet policy would soon switch
to collaboration with the Third Reich. Nevertheless, the section
of the French Press that was steered by Communist agents was
neither willing nor able to understand anything of this; the articles
I submitted to journals of the Left were rejected, and the only
platform I could find was in the review *Esprit*. It was quite obvious
to me that the Politbureau regarded France as beaten before the
battle, and was therefore tacking towards finding some accommoda-
tion with the strongest side.

An obscure journalist, one Benoist-Méchin, the author of a tolerable *History of the German Army*, asked me to meet him. I asked a left-
wing publisher to give me some information about the man, and
was told: 'He is a former composer, a good scissors-and-paste man,
of no particular political complexion.' We met in a café on the
Boulevard St. Michel. This character was young (about thirty-five),
featureless, bespectacled, reserved in speech, and most attentive.
After ten minutes I was absolutely sure that he must be working
simultaneously for the *Deuxième Bureau* and some other organization,
probably German. He told me that he was thinking of writing a
history of the Civil War in the Ukraine.

'Do you know Russian?' I asked him.

'No.'

'Have you travelled in the Ukraine?'

'No.'

'Have you studied the Russian Revolution?'

'Not particularly. . . .'

Our conversation wandered on to current affairs, and I could
see that my interlocutor was primarily interested in the attitude of
the Ukrainian peasantry in case of war. I cut the conversation short,
and said, 'The Ukraine is disaffected, but will defend itself furiously
against any aggression. And besides, what is on the agenda today

is not a war between the Soviet Union and Germany, but rather a new partition of Poland.'

I left Monsieur Benoist-Méchin, double agent, in a state of utter perplexity, since nobody in the relevant departments had this hypothesis in mind. (We never met again; in 1942, Benoist-Méchin became a leading figure in the Vichy régime.)

When it came, the war found the mass of the people in the worst possible confusion of feeling and thought. I was ill and utterly alone. I lived in a working-class district, at Pré-St. Gervais; most of my comrades who lived near by had run off to the provinces as soon as mobilization began, terrified of being bombed. I saw practically no one. Every man for himself, that's it—no time for fooling around. Publications ceased appearing of their own accord. On the day of the general mobilization, I found my way to the Socialist Party's headquarters, in a drinking and dancing quarter below the Place Pigalle; the alley, old and bourgeois-looking, was deserted, the building itself empty. I had been the only visitor there the whole afternoon. Séverac,[1] pallid and resigned, was seeing to the routine business. Maurice Paz told me of a surprising statement by Henri de Man: 'Germany does not want a general war, a settlement can be reached while mobilization is still on. . . .'[2] The P.S.O.P. had lost its influence in the Paris region and was in a serious crisis of morale, having been abandoned by its most prominent leaders. Not one group with any life in it was still on the scene.

At the Gare de l'Est the conscripts were departing, without any singing of the 'Marseillaise', in a silence heavy with anxiety and uninspired pluck. The women were not weeping very much. I shall never forget the old worker I saw staggering up a *Métro* staircase, talking to himself: '*Ah! nom de Dieu! Ah! nom de Dieu!* Two wars in one lifetime!' A cartoon in a pacifist paper showed a bill-sticker pasting up posters for the mobilization and explaining to a boozer, 'It's the war, Ben.' 'Which war?' the other was replying in a stunned voice.

This was a war that nobody was keen on. The wealthy classes

---

[1] Jean-Baptiste Séverac (1879–1951): old Socialist and Co-operative activist; editor-in-chief of *L'Humanité* up to 1918; then of *Le Populaire*.

[2] Henri de Man (1885–1953): Belgian Socialist leader, famous for his *Plan du Travail* (1933), advocating planning within a mixed economy. Collaborated (as adviser to Leopold III) with the German occupying authorities during the Second World War. Retired to Switzerland at the end of the war.

had no desire to fight against Fascism, which they preferred to the Popular Front. The intelligentsia judged that a country like France with a low birth-rate, just beginning to recover from its losses of 1914–18, was in no mood for further bloodshed. The pacifism of the Left reflected the same feeling. The workers and the middle-class folk were vaguely conscious of being betrayed, had no confidence in the Government or the General Staff, and could not follow how it was necessary to fight for Poland after having deserted Socialist Austria, Socialist Spain, and our ally Czechoslovakia. Overnight the most forceful elements in the working-class suburbs, namely the Communists, had become pacifists, 'anti-imperialists' and supporters of the new 'peace policy of the Soviet Union'. Maurice Thorez, the leader of the Communist Party, deserted; Duclos, the Vice-President of the Chamber, left for Moscow, a few deputies resigned from the Party, and the rest went to jail. The general opinion was that there would be very little fighting and that everybody would be quite safe behind the impregnable Maginot Line.

Paris waited calmly for the bombing to start: there were blackouts, long wails from the sirens at night and sometimes in broad daylight, the crackle of the anti-aircraft barrage, descents into the cellar shelters, and ridiculous trench-shelters dug in the public gardens. The rich people were taking themselves off to the Mediterranean coast. A phoney war indeed.

The walls were covered with posters: '*We will win because we are the strongest . . .!*' A right-wing writer, Thierry Maulnier, denounced the fear of victory which dominated the reactionary parties. They knew the chances of our defeat—not without reason—and 'the defeat of Germany would mean the collapse of the authoritarian systems which constitute the principal bulwark against Communist revolution, possibly even the immediate Bolshevization of Europe. . . .' The Royalist *Action Française* remained pro-Italian.

The success of my novel *S'il est Minuit dans Le Siècle* spared me the hazards of internment. I saw Georges Duhamel: he had aged ten years at one stroke, eyelids reddened and voice weak; he was already plumbing the depths of the disaster. I also met Jean Giraudoux; he was unpretentiously elegant, and dejected—his *Appeal to the Workers of France* had, despite his high position in the Ministry of Information, been censored. A great writer, and a member of the Government, wanting to speak 'to the workers'—

what a weird idea! In the same period a comrade of mine who had volunteered for the French Army wrote in a letter that he was 'happy to be fighting for the cause of freedom and democracy'. For this he was severely reprimanded by his commander: 'We are fighting for France and for nothing else!' Jean Malaquais, the author of *Les Javanais*, who was serving on the Maginot Line, told me of the utter passivity of the troops at the front, who had no idea of anything and talked only of women and booze. The most-discussed book of the year was one by Jean-Paul Sartre, an analysis in novel form of a case of neurosis, called *La Nausée*. An appropriate title.

The publishing house of Gallimard had a novel in the press by a young author, dealing with the Spanish Civil War, but decided not to publish it. The subject was too hot: it might upset the Italians. Bernard Grasset were preparing a new edition of my book *L'An Un de la Révolution Russe*, and the Ministry of Information asked them to postpone its appearance until more suitable times; in other words, this was a rather hot subject too. There was an order forbidding too much publicity about my *Portrait de Staline*, which had just appeared. . . . Publishers were refusing any works which were anti-Hitler. There was neither freedom nor intellectual purpose. The war even lacked an ideology.

On the 8th or 9th of May, *Le Figaro* stated that the massing of German forces on the borders of the Low Countries was probably only a bluff. I spent the evening of the 9th at Léon Werth's. He had been an acute and humane romantic chronicler of the last war's aftermath, but he was writing no more; he lived in uncertainty, in ceaseless self-questioning about the values that had disappeared. There Saint-Exupéry, in uniform, stretched his great body on a couch: Saint-Exupéry was still undertaking reconnaissance over enemy territory, and he was devising a new defence-system for aerodromes. He was not sure whether he was of the Left or the Right: reluctant to locate himself anywhere among discredited parties, inhibited by his family name and his relatives, disillusioned by the Spanish tragedy, living out this end of a world with his whole soul, even though his intellect was unable to master its outstanding features. On that particular evening, he was feverishly restless, itching to go and almost silent. I asked him if it was true that for some long months the Allied air force would continue to be inferior to the enemy's. The only answer he gave me was a few despairing words with gestures to match. I went out into the lovely Paris night, literally in agony. On the morning of the 10th, the newspapers reported the invasion of Belgium and Holland.

Within six days the Panzers reached Sedan. Fleeing Belgians told me of the massacre of the French cavalry in the Ardennes: cavalry against tanks and planes! The communiqués invent a new phrase, 'mopping-up operations'. The map shows plainly that the enemy is aiming for the heart of France, and Paris is threatened. On the midday of 3 June the summer sky is filled with the noise of engines: it sounds like an army of the air, but nothing can be seen in the blue above. Then come the dull explosions of bombs bursting, and the crackle of anti-aircraft fire. My wife and I follow this invisible battle from a balcony where the window-panes are trembling. Innocent blood is streaming at this very moment in our midst: at the idea of this, so great a revulsion sweeps over us that everything else is now blotted out of our minds. However, Paris wears no trace of gloom afterwards, but keeps the festive air with which the sun always endows it.

Two factions in the Government begin to clash, almost openly. The clique favouring immediate peace, the clique of reaction and future surrender, demands power for Pétain; the name of the banker Paul Baudouin, unknown up till now, crops up in every conversation. Its opponent is the party favouring resistance, which includes Reynaud, Daladier, Mandel, and Léon Blum. The Socialists are divided, the Paul Faure tendency remaining pacifistic. I hear it said that in certain quarters lists of names have been drawn up for arrest. Mandel, now Minister of the Interior, begins the purge of Paris. Helmeted *Gardes Mobiles*, their rifles loaded, surround the student cafés in the Boulevard St. Michel. Any foreigners whose papers are not in order are packed into lorries which take them to police headquarters. Many of them are anti-Nazi refugees, for the other foreigners' papers are of course quite in order. How can a refugee be in order with this Préfecture of red-tape and petty pestering, a shuttlecock between left-wing influences, right-wing influences, and others more mysterious? The anti-Nazi and anti-Fascist refugees are due to experience yet more prisons: those of the Republic which was their last land of asylum on this continent, which in its death-throes is losing its wits. Spaniards and

International Brigaders who beat back Fascism outside Madrid are treated as if they carried the plague. Meanwhile, with documents in order and purses full, Spanish Falangists, Italian Fascists (still neutrals), and White Russians (and how many actual Nazis were there behind these easy disguises?) walked at liberty through the length and breadth of France. 'Home Defence' is a farce, a horribly symbolic one at that.

Vain appeals reach me from the Belgian frontier. The police are letting the flood of Belgian refugees pass by, but are halting Belgium's anti-Nazi and Spanish exiles in their tracks. The Gestapo is advancing in line with the tanks, but the reply is 'You don't have visas! You can't cross!' A few will get through when the police make themselves scarce. Some of the Spaniards pick up the weapons which the police have abandoned, and start to fight the Nazi tanks. . . . Sneevliet asks me to get him a visa, but in the general stampede there is no one to speak to in Paris. (Sneevliet will be shot, with eight of his comrades, in Amsterdam on 15 April 1942.)

The Press is still making reassuring remarks: 'The Weygand Line will hold fast!'—meanwhile 'German infiltration' has got as far as the Somme, reaching Forges-les-Eaux. . . . Under the sunlight of June, the Champs-Elysées still keeps its smiling face. I am resolved to put off leaving until almost the last train, for I still feel some vague hope that the situation will mend, and I have practically no money. When Paris ends the world ends; useless to see the truth, how could one bear to acknowledge it? On Sunday the 9th, I see Cabinet ministers moving house. Cars, blanketed with mattresses and overloaded with trunks, shoot off towards the city's southern gates. Shops are closed.

On the morning of 10 June, I am in the *Métro* and see men and women on the verge of tears; all one can hear is a murmur of heart-broken rage: 'Oh, the bastards!' Hands, clenched violently, screw up the newspaper which reports Italy's entry into the war; a stab in the back dealt to a man already falling. 'We're betrayed at every turn!' the man next to me says. 'Yes, friend, that is just it.'

Last images of Paris: from the high ground of the Porte des Lilas, the outer suburbs are overshadowed by a strange bluish mist, a suspicious-looking gas or smoke drifting towards Belleville and Montmartre. They say that the petrol tanks at Rouen are burning. The outskirts of the Gare du Nord, empty and pale as evening falls;

the shops with their iron shutters up; people on their doorsteps, listening to the distant moan of shells. All the shopkeepers feel personally threatened: it's the beginning of the end of the world, isn't it? The Boulevard de Sébastopol in complete darkness, practically deserted; underneath, the Réaumur-Sébastopol *Métro* station with its human hotchpotch burdened under an animal despair: the trains are late. . . . Good-bye to all that—let us be off on foot, as best we may. At night, around the Gare de Lyon, we sense violence in the air because, they say, there are no more trains, and in any case no more room in the station. . . . A providential taxi with a one-eyed driver takes us through the Fontainebleau woods, underneath the barrage of shells, along roads thronged with traffic. 'Put your lights out, for God's sake! There's an alert on!' men in steel helmets shout through the darkness, but nobody listens to them. Four of us are making the journey: my wife,[1] my son, a Spanish friend who has joined us at the last moment, and myself. I have raked together 4,000 francs for our escape. (This would be about 100 dollars. . . .)

Our flight is accompanied by a sense of release bordering at times on gaiety. All our possessions have been reduced to a few bundles. Only the other day I was peeved at not being able to find a jotting among my papers; and now, lo and behold, books, personal objects, documents, manuscripts, all disappear at one stroke without effecting any real emotion. (It is true that I am used to it.) A whole segment of old Europe is caving in, events are unfolding in their predestined course. We had been living in a suffocating blind alley. For years now, or so it seems to me, France—and perhaps the whole West—was dominated by the consciousness that 'it could not last'. Nobody believed in anything any more, because nothing in fact was possible any more: certainly not a revolution, with this working class gorged on fresh Camembert, pleasant wine, and ancient ideas which had become mere words—a working class, moreover, ringed on all sides by Nazi Germany, Fascist Italy, Franco Spain, and insular, Conservative Great Britain. And certainly not a counter-revolution either, with this bourgeoisie incapable of daring

---

[1] This is Serge's third wife, Laurette, whom he met in Paris. His Russian wife Liuba had proved to be incurably deranged as a result of the persecution in the Soviet Union, and lapsed into infantilism; Serge had to leave her in a French mental hospital in 1940. She never recovered.

or thinking and, ever since the workers' occupation of the factories, sick with fright as well. Now it is all over: the rotten tooth has been pulled out, the leap into the unknown has been made. It will be black and terrible, but those who survive will see a new world born. There are very few people who have this new sense which modern man is so painfully developing: the sense of history. The folk who are fleeing with us along the highways of France, and on the last trains as defeat sets in, realize all the same that 'it had to happen'.

All at once I re-experience the deepest and most invigorating feeling of my childhood which, I believe, has made a lifelong impression on me. I grew up among Russian revolutionary exiles who knew that the Revolution was advancing towards them, inexorably, out of the depths of the future. In simple words they taught me to have faith in mankind and to wait steadfastly for the necessary cataclysms. They waited for half a century, in the midst of persecution. There is a Spanish friend travelling with us. Between us we can muster quite a fine collection of wrecked régimes. We wake at dawn, in the middle of open country, a thin rain mingled with sunshine falling on our faces, and we decide that, this time, the way forward for the European revolution is already half-clear. Over Nazism, our conqueror, we feel a resounding superiority: we know that it is doomed.

Along with the fleeing army, with the refugees from Paris, Alsace, Lorraine, Champagne, from Belgium, Holland and scores of other places, we invade charming, pious, well-heeled little towns, slumbering around the church and the splendid house of the local rent-collector. Here folk live in the darkness of old houses, skimping on the electricity, never buying a book, but patiently, from the beginning of time, filling out the woollen stocking with cash and amassing their little fortunes. 'Is it really possible?' moan the gossips, 'What's happening? Do you understand anything about it, sir?' The soldiers reply as one man that 'We've been sold out, betrayed, what else?—by the officers who've hopped it with their fancy women, quick as you please; by the General Staff, by the Cagoulards who wanted their revenge on the Popular Front; it's all obvious. . . .' General Staff, militarism, reaction, big bourgeoisie, all have been discredited at one swoop.

We have nothing left now, so we look for some place of sanctuary. Several have been offered or promised to us. It used to be quite the

style for people to invite themselves along to Paris: 'Of course you
must come and stay with me in Dordogne or Gironde if dear old
Paris ever gets too disagreeable for you! You will be able to taste my
little stock of wine!' However, my wife is more or less hounded, ever
so politely, out of a *château* which is the home of an anarchist well-
endowed with worldly goods—this on a day of torrential rain which
pours over the dainty slate turrets, the artificial stream and the
romantic rock-garden. We enter an abandoned farm in the middle
of the woods; a friend, a Socialist journalist, who discloses that he is
its owner, begs us to be off at once: 'Take my car, but get out
quickly. They're coming this way!' We clear off, and this late
Socialist explains to me that he is now a convert to collaboration
with Hitler and to strong government, which must inevitably be
military rule: the power of the utterly bankrupt, in a word. One
sanctuary is still promised me, with a pacifist author. It is a pretty
little house surrounded by flowers, but its door is shut and well-
guarded; the writer has gone to the hills to meditate. The police
arrest us and then let us depart, equally inclined to meditate.
These are not simply personal misfortunes, it happens in almost
every case. Refugees are suspected as enemies by the inhabitants
of the prosperous provinces: they send prices up, gobble the food-
supplies, steal bicycles, and among them, just imagine, there are
Spaniards, ruffians—God help us! We gladly embrace the peasant-
woman (not a wealthy person) who offers us coffee and shelter on a
day of teeming rain, and refuses to take our pennies.

It becomes clear that ready money and the sordid influence of
prosperity have caused a serious moral deterioration. It never occurs
to the syndicalist militants of a certain town to give their adored
meeting-hall over to the cause of hospitality. Various town halls, not
reactionary ones, refuse to pay the refugees' allowance to anyone
from Spain. For people to be refugees twice over is excessive, surely.

The working-class organizations, Socialist Party and C.G.T.,
have melted into nothing. Old-time Socialists concentrate on
keeping their positions in the municipal administrations where they
are serving. Fragments of the far Left—schoolmistresses, anarchistic
tradesmen, freemasons, and Socialists—still continue to think, and
keep solidarity alive. In one small town invaded by the straggling
army—actually Agen—we meet some old '*anarchos*' who have known
me thirty years and more. In the old days, when I turned to support

the proletarian dictatorship they thought I was a careerist; they are happy to realize that they were wrong. We meet together in a secluded spot on the river bank. Moroccan riflemen, idle and sour, wander along by the stream, pondering upon the glory of the Empire. . . .

On a highway of Gascony, amid the chaos of fugitive lorries, some Belgian magistrates, dining on the balcony of a little café, tell me, 'There is going to be a new régime in France—Hitler insists on it.' People weep to hear the loudspeakers announcing the news of the Armistice. Daily I follow the intrigues of the Government at Bordeaux. Some of the Socialists of Agen have returned from there with the latest information. 'Hitler does not want France, now trampled underfoot, to have any more Parliaments. The system of government must be Fascist. That is the unwritten clause in the Armistice. Laval and Baudouin declare that Britain will come to terms within three months. The invasion of the British Isles is well in hand.'

A man can live, and keep his spirits up, in a tent under the rain, as my son and Narciso did. A man can sleep, and sleep well, in a stinking, over-priced hovel next to the slaughter-house, as we did. He can cook his meals in a school and work in cafés; for the Age of Waiting has begun. . . . I go out to work. The problem is to find food for tomorrow or next week. We send S.O.S. messages to Switzerland and across the Atlantic. On our last postage-stamps disappointments and small betrayals rain by the score. Suddenly I become aware of a harsh revelation: that now we political refugees, we cornered revolutionaries, are utterly beaten, because certain of our comrades are no longer our comrades, so demoralized and defeated are they to the quick of their hearts; and among us a squalid battle is beginning for places in the last lifeboat from the sinking ship. However, from Switzerland and America breathtaking replies reach us. These letters, from the poet J.-P. Samson and from Dwight Macdonald—two men I have never seen in my life—seem to clasp my hands in the dark. I can hardly believe it. So then, let us hold on.[1]

---

[1] J.-P. Samson (1894–1964): poet and translator; a socialist militant in the years before the First World War; upon the outbreak of war in 1914 chose exile in Zurich, where he subsequently lived; editor of the independant review *Témoins*. Dwight Macdonald (1906–): American journalist and critic; formerly a Trotsky-ist, later a pacifist, then an independent liberal; edited the journal *Politics* from 1944 to 1949.

Little towns on the south coast are slumbering peacefully as though nothing was happening. The shock of the earthquake has still not touched here. We reach Marseilles three weeks too late: all seats in the lifeboats are taken. In drawing up visa-lists, both in America and here, the leading figures of the old exiled parties were, it seems, determined to exclude the militants of the far Left, whose very names might be compromising to Ministerial eyes. Besides, everybody is making their escape through the political family-network: groupings are of use now only for that purpose. So much the worse for the man of no Party who has dared to think only in terms of Socialism in all its vastness! All of my party, all of it, has been shot or murdered; and so I am alone, a curiously disturbing figure. People meet, people shake hands, and each one keeps for himself and those close to him the address of the American gentleman who sees to visas and relief-work. Faces whose strength shone out to me in the old days, in Moscow, Vienna, or Berlin, I now see twitching hysterically. Think of it: the fourth exile, the seventh flight in twenty years!

Marseilles, flushed and carefree with its crowded bars, its alleys in the old port festooned with whores, its old bourgeois streets with lattice-windows, its lifeless wharves, and its brilliant seascapes, is first and foremost a 'Red city', but its exact shade is Off-Red, Dirty-Red or Racket-Red, so to speak. The Vichy régime has sacked the Socialist city council and the key man in the new administration is Sabiani, a real gangster from Doriot's party. The man in the street knows what's what pretty well: 'Nothing one can do while the Nazi occupation lasts. After that, we settle matters with the bastards. That'll be it—a gay time and some faces bashed in!'

How many exiles are there tucked away in small hotels, at the end of their tether? We have the German emigration, the Austrian, the Czech, the Dutch, the Belgian, the Italian, the Spanish, and two or three Russian ones—plus some Rumanians, Yugoslavs, Greeks, and Bulgarians. Not forgetting the Parisians! Rich Jews of all nations are selling, buying and selling back documents, visas, currency, and tasty titbits of information. Little gangs of specialists supply them with perfect forgeries of dollars on the 'Black Bourse'. And the poor Jews of all nations are running through numberless varieties of terror and courage, anticipating every fate they can imagine lying ahead.

Our mob of fugitives includes first-rate brains from all those classes which have ceased to exist through the mere fact of daring to say *No!* (most of them rather quietly) to totalitarian oppression. In our ranks are enough doctors, psychologists, engineers, educationists, poets, painters, writers, musicians, economists, and public men to vitalize a whole great country. Our wretchedness contains as much talent and expertise as Paris could summon in the days of her prime; and nothing of it is visible, only hunted, terribly tired men at the limit of their nervous resources. Here is a beggar's alley gathering the remnants of revolutions, democracies, and crushed intellects. We sometimes tell ourselves that it would be tremendous if only five in a hundred of these forsaken men could manage to cross the Atlantic, and there rekindle the flame of battle in their hearts. If it had not been for Varian Fry's American Relief Committee, a goodly number of refugees would have had no reasonable course open to them but to jump into the sea from the height of the transporter-bridge, a certain enough method.

Those with the most scars take the shock best. These are the young revolutionary workers or semi-intellectuals who have passed through countless prisons and concentration-camps. They are difficult to rescue, because nobody knows them, because the old conformist parties have no sympathy for them, because the governments of the New World are afraid of them (subversives. . . .), because they possess nothing, and because every police force is out to catch them. Our beggars' alley is full of prowlers—the *Sûreté*, the lodging-house patrol, the Gestapo, the O.V.R.A., the Falangist police. Every week people disappear. Hunger is another prowler to reckon with. But we do not panic. Not many of us have very high spirits, but those who are spent come out to coffee exactly as if they still had some spark of life left.

The Frenchmen, whether intellectuals or militants, have no intention of emigrating for some time. Prisoners of habit, they do not realize the full extent of the catastrophe, and have vague hopes of some tolerable way out. Among the intellectuals there is a general tendency to adapt themselves. Various militants tell me, quite simply, 'Our place is here', and they are right. Among the notable writers, the surrealist André Breton is the only one who is anxious to cross the Atlantic; among the painters, André Masson. It is evident that, in the first wave of confusion, many people are fooled by the 'National Revolution' and the personal glamour of the 'Soldier of Verdun', that old man of over eighty who every morning drinks the bitter cup of defeat, retching with disgust but behaving with a repulsive subservience. In the course of the winter these mists melt away: reality is too insistent. The suppression of the Socialist Press, the stupid re-christenings of the streets hitherto named after Rousseau, Anatole France, Jean Jaurès, and Pierre Curie, the official anti-Semitism, the ruthless rationing, all are instructive. In the Rue Saint Ferréol people crowd in front of a *rôtisserie* to see a single chicken being roasted, a prodigious sight! The gulls of the port are so hungry that they come hovering round windows they know to be charitable. This degrading poverty, fastening upon a country so prosperous, does more to open people's eyes than any propaganda that could be devised.

The propaganda of the Allies, lacking as it does any social content, is inferior to the Nazis' demagogy, which is always talking in terms of the New Order and the 'European Revolution'. However, Wavell's victories in Africa fortunately make up for the shortcomings of the London radio. Gaullism is arising spontaneously and fairly generally; Socialist ideas are sprouting unceremoniously everywhere, even as the Socialist Party collapses into silence. Socialist delegates vote in favour of the Vichy régime whilst Blum goes off to prison and Dormoy to house-arrest. One of the Party's most capable brains, Rossi (Angelo Tasca), an old adversary of Mussolini who worked with Léon Blum and who, a month before the fall of Paris, had argued passionately in my hearing for a creed founded on liberty, has joined with Spinasse in supporting the Marshal's 'national revolution'; *L'Effort*, the organ of these Socialist flunkeys, prints the verbiage of the Nazi agent Marcel Déat. The Paul Faure tendency is equally accommodating, and negotiates with the Marshal; not under any illusions, I think, purely to avoid persecution and the mass dismissal of tens of thousands of left-wing officials and teachers. On this point the negotiations are successful.

Our very existence is hanging from slender threads which may break at any moment. Several times the total occupation of France is rumoured to be in the offing. And the long-awaited visas are not here, still not here! This much must be said: because of their reactionary or bureaucratic leanings, most of the American republics have displayed neither humanity nor sense in their immigration policies. Visas were granted in the merest trickle, in a manner so criminally stingy that thousands upon thousands of real victims, all fine human beings, were left to the mercies of the Nazis. People with money and no political commitments got visas, generally speaking, rather easily; a host of anti-Fascist fighters did not get them at all. Visas for practically every American state were habitually sold, at prices more or less exorbitant; and the Vichy officials conducted a trade in exit-permits. A fine trade this, selling lifebelts on a shipwrecked continent! Thanks to my friends in the United States, I was granted a visa for Mexico by President Lazaro Cárdenas, to whom tens of thousands of Spaniards owe their lives.

With some good friends of mine I was living for the moment in a tumbledown *château*, which we nicknamed *Espervisa*. André Breton used to write poetry in the greenhouse there under the November sun. I wrote some pages of a novel, not, however, from any love of literature. For this age must be witnessed; the witness passes, but his testimony manages to endure—and life still goes on. Others, turned rescuers by profession—who included two soldiers from Dunkirk—worked night and day for the American Relief Committee, overwhelmed by work and the appeals from concentration-camps, and in constant peril themselves. As it was, however, this was a shipwreck with too many castaways.

Once I was arrested at home and released afterwards, twice caught in a street round-up, once listed for the concentration-camp, once interned for several days on board ship, with the staff of the American Relief Committee; I was lucky to be a well-known writer—and with pretty powerful support. I lived in a hotel—the *Hôtel de Rome*—where several refugees with a name enjoyed a tranquillity which was only relative, since several Gestapo agents hung around and the *Sûreté* kept a special watch. Both at the Préfecture and among the police, at least half of the officials were pro-British and discreetly anti-Nazi, and this helped matters along. Meanwhile, at this time, the poets Walter Hasenclever and Walter Benjamin[1] commit suicide. Rudolf Hilferding and Breitscheid are carried off

[1] Walter Hasenclever (1890–1940): German expressionist poet and playwright, said to have influenced Brecht. Walter Benjamin (1892–1940): German aesthetician and poet; committed suicide when arrested by the Spanish frontier police.

out of our midst and handed to the Nazis.[1] The lawyer Apfel happened to die—of a heart attack—right in Varian Fry's office. In the newspapers: suicide or murder of Krivitsky in Washington. Trotsky murdered in Mexico. Yes, this is just the hour for the Old Man to die, the blackest hour for the working classes: just as their keenest hour saw his highest ascendancy. (Russia is just on the eve of entering the war. . . .)

The morale of my Italian friends is first-rate. These are: a bold-hearted young Marxist, an old Garibaldian, full of Latin saws, and Modigliani, an honest old reformist leader with a keen intellect. They can hear the timber of the whole edifice in their part of the world giving off loud cracks, and explain that the moment has come when Fascism's own profiteers are beginning to realize that their only hope of safety lies in turning traitor promptly enough. An Italian senator has just written that the régime has entered its crisis, and that his circle are thinking in terms of a constitutional monarchy: salvation by putting the clock back a quarter of a century, how very easy. Modigliani—stout, with an impressive beard, his manner most patrician, his blue eyes alert and sad, his words measured, always thoughtful, and burdened with experience—Modigliani, at the age of sixty-three, still likes to keep in his inmost heart the hope that some day he can again be of service. All the same his wife Vera, still at his side, is trembling for his sake. Both of them, with their faultless dignity, incarnate the sober, noble Socialism of an age that has passed. (What has happened to them now? They were still in France at the moment when the Nazis took over the unoccupied zone. . . .)[2]

Some of us whose lives are in danger eventually make our exit. The Battle of the Visas which their friends have had to wage for their sake would stand some description: a single escape would provide material for a book of Balzacian proportions, packed with unexpected incidents and dark happenings behind the scenes. I take the last ship to leave for Martinique. Permission to journey by way of Morocco and the French West Indies has just been refused

---

[1] Rudolf Hilferding (1877–1944): prominent German economist and Social-Democratic politician; author of important works on imperialism and finance capital. Rudolf Breitscheid (1874–1944): Minister of the Interior in the German Republic, 1918–19, then a leading Social-Democratic Deputy.

[2] Modigliani succeeded in escaping to Switzerland in 1943 and returned to Italy following the liberation. He died in Rome in 1947.

me, but quite suddenly, within two hours, a transit-visa through Martinique is granted me at the Préfecture. . . . So here we are, my son and I, on a cargo boat converted into an ersatz concentration-camp of the sea, the *Capitaine Paul-Lemerle*. I feel no joy at going. I would a thousand times rather have stayed, if that had been possible: but before liberation of some kind comes its way, the chances are ninety-nine out of a hundred that I shall have perished in some filthy prison. Europe, with its bullet-ridden Russias, its crushed and trampled Germanies, its invaded nations, its gutted France—how one clings to it! We are parting only to return.

On board, forty of us are comrades, out of 300 refugees. The rest of them have no thought except for flight, being unpolitical or, in many cases, reactionary. Out in the Atlantic, past the Sahara coast, the stars pitch up and down above our heads. We hold a meeting on the upper deck, between the funnel and the lifeboats. There are a number of appraisals that we can make. We have fresh news, of the kind that does not get into the newspapers, from Germany, Austria, Spain, and Italy. We can see the partnership between Hitler and Stalin drawing to its perilous end. We have witnessed the failure of the Nazi victory and the Nazi-inspired counter-revolution in France. All around us we have seen the growth of fresh ways of thinking, a fresh eagerness to fight, a vague but powerful consciousness of the immense changes that are necessary. In Spanish waters, the fishermen gave us the clenched-fist salute from their little yachts. In Casablanca port, some friends came up to see me, and to tell me that they were looking to the future.

What can I say that is at all essential, to these forty faces gathered together in the twilight between sky and sea, and blending with the stars? I have a faint inkling of what is really essential: that we have not lost after all, that we have lost only for the moment. In the struggles of society we contributed a superabundance of consciousness and will, which greatly exceeded the forces at our command. All of us have behind us a certain number of mistakes and failings, for creative thought of any kind can proceed only with hesitating, stumbling steps. . . . Having made this qualification, in accordance with which each must search his heart—we have been quite astoundingly right. We with our nondescript little journals, we have often seen clearly where statesmen have floundered in ridiculous and disastrous folly. We have caught a glimpse of man resolving his own history. And we have known how to win, we must never forget that. The Russians and the Spaniards among us know what it is to take the world into their hands, to set the railways running and the factories working, to defend bombarded cities, to establish production-plans, to treat the wretched potentates of yesterday according to their deserts. No kind of predestination impels us to become the offal of concentration-camps—and as for the torturers of the prisons, we know very well how they are put against the wall! This experiment of ours will not be wasted. Millions of men who could not hear us are repeating it after us. There are whole armies in the concentration-camps, there are whole peoples in the prisons and under the terror. Yes, we have lost, but our spirit is strong, we are looking ahead eagerly.

In the Western hemisphere, marvellous landscapes open to our eyes. The sun streams down upon every object. In front of the ship's bows little flying fish, the colour of the sky, dart like dragonflies from the sea. The green mountains of Martinique are spread with dazzling riches. On the very edge of the sea, which has all the hues of the rainbow, the coco-nut trees are climbing high. And here we find yet one more concentration-camp, scorching hot, without drinkable water, guarded by tall childlike Negroes, managed by thieves of policemen. Some of them, Vichy officials, are Nazi to the core. (Now for a lesson in the political economy of the West Indies. The island is owned by a few superlatively wealthy families of big rum-distillers and sugar-growers, who maintain a diluted form of slavery on it. We shall see how long that will last; perhaps for quite some time, since here there is the problem of peoples still in their infancy.)

We feel strangely free in Ciudad-Trujillo, the small, spruce capital of the Dominican Republic. This is lit up unassumingly, and filled with flags, well-shaped girls with every conceivable kind of Eur-african face, and Spanish refugees, comrades of ours, who make us wonder how they manage to live so well. Suddenly, this heavy tropical sky reverberates loud and long with the thunder of a new war, this most evil, most decisive war which the Nazi Empire is now declaring against the Russian people. The Negroes, deeply stirred, gather in crowds before the newspaper posters. Do they too, then, feel unconsciously that they are the citizens of an invisible International? I know the Russian system too well not to expect disastrous reverses. To think that all that has been built, at the cost of so many sacrifices and injustices, is going to perish under Nazi cannonfire. . . . I have no doubt that, because of the massacre of the revolutionary generation (which constituted the Soviet Union's best-trained nucleus of skill), we are now going to face a horribly successful advance. For weeks I find it impossible to think of anything else but the nightmare sweeping over Russia. I can guess that, in these very days, the last of my comrades are being shot in Russian jails—because they were too discerning and because they might, before long, acquire too much influence. (Later I learnt that I had guessed right.) I carry on my work with practically no documentation, in the tropical heat, anxious for the fate of my wife back in France, whose painful battle for visas is not ended. This is what I write:

'Those of these men (the persecuted Oppositionists) who are still alive, if they could battle today for the Russian people, for the factories built by the Russian people with its own sweat and blood, for the old red flags of the Ural partisans and the Petrograd workers—these men, in chains for more than a decade, would do battle with their whole being. And he who is writing these lines, a man who has come out of the same prisons, would be at their side. For today the salvation of the Russian people and its revolutionary achievements is indispensable to the salvation of the world.'

I write that the weakness of Russia before industrial Germany (Russia still being, despite the immense achievements of industrialization, mainly an agricultural nation) would cost her untold sufferings, extending over years; however 'Russia spells an end to the effortless victories, an end to the unchallenged butcheries like Rotterdam—the butchers are now being paid back in kind; an end to the conquests with immediate booty—real trouble is beginning; an end to the hope of peace in the near future, since nobody can really tell any longer when the fighting will end. There are so many factors tending to material and moral attrition. . . . The Nazi Empire has been halted in its tracks.'

I predict the stubborn, ever-renewed war of the partisans and the unconquerable Russian winters. I announce, in July 1941, that 'Stalingrad, a vital strategic point, will be attacked and defended ferociously'; that Japan will probably refrain from attacking Vladivostok 'unless the Soviet power disintegrates altogether. . . . but even in defeat we would judge it far closer to recovery than to anything that could really be called disintegration. . . .'

Two years of war have not given the lie to this work (*Hitler Contra Stalin*) published in Mexico in September 1941; no publisher in New York would touch it. In the second part I ventured into the future and showed how infinitely probable was the 'resurrection' of Russian democracy from its totalitarian noose. A people as great as this cannot die, still less can it survive such an ordeal without reviving into liberty, suppressing the terror at long last, and asking searching questions which will assign the political responsibility for the past.

My journey to Mexico continues, with a few incidents on the way. The articles I published in Ciudad-Trujillo have excited the attention of the town's Communist cell, which is certainly connected with more powerful organizations in America. I am surrounded by a torrent of filthy denunciations—all over again. The police of Haiti go into a fit of terror at the airport and take us into custody; if we had not greeted the affair with such complete coolness we would have been beaten up there and then. They recover a little composure, only to smile nicely at a Falangist gentleman who is passing through with a pretty passport duly stamped by Franco's consuls. Back in the Dominican Republic, and again in Cuba, our luggage is searched and we are interrogated. But where there is nothing to find, the blackest slander loses its power. Everything is cleared up in a matter of days.

The loveliness of Havana, its sensual delight feeding on electricity —this after our pitifully dark European cities. Meetings with friends hitherto unseen. The heady sensation of being in a free country. We arrive in Havana while the battle of Leningrad is beginning, and we are haunted by mental pictures of the fighting over there.

The aeroplane instructs us in a new vision of the world whose lyrical richness could provide material for a renewed art-form to flourish, whether in poetry or painting.[1] But this semi-bankrupt civilization has made it into a killing-machine; it is used for travel only by the rich, who are dead to any kind of enthusiasm. We see them dozing in the comfortable seats of the Douglas aircraft, and all the while we are winging over the Caribbean Sea, the storm-ridden lands of Yucatan, and then the tablelands of Mexico, covered in

---

[1] Serge is here drawing upon the ideas of a Mexican artist named Dr. Atl, whom he met in the course of his exile. Atl was the theorist and practitioner of *aeropittura*, i.e. of landscapes and scenes as observed from an aeroplane.

heavy clouds which are transfixed by shafts of light. Huge, rose-pink and solid, Tenayuca's Pyramid of the Sun stands out suddenly on its flinty plain.

The first face I see at Mexico Airport belongs to a Spanish friend; it is bespectacled, pensive, vigorous and gaunt—Julián Gorkín. When he was in the jails of Spain we fought for eighteen months to save his life. Now he and other comrades, in New York and Mexico, have just fought over fourteen months to guarantee me this journey, this escape. Without them I should have been doomed, almost hopelessly. My destiny has its privileges: this is the second time in six years that this rational miracle of solidarity has been worked on my behalf. We stick together like this, from one end of the world to the other, few in number but sure of one another—and confident in the march of history.

In the Mexican street, I taste a singular sensation. I am no longer an outlaw, no longer a hunted man, due any minute to be interned or to disappear. Only I am told now: 'There are certain revolvers you must beware of. . . .' That can take care of itself: I have lived too long to live anywhere but in the immediate present. For me, the gracious lights of Mexico are superimposed over the prospect of distant cities, restless, devastated, and plunged into black-out, and in these I see men walking, the most hunted men in the world, whom I have left behind me. I know that not all of them have to leave, that those who can stay have a duty to stay (and, no doubt, they are performing this simple duty exceedingly well); I know that some of them have to be killed, statistics requires it to be so. But there are some of them, too, who cannot stay without being killed and who by reason of their experience, their steadfastness, their idealism, their knowledge, are precious for tomorrow's Europe. If the men who were the backbone of the old European Socialism and the young murdered democracies are not saved, the inevitable revolutions to come will be led by ex-Nazis, ex-Fascists, ex-Communists of the totalitarian stamp, or adventurers devoid of ideas or humanism, or men of goodwill who have lost their bearings. This is a simple and urgent political calculation. Why, then, do the Americas find it so hard to open a chink in their doorways to welcome in a few of these warriors?

10

LOOKING FORWARD

I end these recollections on the threshold of Mexico. Life goes on: the struggle goes on. I know that what I have written is at once too scrappy and too concentrated; I have had too much experience to record. To my regret, for lack of space, I have had to miss many portrayals and many details. I have sought to give only what was typical and essential. The environment of my work has been rather hard, appropriately so for a work of this kind: living with difficulty, surrounded by obscure threats, without knowing when or where the work could be published—but at the same time with the conviction that one day it would find its proper use. Possibly, on some secondary points, I may be guilty of lapses of memory; but I have told only the truth, told it as completely as I can.

It has been observed that I show hardly any interest in talking about myself. It is hard for me to disentangle my own person from the social processes, the ideas and activities in which it has shared, which matter more than it and which give it value. I do not think of myself as at all an individualist: rather as a 'personalist', in that I view human personality as a supreme value, only integrated in society and in history. The experience and thought of one man have no significance which deserves to last, except in this sense. Nevertheless, no one should read into these words any yearning for self-effacement; I am sure that one must be oneself, simply and fully, neither abdicating responsibility nor wishing to diminish others. To sum up, nothing of us is truly our own unless it be our sincere desire to share in the common life of mankind.

Out of a little over fifty years, I have spent ten in various forms of captivity, which have usually been harsh. These confinements have taught me the truth of Nietzsche's paradoxical dictum: 'Whatever does not kill me, strengthens me'. I have never had property, and

practically never lived in security. Several times I have lost every
material thing that I cherished: books, papers and personal souve-
nirs. In Brussels, in Paris, in Barcelona, in Berlin, in Leningrad, at the
Soviet frontier, in Paris again, I have left nearly everything behind
—or it has all been taken away from me. This experience has made
me indifferent to material goods, although it has done nothing to
discourage me.

My inclinations have always been towards intellectual work.
Few satisfactions seem to me as great as those of understanding and
expression. Probably my books have been my dearest love, but I
have written much less than I could have wished, and then hastily,
without opportunity to revise, in the thick of the struggle. My books
have undergone a singular fate. In my first fatherland, Russia, and
only because I wished to serve my country without lying, every
single one was suppressed even before publication; and the political
police confiscated the manuscripts of several finished works, the
fruit of several years' effort: among these the novel in which I
thought I had best conveyed the grandeur of the Revolution. On
the other hand, my *History of the first years of the Revolution*, published
in Paris and Madrid, is one of the three or four honest and relatively
complete works on an epoch whose documents have been destroyed,
whose very memoirs falsified, whose witnesses shot. In France and
Spain, my books have had a fine reception; in Spain they have been
burned, in France I do not know what has become of them. In the
United States, with only two exceptions, conservative publishers
considered my work too revolutionary, and left-wing publishers too
anti-totalitarian, that is, too hard on the Stalin régime. My latest
novel, *La Terre Commence à Trembler* . . ., written in my journeyings
across the world, with the single passionate motive of giving life
to human beings about whom practically nothing has been written
up to now, has still not been able to appear, for this double reason.
Although their quality has generally been recognized, my books
have known a life as hard as my own. I have found that the writer
cannot even *exist* in our decomposing modern societies without
accommodating himself to interests which forcibly limit his horizons
and mutilate his sincerity.

I have outlived three generations of brave men, mistaken as they
may have been, to whom I was deeply attached, and whose memory
remains dear to me. And here again, I have discovered that it is

nearly impossible to live a life devoted wholly to a cause which one believes to be just; a life, that is, where one refuses to separate thought from daily action. The young French and Belgian rebels of my twenties have all perished; my syndicalist comrades of Barcelona in 1917 were nearly all massacred; my comrades and friends of the Russian Revolution are probably all dead—any exceptions are only by a miracle. All were brave, all sought a principle of life nobler and juster than that of surrender to the bourgeois order; except perhaps for certain young men, disillusioned and crushed before their consciousness had crystallized, all were engaged in movements for progress. I must confess that the feeling of having so many dead men at my back, many of them my betters in energy, talent, and historical character, has often overwhelmed me; and that this feeling has been for me also the source of a certain courage, if that is the right word for it.

A political exile since my birth, I have known both the real benefits and the oppressive hardships of the uprooted man. Upheaval broadens his perception of the world and his knowledge of men; it blows away his foggy conformities and stifling particularisms; it saves him from that patriotic complacency which really is no more than humdrum self-satisfaction; but, in the struggle for existence, it remains a most serious handicap. I have witnessed the birth of the enormous category of 'stateless persons', that is, of those men to whom tyrants refuse even a nationality. As far as the right to live is concerned, the plight of these men without a country (who are in truth those who are most attached to their own countries and to the country of mankind) can be compared only to that of the 'unacknowledged man' of the Middle Ages who, since he had no lord or sovereign, had no rights and no protection either, and whose very name became a kind of insult. Through their conservative temper, in a time when nothing can any longer be 'conserved' without change, and also through legalistic inertia, most modern states have become accomplices in the persecution of these defenders of liberty. Now at last, when we, the stateless, are beginning to number millions, perhaps things will change. For my own part, I have no regrets at carrying this leaden burden, since I can feel myself to be at one and the same time Russian and French, European and Eurasian, a stranger to no land, despite the law, and recognizing everywhere, in all the diversity of place and person, the unity of the world and of mankind. Even in the earth of Mexico, so profoundly original in its volcanic aridity, I have seen the contours of Russia and Spain; and the *Indio* of this land reveals himself as brother to the toilers of Central Asia.

Early on, I learnt from the Russian intelligentsia that the only meaning of life lies in conscious participation in the making of history. The more I think of that, the more deeply true it seems to be. It follows that one must range oneself actively against everything that diminishes man, and involve oneself in all struggles which tend to liberate and enlarge him. This categorical imperative is in no way lessened by the fact that such an involvement is inevitably soiled by error: it is a worse error merely to live for oneself, caught within traditions which are soiled by inhumanity. This conviction has brought me, as it has brought others, to a somewhat unusual destiny; but we were, and still are, in line with the development of history, and it is now obvious that, during an entire epoch, millions of individual destinies will follow the paths along which we were the first to travel. In Europe, in Asia, in America, whole generations are in upheaval, are involved to the hilt in collective struggles, have become apprenticed to violence and grave danger; endure captivity in its various forms, prove to themselves that the egoism of 'every man for himself' is finished, that private enrichment is no fit aim for life, that yesterday's conservatisms lead to nothing but catastrophe; and they sense the necessity for a fresh outlook tending towards the reorganization of the world.

I give myself credit for having seen clearly in a number of important situations. In itself, this is not so difficult to achieve, and yet it is rather unusual. To my mind, it is less a question of an exalted or shrewd intelligence, than of good sense, goodwill and a certain sort of courage to enable one to rise above both the pressures of one's environment and the natural inclination to close one's eyes to facts, a temptation that arises from our immediate interests and from the fear which problems inspire in us. A French essayist has said: 'What is terrible when you seek the truth, is that you find it.' You find it, and then you are no longer free to follow the biases of your personal circle, or to accept fashionable clichés. I immediately discerned within the Russian Revolution the seeds of such serious evils as intolerance and the drive towards the persecution of dissent. These evils originated in an absolute sense of possession of the truth, grafted upon doctrinal rigidity. What followed was contempt for the man who was different, of his arguments and way of life. Undoubtedly, one of the greatest problems which each of us has to solve in the realm of practice, is that of accepting the necessity to maintain, in the midst of the intransigence which comes from steadfast beliefs, a critical spirit towards these same beliefs and a respect for the belief that differs. In the struggle, it is the problem of combining the greatest practical efficiency with respect for the man in the enemy; in a word, of war without hate. The Russian Revolution, although led by men who were upright and intelligent, did not resolve this problem; the character of the masses had received, from the experience of despotism, a fatal stamp whose effects were imprinted in the leaders themselves. In making this judgement, I do not mean to disown the importance of economic-historical factors; they broadly condition action, but they do not determine its entire quality. There, the human factor intervenes.

Many times I have felt myself on the brink of a pessimistic conclusion as to the function of thinking, of intelligence, in society. Continuously, over a quarter of a century, that is since the stabilization of the Russian Revolution just before 1920, I have found a general tendency to the suppression of percipient thinking. Earlier than that, I was too young to arrive at a fair judgement of the situation in European society before the First World War; but I have the impression that the most daring thinking would have met with a warmer welcome at that period, and consequently found more opportunity to survive.

I do not, after all my reflection on the subject, cast any doubt upon the scientific spirit of Marxism, nor on its contribution, a blend of rationality and idealism, to the consciousness of our age. All the same, I cannot help considering as a positive disaster the fact that a Marxist orthodoxy should, in a great country in the throes of social transformation, have taken over the apparatus of power. Whatever may be the scientific value of a doctrine, from the moment that it becomes governmental, interests of State will cease to allow it the possibility of impartial inquiry; and its scientific certitude will even lead it, first to intrude into education, and then, by the methods of guided thought, which is the same as suppressed thought, to exempt itself from criticism. The relationships between error and true understanding are in any case too abstruse for any one to presume to regulate them by authority; men have no choice but to make long detours through hypotheses, mistakes and imaginative guesses, if they are to succeed in extricating assessments which are more exact, if partly provisional: for there are few cases of complete exactness. This means that freedom of thought seems to me, of all values, one of the most essential.

It is also one of the most contested. Everywhere and at every time, I have encountered fear of thought, repression of thought, as an almost universal desire to escape or else stifle this ferment of restlessness. During the dictatorship of the proletariat, when Red posters proclaimed that 'the reign of the workers will never end', no one would admit any doubt as to the eternity of a régime which was quite clearly exceptional, formed in the course of siege. Our great Marxists of Russia, nurtured on Science, would not admit any doubt concerning the dialectical conception of Nature—which is, however, no more than a hypothesis, and one difficult to sustain at that. The leadership of the Communist International classified as a moral lapse, or as a crime, the slightest doubt as to the triumphal future of their organization. Later, in the heart of the Opposition, with all the integrity of its ideals, Trotsky would not tolerate any point of view different from his own. I say nothing of other sorts of men, victims to waves of mob-hysteria, to the blindness of private interest or the inertia of tradition. In 1918 I was nearly torn to pieces by my French workmates because I defended the Russian Revolution at the moment of the Brest-Litovsk negotiations. Twenty years later, I was nearly torn to pieces by the same workers because I denounced the totalitarianism which had sprung from that Revolution.

I have seen the intellectuals of the Left, responsible for editing reputable reviews and journals, refuse to publish the truth, even though it was absolutely certain, even though they did not contest it; but they found it painful, they preferred to ignore it, it was in contradiction with their moral and material interests (the two generally go together). In politics I have observed the appalling powerlessness of accurate prediction, which brings boycott, slander, or persecution on him who predicts. The role of critical intelligence has seemed to me to be dangerous, and very nearly useless. That is the most pessimistic conclusion to which I have felt myself drawn. I am careful not to state it finally; I blame the feeling on my personal weakness, and I persist in regarding critical and percipient thought as an absolute necessity, as a categorical imperative which no one can evade without damage to himself and harm to society, and, besides, as the source of immense satisfactions. Better times will come, and perhaps soon. It is a matter of holding fast and keeping faith until then.

The participant and witness of our epoch's events must be driven to pronounce against historical fatality. It is evident that the broadest outlines of the historical process are the product of factors outside our grasp and control, which we can come to know only after an imperfect, fragmentary fashion. But it is no less evident that the character, and even in certain cases the direction, of historical facts depends to a very large extent on the calibre of individual human beings. When the Central Committee of the Bolshevik Party met in December 1918 to study methods of attacking domestic counter-revolution, it had a conscious choice to make among the weapons it could present to the new régime. It *could have* instituted public revolutionary tribunals (allowing secret trial in certain specified cases) and, within these tribunals, permitted the right of defence, and ensured judicial strictness. It *preferred* to set up the Cheka, that is to say, an Inquisition with secret proceedings, and to exclude from this body any right of defence and any control by public opinion. In doing this, the Central Committee probably followed the line of least resistance; it also followed psychological impulses which are comprehensible to any student of Russian history, but which have nothing in common with Socialist principles.

Was it possible, in the Russia of 1926 and 1927, to foresee the difficulties which would ensue from the combination of industrial backwardness with agrarian revival? We foresaw them; and it would have been possible to remedy them in time, to some degree. But once again, the men in power preferred to follow the line of least resistance, which is also the line of least foresight, but gives the illusion of putting off serious crisis as fearful invalids put off a surgical operation. The difficulties which had been deliberately ignored still kept growing; provoked a kind of panic or blockage of reason, and necessitated solutions which were not only violent, but hideously inhuman and burdensome, those of total collectivization and totalitarian industrialization. In *Destiny of a Revolution* (1937) I concluded: 'The bureaucracy itself could, it seems, have a less disastrous policy without difficulty, if it had displayed more general culture and Socialist spirit. Its infatuation with administrative and military methods, joined to a penchant for panic in critical moments, reduced its real means. In despotic régimes, too many things depend on the tyrant. . . .'; and 'all that was done in the U.S.S.R. would have been done much better by a Soviet democracy. . . .'

The character of the tyrant consequently lends a catastrophic impetus to political conflicts. The Trials of deception and blood were decided upon by the Politbureau, which laid down the sentences and decreed their execution. This means that no more than *ten* individuals deliberated at leisure whether or not to massacre tens of thousands of citizens who were imbued with a spirit of opposition; they could have decided to deprive these adversaries of political rights or to imprison them. Instead, they resolved upon the use of the cruellest and most demoralizing means possible. In another situation, whose significance is incalculable, the same Politbureau, with the choice of collaboration with Hitler and collaboration with the democratic Powers, both solutions implying grave risks of war and invasion, adopted that solution which removed the most immediate danger by increasing the danger post-dated a few months or years, as has now been proved. In all this, the intelligence and character of men play a supreme role; and the observation follows that their rational intelligence, and also their morality—as defined by human feeling and fidelity to principles representing general higher interests—must be at fault.

I take these examples only from facts—and from men whom I know well. Doubtless the same can be said of the most atrocious and tragic crime of our age: the extermination by the Nazis of the Jews of occupied Europe. Nothing at the present can measure the political, social, and psychological consequences of this crime. Even the idea of the human, acquired over thousands of years of civilization, has been put in question. Man's soul will be branded with the fact; and all that was sufficient for it was provided by a decree deliberated by a few individuals. The totalitarian machine, then, functions like a factory to which an engineer comes, turning a lever to make the current run.

It is necessary to conclude against the existence of fatality, and for the immense power of man and for personal responsibility. It is not a pessimistic conclusion. But it stands as a condemnation of systems which concentrate maddening power in a few hands, force a selection of perverted elements, destroy even an imperfect check upon power by the average man, and paralyse the public conscience.

The men of my generation—those born around 1890—above all the Europeans among them, cannot help the sensation of having lived on a frontier where one world ends and another begins. The passage from one century to another was a giddy one. I remember my astonishment as a child when I saw the first 'horseless carriages' pass in the street. The motor-car was being born. I was a newsvendor during the first aeroplane rally organized in France; that would be about 1909. Blériot's exploit of crossing the Channel by air provoked mass enthusiasm. I knew domestic lighting by paraffin, then by gas, since electricity still penetrated only into wealthy homes. I waited in the street for that magic character, the lamp-lighter, to pass. . . . The illustrated journals of those distant times were full of the portraits of kings and emperors: the Emperor of Russia, the Emperor of Germany, the Emperor of Austro-Hungary, the Empress of China, the Sultan of the Sublime Porte. . . . Across the screens of the first cinemas, regiments used to parade, rather too rapidly, with jerky steps, and these animated pictures dumbfounded us. There was even some talk of X-rays which allowed one to see right through the human body.

When I was fifteen I was much exercised by the discoveries in the field of energy. A popularizer, dealing with the splitting of the atom, wrote: 'Nothing is created, everything is destroyed. . . .' Anxiously, I questioned my father, a Spencerian positivist. He answered, smiling, 'How do you imagine that could be true over infinite time? Everything would have disappeared billions of years ago!' I was reassured; Mach's book on energy became my bedside reading. The solid idea of matter was now overthrown; the First World War destroyed the idea of the stability of the world. The empires crumpled like houses of cards, the emperors were suddenly only poor devils on the run, who could even be shot. The banknote, that talisman, became no more than a scrap of paper—and we were all millionaires, except that a million would not buy a box of matches. Relativity taught a new—and perplexing—concept of time and space.

I have seen the face of Europe change several times. Before the First World War I knew a buoyant Europe, optimistic, liberal and crudely dominated by money. We reached our twenties as young idealistic workers, and we were angry and desperate, at times, because of the Wall: we could see nothing beyond an eternal bourgeois world, unjust and self-satisfied.

The guns thundered, and Europe was at war, a prey to contending hysterias, bleeding from all her veins, and yet, in the middle of the slaughter, pretty comfortably off. Behind the lines business was good, the world was still solid! Paris, ominous at night, but almost gay in the day-time; Barcelona, full of birds, dancing-girls and *anarchos*, the trains packed with tough, worn-out soldiers . . . without knowing it, the world was sliding towards the maelstrom.

Suddenly the Europe of revolutions was born at Petrograd. Our Red soldiers chased the generals' bands across all Europe and all Siberia. Insurrections and summary executions followed in Central Europe. Among the victorious Powers, there reigned the calm, stupid self-assurance of folk getting back to their profitable affairs. 'It will all quieten down, just wait and see!' Businesses, chancelleries, governments, newspapers, the League of Nations, all were stocked in plenty with competent gentlemen whose bodily nourishment was excellent, and spiritual diet less so, only it was bad taste to talk about that. Post-war 'good time', peace of the victors . . . We saw the cracks in the earth open wide; and when we spoke of it, they called us visionaries.

Meanwhile, totalitarian Europe was growing behind our backs. As to that, we were blind. We revolutionaries, who aimed to create a new society, 'the broadest democracy of the workers', had unwittingly, with our hands, constructed the most terrifying State machine conceivable; and when, with revulsion, we realized the truth, this machine, driven by our friends and comrades, turned on us and crushed us. Maturing into merciless despotism, the Russian Revolution no longer summoned the German masses to give the utmost of. their resources and strength. Nazism came to power, aping the Marxism it loathed. Europe multiplied concentration-camps, burned or pulped books, laid reason under the steamroller and scattered abroad, over all its loudspeakers, intoxicating lies.

There followed a dream of confused hopes: the Europe of the Popular Fronts and Moscow Trials seemed convalescent in those very moments when it was doomed. It became increasingly difficult to distinguish between revolution and reaction, between democracy with Fascist trends and Fascism in disguise, between submerged civil war and the rule of democracy, between open civil war and war between States, between intervention and non-intervention, between brands of totalitarianism in opposition but momentarily allied, between the most criminal impostures and the simple truth. This confusion sprang from the impotence of men caught up in the drift towards the cataclysm, and impotence fed in its turn upon confusion.

The era of huge collapses followed. It seemed that no human value could survive—only gigantic war-machines whose function was to establish slavery.

Since I escaped from Europe, other changes have come about. The prestige and effectiveness of the totalitarian Powers have declined. Even their victories seem to foreshadow their future defeat. The horizon begins to clear; the balance-sheet is being drawn up. For the last thirty years, with the existence of discoveries which add prodigiously to man's technical knowledge (without proportionately improving his level of consciousness), we have been entering a cycle of world transformation. In it we are the prisoners of social systems worn to the point of breakdown. Moulded themselves by a defunct world, the best and most clear-sighted of us have often been revealed, in the tempests of the age, as more than half blind. No doctrine has stood before the shock. There is nothing surprising about that: such are the limitations of man and of doctrine. Meanwhile, the broad outlines of history now in the course of realization are breaking clear from the chaos. It is no longer the revolutionaries who are making the world's tremendous revolution; it is the tyrannies that have set it going, it is the actual technique of the modern world that is breaking brutally with the past and throwing the peoples of entire continents into the necessity for starting life afresh on new foundations. That these foundations must be of social justice, of rational organization, of respect for the individual, of liberty, is for me a wonderfully evident fact which, little by little, is asserting itself beyond the inhumanity of the present time. The future seems to me to be full of possibilities greater than any we have glimpsed throughout the past. May the passion, the experience and even the faults of my fighting generation have some small power to illumine the way forward!

Mexico, 1942–February, 1943.

VICTOR SERGE AND GAULLISM

On 31 January 1948 *Le Rassemblement*, the official organ of General de Gaulle's *Rassemblement du Peuple Français* (R.P.F.), published a brief extract from a personal letter written by Victor Serge six days before his death to André Malraux, then as now one of the most prominent figures of Gaullism. (Serge died in November of the year before.) The lines quoted ran: '*I wish to tell you that I judge the political position you have adopted to be courageous and probably reasonable; if I myself were in France, I should be among those Socialists who support collaboration with the movement of which you are a member. The electoral victory of your movement,*[1] *which I foresaw but whose magnitude surprised me, was in my opinion a great step towards the immediate safety of France.*' The extract concluded with a few political generalities.

The publication of those lines came as a tremendous shock to Serge's friends and associates.[2] The Gaullism of 1947 was in several ways even more suspect from a traditional Socialist point of view than the Gaullism of the Fifth Republic; it was a well-drilled anti-Parliamentarian mass-movement with a leader-cult, an ugly proneness to rowdyism, and a corporatist streak in its programme. It was generally held by the Left to be 'soft' towards the ex-Vichyite elements of the population. Any Marxist revolutionary who declared his support for such a movement could be fairly charged with renegacy.

Such a judgement on Serge would be far too harsh; or rather positively misleading. Serge did not, after all, issue any public statement in favour of Gaullism (or, we may add, of any other non-Socialist creed) at any time during his life. The entire evidence in the affair consists of an extract, presented without context, from a

[1] In which the R.P.F. had gained 40 per cent. of all votes cast.
[2] See the editorial comments in *La Révolution Prolétarienne*, April 1948.

personal letter which was not intended for publication. According to his son Vlady,[1] this letter marked a resumption by Serge of personal relations with Malraux. Despite Malraux's record of support for the 'Victor Serge campaign' of 1935–6 (including a personal approach by him to Stalin), their last conversation, in Marseilles before Serge's departure to Mexico, had been of an estranging character.[2] The phrase in the extract describing the R.P.F.'s success as 'a great step towards the immediate safety of France' undoubtedly reflects Serge's deep concern at the post-war strength of the French Communist Party.

While it is legitimate to wonder if Serge might have worded those lines rather differently if he had known that they might be quoted as a political testimonial, the fact remains that he did write them. It is equally a fact that no other statement with anything like a pro-Gaullist construction can be found in Serge's writings or in his associates' recollections of him.

Indeed, in a letter (undated but apparently from October 1946) addressed to the editor of one of the few Paris magazines that was taking his work, Victor Serge expressed grave chagrin at the Gaullist and pro-Western leanings of the journal's publishing policy: 'I have been asking myself if you and I still spoke the same language. What was even more serious is that other articles were flirting with Gaullism, with Christianity (up to your third issue), endorsing British foreign policy and—while deploring the collision of the two blocs—omitting the formulation of any definite critique directed against American imperialism.'[3] In striking contrast to the complacency with which, in the Malraux letter, Serge views an anti-Communist electoral stampede, his warning of late 1946 insists that 'We must not play around with an anti-Communist bloc. . . . The C.P. retains its hold over a large section of the working class. . . . We cannot adopt a purely negative attitude towards the C.P. We shall get nowhere if we appear to be more preoccupied with criticizing Stalinism than with the defence of the workers. The reactionary danger is still real, and in practice we shall often have to act side by side with the Communists.'

[1] In *La Révolution Prolétarienne*, May 1948.
[2] M. Malraux has unfortunately been prevented both by the pressure of his Ministerial duties and by the inaccessibility of his archives from supplying any further context or background to the extract which has been cited.
[3] *Seize Fusillés à Moscou; Lettres inédites* (Paris, 1972, Spartacus edition), p. 125.

It would be facile to conclude that some kind of deathbed repentance had taken place, simply because Serge died shortly after the date of the Malraux extract. Other revolutionaries have been known to commit doubtful acts which have been forgotten or forgiven simply because their perpetrators have lived to redeem themselves in other ways. If Lenin had died in April 1917 on the sealed train provided for his return to Russia by German imperialism; or if Trotsky had died in December 1939 the instant after consenting to travel to the United States to testify before the House Un-American Activities Committee, it would doubtless be suspected—and not only by their detractors—that two more subversives had made their peace with the old order.

Those six lines or so quoted by Gaullists must be judged, finally, against the whole politico-literary tendency of Victor Serge's last period. In June 1947 he had completed a book-length biography of Trotsky in collaboration with the dead leader's widow. In the following two months he wrote the last essay to be published during his lifetime, a lengthy commemorative piece for the thirtieth anniversary of the Russian Revolution.[1] Like nearly all of Serge's later journalism it was written for an inconspicuous, disestablished, small magazine of the far Left. In it the old combative fire is undiminished:

'*A feeble logic, whose finger beckons us to the dark spectacle of the Stalinist Soviet Union, affirms the bankruptcy of Bolshevism, followed by that of Marxism, followed by that of Socialism. . . . Have you forgotten the other bankruptcies? What was Christianity doing in the various catastrophes of society? What became of Liberalism? What has Conservatism produced, in either its enlightened or its reactionary form? Did it not spawn Mussolini, Hitler, Salazar, and Franco? If we are indeed honestly to weigh out the bankruptcies of ideology, we shall have a long task ahead of us. . . . And nothing is finished yet. . . .*' Here too Serge indulges in a violent invective against the American ex-Marxist James Burnham, who had argued that Stalin was Lenin's authentic continuation:

'*The paradox that he has developed, doubtless out of love for a provocative theory, is as false as it is dangerous. Under a thousand insipid forms it is to be found in the Press and the literature of this age of preparation for the Third World War. The reactionaries have an obvious interest in confounding*

---

[1] *Trente Ans Après La Révolution Russe*, in *La Révolution Prolétarienne*, November 1947.

Stalinist totalitarianism—exterminator of the Bolsheviks—with Bolshevism itself; their aim is to strike at the working class, at Socialism, at Marxism, and even at Liberalism. . . .'

Whatever else they may be, these are not the words of a man of the Right, or of any variety of ex-revolutionary penitent.

SELECT BIBLIOGRAPHY

HISTORY, POLITICAL ANALYSIS, AND AUTOBIOGRAPHY

1. *Contra la faim*: Paris, Éditions de l'Anarchie, 1911. (A pamphlet written by the young Kibalchich (Victor Serge) under the pseudonym *Le Rétif*.)
2. *Pendant la guerre civile: Pétrograd mai-juin 1909*: Paris, Bibliothèque du Travail, 1921. (Serge's diary during the siege of Petrograd.)
3. *Les Anarchistes et l'expérience de la révolution russe*: Paris, Librairie du Travail, 1921. (An essay on the problems of revolutionary power and the role of anarchists and libertarians within the Socialist state.) Also as Chapter Four of A. Skirda (ed.), *Les Anarchistes dans la révolution russe*: Paris, Éditions de la Tête de Feuilles, 1973.
4. *La Ville en danger: Pétrograd, l'an II de la révolution*: Paris, Librairie du Travail, 1924. (Another piece on the siege in the Civil War.) Reprinted as an appendix to the 1971 Maspero edition of title 9 below.
5. *Les Coulisses d'une sûreté générale: l'Okhrana*: Paris, Librairie du Travail, 1925. (An account of Serge's discoveries in the Okhrana archives and a warning to the Western labour movements of the extent of police infiltration. Also: reissued as *Ce que tout révolutionnaire doit savoir de la répression*: Paris, François Maspero, 1970.)
6. *Lénine, 1917*: Paris, Librairie du Travail, 1925. Also with a new preface as *Vingt ans après*: Paris, Cahiers Spartacus, 1937. (A historical essay on Lenin's ideas and actions in the year of the Revolution.)
7. *La lutte des classes dans la révolution chinoise*: *Clarté* (Paris), Nos. 9, 11, 12, 13, and 14, May to October 1927; reprinted as *La Révolution Chinoise*: Paris, Éditions Savelli, 1977, with introduction by Pierre Naville and the addition of two further articles by Serge, 'Le bolchévisme dans l'Asie' from *Clarté*, No. 7, March 1927, and 'Canton' from *La Lutte des Classes*, No. 1, February–March 1928, the latter first published under the pseudonym 'Paul Sizoff' (see *Memoirs*, p. 239). An English translation by Gregor Benton with a preface by the veteran Chinese Trotskyist Wang Fan-hsi will be published in 1978 by Pluto Press, London.
8. *Vie des révolutionnaires*: Paris, Librairie du Travail, 1930. Mimeographed reprint, Paris, U.C.I. (Union Communiste Internationale), 1961. (A memorial account of some relatively unknown Bolshevik militants.)
9. *L'An I de la Révolution russe*: Paris, Librairie du Travail, 1930. Also: Paris, Éditions de Delphes, 1965; Paris, François Maspero, 1971. (English translation by Peter Sedgwick: *Year One of the Russian Revolution*; New York, Holt, Rinehart, 1972; London, Allen Lane, 1972.)

10. *Littérature et révolution*: Paris, Librairie Valois, 1932. Also: Paris, François Maspero, 1976, and (in a considerably augmented edition) 1978.

11. *Seize fusillés à Moscou*: Paris, Cahiers Spartacus, 1936. (Pamphlet attacking the first Moscow trial.) Also: Paris, Spartacus, 1972, in a volume including unpublished letters by Serge.

12. *De Lénine à Staline*: Paris, Le Crapouillot, special issue, January 1937. (English translation by Ralph Manheim: *From Lenin to Stalin*; New York, Pioneer Publishers, 1937; London, Secker and Warburg, 1937. Also in an edition with a selection of articles on Russia by Serge: New York, Monad Press, 1973.)

13. *Vingt-neuf fusillés et la fin de Yagoda*: Paris, 1937, special issue of the review *Lectures Prolétariennes* (No. 3, April 1937).

14. *Destin d'une Révolution: U.R.S.S., 1917–1937*: Paris, Bernard Grasset, 1937. (English translation by Max Schachtman: *Russia Twenty Years After*, New York, Pioneer Publishers, 1937, and Connecticut, Hyperion Press, 1973; *Destiny of a Revolution*, London, Jarrolds, 1937.)

15. 'La Pensée anarchiste': in *L'Anarchie; Le Crapouillot*, special issue, January 1938.

16. *L'Assassinat d'Ignace Reiss*: in *L'Assassinat politique et l'U.R.S.S.*, by V. Serge, M. Wullens and A. Rosmer: Paris, Éditions Pierre Tisné, 1938.

17. *La Révolution Russe: Février–Octobre 1917*: Chapter Six in the collection *Histoire des Révolutions de Cromwell à Franco*: Paris, Éditions Gallimard, 1938.

18. 'Deux rencontres': in *Les Humbles*, Cahiers 8–12, August–December 1938, special issue *A Maurice Parijanine* (Serge's reminiscence of Parijanine, his fellow translator of Lenin, Trotsky, etc). Also in *Témoins* (Zürich), No. 23, May 1960. (English translation under the title 'Twice Met' in *International Socialism* (London), No. 20, Spring 1965.)

19. *Portrait de Staline*: Paris, Bernard Grasset, 1940.

20. *Hitler contra Stalin*: Mexico City, Ediciones Quetzal, 1941. (In Spanish.)

21. *Los Problemas del Socialismo en nuestro tiempo*: Mexico City, *Mundo*, 1944. (A set of essays, published in Spanish, by Julián Gorkín, Marceau Pivert and Serge.)

22. *La Tragédie des écrivains soviétiques*: Paris, Les Égaux, 1947. Also in the 1972 Spartacus reissue of title 11 above. In English translation under the title 'The Writer's Conscience' in *Now* (London), No. 7, March 1947.

23. *Le Nouvel Impérialisme russe*: Paris, Cahiers Spartacus, 1947. Also, with four short articles by Serge, in *Hommage à Victor Serge. Le Nouvel Impérialisme russe*: Paris, Spartacus, 1972.

24. *Vie et Mort de Trotsky*: Paris, Amiot-Dumont, 1951. (A biography written in collaboration with Trotsky's widow Natalia Sedova, whose reminiscences are marked off in the text. Also: Paris, Club

des Amis du Livre, 1961, and (as *Vie et Mort de Léon Trotsky*) Paris, François Maspero, 1973. English translation by Arnold Pomerans: *The Life and Death of Leon Trotsky*; New York, Basic Books, 1975; London, Wildwood House, 1975.)

25. *Le Tournant obscur*: Paris, Les Îles d'Or, 1951. (A fragment of Serge's memoirs which Serge left behind in Paris in 1940 and later incorporated virtually unchanged in the complete *Memoirs*; published separately in error.) Also: Paris, Éditions Albatros, 1972

26. *Mémoires d'un révolutionnaire, 1901–1941*: Paris, Éditions du Seuil, 1951. Also (with interesting additional material by Julián Gorkín and others): Paris, Club des Éditeurs, 1957. Sections of the *Memoirs* appeared in an English translation by Ethel Libson in *Politics* (New York), June 1944–June 1945. A second version of the *Memoirs*, revised and corrected by Serge, is published by Éditions du Seuil, Paris, Collection 'Points-Histoire', 1978.

27. *Carnets*: Paris, René Julliard, 1952. (Notebooks from the period 1936–1938 and 1942–7. An English translation from Serge's notebooks by James A. Fenwick, overlapping only partially with the *Carnets*, is to be found in *New International* (New York), September 1949–November/December 1950. This is translated from a somewhat separate selection of Serge's diary entries: *Pages de journal* (for 1936–8 and 1945–7) in *Les Temps Modernes* (Paris), Nos. 44 and 45, June and July 1949.)

28. Victor Serge, Leon Trotsky: *La Lutte contre le stalinisme*. Texts from 1936 to 1939 selected and introduced by Michel Dreyfus; Paris, François Maspero, 1977. (Letters between Serge and Trotsky and from Serge to other correspondents, as well as various articles on the themes of Kronstadt, Spain, anarchism and Trotskyism illustrating the different positions of the two revolutionaries; the collection reproduces as a genuine text of Serge the piece referred to on p. 349 of the *Memoirs*, whose authorship Victor Serge repeatedly denied and which was quite out of keeping with his published views.)

NOVELS

29. *Les Hommes dans la prison*: Paris, Éditions Rieder, 1930. (Drawn from Serge's five years in French jails, 1912–17. English translation by Richard Greeman: *Men in Prison*; New York, Doubleday, 1969; London, Gollancz, 1970; Harmondsworth, Penguin, 1972; London, Writers and Readers Publishing Co-operative, 1978.)

30. *Naissance de Notre Force*: Paris, Éditions Rieder, 1931. (Based upon the Barcelona rising of 1917 and Serge's repatriation to Russia. English translation by Richard Greeman: *Birth of Our Power*, New York, Doubleday, 1967; London, Gollancz, 1968; Harmondsworth, Penguin, 1970); London, Writers and Readers Publishing Co-operative, 1978.)

31. *Ville conquise*: Paris, Éditions Rieder, 1932. (Petrograd in 1919.) Also: Lausanne, Éditions Rencontre, 1964. (English translation by Richard Greeman: *Conquered City*; New York; Doubleday, 1975, London, Gollancz, 1976; London, Writers and Readers Publishing Co-operative, 1978.)

32. *S'il est Minuit dans le Siècle*: Paris, Bernard Grasset, 1939. Paris, Hachette, Le Livre de Poche, 1976. (Deals with the life of the Oppositionist political prisoners in the U.S.S.R. English translation by Richard Greeman to be published by Writers and Readers Publishing Co-operative, 1979.)

33. *Les Derniers Temps*: Montreal, Éditions de l'Arbre, 1946; Paris, Bernard Grasset, 1951. (A novel of dispossessed refugees at the time of the fall of France. English translation by Ralph Manheim: *The Long Dusk*; New York, Dial Press, 1946; Toronto, Longmans, 1946.)

34. *L'Affaire Toulaév*: Paris, Éditions du Seuil, 1948. Paris, Hachette, Le Livre de Poche, 1978. (A brilliant novel of the Purges. English translation by Willard R. Trask: *The Case of Comrade Tulayev*; New York, Doubleday, 1950; London, Hamish Hamilton, 1951; Harmondsworth, Penguin, 1968.)

35. *Les Années sans pardon*: Paris, François Maspero, 1971. (A novel of the Second World War, whose characters live the Communist tragedy on the Russian front, in a besieged Berlin and in a final G.P.U. assassination scene in Mexico.)

Le Terre commence à trembler . . ., mentioned by Serge on p. 372, seems to be an alternative title for *L'Affaire Toulaév* (title 34).

Titles 29, 30, 31, 32, and 34 above were published in a single volume under the title *Les Révolutionnaires*, Paris, Éditions du Seuil, 1967.

SHORT STORIES

36. *Le Tropique et le Nord*: Paris, François Maspero, 1972. (A collection planned by Serge which includes two pre-war stories (*Mer Blanche*, 1932, and *L'Impasse Saint-Barnabé*, 1936), a story about a psychiatric clinic, *L'Hôpital de Leningrad*, and a previously unpublished memoir of Mexico, *Le Séisme*.)

POETRY

37. *Résistance*: Paris, Les Humbles, 1938. Reissued as *Pour un brasier dans un désert*, Paris, François Maspero, 1972. (Poems written in the U.S.S.R., confiscated by the Soviet censor in 1936, and re-composed from memory.)

PUBLISHED CORRESPONDENCE

38. Two of Serge's 528 letters from prison to Rirette are given in E. Michon, *Un Peu de l'âme des bandits*, Paris, 1918.

39. Twelve letters to friends in France, describing conditions in Russia (1926–30) are in *La Révolution prolétarienne* (Paris), July–November 1933.

40. *Lettres à Antoine Borie*, Serge's correspondence with a French sympathizer in 1946–7, is in *Témoins* (Zürich), No. 21, February 1959.

41. *De Kibaltchiche à Victor Serge: Le Rétif (1909–1919)*, a series of letters to E. Armand reflecting Serge's evolution from anarchism to Marxism, presented and introduced by Jean Maitron, in *Le Mouvement Social* (Paris), No. 47, 1964.

42. 'Correspondance Emmanuel Mounier–Victor Serge', letters exchanged between Mounier and Serge over 1940–7, is in *Bulletin des amis d'Emmanuel Mounier* (Paris), No. 39, 1972.

Two letters to Mlle Jeanne Saint-Martin in 1940 and eighteen letters over 1945–7, to the publisher René Lefeuvre, are collected in the 1972 Spartacus edition of title 11 above.

Letters between Serge and Trotsky, Marcel Martinet, Andreu Nin, Leon Sedov and Henryk Sneevliet are published in title 28 above.

WORKS CONFISCATED BY THE SOVIET CENSORSHIP

L'An II de la Révolution russe: uncompleted materials for a work on War Communism.

Les Hommes perdus: a memoir of the French anarchist movement.

La Tourmente: a novel on Russia in 1920, 'in which I thought I had best conveyed the grandeur of the Revolution' (*Memoirs*, p. 372).

A complete bibliography of the works of Victor Serge is in preparation by Jean Rière for his major study *Victor Serge, un voix sous la glace et le granit*.

INDEX